Father Abraham's
Children

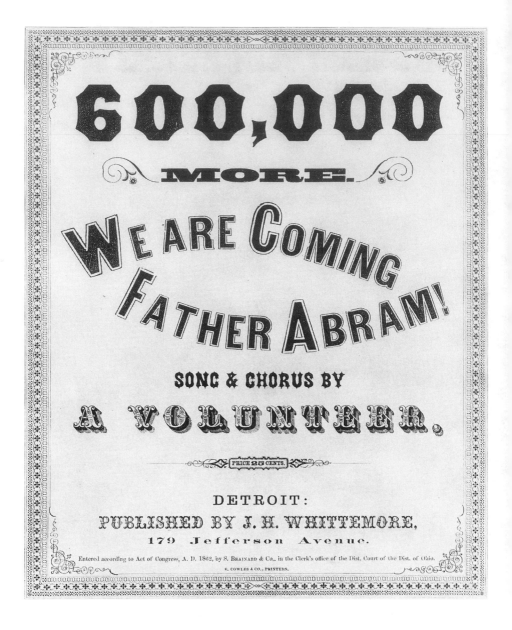

Father Abraham's Children

Michigan Episodes in the Civil War

Frank B. Woodford

New Foreword by Arthur M. Woodford

 Wayne State University Press   Detroit

Great Lakes Books
A complete listing of the books in this series can be found at the back of this volume.

Philip P. Mason, Editor
Department of History, Wayne State University

Dr. Charles K. Hyde, Associate Editor
Department of History, Wayne State University

03 02 01 00 99   5 4 3 2

ISBN 0-8143-2816-4
LC number 61-5852

Grateful acknowledgment is made to the Ford Foundation for financial assistance in the publication of the 1961 edition of this book.

For the 1999 edition, grateful acknowledgment is made to Janet Whitson and David Poremba of the Burton Historical Collection, Detroit Public Library, for their special assistance; to Thomas Sherry for his assistance in photo reproduction; and to Barry Puckett, who compiled the index.

Frontispiece: Marching Song of Union Troops
The title page of a song that became popular in the North early in the Civil War. It was later supplanted by the "Battle Hymn of the Republic" as the leading march and patriotic air of the Union. Courtesy Burton Historical Collection.

Contents

Foreword to the Great Lakes Books Edition

F*ATHER* A*BRAHAM'S* C*HILDREN* was first published on the eve of the 100th anniversary of the Civil War. It was a time of great interest in this period of our history, and a time that saw the publication of hundreds of new books about the War of the Great Rebellion. These books were widely read and many, by authors such as Bruce Catton, became major book club selections and even reached best-seller status.

This interest by the general public in books on the Civil War waned over the next two decades only to be renewed with an even greater vigor in the 1980s and early 1990s with the writings of such noted historians as Shelby Foote, C. Vann Woodward, and of course James M. McPherson. Yet the greatest factor in this renewed interest was not just the writings of noted historians, but it was probably the release of the superb television documentary "The Civil War." Produced by Ken and Ric Burns, this nine-part PBS series came into millions of homes and introduced to a whole new generation of Americans this monumental period of our nation's history.

Following the television series, a flood of new histories (and works of fiction as well) appeared on the shelves of bookstores and libraries across the country. One of the most widely read of these new publications was *The Civil War: An Illustrated History.* This book was written by Geoffrey C. Ward, a former editor of *American Heritage Magazine,* who had teamed up with Ken and Ric Burns to produce this fine volume as a companion piece to their award-winning television program.

With this exposure, a whole range of new books was published—histories of battles and individual regiments, collections of essays and anthologies, and biographies of both political and military figures. It was as if the Civil War had been rediscovered and it was within this context that the decision was made to reprint *Father Abraham's Children.*

The original publication of *Father Abraham's Children* was my first introduction to the research and writing of Michigan history. In April 1961, on the anniversary of the bombardment of Fort Sumpter, the *Detroit Free Press* decided to begin a serialization of *Father Abraham's Children.* The fact that the author of the book was also the paper's chief editorial writer might have had something to do with that decision.

At that time, I was attending college and, having completed a couple of years of engineering school, was asked by the author to prepare a series of maps to be used as illustrations for his articles. Needless to say, this was quite an honor for a young college student to be asked to assist a noted historian. The fact that the noted historian was also my father made it all that more exciting.

In all, my father authored eleven books dealing with the history of Detroit and Michigan. His last book I had the honor of co-authoring with him. Yet of all his writings, *Father Abraham's Children* was most special to my father. Probably because he had long had an interest in the Civil War and his own remembrances, as related in his original introduction, brought to mind a very special part of his life.

I know some of the thoughts my father held about the Civil War and its impact upon the citizens of our state. As a boy I walked the fields of Gettysburg with him and listened as he recounted the stories of the men from Michgian. I also remember evenings around the dinner table as he recalled his "battlefield exploring expeditions" with Messrs. Kunz, Babcock, and Mason. And too, I remember the Christmas of 1961 when I received from Mr. Kunz a U.S. navy seaman's cutlass date stamped 1861.

In addition to being a fine historian, my father was also a gifted writer and storyteller. For these reasons *Father Abraham's Children* retains its freshness even today. With this republication, a new generation of Michiganians will be introduced to these stories from our state's past—*Father Abraham's Children.*

Arthur M. Woodford
January 1999

Foreword

THE PEOPLE of Michigan, like the American people as a whole, were more directly and intimately involved in the Civil War than in any other national conflict.

Most readers of this book will have vivid and sometimes poignant memories of World War II, and many will have experienced the intense excitement and hazards of modern warfare. Some will have sustained severe wounds or the fierce shock of battle, while others will have seen comrades fall beside them. Certain civilians will not have completely recovered from the effects of a fateful telegram from the War or Navy department. To all these and many more, World War II will ever be an unforgettable experience.

But the Civil War came home more keenly and more completely to an even greater proportion of the population than did the total war of the 1940's. In many respects the Civil War was the first modern war, but it differed significantly from the wars of the twentieth century. Michigan was a predominantly agrarian society with hundreds of rural communities where everyone was personally aware when each man departed for the war. Many Michigan men enlisted in pairs or in groups, while companies and entire regiments of volunteers were organized by counties or adjoining areas. The communities as a whole were deeply concerned with the location, activities and welfare of what they considered their own military units. This tended to build community cohesiveness but it also brought widespread anxiety and profound grief when the units suffered heavy casualties. Following major battles the local telegraph or newspaper office became the center of shocking revelation as the casualty lists were posted. The proportion of soldiers who suffered casualties or serious illness was greater than in other American wars.

The governments and peoples of much of Europe followed with great interest both the military and political aspects of the "American War." After First Bull Run European military experts criticized the volunteers as undisciplined and ineffective, but by 1863 and 1864 most military observers considered the typical American soldier, whether Union or Confederate, regular or volunteer, as an exceptionally resourceful and competent fighting man. Many civilian observers were impressed by the tenacity and determination of American troops in the face of heavy artillery and rifle fire. Few military experts had ever seen courage or military persistence to match that displayed at Gettysburg and Chickamauga, at Cold Harbor and the crater below Petersburg.

The Civil War was the most gigantic and bloody conflict ever waged upon American soil. The fighting took place not in distant and virtually unknown places like Guadalcanal or Anzio but within a few hundred miles of Michigan and near familiar name-places like Washington and Richmond, Nashville and Chattanooga. Although Michigan was never seriously threatened with Confederate invasion or guerrilla raids, there were repeated rumors and occasional alarms concerning the possibility of attacks from across the Canadian border in Ontario. Under such circumstances the war could never be far away for the people of Michigan.

The heroism of Michigan men in the Civil War, from privates to generals, made their names and deeds household legends throughout the state and across the nation. On the other hand, many instances of heroic sacrifice and devotion passed unnoticed by either the war reporter or the commanding officer, and hence also by the later historian. Military reporting was largely uncensored, the news coverage was generally excellent, and the speed of the newly invented telegraph literally brought the war home to the civilian population.

The issues of the war were domestic and long associated with the experiences of the people of Michigan. The preservation of the Union may have seemed like a nebulous and unpalatable idea to the Southern Secessionists of 1861 but to most citizens of Michigan it epitomized the political ideals of the young and vigorous republic. The national flag proved to be a great rallying standard both upon the battlefield and at the recruiting assemblage. Southerners and even men from the border slave states might insist that slavery was not an issue directly involved in the war, but the people of Ann Arbor and Marshall and Grand Rapids knew that slavery was the great national curse which had to be destroyed before permanent peace could prevail in the land. In a romantic age these issues seemed doubly real and worth fighting for.

As in all wars the daily problems of personal and group survival took precedence over noble ideals. Individual initiative and group resourcefulness proved to be more significant than precision maneuvers or strict military discipline. Devotion to comrades and to one's military unit (whether company, regiment or division) was often a more potent motivation than loyalty to the lofty cause of national integrity. The average soldier's primary goal was sheer survival, to endure until victory was secured, and his secondary but almost constant concern was with some semblance of everyday comfort and convenience, even in the midst of the blood and sweat of the battlefield or the rain and mud of the bivouac.

There was a kind of unbelligerent, almost civilian, character to certain phases of the Civil War. Officers when captured or wounded would often be treated by their captors as long lost comrades or former classmates, as indeed they sometimes were. Pickets at times would deliberately refrain from firing upon their opposite numbers. As if by mutual consent both sides largely demobilized their major armies during the winter months. Private Lane's account of building "comfortable" winter quarters in Tennessee in November, 1863, reminds one more of a friendly camping or hunting expedition than of fighting a terrible civil war.

Frank Woodford catches the flavor and wide variety of moods which constitute the great national tragedy of the Civil War. His selected episodes cover activities from the truly heroic stand of the 24th Michigan at the battle of Gettysburg to the despicable mob attack upon Negroes in Detroit, the incredible exploit of the young woman who served two years as a "man" in the military ranks, the suspense of soldiers' escape from a Confederate prison, the almost routine slaying of the internationally famous General J. E. B. Stuart and the final roundup of the fleeing President of the Confederacy in May, 1865.

The theme is always Michigan in the Civil War—and not just Michigan or the war separately. Woodford's major emphasis is upon Michigan soldiers, both as individuals and as units, and upon their actions, thoughts and aspirations. He is quite properly not much concerned with politics or economics or international relationships, or even with the grand strategy of the war. To most people, locally or nationally, the war was a series of episodes involving relatives and friends, regiments and armies, rather than a national effort for a lofty cause as interpreted by President Lincoln. Woodford presents just enough background material to set the stage for each dramatic episode. The *dramatis personae* are properly introduced but the introductions are never permitted to distract from the action which is always paramount.

A few of the Michigan episodes are unique, like the shooting of J. E. B. Stuart or the capture of Jefferson Davis, but most of them are typical of the exploits of the soldiers and civilians of the other Northern states. Thus *Father Abraham's Children* becomes an informal case history of the great ordeal for the preservation of the Union.

WINFRED A. HARBISON

xi

Preface

IT IS USUALLY DIFFICULT to put the finger on the exact place or moment of a book's genesis, and this book is no exception.

It may have had its origin many years ago when, as a member of the Boy Scouts of America, I walked alongside the veterans of the Civil War in Memorial Day parades, carrying a bucket of water from which the marching old soldiers might refresh themselves. Or it may have begun when, as a newspaper reporter, I covered some of the last meetings of the Grand Army of the Republic and interviewed old, feeble men about their experiences in a war fought so long before that it had become vague and clouded in their minds.

Maybe it started when Civil War veterans—relatives and neighbors—permitted a small boy to handle their sabers and examine the other relics they had brought back from the battlefields and cherished through the years along with their memories of Shiloh, Gettysburg, and Chickamauga.

It was this kind of personal relationship, I like to feel, which really prompted me to write this book. For, rather than a formal account of Michigan's part in the Civil War, or an analysis of military strategy and wartime politics, it is an attempt to retell some of the stories and reminiscences that are the basis of history and legend.

A good many people participated in the writing of this book, and their help and encouragement demands acknowledgement.

My friend Hazen E. Kunz gave me the free run of his extensive library, and made available to me many useful reference works. James M. Babcock, Chief of the Burton Historical Collection, Detroit Public Library, and his amiable staff, cheerfully and efficiently met all of my requirements and demands, and helped me over many a rough research obstacle. Dr. Philip P. Mason, Archivist, Wayne State University, was always cooperative, and to him I owe a special debt of gratitude for the book's illustrations.

It might be added that Messrs. Kunz, Babcock and Mason were delightful companions on battlefield exploring expeditions.

My thanks also are due to Mrs. Esther Loughin, Chief of the Michigan section of the Michigan State Library, William McCann, of East Lansing, Dr. F. Clever Bald, of Ann Arbor, and Fred Hart Williams, of Detroit, all of whom furnished me with materials and were amazingly prompt in responding to my calls for help.

Finally, I must acknowledge the good counsel and encouragement given me by Dr. Harold Basilius, Director, Wayne State University Press, and those of his associates who helped guide this book from the talking stage to the finished product.

FRANK B. WOODFORD

Detroit, January 4, 1961

If you look across the hill-tops that meet the northern sky,
Long moving lines of rising dust your vision may descry;
And now the wind, an instant, tears the cloudy veil aside,
And floats aloft our spangled flag in glory and in pride;
And bayonets in the sunlight gleam, and bands brave music pour—
We are coming Father Abraham—three hundred thousand more!

—From the Civil War song

"WE ARE COMING FATHER ABRAHAM!"

I

So Much

for Valor

IN THE COLD, gray dawn's mist of April 12, 1861, the shooting phase of the Civil War began when the Confederate batteries rimming the harbor of Charleston, South Carolina, commenced to lob shells into Union-held Fort Sumter.

Defending the fort was a garrison of seventy-two officers and men under Major Robert Anderson. One of the junior officers was Norman J. Hall,* a twenty-five-year-old second lieutenant, from Monroe, Michigan. A recent graduate of West Point, he was a member of the 1st U.S. Artillery.

In the person of Lieutenant Hall, Michigan was on stage when the curtain rose upon the Civil War. Michigan was present at the end also. At Appomattox, when the tattered remnant of Robert E. Lee's army marched by and laid down its guns and battle flags in final surrender, it was the 1st and 16th Michigan Volunteer Infantry regiments that received them.

Appomattox was conclusive, but as far as Michigan was concerned it was not final. Wolverine troops were with General William Tecumseh Sherman during his closing campaign against Confederate General Joseph E. Johnston in North Carolina. When the body of the martyred Lincoln was carried to its grave in Springfield, the honor escort was a Michigan regiment. After the collapse of the Confederacy, the fleeing Jefferson Davis was captured by a detachment of Michigan cavalry.

The search for Lincoln's murderer, John Wilkes Booth, set off the biggest manhunt in the history of the country up to that time. Michigan participated in the chase. The military expedition which followed Booth's trail through Maryland and ran him to earth in Virgina was organized and directed by a

---

* I have gathered together in the Appendix detailed information and documentation which would interrupt the flow of the narrative but which may be helpful to readers with a special interest in certain events or personalities. Topics which receive such additional treatment in the Appendix have been marked with an asterisk.

1

former Clinton County farm boy, Lafayette C. Baker.* General Baker was chief of detectives for the War Department and was one of the Federal government's most energetic and effective intelligence agents.

The troops employed in the search for Booth and his co-conspirators were led by Lieutenant L. B. Baker, cousin to General Baker, and Lieutenant Colonel E. J. Conger. Lieutenant Baker had Michigan roots too, and after the war he was employed in the auditor general's department of the state government. Colonel Conger was the brother of O. D. Conger who was prominent in Michigan public affairs and represented the state, in Congress and the United States Senate.

It was a man from Jackson, Captain Christian Rath,* of the 17th Michigan Infantry, who conducted the execution of four of Booth's co-conspirators— Lewis Payne, David E. Herold, George A. Atzerodt and Mrs. Mary E. Surratt.

Michigan continued to play an important role even after the assassination of Lincoln had been expiated. The 3rd and 4th Michigan Infantry regiments were sent to Texas on occupation and pacification duty, and they did not return to their home state until the summer of 1866. The Michigan Cavalry Brigade,* no longer needed in Virginia after April 1865, was sent into the West to help suppress the Sioux and other hostile tribes. Some of the Michigan troopers were mustered out at Fort Leavenworth, Kansas, late in 1865; the 1st Michigan Cavalry was finally paid off and disbanded at Salt Lake City, Utah, on March 10, 1866.

Between that fateful morning at Charleston in 1861 and the mustering out at Salt Lake City almost five years later, Michigan bore a heavy, tragic burden of war both in the field and at home. She had her heroes—fifty of her soldiers were awarded the coveted Congressional Medal of Honor.* She also had her cravens and scoundrels, the latter exemplified by Milton S. Littlefield, whose early years were spent at Grand Rapids. He earned the dubious title, in the reconstruction era, of "Prince of the Carpetbaggers."

Between such extremes of dark and light, there were thousands upon thousands of Michiganders, at home and on the battlefields, who accepted the obligations which the war placed upon them; who served faithfully and bore the sacrifice—not always uncomplainingly, to be sure, but nevertheless with that measure of devotion which in the end preserved the Union.

During the war period, Michigan was largely an agricultural community. Most of the people were small farmers who owned their own land. But in 1861 there also were the beginnings of an industrial and commercial age. In the Upper Peninsula, copper and iron mining and smelting were becoming important activities, and the war brought a boom, particularly to iron. In 1860,

2

iron ore and pig shipments amounted to $736,496. By 1864, the iron mines were producing at the rate of $1,867,215 a year.

Just prior to the outbreak of the war, the state had 1,979 manufacturing establishments producing at the rate of $500 or more annually. Most industry was concentrated in and around Detroit, which had almost all of what might be described as the state's then heavy industry, including railroad equipment and ship building, and a growing number of boiler shops, foundries, and machine shops. Output of iron and steel products was on the increase.

Lumbering was a major industry, operating in 1860 at the rate of about $10,000,000 a year. Fisheries contributed to Michigan employment and income. At the beginning of the war, the state was shipping upwards of 80,000 barrels of fish a year. Large shipments of dried and salted fish found a market in the South. Fish packing naturally created a demand for salt, and the one industry acted as a spur to the other.

Commerce understandably catered to an agricultural market. Several Detroit firms engaged in lucrative shipping, forwarding, and commission businesses. Mercantile houses were solidly established in Detroit and other leading Michigan cities, supplying the rural stores with everything from dress goods to liquors and farm equipment.

The base of the whole Michigan economic structure, though, remained the family farm. Staple products were wheat, rye, buckwheat, corn, barley, oats, potatoes, butter, hay, maple sugar, wool, peas, beans, cheese, beeswax, and honey. About 1863 fruit farming began to develop in importance. Michigan grown and processed crops found their way to market in New York, moving down the Great Lakes and through the Erie Canal, and some were funneled down the Ohio and Mississippi to the South. Michigan wheat was particularly esteemed in England and France.

General farming naturally suggests livestock raising, and southern Michigan sent large quantities of beef, pork, and mutton to market. During the war, the state was a large meat supplier for the armies. Every farmer needed horses, and horse breeding was important in the agricultural economy. The war drums had barely begun to beat when quartermasters were ranging through Michigan buying mounts for the army. Undoubtedly it was the quality of Michigan horses as much as the riders that enabled Michigan cavalry to perform so brilliantly. Because the state could produce both mounts and the men to ride them, the War Department called upon Michigan for a higher proportion of cavalry regiments than most of the other states provided.

When the call to arms first sounded, Michigan's population (1860 census) was 775,881, placing it tenth among the loyal states. It ranked just behind

Wisconsin and slightly ahead of New Jersey. The 1860 population was concentrated in about twenty counties, all of them south of a line extending west from Port Huron. It was a predominantly native American population, although not necessarily native to Michigan. Of the Michiganders of 1861, more had been born in New York than in any other state. Large numbers had migrated from New England, Pennsylvania, New Jersey, Ohio, and Indiana. Michigan had a substantial Canadian colony, and of the other foreign-born, Germans predominated, followed closely by the Irish, English, and Dutch.

Background, tradition, and economic interest all combined to create a progressive, liberal social and political order which was the antithesis of that found below the Mason-Dixon line. Abolition sentiment, while far from universal, was strong in Michigan, but the belief in the integrity of the Union was stronger. What people believed in hard enough they would fight for.

And fight Michigan did, through four long, bloody years. Out of her comparatively small population, she sent 90,048 men into service. That was twelve per cent of all her people—one man out of each eight men, women, and children whom the census taker counted.

Those men were organized into thirty-one regiments of infantry; * eleven of cavalry; one regiment of engineers and mechanics; one regiment of sharpshooters; fourteen batteries of light artillery; and several miscellaneous companies, some of which were incorporated into regiments of other states. Michigan also contributed its share to the regular army. The 19th U.S. Infantry, a regular army unit, was composed almost entirely of Michiganders. Only 598 Wolverines served in the Navy, a seemingly small number in view of the fact that many Michigan men earned their civilian livelihoods as mariners on the Great Lakes. Perhaps the relatively few Navy enlistments can be explained by the fact that the sailors were needed at home to man the Lakes ships which moved the iron ore, lumber, and other cargoes essential to the war effort. Most Navy recruits naturally came from the Eastern seaboard states where many ships were outfitted and launched. Still, hardly a Michigan regiment went to the front which did not have some seamen in its ranks.

In the interval between the fight at Blackburn's Ford on July 18, 1861— the first major engagement in which Michigan troops were involved—and Appomattox on April 9, 1865, Michigan regiments participated in at least 802 battles or skirmishes. There were few if any major engagements fought east of the Mississippi in which Michigan units did not take part.

There remains one more body of statistics which requires attention. Of the 90,048 Michigan men in service, 14,855, or sixteen and a half per cent, died for their country. Of the total of these casualties, 2,820 were killed in action, 1,387 died of battle wounds, and 10,136 succumbed to disease. An additional 512 were unclassified casualties. To this list must be added the uncounted thousands who came home maimed or in shattered health, to live out their lives in pain and anguish, a burden to themselves, their families, and their communities.

So much for valor!

And now, before examining some of the incidents which followed the attack on Fort Sumter, it would be well to consider some prior matters which helped set 90,048 pairs of Michigan feet on the road to war.

II

Freedom Train

"Slave catchers!"

The cry echoed through the streets of Marshall, Michigan; crackling in the crisp morning air of January 2, 1847.

"Slave catchers!"

The sleepy men of Marshall tumbled out of their warm beds, pulled on their breeches and boots, and reached for their shotguns. They reacted instinctively, like minutemen. Their grandfathers at Lexington and Concord had reacted the same way seventy-two years before in response to the tocsin: "The British are coming!"

In Marshall the shout was taken up and passed from house to house, from street to street.

It was the cry of America's awakening conscience.

There was no need for anyone to direct the footsteps of the men who poured out of their houses. They knew where to go without being told. With expressions of grim determination, they ran toward the edge of town where a cluster of shacks provided shelter for Marshall's community of Negroes.

Shantytown was in an uproar. White men, strangers, were breaking into private houses and dragging frightened Negroes into the street. The center of excitement was at the home of Adam Crosswhite, a mulatto. Crosswhite had a gun and was threatening to shoot whoever approached.

The men of Marshall soon rounded up and disarmed the strangers. But there was still a good deal of shouting and milling around. There were ugly threats about tar and feathers and rides on rails. That from the indignant citizens, colored and white. From the slave catchers there were demands for protection, arguments about property rights, and insistence that the authorities be summoned.

What happened in Marshall that morning had happened before in Michigan and was to happen again many times.

Adam Crosswhite, his wife, and three children were the chattels of a Kentucky plantation owner named David Giltner. They had escaped three or four years before and by means of that mysterious, nebulous operation known as

7

the Underground Railway, they had been passed along from farmhouse to farmhouse, from village to village, across Indiana and into Michigan. At Marshall they thought they had found sanctuary and freedom.

In some way Giltner had traced his five articles of property, and had sent four agents, led by Francis Troutman, to claim them under the Federal law which provided for the return of fugitive slaves. But Marshall had no intention of permitting them to be sent back to Kentucky and bondage. Abolition sentiment was strong in southern Michigan and slave catchers operated at their peril.

Troutman was a cool one. While the mob threatened him and his associates, he calmly asked for names and wrote them down in a little pocket notebook. Members of the crowd weren't afraid to identify themselves; some defiantly spelled out their names so Troutman would make no mistake.

Soon the town marshal and the squire appeared on the scene. Troutman and his aides were escorted to the lockup, where they were lodged while warrants were prepared charging them with breaking and entering, assault and battery, and illegal possession of firearms. It was all very neatly handled; everything was done according to the strict letter of the Michigan law.

By the time Troutman and friends had been able to post bond and win their release, Adam Crosswhite and his family were back on the Underground Railway, headed for Detroit. Arriving there, they were escorted across the Detroit River to Canada where they were safely beyond reach of anyone from Kentucky.

The Underground Railway by which the Crosswhites escaped from the South was an informal association of abolitionists who arranged for and encouraged slaves to escape from their owners, and passed them on from one "station" to another until they were safely in Canada,* or in some northern community where they could be hidden and protected.

The "stations" were usually a night's travel apart. They were farmhouses, barns, haystacks, caves, or clumps of woods; any place where the fugitives could be hidden and fed during the day. When night came the fugitives were concealed in the bed of a wagon and driven to the next stop, or they were guided on foot or by other means to their destination. There were occasions when real trainmen permitted the fugitives to hide in boxcars and ride in style on a railroad which was not underground.

Many—possibly most—of the stationmasters were Quakers; in Michigan that sect was particularly active in the cause. Its best known leaders were Erastus Hussey of Battle Creek, and Mrs. Laura Smith Haviland, who conducted the Raisin Valley Academy in Lenawee County. In Detroit and elsewhere free Negroes worked for the Underground, as did several Jewish families who knew something of persecution from the old country.

The smoothness with which the Underground Railway functioned was due to the courage, devotion, and open handedness of those who operated it, and to the experience they acquired over twenty-five years of smuggling slaves out of the South. An elaborate code was perfected by which a stationmaster could be notified when to look for a shipment of passengers, how many to expect, and something about the condition of the consignment.*

For example, a stationmaster might pick up the weekly paper from a town below him on the line and read an advertisement in the personals column such as this:

"There is a chance to purchase a horse that will suit your purpose. He is a mahogany bay, young, well broken, large, and is just the thing for a minister. You can see him on Tuesday afternoon. Price $100."

The station agent, anticipating a shipment, would understand the meaning of such an ad. It would tell him to expect on the following Tuesday a large mulatto man who was a church member, possessing some education. He would have $100 to help cover his expenses.

Again, a message, perhaps contained in a note, would mention a "light brown filly," referring to a young girl. If reference was made to a bargain, or if it was stated "the price is cheap," those along the route understood that the passenger on the way had no funds.

One message stated: "I have secured for you a pair of black and tan pups —good ratters, but young. They will be ready for you next Monday." This was a warning to be on the watch for the arrival of two children.

Most of the escapees who traveled the Underground Railway in Michigan came from Missouri or Kentucky. Their destination was Detroit. From there they could easily be transported to Canada. There were two main lines in the state. One, known as the "Central Michigan," * came up through Cass County in the southwest corner of Michigan. Its depots were at Cassopolis, Schoolcraft, Climax, Battle Creek, Marshall, Albion, Parma, Jackson, Michigan Center, Dexter, Ann Arbor, Ypsilanti, and Plymouth, with occasional way-stops at other places. From Plymouth, the route followed the Rouge River into Detroit. The other line entered the state near Hillsdale or Morenci, and ran through Adrian and Tecumseh to Ann Arbor and Ypsilanti. When circumstances required there were always variations and alternate routes.

In Detroit the terminal was the livery stable of the Temperance House, a hotel operated by Seymour Finney,* an ardent abolitionist. The hotel was located on Woodward Avenue at State Street. The stable was on the northeast

9

corner of Griswold and State Streets, opposite the building which had formerly been the state capitol of Michigan. On occasion, when Detroit was "too hot" to handle contraband cargo, arrivals were shunted over a spur line to the farm of Peter Lerrich, near Mt. Clemens in Macomb County. From there, when the coast was clear, it was easy to take them across the St. Clair River to Canada.

The Underground Railway was completely frustrating to slave owners and their agents who went north to recover strayed or stolen property. It was common knowledge that the traffic was carried on, but, as if by universal agreement, no one would admit knowing anything about it. By 1855, when the obnoxious Fugitive Slave Law of 1850 had been in effect five years, official impediments were raised, such as the Personal Liberty Law * adopted by the Michigan Legislature. This statute prohibited the use of any county jail for the detention of escaped slaves, and also required county prosecutors to defend fugitives in any legal action brought to reclaim them.

As if to taunt the slave catchers, items frequently appeared in Detroit newspapers announcing the passage of their quarry across the river.

"Twenty-nine fugitive slaves, men and women, from Kentucky and the Carolinas, who had arrived in this city by the underground railroad, passed over the river into Canada yesterday morning about 3 o'clock," said a notice in the *Detroit Free Press* of April 20, 1853.

The February 2, 1854 issue of the same newspaper carried this report:

> Underground Railroad Operations—The night connections of the underground railroad, between this city and Canada, are made by any of the small boats along the wharves to which the passengers take a fancy. On Friday night, the second cutter of the revenue schooner *Ingham* was taken from its winter moorings by some half dozen sable southern gents who arrived by the above road, and who were so anxious to get into Her Majesty's dominions, that they never said "by your leave, sir." The boat has been recovered.

How many slaves found their way to freedom via the Underground Railway through Michigan obviously cannot be exactly determined. But before the Civil War ended the necessity for the system and put it out of business, the number was considerable. An estimate by an operator put the figure at between forty and fifty thousand.* Western Ontario to this day has substantial Negro communities made up of descendants of slaves who escaped by the Underground.

Although Adam Crosswhite and his family were among those fortunate ones who finally found safety and freedom in Canada, their story did not end with their escape.

Giltner, their owner, filed suit in the Federal district court in Detroit against the Marshallites for damages. The names which his agent, Troutman, jotted down in his notebook, provided a list of defendants.

The case came to trial July 21, 1848. But Giltner discovered, as many other slave owners did, that while the letter of the law was on his side, the sympathy of juries was not. It was almost impossible in Michigan to get a favorable verdict for the plaintiff in fugitive slave cases, a fact which angered the South and added to the growing sectional resentment. The Crosswhite jury disagreed and there was no verdict.

But that wasn't the end of the matter. In 1848 Lewis Cass, the senior United States senator from Michigan, and long a political leader of the people of his state, was nominated for President by the Democratic Party. Cass personally stood for moderation. He deplored slavery, but he believed that its extension or prohibition in the territories and new states should be decided exclusively by the people of those territories and states. The preservation of the Union was to him more important than slavery. He sought to avert the kind of split between North and South which followed Abraham Lincoln's election twelve years later. Because the Democratic Party was strong in the South, and because he needed the slave states' support, Cass was in no position to alienate Southern votes by any stand which might be construed as leaning toward abolition. His supporters felt it would be politically disastrous if the home state of their candidate openly offended the South by condoning antislavery activities of which the Crosswhite incident was typical. The Crosswhites, therefore, became a national political issue.

Because of the politics involved, strong influence was brought to bear upon the United States district court, and a new trial was ordered. Justice John McLean, of the United States Supreme Court, was called in to preside. That suggests the lengths to which the Democrats went to assure a favorable outcome. A verdict of guilty was returned by a jury which had been hand-picked. The ringleaders of the Marshall crowd were required to pay damages and costs of $1,925. This sum was raised through public subscription by Whigs and Free Soilers. While members of those two parties used the Crosswhite case to denounce the candidacy of Cass, he carried his own state in the election. He had been successful in sidestepping an issue and had satisfied the South. Nevertheless, the Crosswhite affair served to solidify antislavery sentiment in the North and particularly in Michigan.*

There were other fugitive slave cases which, while lacking the political implications of the Crosswhite matter, added to the general turbulence prevailing during the ante-bellum period and gave additional significance to the work of the Underground Railway.

The same year that the Crosswhite affair occurred, there was another incident which stirred the people of Michigan.

Robert Cromwell escaped in 1840 from his owner, David Dunn of St. Louis, and by means of the Underground Railway made his way to Flint, where he opened a barbershop and prospered. When he fled, he left behind a daughter, the property of Dunn. By 1846, Cromwell was well established and began to think about obtaining his daughter's freedom. He wrote Dunn, offering to purchase the girl for $100. As a precaution (Dunn did not know his whereabouts) Cromwell put a Montreal dateline on his letter. No sooner had he mailed it than he realized his mistake. Regardless of the dateline, the postmark would show it had been mailed at Flint.

Cromwell knew that his error now made it possible for Dunn to trace him. So he sold his barbershop and moved to Detroit. Apparently Cromwell was an enterprising person because he was soon the proprietor of a small restaurant at Brush and Larned Streets.

As Cromwell feared, Dunn went to Flint, investigated, and traced him to Detroit. There he retained a lawyer who must have been more energetic on behalf of his client than he was ethical. The attorney knew that popular feeling would bring on trouble if Cromwell was arrested and dragged into court. So he used subterfuge. He had Dunn bribe a constable to call on Cromwell and tell the Negro that District Judge Ross Wilkins * wanted to talk to him about some property in the neighborhood of his restaurant. The strategy was to get Cromwell quietly into court and before Judge Wilkins, who would have no alternative but to order his return to St. Louis. The Federal law was cut and dried.

Not suspecting anything was wrong, Cromwell appeared at the courthouse. As he entered, Dunn (who was hiding behind the door) seized him, and with the aid of a couple of strong-arm men tried to drag him to the second floor, where Judge Wilkins was holding court. Cromwell resisted, and to prevent his escape from the building his captors locked the courthouse door from the inside.

Cromwell had no intention of being taken to court if he could help it. He put up a valiant struggle in the corridor, shouting for help at the top of his lungs. The commotion attracted a crowd in the street. William Lambert and George de Baptiste, the two colored leaders of the underground, tried to force the courthouse door to rescue Cromwell. Judge Wilkins, whose personal sentiments were all on the side of abolition, hurriedly recessed court and hid in the dusty attic of the building in order to avoid being confronted by Cromwell and having to perform his legal duty.

By this time the mob, composed, it was said, of Negroes and Irish, was getting bigger and uglier. Someone produced an ax, and Lambert and de Baptiste started to smash their way in. With Judge Wilkins hidden and out of the way, his court clerk opened a window and dropped the door key to the crowd. It took only a minute to rescue Cromwell, and another minute to start him on his way to Canada.

The mob, however, was not satisfied. It howled for vengeance and there were open threats to lynch Dunn. That unhappy gentleman fled down the street with the pack at his heels. He was saved from their fury when someone admitted him into a private house. The Negroes of Detroit did not let the matter end there. They went before a justice of the peace and obtained a kidnaping warrant. Dunn was arrested, and, while kidnaping charges might have been hard to prove under the circumstances, he was nevertheless held in jail for six months. Finally brought to trial, he was acquitted and permitted to return to St. Louis. His experience served as a warning to other Southern slave catchers of what they might expect from the authoritites and people of Michigan.

In the end slave owners and their agents just weren't safe in Michigan, and many Negroes found it unnecessary to go to Canada. They found refuge in small towns and in the country, and members of various protective associations formed in the South to recover escaped slaves found it hazardous to interfere with those who sought sanctuary in Michigan.

The representative of one slave owners' association, acting for Kentucky interests, appeared in southern Michigan in 1847, traveling from one community to another in Cass, Calhoun, Branch and other counties. He posed as an attorney looking for a place in which to settle and open a practice. Actually he was a detective. His real purpose in going from one town to another was to locate escaped slaves. He was the advance man for what was to be a large expedition of slave catchers, who were planning to swoop down on southern Michigan and make a wholesale recovery.

After the initial investigation was complete, a band of thirteen armed men "invaded" Battle Creek, posing as the sales crew for a washing-machine company. Somehow their plan leaked out, and Erastus Hussey and several of his associates warned the Kentuckians to leave. A threatening public attitude helped convince them that Hussey was right.

The raiders—that was the term applied to them—didn't give up easily. Pretending to leave, they piled into the wagon or van in which they had arrived, and drove across the Michigan line into Indiana. Then they circled back to Cass County, where the township of Calvin * was almost entirely populated by Negroes, many of them legitimately free. Acting on information previously obtained, they forced their way into the home of Josiah Osborne, a white agent of the Underground, and captured three Negroes he had hidden. A fourth escaped and raised the alarm.

The Kentuckians moved swiftly, invading two other homes of white families, those of Joel East and Zachariah Shugart, where they rounded up five more Negroes, including three men, one woman, and a baby.

By this time the minute men were rallying; men and boys, black and white, turned out with shotguns, pitchforks, and billets of wood. Soon three hundred of them had assembled, and they were in no mood for argument or parley. The heavily outnumbered Kentuckians surrendered meekly and were marched off to Cassopolis, the county seat. The Negroes were sent to a tavern, where part of the vigilante force guarded them. The slave agents were taken before a justice of the peace and charged with kidnaping, trespassing, and assault and battery. They were tried on the spot and convicted, and then released under bond to leave the state and not return. It was an easy solution; there really wasn't room in the lockup to accommodate so many.

Considerably subdued and shaken, the Kentuckians started home. They almost didn't make it. Several Negroes hid in a cornfield along the road over which they had to pass, and prepared to ambush them when they came by. Some of the same group which had protected the Negroes got wind of the intended ambush and broke it up, giving as much protection to the harried Kentuckians as they had given but a short time before to the Negroes.

The Cass County affair attracted nationwide attention, and provided Henry Clay with material for a rousing speech, in which he denounced the entire state of Michigan as a hotbed of radicalism. The Kentucky legislature adopted a resolution demanding redress. Later, in 1849, the Kentuckians recovered their courage and took their complaint into Federal court in Detroit, seeking to have several of the Cass County Negroes turned over to their proper owners. Their legal efforts proved no more successful than their direct action had been. Their suit was dismissed and again they went home empty-handed.

Michigan simply wasn't in the mood to accommodate either the persecutors or the prosecutors of runaway slaves.

The antislavery agitation in the North reached a grand climax when the fanatical John Brown and twenty-two followers staged their ill-advised, ill-fated raid on Harper's Ferry, Virginia. That event, which inflamed North and South alike and pushed the country toward civil war—made it, in fact, almost inevitable—had its antecedents in Detroit.

On the evening of March 12, 1859, the celebrated Negro orator and abolition leader, Frederick Douglass, was billed to deliver a lecture in Detroit. There was every prospect that the hall would be filled. Even those who opposed abolition, or who had no particular convictions on the subject one way or another, attended because Douglass was a celebrity. Such discourses as he customarily delivered were in those days regarded as entertainment, and he was a major attraction. Seated in the audience was a gaunt man, heavily bearded, with an eagle eye from which flashed the fire of righteousness. Garbed differently, he could have been perfectly cast as an Old Testament prophet. His name was John Brown.

Brown had arrived with five white followers from Missouri, by way of Iowa and Illinois. Somewhere along the way his party had picked up fourteen slaves, whom he brought through the Underground and delivered in Detroit for forwarding to Canada. Some accounts say Brown, by coincidence, reached Detroit on the day of Douglass' lecture. Others put the time of arrival two or three days earlier and indicate that he accompanied his shipment of contraband to Chatham, a Canadian county town sixty miles east of Detroit. He is supposed to have stayed there with Elijah Willis, a Negro publisher and leader who was regarded as head of the Negro community in West Canada, and to have returned with him to Detroit on March 12 purposely to attend the Douglass lecture.

At any rate, after the lecture, Brown, Willis, and Douglass went to the home of William Webb at 185 East Congress Street, where several other men active in the Underground movement also assembled. In the company, besides those mentioned, were William Lambert, George de Baptiste, John P. Richards, Dr. Joseph Ferguson, and the Reverend William C. Monroe.* They met by design to hear Brown outline a scheme which for some time had been taking form in his mind.

His plan as he described it was to recruit a group of reliable men and attack and capture Harper's Ferry. His raid would be the signal for a general revolt of slaves throughout the South. Harper's Ferry, with its Federal arsenal from which Brown could distribute arms, would become the focal point of the uprising. There the slaves would assemble, and in that mountain fastness they could resist whatever forces might be sent against them.

It has sometimes been said that the idea of the raid was born that night at Webb's. Actually, Brown already had his plans well worked out in his own mind; what he wanted from his Detroit friends was advice, money, manpower, and moral support.

The group's reaction to Brown's scheme was varied. Douglass thought it was reckless and certain to fail. He wanted nothing to do with it. Brown accused him of cowardice and finally, under that kind of pressure, Douglass reluctantly gave his approval but refused to take an active part in the plot.

George de Baptiste, the firebrand of the group, had demonstrated his flair for street fighting and mob action in earlier escapades such as the Cromwell affair. He proposed even more drastic measures: A terror campaign was to be conducted in the South; on an appointed Sunday, churches all through the South were to be blown up and their assembled congregations sent heavenward with charges of black powder. Brown wisely vetoed that idea, pointing out that scores of innocent people would be slaughtered and public opinion, upon which he counted, would turn against him.

In the end the gathering endorsed the Harper's Ferry raid and promised to find a recruit in Chatham.*

The raid on Harper's Ferry was carried out on October 16, 1859. When news of the assault flashed with electrifying effect over the wires, it did not create much surprise among the Negroes of Detroit. They had been anticipating it. Neither, probably, did the outcome—disastrous from Brown's standpoint—run contrary to the real expectations of Brown's fellow conspirators. If the antislavery people wanted a martyr, they had one now. Public feelings, North and South, were stirred as they seldom have been before or since, although emotions naturally ran in sectional channels. A Kentuckian, visiting in Detroit, wrote Governor Wise of Virginia, warning him that a large armed force had been recruited and was drilling in Michigan, and soon would be marching to rescue Brown.

There may have been some talk in Detroit about such an expedition, but none was organized.*

They hanged John Brown on December 2, and his death was a sharper weapon for the abolitionists than any knives or bayonets in the hands of would-be rescuers.

Michigan listened to the tolling of bells in a score of towns, and agreed with Henry Wadsworth Longfellow, who that day wrote in his diary:

"This will be a great day in history: the date of a new Revolution."

True enough! Michigan regiments were soon tramping to the cadence of a stirring war song: "John Brown's body lies a mould'ring in the grave, but his soul goes marching on!"

III

Reveille

in Michigan

A WAR HAD begun in Charleston harbor. The deep-throated roar of the Confederate batteries bombarding Sumter, and the answering bark of the fort's guns, stirred distant reverberations in the streets of Michigan towns and in her country lanes.

At first people received the news in stunned silence. They gathered outside the newspaper offices, waiting for the latest bulletins to be posted, or they stood around the railroad depots, listening while the clacking telegraph instruments told of new developments.

Since the previous November many people had felt that war was inevitable. Abraham Lincoln's election at the polls set the course of future events. Now the waiting was over; the time for moderation, for conciliation, had slipped beyond reach. The moment of truth had arrived, and its impact was sobering.

When later news arrived that Sumter had been surrendered, the first feeling of shock gave way to other moods—indignation, anger, and the exhilaration of spirit which painted the prospect of war in heroic colors.

The *Detroit Advertiser,** spokesman for Michigan Republicanism, replied to the rebel challenge with a verbal salvo which fairly reflected the public feeling.

"There can be no more hesitation in the mind of any patriot as to the duty which the emergency imposes," the paper declared. "The Stars and Stripes must be sustained at all hazards and at every sacrifice. . . . The man is a traitor who shrinks now from rendering loyal service to the authorities which are intrusted with the honor and integrity of the nation."

The *Detroit Free Press*, the Democratic Party organ, was more restrained. In its April 14, 1861 edition, it pointed out that the disaster befalling the country could have been averted, but "while we condemn the wretched fanaticism and folly and wickedness which have produced the national calamities, and lament and deplore the fratricidal conflict, it is nevertheless our duty to support the government in a contest for its own preservation. . . ."

On the 15th, the *Advertiser* carried the news of Sumter's capitulation and Lincoln's call for 75,000 volunteers for three months' service. "That a civil war is absolutely raging at this moment in the United States . . . is a fact almost too astounding to believe," it cried.

All over the state, in towns large and small, patriotic rallies answered the President's call to arms. Bands played; civic leaders exercised their best oratorical talents.

"Resolved," shouted C. I. Walker to a Detroit mass meeting on the 15th, "that we hereby pledge our undivided loyalty to the maintenance of the government and its laws, and in the present crisis we avow our united purpose, if need be, to devote our lives, our fortunes and our sacred honor to the support of the integrity of the government and the honor of its flag."

Although there was a certain lack of phraseological originality in the Walker resolution, it charmed the crowd nevertheless. A copy was sent to A. Lincoln, White House, Washington, D.C. He, no doubt, derived great comfort and satisfaction from it.

The *Free Press* continued in sardonic vein to view what it considered a manifestation of mass hysteria. Instead of war meetings, it suggested that peace meetings would be more appropriate.

"What have the people of the two sections to fight about?" the *Free Press* editor asked. "Why should they cut each other's throats? Why should they rush to arms, lay waste each other's fields, burn each other's cities and towns, and leave each other's bones to bleach on desolated plains?"

To the *Free Press,* the war which had hardly begun was already a bloody business. The sad part, the paper pointed out, was that nobody realized where the headlong rush to war was leading.

> Those who are going to enlist expect to have a fight with somebody or other, but they don't appear to know exactly who or what for. A mild-looking blue-eyed little man told us yesterday that he was going to "have his rights and stick to the constitution." He had enlisted, or was about doing so, but of course didn't know whether the government would number him as one of the seventy-five thousand, or dispatch him to defend the western frontier from the Indians.

The *Free Press* had some reason to question Michigan's ability, if not her motives, for making war. Like the other Northern states, Michigan had nothing at hand to support a military posture. The state treasury was empty and the Legislature was not in session. The militia consisted of twenty-eight scattered independent companies with a total strength of 1,241 officers and men. For the most part, the militia companies were more social than military organizations, sporting fancy uniforms of their own design, and bearing dashing designations such as the Detroit Light Guard, the Michigan Hussars, the Coldwater Cadets, the Flint Union Greys, and the Hudson Artillery.

These companies were local rather than state units. The state spent less than $3,000 a year for military purposes, and the militia of 1861 bore no resemblance whatever to the National Guard which later provided a nucleus for a citizen army in two world wars.

Nevertheless, the militia companies were full of fight, regarding themselves as the backbone of the North's cause as, indeed, for the moment they were. Individually, the members were not only ready but eager to serve for ninety days in answer to Lincoln's call. Belonging to some of the companies were graduates of West Point who had left the army for civilian pursuits, and some veterans of the War with Mexico. It was these one-time professionals, prompt to return to their old trade of soldiering who provided the state with its most competent and distinguished military leaders.

While there were men enough and more for immediate needs, there was an almost complete lack of equipment, arms, and serviceable field uniforms. And of organization above the company level there was virtually none. A rush was made on the bookstores and every available copy of Hardee's *Tactics* * was snatched up; old brass cannon left over from the territorial Indian wars were polished up. Muskets and shotguns of ancient vintage were brought out of storage. They would serve to drill with, even if they were not exactly lethal as far as the rebels were concerned.

But if Michigan lacked everything else, it had one great asset. That was its war governor, the energetic, capable and wholly dedicated Austin Blair.* To Michigan he became what Lincoln was to the Union.

Blair was a native of Caroline, Tompkins County, New York. Of Scotch ancestry, he was born February 8, 1818. His father George and his mother Rhoda migrated from New England and were said to have built the first cabin in Tompkins County. The parents, like so many pioneers who came out of New England, were militant abolitionists, and young Austin inherited their strong antislavery sentiments.

When he was old enough Austin was enrolled in the Cazenovia (New York) Seminary. He followed more advanced studies at Hamilton and Union Colleges, and it was from the latter that he graduated in 1837. Two years later he was admitted to the bar in Tioga County, New York. But the West beckoned to him as it did to so many of his New York State neighbors. In 1841 he moved to Michigan and hung out his shingle in Jackson. There he became an active member of the Whig Party and a follower and admirer of Henry Clay.

Although Blair was an attorney by profession, he was a politician by inclination, and it was into the fields of public service that his true interests soon led him. In 1844 he was elected to the Michigan Legislature, where, as a Whig, he was associated with a liberal faction which advocated granting Negroes the franchise. Blair also played a leading part in the movement to abolish capital punishment, and supported legislation designed to nullify at the state level the enforcement of the Federal fugitive slave laws.

At heart he continued to be an ardent abolitionist, and in 1848 he became a member of the Free-Soil Party. The Whigs soon after that time virtually disappeared as a political force. Those who were left, consolidated with Free-Soilers, abolitionists and liberal Democrats to form the Republican Party as a medium for the expression of their political views. Blair was one of those who attended the famous organizational meeting of the Republican Party "under the oaks" at his home town of Jackson, Michigan in 1854. From that time on he was identified with the Republicans—invariably with the party's most liberal wing. One of the first Republicans elected to office, he was sent to the Michigan Senate in 1855, and for the next four years he was the majority leader in that chamber.

In 1857 Blair was a candidate for the United States Senate, but he was passed over in favor of Zachariah Chandler. He continued to maintain his place of authority in the party, however, and in 1860 he led the Michigan delegation to the Republican national convention in Chicago. There he was a staunch supporter of the candidacy of William H. Seward for the presidential nomination and he admitted that he was bitterly disappointed when the convention chose Abraham Lincoln.

Nevertheless, Blair was too loyal a party man to allow his chagrin to interfere with his campaign efforts on behalf of Lincoln. To give the national ticket strength in Michigan, he permitted his name to go on the ballot as candidate for governor. Elected, he took office January 3, 1861, and for the next four years—two terms—he devoted himself whole-heartedly to the Union cause. Along with Andrew of Massachusetts, Curtin of Pennsylvania, Morton of Indiana, and Yates of Illinois, he was one of that band of Northern governors upon whom Lincoln leaned heavily, and who gave him firm, unwavering support.

Austin Blair's election did not usher in any sudden or unexpected change in the political climate of Michigan. The general principles for which he stood, as far as national and sectional issues were concerned, were not very different from those of his immediate predecessors. The people had been conditioned to a firm attitude toward the South; in fact, they voted for such men as Blair and Lincoln because these men's views reflected public thinking.

Governor Moses Wisner of Pontiac immediately preceded Blair in the gubernatorial chair. In his valedictory address to the Legislature, he expressed sentiments which were shared by most of the people.

"This is no time for timid and vacillating councils when the cry of treason and rebellion is ringing in our ears," Wisner said. "The constitution, as our fathers made it, is good enough for us, and must be enforced upon every foot of American soil. Michigan cannot recognize the right of a state to secede from this Union. . . . I would calmly but firmly declare it to be the firm determination of Michigan that the Federal constitution . . . must and shall be preserved."

Wisner was the man to back his convictions with action. He did not hesitate to hazard his life for what he believed. A little more than a year after he left office, he accepted the colonelcy of the 22nd Michigan Infantry, and died in the service of his country in Kentucky, January 4, 1863.

In his inaugural address, Governor Blair picked up where Moses Wisner had left off.

"The Federal government," he said, "has the power to defend itself, and I do not doubt that that power will be exercised to the utmost. It is a question of war that the seceding states have to look in the face."

From the tone of these speeches, delivered almost four months before Sumter was fired upon, it is evident that Michigan was being prepared for what eventually had to come.

Blair was at his home at Jackson on April 15 when he received President Lincoln's telegram, calling for 75,000 volunteers for three months' service. Michigan's quota was one regiment of ten companies, about eight hundred men. Blair immediately took the train to Detroit, arriving on the 16th. He proceeded directly to the office of H. M. Whittlesey, a member of the Detroit Light Guard. Joining him there in a building on Griswold near Congress were several civic, state, and military leaders, including Alpheus S. Williams (a Mexican War veteran, destined to become Michigan's only army corps commander), Mayor Buhl, Adjutant General John Robertson, William D. Wilkins, H. L. Chipman, Orlando Bolivar Willcox (a former West Pointer), James E. Pittman, and State Treasurer John Owen. The question which Governor Blair laid before this group was not whether Michigan should comply with the President's summons, but how.*

Alpheus Williams—the nominal head of the militia with the rank of brigadier general—and Willcox were professional soldiers, or at least the closest to professionals that Michigan had at the moment. Whittlesey, Wilkins, and Pittman were amateurs, but they were experienced businessmen and their voices carried weight in the community. Their judgment could be trusted. Owen was not only the state treasurer, he was also a prominent industrialist and business leader. It was to these men that Blair turned for advice. First of all he wanted to know how much it would cost to equip a regiment and put it in the field. The opinion around the conference table was that the state would need $100,000.

All heads turned toward John Owen. There was little he could say except to remind all of them that the treasury was empty. Someone—probably Owen —suggested that the public might be asked for an interim loan until the Legislature could be convened and money could be properly appropriated. It was decided to try to raise $50,000 in Detroit and an equal amount outstate. Actually, all that could be asked of the citizens was to sign pledges upon which a loan could be negotiated. That was a most unusual way to transact state business; in fact, the legality of the plan was highly doubtful. Only the Legislature could bind the state to make the loan good.

Nevertheless, it was the only practical solution to a situation which constituted an emergency, and Owen was instructed to get busy. Before the meeting in Whittlesey's office broke up, $23,000 had been pledged by those in the room. The balance did not come easily. The subscription rolls remained open until July, and the total amount pledged was $81,020. Lewis Cass, Michigan's elder statesman, and the H. A. Hayden Company of Jackson, made the largest pledges, $3,000 each. E. B. Ward, reputed to be Detroit's wealthiest man, signed up for $2,500, and there were many other pledges of $1,000 and more. From those big sums the pledges scaled down to such modest amounts as $25 and $50. Among well-known firms and individuals on the list were Richmond & Backus, G. & R. McMillan, C. C. Trowbridge, T. H. Eaton, Dr. Herman Keifer, all of Detroit; J. W. Begole of Flint, eventually to become governor of Michigan; James Clements and Henry Tappan of Ann Arbor, and Erastus Hussey of Battle Creek, the abolitionist leader. One Detroit firm, presumably short of cash, offered to contribute one ton of grapeshot, barreled and delivered on any dock in the city, free of charge, "for the express purpose of dealing death to all traitors."

Meanwhile, having disposed of money problems, Governor Blair and his conferees turned their attention to other matters.

First, there was a proclamation to be written and issued, calling for ten companies of infantry to be mustered into Federal service for ninety days. Adjutant General Robertson, who held his post throughout the entire war, was told to accept the first ten uniformed militia companies which volunteered. All companies were advised to recruit up to full strength as quickly as possible. Each was to consist of a captain, a first lieutenant, a second lieutenant, four sergeants, four corporals, two musicians and sixty-five privates. Companies not immediately accepted in the first call were to be placed on a stand-by status, to be organized into additional regiments if needed.

Company or line officers were to be elected by the ranks—common procedure in the militia at that time. Field or staff grade officers were appointed by the governor.

"It is confidently expected," Blair said in his proclamation of April 16, "that the patriotic citizen soldiery of Michigan will promptly come forward to enlist in the cause of the Union, against which an extensive rebellion in arms exists, threatening the integrity and perpetuity of the government."

The governor's confidence in the patriotism of his people was not misplaced, with regard either to the militia or to the civilians. Throughout the state the volunteer companies met and democratically voted to offer their services. They opened their armories and began to recruit.

War fever mounted by the hour. United States District Judge Ross Wilkins summoned all Federal office and job holders in Detroit before him and administered to each an oath of loyalty to the Constitution. He felt this to be necessary because of the number of government officials in Washington and the South, civil as well as military, who were transferring their loyalties to the Confederacy.

Ordinary citizens had the opportunity to express their sentiments of loyalty on April 18 at a public flag-raising ceremony in front of the Detroit post-office at Griswold and Larned. An April shower failed to dampen the enthusiasm of several hundred men and women who jammed the street. The Light Guard paraded, and the City Band blared patriotic airs, including "The Star-Spangled Banner" and a lively new popular tune, "Dixie."

"Old Glory floated everywhere," a witness to the current excitement reported. "The shipping was adorned with it as on a holiday; every flagstaff bore it; it floated across the avenues, from the roofs of houses, from cupolas, from all public places and in all conspicuous positions. Omnibus men decorated their vehicles and horses with it; draymen and wagoners exhibited a similar partiality for it; shops, stores, offices, public halls and all like places were festooned with it. Those who did not have a flag were eagerly inquiring for one. Sailmakers were driven with the great demand, and the supply of bunting became exhausted."

Draped across the front of the post office was a large banner bearing the words "The Union—one and perpetual; what God has joined together let no man put asunder."

The *Advertiser* observed that everyone was wearing a large red-white-and-blue rosette pinned to his lapel.

What was happening in Detroit was being repeated in scores of towns and villages throughout Michigan. Drums beat, fifes shrilled, veterans of former wars got out their old uniforms and paraded, and orators made the most of their opportunities. In Manchester, a town of 1,500 people, a big rally was held on the evening of April 17. The principal speaker, Jabez H. Fountain, who the day before had been appointed quartermaster general by Governor Blair, turned up looking every inch the war hero with a bandage around his head. He had been cut by flying glass when the enthusiastic citizens of nearby Clinton fired a cannon too close to his railroad car and shattered the windows.

Everywhere the atmosphere was charged with excitement—so much so, in fact, that it is doubtful that many people noticed a small item in the personals column of one of the Detroit newspapers. Or, if they did read it, they could not have attached any particular significance to it. The item stated:

"We regret to learn that Capt. George G. Meade,* Topographical Engineer, commanding the survey of the North-west Lakes, has been ordered to lighthouse duty at Philadelphia, Pa."

Captain Meade and many of his former Detroit neighbors would, before long, have the opportunity to renew old acquaintance in a little town in Pennsylvania which had no lighthouse.

Its name was Gettysburg.

IV

Thank God for Michigan!

WILLIAM H. WITHINGTON * went to war, but on the way he stopped long enough to buy a corset for his wife at Mrs. McAdams' shop in Jackson, Michigan. To remind himself of what he had to purchase—a "No. 28, fasten in front with strap, $2"—he jotted down the essential information and specifications in his little pocket notebook. On the opposite page, he registered the number of his service revolver. It was 1107. Withington was a careful man; a written record was much more reliable than a frail memory.

Having done his errand at Mrs. McAdams', Withington boarded the Detroit train. The date was April 16, 1861. He made the journey, in all probability, with his fellow townsman, Governor Austin Blair, whose business in Detroit was urgent.

Besides being an up-and-coming businessman of whom everybody in Jackson expected great things, the twenty-six-year-old Withington was captain of the local militia company, the Jackson Greys. It was in his capacity as a military man that the governor might have wished his company. Governor Blair was embarking on a fateful journey. He was on his way to meet his advisers and see what could be done about raising an infantry regiment to fill Michigan's quota under President Lincoln's call for 75,000 volunteers for three months' service.

The call to arms came as no great surprise to Captain Withington. He had been expecting it, and, with the thoroughness which was typical of everything he did, he started early to get ready for war. A native of Dorchester, Massachusetts, there was enough Yankee in him to make him methodical and precise. The entries in his notebook reveal a good deal about him. A careful man with a dollar, as every young man on his way up should be, he noted every penny he spent.

For example, on January 2, 1861, he gave his wife Julia her allowance of forty dollars, but he also spent (was it recklessly?) nine cents for apples and a newspaper. And although he stayed at his office until 8:30 that night, he went to the theater later. The admission was twenty-five cents. He didn't get home until 11 o'clock, but he failed to mention what Julia said about that. Perhaps the gallon of ice cream for which he paid two dollars was a peace offering.

The following week Withington paid his dues to the Jackson Greys—another twenty-five cents. It was a sound investment, because on February 15 he was elected captain of the company.

What Withington had been anticipating happened April 15. When the news of Fort Sumter's surrender was announced, the Jackson Greys assembled immediately in their armory and voted to offer their services, which, their captain proudly recorded, "were tendered by me to the Gov. this day." It was with satisfaction that he pointed out that in the aye-and-nay voting on the question all thirty-one votes were ayes.

The next morning, when Withington boarded the train, recruiting had already started, and when he returned from Detroit on the 17th, he "found enlistments going on with a rush." He promptly took charge and "examined and selected my men."

When it came to raising a company of volunteers or buying a corset, Withington gave the matter at hand his close personal attention.

The enthusiasm with which the Jackson Greys embraced the goddess of war was duplicated all over Michigan in every town which had a militia company. Each unit was as eager as Withington's to offer its services. Each began to fill up its ranks to the authorized strength of seventy-eight men with a spirit which was as competitive as it was patriotic. Orders were that the first ten companies ready would be accepted; the laggards would have to wait until they were needed.

First of all, though, there were certain necessary preliminary steps which had to be taken before a regiment could be put in the field. There had to be a staff. Governor Blair took care of that by appointing one while he was in Detroit on April 16. Alpheus S. Williams, or "Pap" Williams, as his men called him, a fatherly veteran of the Mexican War, was made brigadier general. Later he would command a Union corps. For the moment, however, he established headquarters on the third floor of the Detroit post office. William D. Wilkins, who had also served in the Mexican War, was made brigade major and inspector, and Henry M. Whittlesey was appointed assistant quartermaster with the rank of captain.

There was immediate work for both officers. Wilkins was sent out to inspect the militia companies in the towns along the lines of the Michigan Central and Michigan Southern Railroads, to determine which ones were ready to be mustered in. Proximity to transportation, rather than priority in offering their services, apparently was the principal qualification that established which of the state's companies would be accepted. Captain Whittlesey, his pockets stuffed with the money that Treasurer John Owen had been able to borrow or beg, set off to New York to purchase cloth for uniforms.

The week following Governor Blair's call for troops was one of feverish activity and excitement. In the preparations to go to war, the experiences of the Detroit Light Guard were typical of what all the militia companies went through.

The Light Guard * was a venerable military association which traced its origins back to the Black Hawk War when it was organized as the Brady Guard. Prior to the outbreak of the Civil War it was primarily a social organization which attracted gentlemen of standing in the community as members. Military training consisted of occasional drills and parades, but much more frequently there were dances and banquets. Now and then, the Light Guard journeyed to another city to fraternize with some other militia company, playing host in turn, and trying to outshine the other in a display of hospitality. Several militia companies occasionally joined in a summer encampment for three or four days, and vied for prizes in drill competition.

An encampment was held for three days in Jackson in August 1860, and the Light Guard attracted "much attention by their uniform step and steady line." There were nine companies present with a total of two hundred and thirty-eight men. The Detroit contingent consisted of thirty-three "muskets." Each man received a bouquet from the belles of Jackson, a token which fired the Detroiters up to such a pitch that they handily won the competitive drill prize —thirty-five dollars. Most of the money, unfortunately, had to be paid to farmers to reimburse them for fences torn down to supply firewood.

A few weeks prior to that encampment, the Light Guard was visited by the Chicago Zouaves. The guests were met at the railroad station and escorted to the Michigan Exchange Hotel for breakfast. An afternoon parade was held, up Woodward Avenue to Grand River, and thence to the cricket field near Third.

"Men, women and children followed, all eager to view the famed Zouaves," reported an observer of the gala event. "They drilled for an hour and a half, and went through some thirty different evolutions amid the applause of the spectators of whom there were about 5,000 present. The drill was all that the most experienced military critic could have desired."

That night the Zouaves slept in the Light Guard Armory, and the following morning left Detroit for an eastern tour.

Being a member of the peacetime militia was something like belonging to a uniformed lodge or fraternity.

Then came April 1861, and everything changed!

The Light Guard met in its armory on Woodbridge Street the evening of April 17 and, as Withington's Jackson Greys had done two days earlier, voted to "tender our services as a company to the commander-in-chief of the Michigan Militia, and ask to be enrolled in the regiment called for in his proclamation of the 17th inst."

Several of the members, substantial business and family men, some well on towards middle age, had to resign because of their personal circumstances. A number of them, including Captain James E. Pittman, then formed what amounted to a Light Guard auxiliary, or home guard company of gray beards. This left the ranks pretty well thinned out, and the recruiting which started on the morning of the 18th resulted in the formation of an almost brand-new company. Before the older men withdrew, however, they exercised their prerogative of electing new officers.

For captain they chose Charles M. Lum, thirty-one years old. He had been first sergeant of the old company. John D. Fairbanks, who at forty-three was the oldest man on the roster, became first lieutenant, and William A. Throop, twenty-three, was elected second lieutenant. George W. Grummond succeeded Lum as first sergeant.

The rolls were filled by April 19 with seventy-five of the most promising applicants from the throng which clamored to join.

"Recruits came in by the hundreds, and many were so anxious to enlist with the famed Light Guard that money was liberally offered for the honor and privilege." So said Frederic Isham, a Detroit newspaperman who later went to the front as a war correspondent.

Of those accepted, almost all were Detroit residents. The average age of the company was twenty-three. Columbus Starkweather, Otis Cook, and Irving Garrison, at eighteen, were the "babies" of the company. Eventually, twelve men were dropped, but for every vacancy thus created there was a score of eager applicants.

Training began immediately, and on April 20 rookies with two left feet were learning the rudiments of squad drill in the open spaces of Campus Martius, the plaza adjoining City Hall. At brigade headquarters, General Williams was working around the clock in an effort to clear away details and wade through the paper work involved in completing the regimental organization. Recruits who considered themselves as seasoned veterans after two or three days in the awkward squad became impatient. They had expected to be off for the front within a few hours after enlisting. They didn't know that General Williams had received instructions from the War Department not to rush matters. The Michigan regiment, he was told, wouldn't be needed in Washington before May 20.

A second company, the Michigan Hussars, was formed in much the same manner as the Light Guard. Being a new unit, the Hussars lacked the prestige and social standing of the senior company, and therefore received much less attention from the public and the press. Its ranks may have been filled by men who were turned away by the Light Guard.

Old campaigners, watching the preparations and recalling their experiences in former wars, were free with suggestions to the recruits about how to survive the rigors of the field. The newspapers were glad to pass these tips along, and the *Free Press* (April 25, 1861) printed the following sound advice from an "Old Soldier."

1. Remember that in a campaign more men die from sickness than by the bullet.
2. Line your blanket with one thickness of brown drilling. This adds by four ounces in weight and doubles the warmth.
3. Buy a small India rubber blanket (only $1.50), to lay on the ground or to throw over your shoulders when on guard duty during a rain storm.
4. The best military hat in use is the light-colored soft felt; the crown being sufficiently high to allow space for air over the brain.
5. Let your beard grow, so as to protect the throat and lungs.
6. Keep your entire person clean; this prevents fevers and bowel complaints in warm climates. Wash your body each day if possible. Avoid strong coffee and oily meat.
7. A sudden check of perspiration by chilly or night air often causes fever and death. When thus exposed do not forget your blankets.

April 24 brought the awaited general order forming the regiment—the 1st Michigan Infantry—and listing the companies which had been selected,* giving them their designations. They were: Company A, Detroit Light Guard; B, Jackson Greys; C, Coldwater Cadets; D, Manchester Union Guard; E, Steuben Guard (Ann Arbor); F, Michigan Hussars (Detroit); G, Burr Oak Guard; H, Ypsilanti Light Guard; I, Marshall Light Guard; K, Hardee Cadets (Adrian).

This general order also named the regimental officers. They were Colonel Orlando B. Willcox, Detroit; Lieutenant Colonel Loren L. Comstock, Adrian;

Major Alonzo F. Bidwell, Coldwater; Surgeon William Brodie, Detroit; Assistant Surgeon Cyrus Smith, Jackson; Adjutant John D. Fairbanks, Detroit, and Quartermaster Edward Grey, Detroit.

"The makeup of the companies," said the state adjutant general, "was composed of young men from all the professions and trades, and really embraced a class of the most respectable of the community." He might have added that for the most part the members of the 1st were from the first families, the socially elect, of their various towns.

From April 18 to 24, all drilling was in company armories, but after the formation of the regiment, a shift was made from the companies' home bases to Fort Wayne, the army post on the Detroit River near the western limits of the town. It had been the intent from the beginning to use the Fort as a mobilization and training center. A "Camp of Instruction" for officers had already been established there on orders of General Williams. In April 1861, no regular army garrison was stationed there, and for several days before April 24 the custodians had been busy getting the place in order.

The two Detroit companies, A and F, were ordered to march from their armories to the Fort at 10 a.m. on Wednesday, April 24. The Light Guard however, was delayed several hours until a supply of muskets could be obtained so that it could present a properly martial appearance as it paraded through the city streets. The out-state companies were instructed to leave their homes on the following Monday, April 29, and by that afternoon all ten companies had reported in and Colonel Willcox took command of his regiment. Later the same day a detail of regular troops which had been stationed at Mackinac joined the 1st Michigan at Fort Wayne. Their arrival was delayed by their transport running aground on Belle Isle. Several hours were required to free the vessel.

Willcox and his officers had a problem of discipline on their hands from the outset. The light-hearted rankers, fresh from their roles of store clerks, bookkeepers, students, and young gentlemen about town, weren't accustomed to the restrictions of military life. They regarded their induction as the beginning of a joyous, carefree outing which would reach an exciting climax some afternoon when they would smash the rebellion with one blow.

Companies A and F discovered they didn't have much to do at the Fort before the rest of the regiment arrived. Playing cards and reading soon palled, and the men saw no good reason for not returning to town for an evening of pleasure. Strict orders had been given that no one was to leave the Fort without a written pass. That posed no problem. The men simply wrote out their own. A stop was put to that after twenty men had passed the guard, but others discovered a convenient exit through an unwatched sally port. Most of them spent the night in Detroit, but all were on hand in the morning for reveille.

The first few days were devoted to giving the recruits the outward appearance of soldiers. On May 1, the first consignment of rifles arrived and was distributed. The arms which the men had brought with them were turned over to the home guards. The new weapons, described only as "minie guns," were probably Springfield 1855 muzzle-loading rifles of .58 caliber.* This assumption is based on the statement that the regiment was equipped with the most up-to-date weapons. The records fail to show where they came from. At the beginning of the war many of the arms were furnished by the various states, but the rifles of the 1st Michigan may have been Federal issue, sent down from the United States Arsenal at Dearborn.

It was time to put away the fancy uniforms of the independent companies which the men had been wearing since they moved into the Fort. The colorful trappings of hussars, dragoons, and zouaves were shipped home and the new uniforms were donned.

Captain Whittlesey had returned to Detroit with $20,000 worth of cloth which he had purchased from the A. T. Stewart Department Store in New York. Detroit tailors, working on contract, made up to each man's individual measure the uniforms, which were described as "gray petershams for overcoats, navy blue for coats and navy flannel for pants." The headgear was the familiar kepi or forage cap, and the ladies of Detroit held sewing bees at which they made havelocks for the men. These, it was said, would be most useful as protection against sunstroke when the regiment marched victoriously through the hot, sunny South.

Along with the 1st Michigan and the few regulars, the Coldwater Light Artillery,* which eventually became Battery A, 1st Michigan Light Artillery, also was assigned to the Fort. It had gone to Detroit with the Coldwater Cadets. Altogether, about a thousand troops were crowded into a space which lacked facilities for that many. To relieve the overcrowding, the passenger steamer *Mississippi* was borrowed from the Michigan Central Railroad and moored alongside the Fort. It was used to quarter four companies, and provided a mess hall for the entire regiment.

At first the mess was catered by a hotel man, Hiram R. Johnson. It came as something of a shock to the young gentlemen to discover they were expected to eat at bare pine tables "with tin cups and plates, with iron spoons and cutlery." The menu was described as similar to that served in the average

31

dollar-a-day hotel. Apparently it did not compare favorably with mother's cooking. The soldiers' indignation exploded into a small riot one day when their dessert consisted of rice pudding instead of pie!

Gradually, however, the regiment began to shake down. Squad drill gave way to company and battalion exercises, and the 1st Michigan began to feel very soldierly. The Fort was visited daily by hordes of admiring civilians— friends, relatives and plain sightseers who were impressed by the progress the troops were making. The easiest access to the Fort from the city was by boat, and the Windsor ferry line scheduled regular trips, with hourly sailings on Sunday. One day alone it was estimated that ten thousand people visited the Fort. A Detroit newspaper offered this description of what they saw:

> The Fort . . . has assumed a military aspect. Approaching it by road, the first object that calls attention is the group of tents pitched outside the Fort for the use of the guard, for which, every 24 hours, 22 men are detailed. . . . Upon entering the Fort a busy scene presents itself. In one place a company, fully armed, may be seen exercising in the manual, in another an awkward squad is receiving its first lessons in the facings, and in another a platoon is being hurried up on double quick step; yet out of this seemingly chaotic element, order is being brought.

The public, like the reporter for the *Advertiser*, saw nothing naive or affected in the habit of the Light Guard whose members "have now been at the Fort for several days" and who "love the old flag that floats above one of the bastions, and several times a day they gather around the flagstaff and sing the 'Star-Spangled Banner!' Such men will not stand quietly by and see that flag insulted."

Actually there was little time for choral exercise. The daily routine was strenuous. Reveille sounded at sunrise; sick call was at 6:30, and breakfast at 7. The guard was mounted at 8; dinner call came at 1 p.m., and evening parade was held one hour before sunset. Tattoo was blown at 9, and all hands were expected to be on their straw-stuffed pallets half an hour later.

On May 1, the regiment was mustered into Federal service. That required new physical examinations, and there was a weeding out of the unfit and the under-aged—some of the recruits having lied about how old they were. There were also opportunities, before induction, for second thoughts, and those who wished to do so were permitted to resign. Few availed themselves of that privilege, even though there were applicants willing to pay generously for a place in the ranks. John Stephens, a prosperous Detroit merchant, went to the Fort with his son Billy, who yearned to be a soldier. The elder Stephens offered to pay any member of Company A the sum of $300 in gold to step out and give his place to the boy. There were no takers. Billy finally went to war as a civilian quartermaster clerk.

After three weeks of preparation, the 1st Michigan was deemed ready. Orders were issued to start for Washington on May 13, and to go by way of Cleveland, Harrisburg, and Baltimore. Now excitement really mounted. Everyone was in a lather of last-minute preparations; friends and relatives came in droves for final goodbyes, and on the night of departure, it was said, the "pillows of their sisters and sweethearts were wet with tears."

Departure time was late afternoon. At 5 p.m. two Michigan Central steamships, the *Illinois* and the *May Queen,* drew alongside the Fort, and the 1st Michigan, 798 strong, went aboard. Slowly the two vessels moved up-river to the foot of Woodward Avenue, where a brilliant fireworks display was touched off as a civic farewell. Then, with much cheering and handkerchief waving, with the regimental band stationed in the bow of one of the ships, playing "The Girl I Left Behind Me," the two vessels turned their prows downstream.

The 1st Michigan was off to war!

The self-esteem which the regiment carried with it was not lessened during its trip East. Cleveland offered a warm welcome on the morning of the 14th. After breakfast, a large crowd gathered at the depot to see the men entrain for Pittsburgh. So cordial was the reception, that Private Thomas O'Neil, an Ypsilanti boy of Company H, missed the train, and was marked down as the regiment's first deserter. Later he was arrested and escorted to Washington by a United States marshal. He had not deserted, O'Neil insisted at his court-martial. He had only "got on a bit of a spree."

Cleveland papers commented on the smart appearance of the 1st Michigan and its fine equipment, and deplored the fact that Ohio troops fell far short of measuring up to the Michiganders.

It was much the same story in Pittsburgh and Harrisburg. At the latter city, the regiment bivouacked at Camp Curtin, a fairgrounds converted into a cantonment. It was already filled with Pennsylvania rookies, and the 1st Michigan created a sensation with its soldierly appearance. By comparison, the Wolverines looked like veterans. In fact, all along the route east, the 1st Michigan passed regiments from other states which had been sidetracked into camps because they lacked arms and uniforms and were deemed unfit to be sent to Washington.

Word ran ahead of the Michigan troops, telling of their approach, and people lined the railroad tracks through Ohio and Pennsylvania to see them pass. At every stop delegations brought food to the men; young ladies presented locks of their hair and occasional kisses to the gallant-looking fellows from the Wolverine state who, in turn, were feeling more heroic by the minute.

At Harrisburg the regiment was issued rations and for the first time was told to do its own cooking. This was a new and baffling experience, and the results were something less than a gourmet's delight. Despite orders not to leave camp, many of the men chucked underdone beef and scorched coffee into the bushes and lit out for restaurants in town.

Colonel Willcox and staff were being entertained by Governor Curtin of Pennsylvania at a late dinner in a fashionable Harrisburg hotel. During the course of the festivities Willcox did a little boasting about the firm discipline with which he controlled his men. As proof he declared that the regiment was caged up in camp, strictly observing his orders to remain there. The Colonel was in the midst of this self-congratulatory dissertation when its effect was completely spoiled. For at that moment about twenty privates of the 1st Michigan filed into the dining room and sat down. The Colonel's face "when his eye fell on us—was a 'sight for the gods!' ", one of the men recalled later.

At Baltimore secessionist sympathy was strong, and some New England troops, passing through a few days earlier, had been roughed up. As a precaution the 1st Michigan, upon arriving there, was issued ammunition and ordered to load its guns. Then, with the band at its head, playing the "Star-Spangled Banner," the regiment marched across town from one depot to another. There were no unpleasant incidents. On the contrary, the *Baltimore Clipper* had only complimentary things to say about the 1st, calling it "the finest in appearance of any who have yet reached this city."

It was 10 o'clock the night of May 16 when the Michigan regiment arrived in Washington, but even at that late hour it was warmly welcomed. In those uncertain days Washington was in a state of perpetual jitters. Rebel flags could be observed from time to time on Arlington Heights across the Potomac. Many Washingtonians sympathized openly with the South. There was no assurance that enough loyal Union troops could be assembled to hold the city against a Confederate coup or attack.

Then, out of the night, came those fine, soldierly-looking men from Michigan, the first Western regiment to reach Washington. Loyal citizens breathed easier.

"The Michigan Rifle Regt. came into town last night about 10 o'clock, marching from the depot up the Avenue to Eleventh Street," the Washington correspondent of the *New York Evening Post* informed his newspaper. "They were preceded by a splendid band of music which soon aroused our citizens, and long before they had reached the quarters assigned to them, hundreds of people were out to give them welcome. The enthusiasm of the crowd was irrepressible, for this was the first Western regiment that had arrived at the capital."

To a lonely, burdened man in the White House, the band's blare and the tramp of feet brought the answer to a question which had bothered him: Would the Western states remain loyal to the Union and support it with men and resources?

Now he knew.

"Thank God," said Abraham Lincoln, "for Michigan!" *

V

The Ordeal of
Colonel Willcox

SITTING RAMROD STRAIGHT in his saddle, Colonel Orlando Bolivar Willcox led the 1st Michigan Infantry across Washington's Long Bridge over the Potomac and into Virginia.

It was a proud moment for the handsome West Pointer because his regiment had been chosen to be the vanguard of the Grand Army. It was the first Union force to invade that part of Virginia which, for the next four years, was to be one of history's bloodiest battlegrounds.

The date was May 24, 1861.

In less than two months, the 1st Michigan with the rest of the Union army would stream back across the Long Bridge, seeking haven in Washington, defeated and humiliated.

That would be July 22, 1861.

Between those two dates Willcox and his men from Michigan were to get a taste of what war really was like. They would learn that to bring the South to heel was going to involve much more than parades, neat new uniforms, and heroic posturing in front of pretty girls.

For Orlando Willcox it would not be the fulfillment of a glorious destiny, but rather the beginning of a long, bitter ordeal: blood and pain and dreary months behind gloomy prison walls, not as a prisoner of war, but as a convicted felon.

But let's go back to the beginning.

Soon after the 1st Michigan arrived in Washington, Willcox called on the ancient and venerable General Winfield Scott, commander-in-chief of the United States army. As a young lieutenant, Willcox had served under Scott in the war with Mexico.

"Where do you wish to make your camp?" wheezed old "Fuss and Feathers," as Scott was familiarly known.

"Yonder," replied Willcox quietly, pointing across the Potomac to Arlington Heights.

"Patience," sighed the old warrior. "You'll get your chance."

The opportunity came eight days after Willcox and his men got to Washington, the first Western regiment to reach the capital. Other troops had preceded them; still others followed close on their heels. Most of them were boys from New England and New York. They presented a motley military array. There was the 11th New York, better known as the Fire Zouaves, a regiment recruited by the dashing Colonel Elmer Ellsworth from among the fire companies of New York City. They were uniformed in the colorful zouave costume of baggy red pants, short blue jackets, white spats, and red fezzes. These brilliant uniforms added a splash of color to parades, but they also made good targets. The 1st Michigan would see a good deal of the Fire Zouaves in the next few weeks.

Then there was the 79th New York. They called themselves the New York Highlanders. A body of fierce and quarrelsome Scots, they arrived in Washington wearing kilts but changed into trews when they went into battle. Other New Yorkers and some of the New Englanders wore uniforms of cadet gray, which led to confusion. In battle it was almost impossible to distinguish them from the Confederates. But then confusion reigned on the other side of the battle line too. Many of the rebel officers, in the early stages of the war, insisted upon going into action in their blue uniforms of the Old Army.

Willcox received his marching orders late on Thursday, May 23. Appearance of Confederate riders on the south side of the Potomac, almost within musket shot of the White House, did nothing to relax Washington's taut nerves. Military experts, professional and arm chair variety alike, urged occupation of the south bank by the Federals. It was really sound advice. If there was to be a movement by Union troops into Virginia, a bridgehead would be necessary.

Each of the privates of the 1st Michigan was issued forty rounds of ammunition and one day's cooked rations. Overcoats and heavy baggage were loaded in the wagons, and the regiment fell in. In light marching order, it was led by Willcox just after midnight through Washington's dark streets to the Long Bridge. There he halted and sent scouts ahead to see what kind of reception Virginia had prepared. It so happened that all was quiet along the Potomac that night. The 1st Michigan crossed without incident or opposition and took the road to Alexandria, eight miles away.*

Alexandria was a rebel town and the 1st Michigan was ordered to occupy it and clear it of any enemy troops that might be loitering there. The Wolverines weren't expected to carry out that assignment without help and support. Marching with them under Willcox's command was a two-gun section of artillery. The Fire Zouaves had instructions to board a river steamer at Washington and land at Alexandria at the same time the 1st Michigan marched in by road. During the night thousands of other Federal troops followed the Michiganders across the Potomac and occupied other sectors along the river. Consequently, by morning a fairly substantial force had been built up on the south side, and the bridgehead as well as the approaches to Washington were secured.

The 1st Michigan entered Alexandria at sunrise. The Zoo-Zoos, as the Michiganders called the Fire Zouaves, came ashore at the same time and spread out along the water front. The whole enterprise had been planned with careful secrecy and was executed with precision. The Confederates were completely surprised.

Willcox hurried his column toward the center of town, his first objective being the railroad station. A small body of rebel cavalry, caught unawares, frantically endeavored to form a line of resistance in front of the old slave market. The detachment consisted of about thirty-six men, commanded by a Captain Ball.

Willcox didn't hesitate. He placed his two guns in position to sweep the street and sent a strong detail on the run through the back alleys, effectively cutting off the horsemen's retreat. Being a reasonable and sensible man, and faced with no alternative but to be blown to blazes, Captain Ball handed over his sword—"very gracefully," as one reporter stated—and he and his men were made prisoners.

For the moment everything was well in hand. The mayor of the town was routed out of bed and easily persuaded to surrender his city. He watched as the American flag was run up over the market place. Willcox, the senior officer in charge of the expedition, proclaimed Alexandria to be under martial law and detailed Company H (the Ypsilanti Light Guard) as a military police force.

An unfortunate incident then occurred, marring what was otherwise a routine operation. The Zouaves' commanding officer, the twenty-four-year-old Colonel Elmer Ellsworth, advancing from the boat-landing to the center of town, observed a Confederate flag flying from the roof of a local hotel, the Marshall House. Accompanied by an aide, the regimental chaplain, a *New York Tribune* correspondent, and a squad of soldiers, he entered the building. Ellsworth, the chaplain, and the newspaperman went to the roof, leaving Private Francis Brownell at the foot of the garret stairs. Hauling down the flag, the colonel tucked it under his arm and started back downstairs. As he reached the bottom step, the hotel proprietor, James T. Jackson, a fanatical secessionist, fired a shotgun blast from the doorway of one of the rooms, instantly killing Ellsworth. Brownell, in turn, shot and bayoneted Jackson to death on the spot.

Willcox had sense enough to realize that Jackson's act was that of a hothead and did not represent an attempt at organized resistance on the part of the inhabitants. He calmed down the troops of his own and Ellsworth's regiments and prevented any retaliatory measures against the citizens.

Back in Michigan, the papers lamented Ellsworth's death, but at the same time they cheered Willcox's "victory."

"To Michigan belongs the honor of attacking and subduing the first armed city of the rebels attacked by the Federal forces," trumpeted a Detroit paper.

In the light of what was soon to happen, it was a good idea for Michigan to wring every drop of satisfaction out of that exploit. Exultation would change soon to despair and disillusionment.

Having subdued Alexandria with the loss of only two lives, the 1st Michigan felt very pleased with itself, although the men, as a correspondent reported, were "much fatigued." With the city safely under Federal control, the regiment moved to Shuter's Hill on the outskirts. There, within sight of Washington, in a pleasant grove of trees, they threw up earthworks and made their camp. The Zouaves were quartered nearby, and before long the two regiments were incorporated into a brigade under the temporary command of Colonel Willcox. The 1st Michigan was taken over by Major Bidwell, Lieutenant Colonel Comstock being absent.

Since Willcox was military governor of Alexandria, he made his headquarters in the city, while his brigade was camped outside of town. The force under him was large enough to discourage any ideas of resistance, so that he was able to treat the people with moderation and consideration. Only once did he have to remove his velvet glove and crack down. That was when the editor of Alexandria's *Virginia Sentinel* refused to publish an official proclamation. Willcox solved the problem by seizing the paper and operating it with a crew of volunteers from the ranks, men formerly employed by the *Detroit Free Press*.

There was some sporadic enemy activity outside of town by guerrillas or bushwhackers who sometimes grew bold enough to take pot shots at the Federals. Details were sent out after them and some of the farmers in the neighborhood were arrested on suspicion of being involved. Detachments of the 1st and the Zouaves patrolled the railroad which ran between Alexandria and Manassas Junction, and guarded the bridges in the Union sector. A company of the 1st was sent to Mt. Vernon, where an outpost was established on the grounds of George Washington's mansion.

For the next four weeks the Michiganders enjoyed a relaxed kind of war. Aside from patrol duty and massive doses of drill, the men led a comfortable existence. Visitors came from Washington, and there were even a few from Michigan. Citizens of Michigan residing in Washington gave the regiment a fine stand of new colors. The Fourth of July was celebrated in high style with a "feu de joies" at sunrise, followed by the playing of the national anthem by the regimental band. At 9:30 in the morning, the regiment was formed for dress parade and was led in prayer by the chaplain. Lieutenant John W. Horner of Adrian, having a flair for such things, read the Declaration of Independence. The regiment then sang the "Star-Spangled Banner," and Colonel Willcox delivered a stirring oration. The formal ceremonies ended with all hands singing the doxology, Old Hundred.

The afternoon was given over to more earthy pleasures. Company A, staging its own celebration, passed the hat and collected enough to buy nine gallons of "commissary" and a supply of plug tobacco.

Captain Withington of Company B looked after his men with fatherly care during the Alexandria interlude. He doled out spending money to those who were broke, giving them amounts ranging from twenty-five cents to ten dollars and, meticulous as always, jotted down in his little notebook the names of the recipients and the amounts advanced. He also made occasional purchases for the mess, providing little luxuries such as lemonade (25 cents), cakes and pies (25 cents), and "cakes for the sick" (5 cents). It was with considerable relief that Withington drew his first pay on July 12. It amounted to $142.

At this time Colonel Orlando Willcox was thirty-eight years old, in the prime of his intellectual, physical, and military life. That he found great satisfaction in his command responsibilities cannot be doubted. It was what he was trained for; the West Point education and tradition were so strong that he made the metamorphosis from civilian to military status with uncomplicated ease and probable relief.

Willcox was born in Detroit, April 16, 1823, one of several children of Charles and Almira Rood Powers Willcox. The Willcoxes prospered and became people of substance in the community. Orlando and his elder brother Eben added distinction to the family name.

Orlando entered West Point in 1843 and graduated in 1847. He ranked eighth in a class of thirty-eight, which suggests, as was indeed the case, an active, intelligent mind. A certain romantic cast later manifested itself in some modest literary accomplishments.

Upon graduation Willcox was commissioned a second lieutenant in the 4th U.S. Artillery just in time to be posted off to the war in Mexico. He served with Lloyd Tilghman's Maryland Volunteer Battery and with Lovell's Battery of the 4th Artillery.

In 1850 he was promoted to first lieutenant; there followed about six years of service, mostly on the Western plains. He took part in expeditions against the Arapahoes and, briefly, against the Seminoles in Florida. Those experiences gave him an insight into and understanding of Indian warfare which he used later to advantage. He was the author of an artillery manual, and ventured as well into the field of romantic fiction with two novels.

During part of 1856 and 1857 Willcox was assigned to units of artillery on coastal defense duty. It was an unglamorous and not very rewarding occupation and after a time the life began to pall. Promotion came slowly; there was no assurance that he would ever advance beyond the rank of captain. Besides, he now had family responsibilities. No matter where the army took him, Willcox always maintained close ties with Detroit. In 1852 he had married a Detroit girl, Marie Louise Farnsworth, the daughter of Chancellor Elon Farnsworth, head of one of Michigan's most distinguished families.

Orlando's brother, Eben Willcox, was a lawyer and by 1857 had become a prosperous and influential member of the Detroit bar and a leader in the city's civic life. With the connections which Orlando's father-in-law and brother were able to provide, and with the demands of family life—he and Marie Louise had six children—it is not surprising that toward the end of 1857 he resigned from the army and returned to his native city.

He began the practice of law in association with Eben. Their offices were in the Rotunda, a veritable nest of legal lights on lower Griswold Street. Orlando and his family lived with the Farnsworths at 426 Jefferson Avenue near Hastings Street—a fashionable part of town. As a lawyer Orlando may have been able; it is doubtful if he was happy. The sedentary life must have bored him, and it can be surmised that he often looked back with nostalgia to the life of adventure and activity which he had abandoned.

That he followed with interest the drift of political affairs during that period of mounting sectional tension, cannot be doubted. There is no evidence that he was politically minded, but his brother and many of his friends were. He must have anticipated what was coming, and it was probably with eagerness that he accepted Governor Blair's invitation to take command of the 1st Michigan Infantry.

If, during the days in Alexandria, Willcox was inclined to reflect upon the recent course of his career, he had reason to feel satisfied with himself. He had whipped together a regiment which had been widely acclaimed as a crack outfit. He had conducted himself well during the capture of Alexandria and during the period of occupation which followed. He had been rewarded with the command of a brigade, and there was no reason why he should stop there. Everyone knew there soon would be a major clash between the Union and Confederate forces, and Willcox felt himself to be ready for any test which he and the 1st Michigan might face.

The trial wasn't long in coming. By July 1, the Union had about 80,000 troops massed in and around Washington. The people of the North demanded to know why so formidable a force had not already marched to Richmond and crushed the rebellion. Political pressure on Lincoln to take the initiative mounted, and the President bowed to it despite the warnings of his military advisers that the army was not ready. Preparations were made for an advance. The Grand Army, forerunner of the Army of the Potomac, was created and its command was given to Brigadier General Irvin McDowell. Four divisions were organized. Willcox's brigade was strengthened by the addition of two more regiments, the 38th New York and the 4th Michigan. The latter left its training camp at Adrian, Michigan on June 25, and arrived at Washington on July 2. These two new units, along with the 1st Michigan and the Fire Zouaves (11th New York), became the Second Brigade, 3rd Division, commanded by Colonel Samuel P. Hcintzclman.*

The Confederates were under equal political pressure to strike the one blow which Southern fire-eaters confidently believed would result in the capture of Washington and the end of the war. They had a force under General Joseph E. Johnston in the lower Shenandoah Valley, and another based at Manassas Junction where General P. G. T. Beauregard had established headquarters. Beauregard's troops were strung out along the Warrenton Turnpike, with outposts at Centreville and Fairfax, the latter about fourteen miles west of Alexandria.

As early as May 31 Michigan newspapers were predicting that "Federal troops will occupy Manassas Junction tomorrow night, driving away the rebels who have congregated there." Although the Union army was not prepared to move that soon, it was obvious to each side that when the proper time arrived, the fight would be for control of Manassas. Its importance lay in the fact that two railroad lines converged there. One ran south and made connections with Richmond; the other tapped the Shenandoah Valley.

Although he felt he was being rushed, McDowell accepted orders to make the first strike. In a sense, he was forced to do so as a measure of desperation. Many of the three-months enlistments were about to run out and he faced the possibility of having a depleted army on his hands. All new troops were being recruited for three years, and the three-months men were being asked to sign up for the extended period. The 1st Michigan had started to enlist for three years on June 28.

The first major move came on July 17 when Willcox's brigade marched away from Alexandria and moved into Fairfax on the Centreville pike, cleaning out the Confederate pickets stationed there. The rest of the army followed, and on the 18th McDowell's force was concentrated at Centreville.

The turnpike bypassed Manassas, which was a short distance south of it. It ran from Centreville to Groveton and then on to Warrenton. Between Centreville and Groveton, about six miles apart, was a rolling terrain, part open fields, part wooded. Through it meandered a small stream know as Bull Run.

West of Centreville about four miles, the pike crossed Bull Run over a stone bridge. Whichever side controlled the bridge controlled the road. It was the key to the fight which was shaping up. The Confederates occupied ground south of the turnpike, and on July 18, while attempting unsuccessfully to establish a foothold on that side, a Union force became involved in a sharp skirmish. In that affair, dignified by the designation of the "Battle" of Blackburn's Ford, the 2nd and 3rd Michigan regiments were engaged. It was there Michigan had its first casualty of the war. The 2nd and 3rd Michigan with the 1st Massachusetts and the 12th New York comprised Richardson's Fourth Brigade of Tyler's Division.

On the morning of July 21 McDowell started his untested, cumbersome and half-trained military machine in motion for the grand assault. The bugles called Willcox's brigade out of their blankets at 1 a.m., and long before the last star had faded three of his regiments were formed. The 4th Michigan had been left behind at Fairfax Court House. There was the inevitable delay, and it was 4 o'clock before the brigade began to march along the Centreville pike with the rest of Heintzelman's division. The 1st Michigan was led by Major Bidwell, with Captain Withington as acting major.

Before long sounds of heavy firing were heard up ahead. The battle had begun with grim purpose on each side. The rattle of muskets furnished the treble for the swelling crescendo of the artillery's bass. Willcox's men had not gone far when they were halted at the side of the road, and, as they stood waiting, they caught their first unnerving sight of the flotsam of battle drifting past toward the rear—the wounded, limping or being carried, the wagons with the dead.

Early in the day Beauregard had been reinforced by Johnston's army, which had ridden the train down from the Shenandoah—demonstrating clearly why control of Manassas and the rail lines was so important. The formidable rebel force made crossing the stone bridge a major undertaking.

44

McDowell looked the situation over and decided his best hope lay in flanking the rebels and, if possible, working around to their rear, getting between them and Manassas. His map showed a route by which this might be accomplished.

Heintzelman's division was ordered to make a wide detour to the right and swing north and west about eight miles to a crossing known as Sudley's Ford. There they would find a road running north and south which would intersect the Centreville-Groveton pike approximately two miles beyond the stone bridge. Tactically, the plan was well conceived. With seasoned troops, well led, it might have succeeded.

Heintzelman set off on a rapid, forced march, Willcox's men eating dust behind Franklin's brigade. The sun arched high and beat down unmercifully. It was one of those hot, humid days on which a marching man can boil in his own juices. Soon the perspiration-soaked men, their canteens dry, began to shuck their knapsacks, coats, and other gear, dropping it at the side of the road in the expectation of recovering their property on their return.

On and on they plodded, and for raw, untrained troops they marched remarkably well. By noon, Major Bidwell reported, the 1st Michigan had crossed Bull Run at Sudley's and was near the intersection of the Centreville and Sudley roads. Ahead of them the battle sounds grew louder and more furious. Two Union batteries had been planted nearby in a field in the southeast angle of the road intersection, and it was there that the fighting raged. To meet this new threat to the Confederate left and rear, Johnston's men from the Shenandoah were brought up. They extended the rebel line so that it overlapped the Union right. It was the Federals' turn now to be in danger of being flanked. One of Johnston's brigades was commanded by a professor at the Virginia Military Institute who from that time on was to be known as "Stonewall" Jackson.

The two Federal batteries got into trouble and Willcox was directed to go to their assistance. He threw the Fire Zouaves in; they advanced in good order but found the enemy well posted. The New Yorkers were greeted with a heavy blast of fire. They answered with one volley and then fell back, as Willcox said, "bewildered and broken." Willcox set out on a desperate hunt for reinforcements.

"Recrossing the Sudley Road," he later stated, "I met the 1st Michigan, Major Bidwell commanding, and marching back with this regiment we found the enemy now drawn up in a thin line across the field and in possession of the battery; advancing to the fence on the roadside the 1st Michigan opened fire, the right wing fell back to reload, owing to a blundering order, but the left stood firm, expelled the enemy and retook the battery."

So far so good! But there was more work, much more, awaiting the 1st

Michigan. The regiment now was holding the extreme right of the Federal line. Cocke's Virginia brigade was in front, and the brigades of Jackson and Kirby-Smith, supported by a body of cavalry under a young rebel colonel, J. E. B. Stuart, were swinging around the right flank and moving into the rear of the Michiganders.

Just then Colonel Heintzelman rode up, and one quick glance told him of impending disaster. To relieve pressure on his division's front and open an escape gap, he directed Willcox to lead the 1st Michigan obliquely to its left, across an open field, and cover the demoralized Zouaves. He promised to send another regiment to aid the 1st Michigan, but it was slow in coming up and when it did arrive it went into the line too far to the left of the Michiganders to give them effective support.

Willcox did not hesitate. Riding in front of the 1st Michigan, he shouted to it to follow him. The regiment's left wing responded gallantly. The right wing managed to re-form and also advanced. The Confederates were driven back to a fringe of woods where they uncovered a masked battery. The 1st Michigan fell back slowly, firing as it went, suffering heavy casualties. Three times more Willcox rallied his men and sent them charging ahead; each time they were repulsed. Actually, each of the 1st Michigan's assaults was against vastly superior numbers of the enemy, formed in a concave line which brought Willcox's men under fire from three sides. The task given the Wolverines should never have been assigned to less than a full brigade. It was too much for green, untried troops, worn to near exhaustion by a march of better than fifteen miles under a broiling sun.

The 1st Michigan took an even five hundred officers and men into that fight.* Six were killed, four officers and thirty-three men were wounded, and five officers and sixty-five men were captured or reported missing.

The *Detroit Free Press* said of the 1st that "the action of the regiment all through the day was in the highest degree honorable, brave and gallant, and reflects the greatest credit upon the state that furnished it."

The failure of the 1st Michigan just about marked the end of the battle. Heintzelman withdrew, marching back to Sudley Ford, and soon the entire army, beaten and disorganized, was in full, panic-stricken flight toward Centreville and Washington.

The story of that retreat which deteriorated into a rout, needs no retelling. The 1st Michigan marched back to Centreville in fairly good order, but beyond that point the men began to straggle. They arrived at Washington the following morning in groups of half a dozen, "having marched," according to a spectator, "nearly sixty miles in twenty-four hours, without sleep, with no food but hard bread, and no drink but muddy water, and a little at that, for thirty-six hours."

The news of the disaster reached Detroit on July 22. It was as though the sky had fallen. Frantic crowds mobbed the office of the *Detroit Free Press,* snatching extras from the hands of the newsboys before they could get out on the street. A police detail was summoned to the building to maintain order. The rumor spread that "the First is all cut to pieces." In an effort to restore calm, the paper posted a bulletin, which stated: "It is confidently believed that the report in relation to the killed and wounded has been greatly exaggerated and that the number will be found very much less by the official returns than at present anticipated."

No attempt was made, however, to minimize the defeat. The *Free Press* frankly admitted: "We are beaten; it is a defeat and a rout."

"It cannot be denied," said the *Advertiser* on July 23, "that we have met with a most disastrous defeat at Manassas Junction. . . . May Providence spare our city and country another such a day."

As for Colonel Willcox, he was left with the cup of bitterness from which there was naught left to drink but the dregs of pain and despair. As he stated later, he "was spared witnessing the disaster which further pursued our arms."

When the final charge of the 1st Michigan was shattered, Willcox's horse was shot under him. Picking himself up, he started to follow his men, but another rebel bullet, finding its mark, smashed into his arm, severing an artery. His men saw him fall and presumed he was dead. Only Captain Withington who was nearby went to his aid.* Withington attempted to lift the wounded man and carry him from the field. He had gone only a few steps when Colonel R. T. Preston's victorious 28th Virginians swept down on them, and both Union officers were captured.

What happened after that is best told by Withington. The story of the following weeks can be reconstructed from the penciled notes which the captain of the Jackson Greys found time to enter in his memorandum book day by day.

Both prisoners were taken to the Lewis farmhouse, which stood on the battlefield less than a mile from where Willcox had been wounded. He was given the best medical care the Confederate staff surgeons could provide. Though his injury was painful and it was apparent he would need much attention, his wound was not expected to be fatal, nor was amputation necessary. He was kept at the Lewis house until August 1, with the faithful Withington permitted to stay and nurse him. Confederate officers, friends from old army days, called upon him and could not do enough in the way of small courtesies. They sent letters to his wife and to Julia Withington, easing the concern each had felt at the first reports that their husbands were dead.

The day after the battle, which Withington described as "a day of horrors," he assisted in bringing in the wounded whose groans "resound through the house day and night." He was permitted to roam around freely under parole, and visited nearby hospitals, where he found a number of Michigan men. Within a week, Willcox was well enough to be moved, but other injured officers were not, and the Confederates wanted to send them to Richmond in a body. Withington chafed at the delay, mainly because conditions at the Lewis house were becoming unbearable.

"The putrification about this house is horrible," he wrote. "The wounded men are covered with m[aggo]ts."

Finally, on Thursday, August 1, Willcox and Withington started for Richmond, arriving the next day after a slow, bumpy train ride from Manassas Junction. Willcox was sent to the general hospital, and again Withington was allowed to accompany him.

They continued to be looked after with great solicitude by everyone. Friends and strangers called and brought food. Even Governor Letcher of Virginia dropped in to pay his respects to the two prisoners. For more than a month Willcox recuperated luxuriously, with Withington the secondary beneficiary. On August 25, a Mrs. Tally sent in their Sunday dinner—duck and chicken with vegetables and custard. The same day a Major Bagley had two gallons of whisky delivered to Willcox. The two men spent their time reading, playing chess, and writing letters.

Then, on September 10, this congenial existence came to an abrupt end. Without notice or explanation, Willcox, Withington, and several other prisoners were coldly informed that they were being transferred to prison at Charleston, South Carolina, and at 3 o'clock that same afternoon they were put aboard a heavily guarded train.

Close-mouthed, stern-eyed guards now treated the prisoners as though they were convicted criminals. When the train reached Wilmington, North Carolina, their cars were shunted onto a siding where they remained all night. It was stifling in the coaches, and the men were refused permission to step on the platform for a breath of air. Withington compared their car to the Black Hole of Calcutta.

They reached Charleston the following day and were taken directly to the town jail, where thirty-four prisoners were jammed into three small cells.

"No furniture but a bucket," Withington noted indignantly. "No plates or cups. Bed bugs soon appear. Breakfast at 11—hard bread and bacon. Ditto with rice in the afternoon."

Home-cooked meals no longer were brought in by kind friends and well-wishers. If the prisoners wanted decent fare they had to buy it. In fact, by September 15, the authorities ceased furnishing any food except salt and sugar. A fifteen-minute turn around the jail yard was the extent of their daily exercise.

There was an explanation for this sudden change. The Union men were no longer looked upon as prisoners of war, but as hostages for prisoners held by the Federal government under sentence of death for piracy.

Soon after the formation of the Confederacy, Southern privateers were commissioned and sent to sea to raid Northern commerce. Some of those maritime guerrillas operated in the Caribbean, hunting ships that transported gold from California. Others worked along the Atlantic coast, and on May 11 two privateers were captured off Long Island.

The Federal government refused to recognize the belligerent status of those raiders, and the *Detroit Free Press* agreed that Washington showed the proper spirit "by ordering every man engaged in the work, who shall be captured, to be strung to the yard-arm and hung as a pirate."

At least one of the captains of the rebel raiders, a man named Smith, was sentenced to be executed and the Confederacy announced there would be reprisals if the sentence was carried out. The group of Bull Run prisoners of which Willcox and Withington were members were picked as hostages.

After being held in the common jail at Charleston about a week, the prisoners were transferred to Castle Pinckney, a fortification in the harbor. Conditions there were much better. Quarters were not so crowded, and there was freedom to roam around the ramparts. Still, they were closely guarded, and their warders refused their request to apply to the Union fleet hovering offshore for money, blankets, and other necessities.

Withington's spirits, already low, drooped further when he got hold of a newspaper with an account of the reorganization of the 1st Michigan and its new list of officers.

"With great surprise & pain," he wrote, "I found my name entirely omitted. What can that mean? There must be some reason for it & I will wait until I know."

Early in October they were unexpectedly shifted back to Charleston and—Withington's words—"again thrust into the despicable jail." They learned the reason quickly enough.

"Pleasant news this morning," the captain wrote. "An order for the selection of officers to stand for the privateers is published. It includes all the field officers here, Col. Willcox not excepted."

A few days later, November 19, five officers were picked out to be the sacrificial lambs and were put into solitary confinement in ordinary felons' cells.

They were Willcox, Colonel Michael Corcoran of the 69th New York, Colonel W. E. Woodruff and Lieutenant Colonel G. W. Neff, both of the 2nd Kentucky, and Major James D. Potter of the 38th New York. Alarmed by this ominous turn of affairs, Withington persuaded his guards to allow him to send a letter to Eben Willcox, warning him of his brother's plight.

For ten days the hostages were kept locked up. On November 29 they were informed that the privateer captain, Smith, was to be hanged that day in the North. Colonel Corcoran was chosen to answer for his life and began preparing himself for death. "Col. C is attending seriously to spiritual matters," Withington noted.

Last-minute influence was exerted in Washington and the privateers were not hanged. The Federal prisoners at Charleston were reprieved, but they did not learn of their change of fortune immediately. Further political pressure was applied on the Federal government, and once more rumors of exchanges began to circulate. Gradually the status of the Bull Run men reverted to that of prisoners of war and their treatment improved. They were permitted to receive boxes and trunks of food and clothing from the North, money was sent to them, and Willcox was allowed a visit from his sister, Mrs. Taylor, who came from her home in Texas to see him, probably to intercede for him.

Even so the ordeal wasn't entirely over. When Charleston was menaced by Union forces, the men were transferred again on January 1, 1862, to the jail at Columbia, South Carolina. Thirty days later Withington was exchanged and started on his way North and home.

Orlando Willcox was less fortunate. For him there remained many dreary months of imprisonment. But finally, on August 19, 1862, he was exchanged too.* When he returned to Detroit, arriving August 27, he was given a hero's welcome. Thousands of people from all over lower Michigan poured into town to greet him. They came by special train and boat to watch the triumphal parade in his honor, led by the 1st Michigan band. The climax was a huge rally in Campus Martius.

As Michigan's first authentic war hero, Colonel Willcox was entitled to the tribute which was paid him. And in honoring him the citizens of Michigan honored his regiment, the 1st Michigan Infantry. As a military unit, it had no reason to be ashamed of its conduct at Bull Run, and there was no cause for Willcox to feel that in the first test of battle he or his men had failed.

The 1st Michigan had, indeed, been beaten and driven from the field at Bull Run. But that was not the end of the 1st. It returned to Detroit—without Willcox, of course—August 7, 1861, and was mustered out as a three-months regiment. This was only a formality, however, because it already had been reorganized as a three-year outfit. It came home mainly to recruit, re-equip, and prepare for new tasks. On September 16 it was on its way back to Virginia.

As a three-months regiment, the 1st Michigan was no conglomeration of glory-seeking ninety-day wonders. Its men were fired with an eagerness to support the flag, and that fire never cooled. The 1st's great distinction was the number of its men who rose to commissioned rank during the four years of the war. Of its original roster of 798 men, 154—or nineteen per cent—won shoulder straps and served as officers in forty-one different regiments. Nearly every Michigan volunteer regiment, cavalry and artillery as well as infantry, had officers who came from the ranks of the 1st Michigan. Company A, the old Light Guard, alone contributed thirty officers to the Union army. The amateur soldiers of the ten militia companies who were mustered in as the 1st Michigan for three months, provided an invaluable cadre upon which the state's volunteer system was built. Its men held every grade of rank from second lieutenant to major general. It produced ten colonels.

Willcox must have thought many times of his regiment's performance on that terrible day at Bull Run. And he must have felt a warm pride in his men. For Heintzelman's report on the battle stated that "the 1st Michigan, on the extreme right, held the most advanced position we occupied that disastrous day."

Willcox himself, when he had the opportunity to submit his own report, made this proud claim for his regiment: "The 1st Michigan deserves the credit of advancing farther into the enemy's lines than any other troops, as their dead bodies proved after the battle."

Those who inspected the field on July 22, before the dead were buried, could substantiate Willcox's claim.

Defeated the 1st Michigan was, but in defeat the regiment set a proud and gallant example for tens of thousands of other Michigan troops, for whom they marked the road to glory.

VI

A General

Wins His Spurs

THE 2ND Michigan Volunteer Cavalry had galloped around just enough by the spring of 1862 to give its troopers the impression they were a ripsnorting, hell-for-leather outfit.

That explains why the 2nd was inclined to look down its long Michigan nose when its newly appointed colonel rode into camp near Corinth, Mississippi and took command on the evening of May 26, 1862.

The new arrival didn't exactly cut a prepossessing figure; he wasn't a cavalryman's dream of what a commanding officer ought to look like. He was short, stocky, thick in the chest, with a pugnacious chin which complemented his sandy red hair and other obvious Irish attributes of countenance. He was no spit-and-polish officer, that was certain. He was wearing an old infantry jacket with a pair of borrowed eagles on his shoulders. His baggage consisted of a haversack stuffed with coffee, sugar, and hard bread.

He wasn't at all to the taste of the 2nd, and the men weren't reticent about saying so.

"Just who," they demanded, "is that bandy-legged little mick?"

They found out.

His name was Philip H. Sheridan, and until that afternoon he had been an obscure commissary captain with an infantryman's insignia on his collar.

It wasn't long, though, before the 2nd was impressed by the fact that the new colonel was a real boss soldier. It wasn't long, either, before the entire North knew about him. So, to its dismay, did the Confederate army.

His arrival in camp was the beginning of one of the most distinguished careers in the Union army. From that day until long after the war, as long as there were two Michigan veterans to hash over old campaigns in a G.A.R. hall, the 2nd basked in reflected glory.

And why not? After all, it was the 2nd that gave Phil Sheridan a leg up to fame.

The 2nd Michigan was organized by the Honorable F. W. Kellogg of Grand Rapids, who represented a western Michigan constituency in Congress. Its recruits came mostly from the small towns and farms of central Michigan. They were accounted a rough lot—lumbermen, woodsmen, trappers, and farmers. In their short cavalry jackets and ridiculous cocked hats with dangling black plumes (soon to be discarded for the more utilitarian forage caps), they were a cocky bunch, quite willing to concede they were God's gift to Mr. Lincoln, and willing to do battle with anyone who held a contrary notion.

They were mustered, 1,163 strong, at Grand Rapids in November 1861. It may be surmised that Grand Rapids saloonkeepers sighed and the parents of Grand Rapids maidens breathed easier when the 2nd boarded the train for St. Louis. When they arrived they were sent to nearby Benton Barracks.

Other than its supreme self-confidence, the 2nd's principal asset when it left Michigan was its weapons. Somewhere the Michigan quartermaster-general had scrounged enough Colt repeating rifles to equip about two-thirds of the regiment. In addition each man had a Colt revolver. Thus the 2nd had a fire power enjoyed by relatively few Union regiments at that early period of the war.

The 2nd was organized and fielded without a colonel. At St. Louis a regular army captain with luxurious whiskers, Gordon Granger,* was given command. Granger was an old pro—a veteran of the Mexican War, in which he had distinguished himself during General Scott's campaign from Vera Cruz to Mexico City.

A West Pointer, Granger had some sound ideas about what was expected of cavalry—ideas which paid off well when later he commanded divisions and a corps. He had the theory—unique at that time—that cavalry was supposed to be able to fight effectively, to meet infantry and drive it from its ground. And fighting involved something more than wild, colorful cavalry charges which, when directed against well-positioned troops, generally accomplished little more than to kill a lot of cavalrymen.

Granger drilled the 2nd until the men rocked with fatigue. He taught them, among other things, to fight dismounted. It was effective schooling, although it was a little hard on the 2nd. The regiment saw its first action in January 1862, and after some uneventful skirmishing during the spring in northeastern Mississippi Granger was promoted and given a brigade. The 2nd wasn't exactly sorry to see him go, although the men did respect him as a capable leader.

Now it became necessary to find someone to take Granger's place. That wasn't easy. The War Department was not enthusiastic about assigning regular army officers to command volunteer regiments. It had plenty of use in its own establishment for all the good men available. General Halleck, who commanded Federal forces in the area, didn't have an experienced man for the 2nd. The leaderless regiment moved down near Corinth, where it idled for many days and where its morale became dangerously low.

That was the situation in the latter part of May when Governor Austin Blair, his staff, and a party of bigwig civilians, went South to visit the army and inspect Michigan troops. On the 25th Governor Blair was at Pittsburg Landing aboard a steamer, ready to start his return journey.

It was at that point that the 2nd's fortunes took a turn for the better.

Captain Russell A. Alger of Company C was acting field officer of the day. He had spent most of the previous night inspecting the pickets, and early on the morning of the 25th he rode up to Granger's brigade headquarters to report on conditions in front of the regiment. Granger invited him to stay for breakfast, and the conversation naturally turned to the fatherless condition of the unhappy 2nd.

"I've found a man who will make your regiment a good colonel," Granger remarked.

"Who is it?" Alger asked.

"Captain Phil Sheridan," was the reply. "He's now at Halleck's headquarters, acting as a commissary on his staff. He's just the man you want, but I doubt whether Governor Blair will commission another regular officer to command a Michigan regiment."

Alger knew what he meant. Governors of the loyal states, including Michigan's Blair, had received too many complaints from their constituents in uniform about the overly strict discipline the regular officers imposed. It cramped the style of the volunteers.

But Alger believed an emergency existed and thought that Governor Blair might see it that way. Alger had been active in Michigan politics and was confident Blair would listen to his recommendation.

"Very well," Granger told him. "I'll give you a letter to him, asking Sheridan's appointment. He is now at Pittsburg Landing, and leaves for the North by steamer at 2 o'clock."

It was then early morning, and Pittsburg Landing was twenty miles away. Alger excused himself and, accompanied by Lieutenant Frank E. Walbridge,* the 2nd's quartermaster, set off at a brisk pace. They reached Pittsburg Landing thirty minutes before the boat was to leave and found the Governor in his cabin.

Blair was hesitant but Alger was persuasive, and, as the boat's whistle blew the departure signal, the Governor gave in. Turning to his adjutant general, John Robertson, he instructed him to draw up the order, promising that the formal commission * would follow along. Robertson wrote:

> Pittsburg Landing,
> May 25, 1862
>
> Captain Philip H. Sheridan is hereby appointed colonel of the 2nd Michigan Cavalry. He is directed to take command at once.
>
> John Robertson,
> Adjutant General

Alger took the paper and jumped ashore just as the steamer pulled away from the bank. He and Walbridge mounted their horses and started the long ride back to camp. They rode hard all afternoon and evening. Alger literally rode his horse to death. He obtained another and arrived at Granger's headquarters around midnight. Granger suggested they take the appointment to Sheridan, who was with Halleck several miles away.

They found him and handed him the paper which not only made Sheridan a colonel but also made him the happiest man in the army. He had to obtain Halleck's approval, and the commanding general was sorry to lose him. Sheridan had been an efficient commissary and he had particularly endeared himself to Halleck by keeping the general's table always supplied with fresh meat. He was the only commissary Halleck had who was able to manage that difficult feat in the field.

Phil Sheridan was the son of Irish immigrant parents who first settled at Albany. Shortly after he was born the family moved to Ohio. Sheridan wangled himself an appointment to West Point, where he distinguished himself chiefly by a pugnaciousness which kept him in constant trouble. He should have graduated in 1852, but he got into a brawl with a cadet officer with whom he had picked a fight. He was soundly thrashed by the cadet, and then was suspended for a year by the Academy authorities. So he graduated a year late, with the class of 1853.* As a second lieutenant he was assigned to the First Infantry.

There was a short tour of duty on the Texas plains, after which Sheridan was sent to California and Oregon. His duty there primarily was to police Indians, a job which he did most creditably with the assistance of a squad of dragoons. He found horse soldiering greatly to his liking. When Sumter was fired on he was recalled and in due time assigned to Halleck's staff, where he fretted because he had no opportunity to command troops in the field. His appointment as colonel of the 2nd Michigan came as a complete and happy surprise.

On May 27 the 2nd was brigaded with the 2nd Iowa under Colonel Washington L. Elliott and was ordered to proceed south of Corinth to Booneville, a station on the Mobile & Ohio Railroad. The mission was to scout the area in the Confederate rear and to cut the railroad on which the rebels relied to bring their supplies to Corinth. This assignment was effectively carried out; rails were torn up, heated, and twisted around tree trunks. Scores of freight cars were burned, and large quantities of supplies and arms were destroyed. Several hundred prisoners were captured but, as there was no way to get them back to the Federal lines, they were released. Sheridan brought his regiment back to camp at Farmington, Mississippi, where early in June he learned that General Beauregard had withdrawn his Confederate forces from Corinth to a point below Booneville, some twenty miles away. Beauregard, his communications slashed by Sheridan's raid, decided to move to safer territory.

This first expedition gave Sheridan and the 2nd Michigan a chance to get acquainted.

"I believe I can say with propriety," Sheridan stated, "that I had firmly established myself in the confidence of the officers and men of the regiment and won their regard by thoughtful care. I had striven unceasingly to have them well fed and well clothed, had personally looked after the selection of their camps, and had maintained such a discipline as to allay former irritation."

The 2nd began to get enthusiastic about Sheridan. He worked them half to death, but he shepherded them with fatherly care. His credo * as a commanding officer was remarkably simple, and his Michiganders responded to it. Sheridan summed it up this way:

"Men who march, scout and fight, and suffer all the hardships that fall to the lot of soldiers in the field, in order to do vigorous work must have the best bodily sustenance, and every comfort that can be provided. . . . Whenever my authority would permit I save my command from needless sacrifices and unnecessary toil. . . . Soldiers are averse to seeing their comrades killed without compensatory results. . . . They want some tangible indemnity for loss of life, and as victory is an offset the value of which is manifest, it not only makes them content to shed their blood, but also furnishes evidence of capacity in those who command them. . . .

"My regiment lost very few men since coming under my command, but it seemed, in the eyes of all who belonged to it, that casualties to the enemy and some slight success for us had repaid every sacrifice. . . ."

In other words, Sheridan and the 2nd Michigan entered into an unspoken, unwritten, but still clearly acknowledged compact. If the regiment would do its duty when called upon, Sheridan would provide it with victories.

Granger's training and Sheridan's leadership made the 2nd a crack fighting machine, as it soon proved to the satisfaction of everybody except the Confederates.

The 2nd Michigan and 2nd Iowa, after a short rest, were ordered to follow the withdrawing enemy and keep an eye on his movements. About this time Colonel Elliott was promoted to brigadier general and given another assignment. Sheridan, assuming command of the two regiments, led them back to Booneville, the most advanced position of the Federal army. There he established his camp on the north edge of the town beside the railroad.

Booneville was strategically located. Not only did it have the railroad, but it was the junction for several major turnpikes. Beauregard's main position was at Tupelo and Gunstown, fifteen miles south of Booneville, but his cavalry was constantly prowling around the network of roads. It was unfamiliar territory to Sheridan, and the maps with which he had been supplied were woefully inadequate. For two weeks he did little except make new ones, until he knew the exact features of the terrain, the location of every bypath, clump of trees, hill, and farmhouse for miles around.

This was the situation, then, on July 1, 1862, when Beauregard decided Sheridan was a nuisance. Knowing he had only a small force, the Confederate chief ordered General J. R. Chalmers with a full cavalry division—about six thousand men—to clear Booneville.* Actually, Sheridan's force was weaker than the rebels realized. He had a total of twenty-two companies, half from the 2nd Michigan, half from the 2nd Iowa. In all, there were 827 men, many of whom were sick. In addition, he was so far in advance of Halleck's main force as to be virtually out of touch with it. It looked to the Confederates as if it would be easy to gobble him up.

The fight started before noon. Chalmers, supremely confident, led his division along the Blackland road, which entered Booneville from the west. About three miles out of town on that road Sheridan had stationed pickets under Lieutenant Leonidas S. Scranton,* a Grand Rapids man attached to Company F. Scranton's few men were quickly pushed back to the edge of town, where support was provided by three companies of the 2nd Michigan led by Captain Archibald P. Campbell * of Company K. Campbell dismounted his men, as Granger had taught him to do, and established a line across the road, partially shielded by a cover of trees. He notified Sheridan that a fight was brewing. Sheridan ordered him to hold on until help could be brought up. He then rounded up all available men of the 2nd Michigan and sent them to Campbell's support. Part of the 2nd Iowa was placed on the left of Campbell's line, and the rest of that regiment was assigned to guard the camp and the wagon park.

At the same time Sheridan sent off a telegram to his division commander, General A. Asboth, stating that he was under strong attack by Chalmers with ten regiments, and asking for reinforcements, particularly artillery. Asboth, of course, was back near Corinth where he could be of little help.

Chalmers drove in hard after the first preliminary skirmishing, and he got the surprise of his life. He was met by a hair-curling fusillade from the 2nd's Colt repeating rifles, and wide gaps were opened in his line. Time after time he rallied and charged in again, only to get the same reception. Each of Sheridan's men got off five fast shots from the repeating rifles and followed them up with six more from their Colt revolvers.* Chalmers hadn't known the 2nd was armed with those weapons; his men had never before run into such a shattering fire.

When Chalmers realized what he was up against, he revised his tactics. He divided his force and sent part of it slipping around Sheridan's left flank, entering the town and getting perilously close to the camp. This he accomplished despite gallant resistance by the 2nd Iowa, which met the enemy with clubbed rifles. Meanwhile Chalmers maintained pressure on the Blackland road, trying by sheer weight to overcome the fire power of the 2nd Michigan.

His position desperate and growing worse, Sheridan pulled a trick out of his own hat. Riding back to camp, he routed Alger out of a sick bed. Spreading out a map, he pointed to a path in the woods which paralleled the Blackland road. It was really no more than a woodcutters' trail which he had discovered when he was mapping the countryside. All that intensive map work was now to pay dividends.

He instructed Alger to take two saber companies from each regiment, a total of ninety men, and ride out that trail three miles from Booneville until he was well in Chalmers' rear. Then he was to turn back up the Blackland road and in exactly one hour from the time he left, hit Chalmers from behind. Under no circumstances was he to deploy his men. He was to come driving in hard in column, making as much noise as he could when he began his charge. When Sheridan heard him, he would also charge, hoping that the simultaneous assault from front and rear would confuse the enemy and persuade him to go away from there.

It worked! There was an hour of nerve-tingling suspense after Alger moved out. At the zero minute Sheridan sounded the charge, and at precisely that moment Alger's column came belting down the Blackland road, howling like a band of Kiowas and scattering rebels all over the landscape.

Sheridan was in luck. Just as the synchronized attack was launched, he received help from an unexpected quarter. At the psychological moment a train

59

pulled in from Corinth carrying forage for his horses. Sheridan instructed the engineer to blow his whistle as long as he had any steam, and he told the train crew to yell at the top of their lungs. Knowing reinforcements had been called for, the Federals thought they were getting help and began to smite the foe with increased enthusiasm. The Confederates were taken in by the ruse, assuming the train whistle meant that support for Sheridan was arriving. The prospect of reinforcements who might also be armed with those murderous repeating rifles was contemplated by the rebels with profound melancholy. They turned around and started for some place else—any place as long as it was far, far away.

When the noise quieted down, the first thing Sheridan did was send another telegram to Asboth, canceling his earlier call for help.

All told, Sheridan's casualties were forty-one—not bad in view of the odds he had faced. Exactly how many Confederates were killed and wounded was never known for sure. Sixty-five dead were left on the field; later forty severely wounded were picked up in farmhouses along the Blackland road.

For a while Sheridan thought Alger was one of his casualties. When the saber companies were counted Alger was not present. In the wild charge down the road he had been knocked from his horse by the low-hanging branch of a tree. He was out cold for a few minutes; when he regained consciousness he found it expedient to remain hidden in the underbrush so as not to be found by the retreating enemy. After the melee was ended, Sheridan sent out a search party to find his body. Instead they brought in a groggy Alger, suffering nothing worse than a bump on the head and a few assorted bruises on other parts of his anatomy.

Sheridan wryly attributed Alger's mishap to the fact that he had neglected to flank a tree.

Booneville didn't change the course of the war. It was one of thousands of similar local actions involving relatively small bodies of men on each side. At best it produced results of only minor tactical advantage. But from the standpoint of the 2nd Michigan, it was something to be proud of. Sheridan observed that "the victory in the face of such odds was most gratifying." It gave him a feeling of satisfaction which lasted for a long time. He dealt with the battle at Booneville in his memoirs at much greater length and in much more detail than many of his later victories of far greater consequence.

Booneville made Sheridan. It started him on a career which became one of the most distinguished in the annals of American arms. General Halleck commended him for gallantry to the Secretary of War. General Rosecrans of the Army of the Mississippi cited the 2nd Michigan and the 2nd Iowa and their leader in general orders which were read to every unit of the army. "The coolness, determination and fearless gallantry displayed by Colonel Sheridan and the officers and men of his command, deserve the thanks and admiration of the army."

There were to be more tangible rewards. Rosecrans and four other generals addressed a petition to Halleck, who was called to Washington in early July to become general-in-chief. It stated: "Brigadiers are scarce; good ones scarcer. . . . The undersigned respectfully beg that you will obtain the promotion of Sheridan. He is worth his weight in gold."

The promotion was promptly forthcoming; it was dated back to July 1 in recognition of Booneville. In orders bearing the same date, Campbell was made colonel of the 2nd Michigan, and Alger was advanced to major.

So everybody except the enemy got his share of glory that day, and Michigan, basking in the reflected distinction of her soldier sons, didn't forget the man or the occasion.

The *Detroit Tribune* of April 8, 1865, the day before Lee's surrender at Appomattox, offered the following citation of its own:

"General Sheridan stands now very high in the court of fame, yet Michigan will always rejoice that in his humbler days she gave him an opportunity to rise, and honored herself by discerning his merit."

VII

March Terror

SOME ATTRIBUTED it to war nerves, others to just plain cussedness. Whatever the cause, the result was civil disturbance in Detroit which jeopardized the war effort and, for a few hours, threatened to destroy a substantial part of the city.

The occurrence went into the history books as the Riot of 1863.* A disgraceful affair, it manifested itself in an attack on the Negro community and took a toll of life and property. It started about noon on March 6, 1863, reached the peak of its fury between four and nine o'clock in the afternoon and evening, and subsided before midnight. It was stamped out by the arrival of Federal troops and a modified form of martial law.

It could and should have been prevented, but hindsight does not compensate for damage done. Tensions had been building up for a long time and authorities should have been forewarned and alert. During 1862 the war had gone badly for the North and little but bad news reached the people from the front. There were calls for more troops and talk about conscription. Prices were inflating and the laboring element was beginning to feel the pinch. Tempers were edgy as early as the evening of July 15, 1862, when a rally was held in Campus Martius to stimulate recruiting. Only a day or two before, Lincoln had asked for an additional 300,000 men. Michigan's quota was six regiments, and officials and civic leaders were frankly worried about the state's ability and willingness to respond.

The rally started with the platform full of dignitaries, primed for spread-eagle oratory. There was the venerable Lewis Cass—Mr. Michigan himself; Mayor William C. Duncan, Congressman William A. Howard, Recorder's Court Judge Henry A. Morrow, and Eber B. Ward, Detroit's wealthiest citizen and foremost industrialist.

When the meeting got under way, it was evident that troublemakers were in the crowd. Derisive hoots of "Bull Run!" greeted the speakers, who found it difficult to make themselves heard. The *Detroit Advertiser and Tribune* said the disturbance was caused by Northern friends of Jefferson Davis, "their pimps and others." The outraged *Advertiser* attributed the trouble to a circulating rumor that "six hundred Irishmen had already been drafted, and that the meeting of Tuesday evening was called for the purpose of adopting measures to enforce the draft." Organized by "traitors" or not, the demonstrators were strategically dispersed through the crowd with the result that the disorder appeared to be spontaneous and was hard to control.

The speakers made a few brave attempts to talk down the hecklers, but had to give up. As the dignitaries left the platform they were rushed and manhandled. Even old Cass, then in his eightieth year, was pushed around. But most of the demonstrators' venom was reserved for Eber B. Ward. As the city's richest man and its largest employer, he was a natural target for resentment. The mob, or that portion of it bent on mischief, made a rush toward Ward, and there were shouts of "Kill him!"

His friends and a few constables on duty, together with Sheriff Mark Flanigan, managed to get Ward across the square into the Russell House. Outside, the mob, which was by now worked up into a fine frenzy, howled threats and imprecations at the tycoon and surged toward the hotel entrance. They were stopped by the monumental Sheriff Flanigan, a ham-fisted, six-foot-four Irishman, who drew a pistol and invited them to come on. The crowd paused thoughtfully and, while Flanigan stood guard, Ward was smuggled out the back door and escorted safely to his palatial mansion on West Fort Street at Vinewood.

The affair of July 15 was only a symptom and a prelude to something much worse. By the following March, the war news hadn't improved. The turning points of Gettysburg and Vicksburg were still four months in the future. The draft had become a reality; the full text of the conscription act was published in the *Detroit Free Press* on the morning of March 5. Labor was increasingly uneasy, and most of the town's mechanics had gone on strike a day or two earlier, mainly in support of the employees of the Detroit Locomotive Works, who were demanding a raise of twenty-five cents a day.

Moreover, many in the city were not in sympathy with the war; some were downright disloyal. There was a growing suspicion that the real reason for the fighting was to free the Negroes rather than to preserve the Union. Some workers were fearful of the competition of cheap Negro labor. There had been demonstrations against the colored in other Northern cities.

Altogether, conditions were ripe for an explosion.

William Faulkner triggered it.

On February 26 Constable Dennis Sullivan arrested Faulkner on the complaint of a mother that he had raped her nine-year-old daughter, Mary Brown. Mary and a playmate her own age, Ellen Hoover, had gone out to mail a letter on Michigan Avenue. On their way they passed Faulkner's saloon and, according to testimony, were enticed inside, where the Brown child was assaulted.

Such a crime was enough to revolt the townspeople under any circumstances. What made things much worse was that Faulkner was said to be a Negro, although he denied it and claimed to be of mixed Spanish-Indian blood. At any rate, the damage was done and, while Faulkner was held in jail awaiting trial, racial tension mounted like the pressure inside a volcano.

Faulkner's trial began the morning of Friday, March 6 in Recorder's Court,* which occupied a small room in the City Hall, then located on the east side of Woodward Avenue, approximately where Detroit's Soldiers' and Sailors' monument now stands. The courtroom was packed and from time to time the spectators were reprimanded for noisy conduct and warned against demonstrating. Outside, a crowd of about a thousand gathered. The evidence against Faulkner was based almost entirely upon the testimony of the two children. Faulkner denied all charges and maintained that his predicament had been brought upon him by people who sought to obtain his property.

At the time of the trial Detroit had no regular police department. Law enforcement was in the hands of a deputy sheriff and a constable in each of the city's wards. All available officers were assembled at City Hall as the attitude of the mob in the street became ominous. It was feared an attempt would be made to lynch Faulkner.

The trial ended early Friday afternoon. After ten minutes' deliberation the jury brought in a verdict of guilty. A sentence of life imprisonment was immediately passed. The problem then was to get Faulkner safely back to the county jail, which stood then, as it does today, at the intersection of Beaubien and Clinton Streets, just a few steps off Gratiot Avenue. The howling mob in the street was too big for the city officers to cope with, so a company of the provost guard was marched down from the barracks at Clinton and Joseph Campau Avenue to provide an escort for the prisoner.

As the detail surrounding Faulkner marched through the streets, the crowd followed and began to shower the prisoner and the soldiers with bricks and paving stones. Faulkner was struck and knocked down but was not seriously injured. Stones bounced off some of the members of the guard. By the time the procession reached Gratiot and Clinton, the rain of missiles was so heavy that the commanding officer of the provost guard, Lieutenant Van Stan,* halted his men and faced the mob with muskets leveled and bayonets fixed. He directed the angry throng to disperse and was answered by hoots of derision and more bricks. He then ordered his men to fire a blank volley, which only made the mob angrier and more menacing. More shots were fired—this time live ammunition was used—directly into the crowd. Accounts of the shooting vary; some witnesses called it a volley, but other evidence suggests only a couple of shots were fired, one of them by Van Stan.

Regardless of the volume of fire, the inevitable happened. A bystander, having no part in the demonstration, was struck. He was Charles Langer, a twenty-four-year-old photographer who operated a daguerrotype studio at Woodward and Larned. He was killed instantly by a bullet in the stomach.

While attention was momentarily centered on the unfortunate Langer, Faulkner was hustled into the jail and the provost guard, without further trouble, marched back to the barracks. But the mob was infuriated and entirely out of hand. Following its leaders, and shouting "Kill the niggers!" it raced down Beaubien Street toward Fort and Lafayette Streets, the heart of the Negro colony. Houses were stoned, windows broken, and fences pulled down. Negroes caught on the street were beaten, men and women alike.

In the block between Fort and Lafayette, Whitney Reynolds had a cooper's shop where he employed four or five fellow Negroes. Adjoining the shop was Reynolds' home, which he, his wife, and his mother shared with at least one other colored family. Reynolds was not home on the day of the riot; he had gone to Oakland County to purchase lumber. But his helpers were all at work when the mob descended upon the establishment.

The workmen slammed the door and attempted to barricade the building. By some unlucky chance, there was a shotgun in the shop. One of the Negro workers panicked and fired through a window. The shot apparently injured no one seriously, but it brought the crowd to a new pitch of frenzy. The rioters battered down the doors and swarmed inside. The Negroes attempted to escape by a rear entrance into the Reynolds house. Some of them were badly beaten, and one, Joshua Boyd, had his skull split by an ax. Boyd was an elderly colored man, recently escaped from slavery in western Virginia. He was endeavoring to accumulate enough money to purchase the freedom of his wife and children, who had been left behind.

Someone in the mob now got the idea of setting the building on fire. Both it and the adjoining home were soon blazing fiercely. The women remained inside as long as possible, then came out appealing to the crowd for mercy. They were roughly handled. An infant was torn from the arms of one woman, tossed back and forth in the air, and finally thrown fifteen feet to the pavement. One casualty of the fire was $1,200 in currency which Reynolds had hidden away, and with which he financed the operations of his shop.

The sight of the Reynolds building in flames whetted the appetite for destruction, and soon several structures were ablaze. It was reported later that fires were set almost simultaneously in places several blocks apart, suggesting that organized planning was behind the arson.

The town constables were unable to cope with the situation. Fire companies appeared, but crowd interference prevented them from being very effective. More often than not the firemen had to fight off the rioters to prevent their equipment from being smashed. At one fire the company was warned by non-rioting businessmen to pay no attention to the burning Negro buildings, but to confine their efforts to preventing the flames from spreading to the property of white people.

Afternoon wore on into evening. The streets of the lower east side were a shambles. Here and there beaten Negroes lay in alleys and gutters, and there was rumor of a general massacre of the colored population.

"About 7 o'clock," said a newspaper account, "the flames of the conflagration illuminated the entire city, and appearances seemed to indicate that the principal portion of the Third Ward was on fire and would be totally destroyed." There was reason for concern; houses and business buildings in that section, as in most of the city, were frame, and a fire, once out of control, could cause widespread damage.

About this time there began a general exodus of Negroes to Canada. Draymen and ferrymen jacked up their rates and reaped a harvest by gouging the distraught colored people who were fleeing for their lives.

Meanwhile public officials and the respectable element of the citizenry sat on their hands and for unaccountable reasons took no measures to stop the disorders, although within a few days the clergy and other leaders would be holding public meetings, expressing horror and indignation, and passing resolutions demanding punishment of those responsible. A few white families, more courageous or with deeper feelings of humanity, took frightened and injured Negroes into their homes and provided shelter and medical care. St. Mary's Hospital received a number of emergency cases. Mayor Duncan was absent from the city, and Acting Mayor Francis B. Phelps appeared paralyzed by indecision. Finally, however, somebody decided that outside help was needed and the call went out for troops to Fort Wayne, to Ypsilanti, where the 27th Michigan Infantry was training, and to the local militia companies—the Scott Guard, the Light Guard and the Lyons Guards. The latter, about fifty strong, was first on the scene and was assigned to guard the jail.

The only man who seemed to know what he was doing was Constable Dennis Sullivan. Sheriff Flanigan had become a lieutenant colonel and was at the front with the 24th Michigan Infantry. But Sullivan was cut from the same cloth as the absent sheriff. He was big, tough, without fear, and he had the true cop's sense of outrage at the sight of hoodlums running wild. He was everywhere at once. The mob, like all of its kind, was fluid and constantly shifting, breaking up into small street gangs and reuniting into larger ones when new avenues of mischief brought them together. Whenever Sullivan found such a group, he waded in, his huge fists swinging. More than one rioter went down with a cracked head, and, of about twenty arrests, most were made by Sullivan.

At one point he attained heroic stature. The screaming mob took after an ancient colored man, Ephraim Clark, sexton of St. Matthew's Episcopal Church, which served the Negro parish in the lower end of town. The old man sought sanctuary in the church, and the crowd threatened to burn it down. They probably would have except that Sullivan came on the scene and, with his back against the door, held off the mob of several hundred at pistol point.

There were other demonstrations of individual courage. Some of the volunteer firemen battled the crowd as hard as they did the flames. A Michigan Central Railroad fireman, Edward Crosby, trying to defend a colored man, defied the mob and got a face full of buckshot for his trouble.

There was a great deal of vandalism and looting. Shops and houses were broken into, furniture was tossed into the streets and smashed, feather beds were ripped open. Whatever was of value was carted away and many valuable and useful household articles disappeared from dwellings before the torch was applied.

Instead of diminishing, worn out by its evil labors, the mob grew as night fell, and the ravaged area broadened. From the Fort-Lafayette district, the demonstrators surged uptown, and before 9 p.m. there was rioting in the neighborhood of Miami (now Broadway) and John R. Streets. It began to look as if the trouble would spread into the better business and residential districts along Woodward Avenue and across into the west side.

But 9 o'clock was the peak. At 8 p.m. a detachment of fifty regulars of the 19th United States Infantry, with two small cannon, arrived from Fort Wayne. A few minutes later a special train pulled in from Ypsilanti with five rifle companies of the 27th Michigan. With bayonets fixed, the troops formed patrols, spread out through the troubled part of town and began to clear the streets. The sight of this determined authority was discouraging to the mob. It began to dissolve. By 11 o'clock the city was as quiet as on any ordinary night.

Quiet perhaps, but the ugly scars remained. A considerable area had been wrecked and the streets were littered with debris. Between thirty and thirty-five buildings had been burned to the ground and several others had been damaged by fire. An estimated two hundred Negroes were without shelter. Some of them were forced to go into the country and find refuge where they could. How many were injured was never determined. It was a miracle that there were not more fatalities. Only two died—Langer, the bystander, and Boyd, the unoffending Negro.

A coroner's inquest later made a half-hearted attempt to fix the responsibility, but nothing came of it. Witnesses were unable to identify members of the mob, or at least they said they couldn't. Almost everyone agreed that the rioters were young men and boys. Some of the latter were described as youngsters of ten years and upwards through the early teens. A reporter observed that they were "young fellows, brought up in the street school."

The *Advertiser and Tribune* said the mob was made up largely of Irish; the *Free Press,* which rarely agreed with the *Advertiser* on any subject, thought the rioters were principally Germans who had become outraged at the death of Langer.

In all probability those who took part in the riot could not be given nationality labels. German and Irish immigrants made up the mass of the laboring class, and undoubtedly elements of each group were represented. Detroit was a river town and had a tough waterfront, full of sailors, floaters, and vagabonds of every description. The general population of Detroit contained mob ingredients. Some witnesses also said they saw several soldiers in uniform running with the pack.

The riot was like an emotional purge. The 27th Michigan stayed around for a few days but kept out of sight. It wasn't needed after Friday night. By Saturday everything was calm, and the citizens of all classes behaved as if they were heartily ashamed of themselves. By the following Monday, even the *Advertiser and Tribune* had forgotten the racial aspect of the riot and was attributing the trouble to Copperheads and secessionists who, it firmly believed, were aided and abetted by its arch-foe, the *Free Press.* It saw the outburst as a deliberate plot to create a home-front situation in which "the administration, it is calculated, would be powerless between a determined enemy in front and civil war in the rear, and so would be compelled to accept terms from, and yield to the control of, the Democratic leaders."

Democrats, it went without saying, were dyed-in-the-wool traitors in the eyes of the radical Republican editors of the *Advertiser.*

Whatever the cause, and whoever was responsible, Friday, March 6, 1863, was a black stain on Detroit's escutcheon. There was to be nothing like it again until another war, eighty years later, produced an equally shameful episode which had many parallels with that of 1863.

Meanwhile, what of William Faulkner?

He was safely under guard in the jail throughout the riot, protected by a cordon of home guards each of whom had been individually deputized. When the excitement had subsided and order had been restored by troops, Faulkner was put aboard a special train at 2 a.m. Saturday and hustled off to the state prison at Jackson.

His story, however, did not end there. Many people in Detroit, on sober reflection, began to wonder if justice had been done in Faulkner's case. In time, an investigation was started; the little girls, his accusers, were requestioned and admitted their testimony was a fabrication. Faulkner was pardoned and returned to Detroit. Several well-to-do men, their consciences still bothering them, got together enough money to set Faulkner up in the produce business. He opened a stall in the central market in Cadillac Square and operated it successfully until his death in 1878.

If he bore any rancor or resentment, he never showed it.

VIII

Private Lane's

War

WHEN THE Union army wasn't marching or fighting, it was writing letters home or recording experiences and observations in countless diaries.

The men of the North were, on the whole, more literate than the citizen soldiers of previous wars. That is understandable because by 1861 educational facilities were available to almost anyone who wanted to take advantage of them. By the time the Civil War began Michigan had a public school system which was better than most. Relatively few young men who had reached military age by 1861 lacked some schooling.

The vast majority of Michigan's soldiers—eighty per cent to be exact— were natives of New England, New York, New Jersey, Pennsylvania, Ohio, Indiana, Michigan, and Canada, in all of which educational standards were relatively high. Accordingly, it may be assumed that most of them had been exposed in some degree to the three R's and school. Thus, when the average soldier "took pen in hand," as he frequently did, he was quite capable of expressing himself.

The flood of mail which went home from camps and battlefields, the volumes of on-the-spot diaries, could they all have been preserved, would be the best possible record of the war. Historians may search and ponder but they have no firsthand knowledge of the events about which they write so profoundly. Generals and statesmen did write their memoirs, but they said only those things which put them in the best possible light. The true history of the Civil War was written by the common soldiers, the men who did the fighting and who had no reason to color their accounts in order to court the favorable opinion of posterity.

Fortunately, here and there, such a record was preserved, like, for instance, the diary of Private David Lane, Company G, 17th Michigan Volunteer Infantry. In some ways Lane was unusual. He was older than most of his comrades and hence his observations were more mature. He was obviously well educated, and he was highly articulate, as his diary proves. He possessed a sense of humor and, what is most important, he understood what he was fighting for. He was a dedicated soldier—to the point of occasionally sounding almost stuffy. But because he was dedicated he was undoubtedly a good soldier.

Otherwise, his feelings and impressions seem to have been those of the average man suddenly torn from civilian pursuits and thrown violently into a life which was strange, hard, and disagreeable. He found himself in the center of epochal events, major campaigns, and important battles. Yet, like almost all enlisted men, he knew little about what was happening beyond the range of his own vision. The value of his diary lies less in his accounts of action —he naturally had no time to make entries during or immediately after battles—than in his impressions and descriptions of camp life and the ordinary routine of a soldier. Great stratagems were of less concern to him than the fellowship of the campfire, the adequacy of the commissary, and the sounds and smells of an army of thousands of men.

Lane's diary covers a period of two and a half years, the most dramatic and difficult years of the war. During that time he experienced hardship. He knew the soldier's boredom and frustration from waiting and doing nothing for long, dreary hours at a time. He knew homesickness. He was disgusted by the stupidity and ineptitude of his superiors. In all, he was a very human being in a blue uniform.

David Lane was born in Broome County, New York, March 4, 1824. When he was ten years old, his parents, Nathan and Clarissa Lane, moved to Michigan. They located first in Ann Arbor; two years later they went to Jackson County, where they settled on a farm in Sandstone Township. When Lane became of age, he taught school until the outbreak of the war. He had married Minerva Crawford and had four children, all born before he enlisted. He was thirty-eight years old when he joined up from a sense of high conviction and marched away, leaving his family. During his entire period of service he had only two short furloughs, After the war Lane returned to Jackson and was employed at the State Prison of southern Michigan. In 1881 he held the position of "yard master."

The 17th Michigan Volunteer Infantry was composed largely of men from the south central part of the state. Under Colonel William H. Withington the regiment was mustered at Detroit in May 1862, and trained at Fort Wayne.* It left the state August 27 with 982 officers and men on its rolls.

From that time on the 17th was a wide-ranging outfit. It was blooded at South Mountain, where its losses were heavy and its performance, for a green regiment, was admirable. At South Mountain it earned the official designation of "the Stonewall Regiment." That fight occurred during McClellan's Maryland campaign, which had its climax at Antietam, another battle in which the 17th was engaged. At that time it was part of the 1st Brigade (8th Michigan, 17th Michigan and 20th Michigan), 1st Division, IXth (Burnside's) Corps.

After Antietam the 17th was at Fredericksburg, but did not participate in that fight for reasons explained by Lane. In 1863 the regiment was detached from the Army of the Potomac and was sent west to join Grant at the siege of Vicksburg. That duty completed, the 17th saw a winter of hard fighting (1863–64) in eastern Tennessee, particularly around Knoxville. It then returned to Virginia and finished out the war in the long and costly operations in front of Petersburg.

But this is not a history of the 17th. It is the personal story of Private David Lane, told in excerpts from his diary, which was privately published in 1905 under the title of *A Soldier's Diary, 1862–65—The Story of a Volunteer.*

But let Lane tell it in his own words.

Fort Baker, D.C., Aug. 31st, 1862

I enlisted August 12, 1862, was mustered into service of the United States on the 18th, and was assigned to Company G, of the Seventeenth regiment of Michigan Volunteer Infantry, then in barracks at Detroit, Michigan. Of the ninety-three enlisted men enrolled in Company G, sixty-five were farmers, ten laborers, five carpenters, six shoemakers, three clerks, one baker, one miller, one tinner, and one professional soldier. They range in age from the smooth-faced boy of sixteen years to the fully developed man of thirty-eight. I judge about the same ratio will apply to the other companies of the regiment, with the exception of Company E, which is composed largely of students from the State Normal College at Ypsilanti. The regiment is largely made up of men verging on middle life, who have left business, wife and children, dearer to them than life, sternly resolved to meet death on the field of battle, rather than suffer rebellion to triumph and the Nation be torn asunder. We left the barracks at ten o'clock in the forenoon of August 27th, marched three miles to the wharf, where we left our baggage; then escorted General Wilcox [sic] around the city until five o'clock p.m., when we marched on board the steamer *Cleveland,* bound for the City of Cleveland. . . .

[*Baltimore was a city of divided sentiments but those favoring the Confederacy predominated. As a result, Union regiments passing through on their way to the front were occasionally assailed by mobs. Appearance of the first Northern regiments set off riots in which citizens and soldiers were killed. It was, then, with a feeling of expectancy that the 17th Michigan passed through Baltimore en route to Washington.†]*

. . . We had expected a row in Baltimore, and were prepared for it, but nothing transpired of a more serious nature than a few personal encounters. One hot-headed fellow jumped on board the officers' car and demanded to see their colors, cursing Unionists and swearing vengeance. Lieutenant Somers, stirred by righteous indignation, struck him a heavy blow in the face and knocked him headlong from the car. A crowd gathered, swords and pistols flashed in the gaslight, epithets were exchanged, and there the matter ended.

[The 17th, still a green regiment, was rushed into battle three weeks after its arrival at Washington. Lee had defeated Pope at Second Bull Run on August 29–30 and, having secured the initiative, he resolved to exploit his advantage by invading the North. He crossed into Maryland near Sharpsburg, and the Federals, now under McClellan's command, moved north and west through Frederick to intercept him and gain the passes through South Mountain. It was there on September 14 between Sharpsburg and Middleton that the 17th saw its first action. After that fight, it was at Antietam, and then moved to Maryland Heights, the high ground along the Potomac overlooking Harper's Ferry.]

Maryland Heights, Va., Sept. 21st, 1862

Toward evening of the 13th we left Frederick City and marched out on the National Turnpike toward South Mountain and halted for supper and a few hours rest near Middleton. It was nearly midnight. We had made a rapid march of several miles, and were tired and hungry as wolves. Hardly had we stacked arms when Lieutenant Rath inquired: "Where's John Conley?" * John could not be found; he was already off on an expedition of his own. "Well, then," said Rath, "send me the next best thief; I want a chicken for my supper." Our foragers soon returned; the Lieutenant got his chicken, and we privates were fairly well supplied with the products of the country. . . .

The battle of Antietam was fought on Wednesday, September 17th, three days after South Mountain. The Seventeenth did not lose so many killed—eighteen or twenty, I think, although the list is not yet made out and eighty or ninety wounded. Company G lost three killed. . . . We crossed the Antietam River about 1 p.m., and about three o'clock charged up the heights, which we carried, and advanced to near Sharpsburg. Here, our ammunition giving out, we fell back behind the hill and quietly sat down 'mid bursting shells and hurtling balls until relieved. As we sat waiting, a spent ball—a six pounder—struck a

† For the rest of this chapter, the italicized, bracketed portions are my own comments. F. W.

tree in front of us. Not having sufficient momentum to penetrate, it dropped back upon the toe of my comrade on my left. With a fierce oath he sprang to his feet and shouted, "Who the h--l? Oh!"

October 3d, 1862

We had a grand review this morning, in honor of the President, who favored us with his presence. My curiosity was gratified by seeing a "live President," and, above all, "Old Abe." He looks much better than the likenesses we see of him—younger and not so long and lank.

[*After Antietam Lee returned to Virginia, and the main Federal army followed him. Both armies resumed the same relative positions as before Second Bull Run. The 17th marched back to Pleasant Valley on the Little River Turnpike west of Chantilly.*]

Pleasant Valley, October 9th, 1862

I am frequently asked how I like soldiering. For a wonder, I am not disappointed. If anything, it is more endurable than I expected to find it. There are hardships—as a matter of fact, it is all hardship—but I was prepared for all that. I expected to suffer—to endure—and find myself the gainer by it. While others say: "If I had known, I would not have enlisted," I can say with truth I am glad I did. If I can be of service to my country I will be satisfied. That which troubles and annoys me most, others do not seem to mind. It is the intolerable, nauseating stench that envelops a military camp. My olfactories have become so acutely sensitive I can smell an encampment "afar off." Many complain of the strictness of military discipline. That does not trouble me. The law is a "terror to evil doers." I am thankful for the many kind friends I have found here. I hail with delight the President's [Emancipation] proclamation. I believe it is a step in the right direction.

Pleasant Valley, October 17th, 1862

We have heard heavy cannonading all day, but have not learned the result. It is rumored that we will move in a day or two—perhaps tomorrow. Where we go, rumor sayeth not. Our men say it does not matter where, so they take us where work is to be done. Two men deserted from Co. G yesterday and two today. This splendid regiment that left Detroit two months ago nearly one thousand strong, mustered today, at inspection, two hundred and fifty-six men fit for duty. There are more sick than well, the result of insufficient supplies, and brutal, needless exposure of the men by officers high in rank.

[*Failure of the Army of the Potomac to gain a decisive victory affected the*

75

morale of the soldiers. It plunged lower still after Burnside's disaster at Fredericksburg, December 13, 1862.]

Camp Near Lovetsville, Va., October 28th

As I passed from group to group through the brigade, I noticed a feeling of discontent, caused by a lack of confidence in our leaders. The men seem to feel we are being outgeneraled; that Lee's army, and not Richmond, should be the objective point; that the rebellion can never be put down until that army is annihilated. When I returned to our company the boys had arranged it all—the President is to retire all generals, select men from the ranks who will serve without pay, and will lead the army against Lee, strike him hard and follow him up until he fails to come to time.

Camp near Fredericksburg, Dec. 28th, 1862

The battle of Fredericksburg has been fought—and lost. We are now engaged in the laudable occupation of making ourselves comfortable; building log huts to protect ourselves from the cold storms of winter. Our brigade—the First—was not engaged at Fredericksburg. We were commanded by Colonel Poe,* a graduate of West Point, a man thoroughly versed in the art of war. He saw the utter hopelessness of the struggle, and, when the order came to advance, he flatly refused to sacrifice his men in the unequal contest. Of course, he was put under arrest, and will be court-martialed, but he saved his men. . . . This whole army, for the time being, is thoroughly demoralized. It has lost all confidence in its leaders—a condition more fatal than defeat.

[*After Fredericksburg both sides, for the time being, were willing to accept a stalemate in Virginia. Not so, however, in the West. Beginning in November 1862, General U. S. Grant with the Army of the Mississippi began working his way south toward Vicksburg. After a difficult winter campaign Grant was ready to deliver the final blow against Vicksburg in the spring of 1863. To assist him, the IXth Corps, including the 17th Michigan, was detached and sent West. In April it was encamped at Lebanon, Kentucky, from which point it started its advance into Mississippi.*]

Lebanon, April 13th, 1863

We had a riffle of excitement yesterday in camp. Early in the morning the Eighteenth and Twenty-Second Michigan Regiments were ordered to leave for Murfreesboro, Tennessee. The officers of these regiments, in common with others, have employed Negroes as servants. Kentucky is violently opposed to the President's emancipation Proclamation. Here was a fine opportunity for a Kentucky General to show the "Abolitionists" that his state was not included in that pronunciamento. As the Eighteenth was about to board the cars, General Manson, commander of this post, ordered them to halt and deliver up all Negroes in the regiment. Upon inquiry it was found that all, except one, were Kentucky Negroes, and were given up. This did not satisfy; he must have the free man also. The Sixteenth Kentucky Infantry and the Twelfth Kentucky Cavalry are doing post duty here. These General Manson ordered to form into line of battle, and again demanded the surrender of the Negro. But Michigan was not to be intimidated. Colonel Doolittle resolutely refused, formed his men for battle with loaded guns and fixed bayonets, and defiantly bade the Kentuckian to "come and take him." Not caring to attack with only two to one, General Manson sent out for the Seventy-ninth New York to come and help him, but the gallant Colonel of that regiment replied: "I am not fighting Michigan men." In the meantime General Burnside had been telegraphed for orders. He replied: "I have nothing to do with it." Colonel Doolittle then telegraphed the War Department, and is now awaiting orders. The Eighteenth lay with their arms beside them all last night, apprehensive of an attack. They kept the Negro.

[*The 17th reached Haines Bluff, Mississippi, on the banks of the Yazoo, a short distance above Vicksburg, about June 1. From that date until July 4, when Confederate General Pemberton surrendered the city to Grant, the 17th was on the outer perimeter of the Union siege lines.*]

Haines Bluff, June 21st, 1863

Last night Pemberton conceived the brilliant idea of turning loose four or five hundred horses and mules, creating a stampede among them, and, when Grant's lines opened to let them through, as certainly would be done, if he suspected nothing, why out they would rush, artillery, infantry and all, before the lines could close again, and thus escape. But Grant was wide awake, fell back a mile or two to give himself room to work, opened his lines for the horses to pass through and the Rebels to pass in, then closed on them and had them trapped.

Haines Bluff, June 24th

I have not seen an alligator yet, but some of our men have seen him to their sorrow. Soon after our arrival some of the men went in to bathe and wash off some of the dust of travel. They had been in the water but a few minutes when one of their number uttered a shriek of terror and disappeared. Two of his comrades who happened to be near by seized him and dragged him to the shore. The right arm was frightfully mangled, the flesh literally torn from the bone by an alligator. Since that incident bathing in the Yazoo is not indulged in.

July 3rd, 1863

We are now twelve miles from Vicksburg. . . . I can still hear the thunder of artillery, morning and eve. . . . If Grant celebrates the Fourth inside of Vicksburg, he must do something decisive soon. He may be doing that very thing this minute. When I began writing, his cannon kept up a continual roar. It has almost ceased. Perhaps he is now storming their works.

[*While Grant was besieging Vicksburg, General Joseph E. Johnston with a large Confederate force, was at Jackson, Mississippi, forty miles away. He was prevented from coming to the beleaguered city's rescue by Sherman. After Vicksburg fell, reinforcements which included the IXth Corps were sent to Sherman to deal with Johnston. It was a short campaign; Jackson was captured, Johnston was chased off, and by July 22 the 17th Michigan was back at its former station at Haines Bluff.*]

July 4th, 1863

"Be ready to march at a minute's notice," is the order. At the same time we learn that Vicksburg has surrendered; that Johnston is in a trap, and that we are to help "bag the game." So away we go, in light marching order. We marched eight miles and camped for the night.

July 5th, 1863

We have moved about one and one-half miles today. No doubt our northern friends think they have seen dusty roads, but if they could have seen us yesterday or today, they would have thought the dustiest time they ever saw was clean and airy in comparison. The road, and two or three rods on either side, was beaten into the finest powder, and the feet of the men and horses caused it to rise in sooty clouds, which enveloped us in their stifling, smothering folds. There was no breeze to carry it away—no possibility of avoiding it. When we halted at night every man of us was a "free soiler," and carried enough dirt on his person to make a "garden spot." Thanks to a kind providence, water is plenty at this place, and we soon washed and forgot our miseries. One of the boys killed a huge rattlesnake a few feet from where I am writing.

Near Jackson, Miss., July 11, 1863

In crossing a level stretch of cleared land, by looking back, I could see the whole brigade in motion, winding along like a huge serpent and extending nearly a mile in length, and a feeling of pride and exultation surged over me as I saw, once more, the grand old Ninth Corps advancing on our country's foe, and led, too, by the glorious Seventeenth.

Haines Bluff, Miss., July 23d, 1863

We arrived at our old camp yesterday—twenty days from the time we left it—the toughest twenty days of our experience. A dirtier, more ragged and drilled-out lot of men I hope never to see. The first thing I did, after eating a little hardtack and drinking a cup of coffee, was to bolt for the spring, build a fire, boil my shirt, pants and socks, scrub myself from head to heels, put on my clothing wet—though not much wetter than before—and return to camp a cleaner, therefore a better man. There have been times when we could not get water to wash our hands and face, to say nothing of our clothing, for a week or more.

[*The Vicksburg campaign ended, the 17th went back to Kentucky to rest. There was little work to be done in camp, and the soldiers found opportunity to indulge in horseplay and deviltry.*]

August 24th, 1863

Of course, we drill; it would be hard to imagine a military camp without drill; but it would make a horse laugh to see us do it. We fall in line, march to the parade ground and halt under the shade of a big tree. A Sergeant puts us through the manual of arms about five minutes; then stack arms and rest. The remainder of the time is spent in lounging in the grass until the bugle sounds recall. . . .

August 25th, 1863

We are still in camp, where each day is like the preceding one. . . . Those who love fun, and have a natural penchant for mischief, have abundant opportunity to indulge. I have never heard Billy Dunham * complain of ennui. So long as guards are to be "run," melons to be "cooned," peach orchards to be "raided," or a peddlar to be harried, tormented and robbed, Billy is in his native element. Peddling to soldiers is not the most agreeable business in the world, especially if said soldiers happen to be, as is often the case, on mischief bent. I have seen a crowd of soldiers gather around an unsuspecting victim, a few shrewd, witty fellows attract his attention, while others pass out to their accomplices melons, peaches, tomatoes and vegetables, and when the poor fellow discovers the game and gathers up his "ropes" to drive away, the harness falls to the ground in a dozen pieces, the unguided mule walks off amazed, the cart performs a somersault and the poor peddlar picks himself up and gazes on the wreck in silent grief. At sight of his helpless misery the wretches seemingly relent; with indignant tones they swear vengeance on the "man who did it;" help him gather up his wares while he secures his mule. This is soon done, for his "stock" has grown small and "beautifully less." He smothers his rage from prudential motives, throws the "toggle" on his mule and prepares to depart. Alas, the millennium has not yet come. His cart wheels, refusing to perform their accustomed revolutions, start off in opposite directions while the air is rent by the screams and derisive yells of his tormenters. When once begun, the amusement continues until the stock is exhausted.

[*September 1863 found the 17th heading into eastern Tennessee where the Confederates were threatening around Knoxville. For the next six months— until March 1864—the regiment saw some hard fighting and was part of Burnside's force which was besieged in Knoxville. In December Lane was assigned to hospital duty. He served intermittently thereafter as a nurse in general and field hospitals until the end of the war.*]

Loudon, Tenn., September 14th, 1863

As we were starting, this morning, we came upon 2,300 prisoners taken at Cumberland Gap. They were free to talk, and a more ignorant lot of semi-savages I never met. We could not convince them that Vicksburg or Port Hudson were in our possession. They were very "frank," and indulged freely in epithets and pet names.

Lenoir, Tenn., Oct. 29–Nov. 10, 1863

We fell in at 1 o'clock today, marched about a mile to a beautiful grove near a large spring of never-failing water. Here our division formed in line and stacked arms, with orders to remain in line until further notice. Lieutenant Colonel Comstock soon called our regiment to "attention," ordered company commanders in front of center, and then and there revealed to them the long-wished-for intelligence. . . . "Our fall campaign is closed. Prepare yourselves comfortable quarters for the winter." For a moment there was a silence that could be felt, then a shout went up that "rent the heavens and shook the everlasting hills. . . ."

We are working like beavers, building our little houses. They are to be eight feet by ten, and will accomodate four persons. Nothing can be heard but the clatter of axes and the crash of falling timber. . . .

No sooner was the order to build winter quarters given than the men scattered in all directions in search of material. There are many foresaken buildings in this vicinity. These were visited, the siding ripped off, floors torn up, chimneys, if brick, pulled down and the material appropriated. Hundreds of men worked all night, and by morning had enough lumber to build bunks, floors and gable ends to their buildings. The reason for this all-night work was to get the start of the officers. They knew, by past experience, all building material would soon be put under guard for use of the officers. A large brick storehouse at the depot had been burned. This was seized by headquarters. Not a brick could be obtained, only as it was stolen in the night. Just the same, the boys all had brick chimneys.

Not being disposed to work nights or Sundays, my tent mates and myself did not begin to build until Monday morning. In the forenoon we cut our logs and carried them about half a mile on our backs. In the afternoon two of us laid the foundations, while the other two went with the Sutler's team for a load of stone for our chimney. They also picked up a few boards. Tuesday we began to build in earnest—two at the house and two at the chimney—carrying them both up together. At night it was ready for the roof. Wednesday we "chunked and daubed" it, and put on the roof, built our bunks, and, toward night, moved in. Thursday we finished the chimney, put up shelves, etc. We have a warm, comfortable house, seven logs high, roofed with two thicknesses of tent cloth, which makes a very good roof. Our bunk is in one end, and occupies four feet across it, leaving a room six by eight feet. We have a splendid fireplace—back and jambs of stone, the top of sticks. In one corner are shelves for our dishes. On one side of the room is a drop table, which we button to the wall when not in use. Our bunk is not made of poles, rough and crooked, like those of last winter, but of pine boards, soft and luxurious.

[*No sooner had winter quarters been completed, than the regiment was ordered out to meet the threatening Confederates. Gradually the Federals were forced back into Knoxville, where they were cooped up all winter.*]

Lenoir, Tenn., November 14th, 1863

Toward night the wind changed, and it was bitter cold. And there we sat, two hours or more, cold and hungry, having eaten nothing since morning. The men began to grow impatient. The First Brigade were on our left and fires burned brightly all along their line. Why could not we have fires? Tom Epley of our company, thought we could, and away he goes for a coal of fire, while others gather wood and kindlings. But our lynx-eyed Adjutant discovers it, and down he comes. "Who built that fire?" says he. "I did, sir," says Tom. "Didn't you know 'twas against orders?" "No, sir; I thought the order was one fire to a company, sir." "You must put it out." "Then how the h--l are we to cook? Do you think we can march all day in the rain and mud and eat flour and raw beef?" "It's tough, boys," says the Adjutant, "but that's the order." Tom did not put out the fire but built it larger, and soon the order came, "One fire to a company."

Knoxville, November 25th, 1863

The enemy have advanced their sharpshooters to within one-fourth of a mile of our line. On the 20th they got possession of a house, just under the hill in our front, and annoyed us exceedingly. Colonel Comstock was ordered to burn it; he called for volunteers to perform the perilous feat. Instantly a company was formed, headed by A. J. Kelley, of Company E, and led by Lieutenant Josiah Billingsly. The house was set on fire and burned to the ground, but the heroic Billingsly was killed by a shell on his return.

Their sharpshooters had now advanced so near the men were forced to remain all day in their rifle pits. Every man who showed even his head became a target.

Yesterday morning, after it became fairly light, I jumped up on the embankment in front of me, as had been my custom, to see what advancement the enemy had made during the night. I took one quick glance around, and as I looked I saw two curls of smoke directly in front of me; and on the instant one bullet whistled over my head; another dropped into the sand at my feet.

This morning Lieutenant Colonel Comstock received a mortal wound from one of them. A number of our boys have been wounded. The first four or five days of the siege our men divided up into reliefs and went to the bank, in the rear of our pits, to cook and eat their food. On the 24th, as I was eating my breakfast, a rifle ball struck a camp kettle standing beside me and spilled its contents. About that time one of my comrades was struck in the face, the ball passing through both cheeks, nearly cutting off his tongue. Inspired by these gentle protests, we moved our kitchen over the brow of the hill, where we could cook and eat our "flapjacks" undisturbed.

Knoxville, Tenn., December 21st, 1863

I have been three weeks "head nurse" in the first ward of the First Brigade hospital.

Knoxville, January 6th, 1864

This has been a day of unusual excitement in Knoxville. A legal murder has been committed in public. In other words, a Rebel spy has been executed.

His name is Dodd, of the Eighth Tennessee Cavalry. I did not witness the execution. I did not feel like it. I saw the procession as it passed my door. First, a regiment of soldiers; next a cart with the victim sitting on his coffin; behind, another regiment with fixed bayonets. On each side, the street was crowded with men and women, eager to see a fellow mortal die. I am forced to see enough human misery. Would God I might never see more. . . . Will it ever end? Perhaps, when political intrigue can keep it going no longer.

Knoxville, February 7th, 1864

I have just returned from attending divine service at the Soldier Chapel, an old shaky building, without fire. We are to have preaching every Sabbath and prayer meeting every day. The Christian Commission is beginning to make itself felt here. Their agent visits us every day, distributes tracts, papers, writing paper, envelopes, etc., gives us good advice, sings patriotic and other airs, prays with and for us, and does it in such a kindly, benevolent way that he has won all hearts.

February 10th, 1864

We at the hospital are well provided with reading matter by the Christian Commission. They have a soldier's reading room, supplied with piles of Northern papers, periodicals, and many religious works. There is also a table supplied with writing materials, all free. If we have no stamps, these friends of the soldiers stamp our letters. If we are sick—unable to write—they offer to write for us. Adjoining the rooms of the Christian Commission are those of the Sanitary Commission, another beneficent association for the benefit of sick and wounded soldiers. All delicacies our poor fellows receive come through their instrumentality. This is the great dispensary of all those countless gifts in the shape of clothing and eatables which the benevolent people of the North so freely bestow. The articles to be distributed are first turned over to the Surgeon in charge, he keeping enough for himself and assistants, then the cooks take out enough for themselves and friends. The balance, should there be a balance, goes to the soldiers. I know the above to be true, from personal observation.

The Christian Commission manage differently. Their agents give to the soldiers such things as they may stand in need of.

[*In mid-1864, Grant began to apply the squeeze to the Richmond defenses in a series of campaigns which finally throttled the Confederacy. The 17th Michigan was part of these operations. After its return from Knoxville in March 1864, the regiment rested and retrained for about a month at Annapolis,*

Maryland. It then rejoined the Army of the Potomac. It was in the Wilderness in May, and then was along the line of the Rappahannock, where Lane suffered a misadventure which he describes. After that, Grant began his sideslipping movement, crossing the James River in June and laying down a massive siege of Petersburg, the key to Richmond. For nine months the 17th was engaged at Petersburg. During most of that time, as Lane explains, he was doing hospital duty or acting as company clerk. His combatant status was just about ended. Nevertheless, he occupied a ringside seat at what proved to be the death of Lee's army and of the Confederacy.]

Fredericksburg, May 17th, 1864

The morning of the eighth of May dawned bright and beautiful. Ten o'clock came, and with it the Rebels. But, thank God, they were not guerillas, but a regiment of Stuart's cavalry, commanded by General Chambers. They file around us. A major visits every tent, takes the name, regiment and description of every man—an officer follows and administers an oath by which we bind ourselves to not take up arms for or assist or aid the Government of the United States in its war with the Confederacy until duly exchanged, and we are paroled "prisoners of war."

We were treated with the utmost courtesy by officers and men. In the afternoon of the same day we beheld with joy a train of ambulances coming in, under a flag of truce, to our relief.

[After his capture, Lane observed his parole for several months. Although he remained with his regiment, he no longer bore arms. Working in the hospital and keeping records for his company commander satisfied his conscience. If he did not always strictly observe the terms of his parole, he apparently felt no qualms; the Confederates were no longer in much of a position to do anything about breaches.]

Petersburg, September 28th, 1864

About two miles from the hospital, two large mortars are planted—one thirteen-inch, the other fifteen-inch bore. From them to Petersburg is two and one-third miles. One evening—it was very dark—I happened to be looking in that direction, when I saw a thread of fire leap from the woods where the mortars lay concealed, describe a half circle against the darkened sky, ending in a lurid light far away over the city. After this came the rushing, roaring, screaming sound flying through the air in swift pursuit. If any harm was done it was all over with before the report reached me.

Camp near Petersburg, Oct. 7th

In speaking of Grant last spring I said, "I suspend judgment for the present." Since that time he has exhibited qualities that prove him to be, with scarcely a rival, the military genius of the age. We talk of Sherman's campaign in Georgia; of Sheridan in the Valley; of Mobile and Charleston. There has been but one campaign against the rebellion. The whole—north, south, east and west —had been guided and directed, under God, by his far-seeing mind. I believe we have at last found the man who is capable of directing the energies of his country and leading us on to victory and peace.

Peebles House, Va., November 8th, 1864

Of one hundred and ninety-four votes polled today, only forty-six were polled for McClellan and Secession. One week ago they claimed a majority. At that time, in Company G, eleven out of eighteen loudly proclaimed fidelity to the "Hero of Malvern Hill." Today, in this same company, three votes were polled for him. I think I can say with truth, and without egotism, the result is largely due to my efforts. I devoted my time mainly to the recruits throughout the regiment, visiting them in their tents, seldom leaving one until I had obtained a promise that he would not vote for "Little Mac." Faithfully they kept their word in nearly every instance.

The day was fine. At sunrise the regiment assembled, chose inspectors, clerks, etc., and proceeded to business. I never knew an election to pass off so quietly. No drunken brawls, for whiskey could not be obtained. General Willcox and staff came over and deposited their votes. It had been confidently asserted that Willcox would vote for McClellan, but he called for an "administration ticket" and deposited it in the ballot box. No partiality was shown to rank; several officers were challenged and had to swear in their votes.

November 13, 1864

There is much talk in the newspapers of a Thanksgiving dinner which is to be given the Army of the Potomac and the James by volunteer contributions of the people of the North. It is a gigantic undertaking, but can be accomplished by the aid of Adams Express Company, who, I understand, have offered to deliver free of charge. . . . Wagon loads of express boxes arrive at Division Headquarters nearly every day. Nearly every man in our regiment has received a box filled with "creature comforts." I had the pleasure of testing the quality of some Michigan butter today, sent to a Mr. Hopkins, of Oakland County. He was so unfortunate as to get a furlough on the day of its arrival, and left it in care of his tent mates, enjoining them to be sure and not let it spoil. They are doing all in their power to prevent it, with fair prospects of success. About one-fourth of the sixteen pounds is already saved.

November 23d, 1864

I must stop writing and draw our company ration of soft bread, which is issued twice a week. We also get mackerel once a week, codfish once, with now and then one potato and one onion per man.

November 26th, 1864

A dinner of roast turkey in the army! I am inclined to think it unparalleled in the annals of warfare. There were liquors of almost every brand; turkeys both roast and raw; chickens with rich dressings; pies, cakes, fruits and sweet-meats—enough, as intended, for every soldier in the army.

Now for the result.

We drew, for thirty-three men in Company G, twenty pounds roast turkey, thirty green apples; four pounds potatoes; seven cookies; three doughnuts; seven papers fine cut tobacco; three papers smoking. The regiment drew in proportion.

[*The end of the war was clearly in sight by the end of March 1865. With the fall of Petersburg and Richmond, it was only a matter of days. Lee began his last retreat, which ended with his surrender at Appomattox Court House, April 9, 1865. The 17th Michigan was not at the surrender scene, having remained at Petersburg. But Lane's reaction to the joyous news was probably typical of that of every man in the Army of the Potomac.*]

March 17th, 1865

Military affairs here are approaching a crisis. Everything betokens immediate action. Quartermasters have sent all superfluous baggage to Washington, and have everything packed, ready to move. Officers and men are sending home their "extras," by orders from Headquarters. The Second and Fifth Corps struck tents at 12 o'clock last night, but had not moved at noon today. The Ninth Corps has been engaged for several days in throwing up breastworks to protect their flank, which shows that we are to hold these lines, while all troops on our left will be cut loose and sent to some other point. Furloughs continue to be granted as freely as last winter, which shows Grant is not short of men. . . .

A flag of truce came inside our lines the fifteenth inst. Rumor says, "Peace Commissioners."

March 19th, 1865

A little after noon the rain began to fall; gently at first, and continued through the day, so warm and pleasant; but as the sun went down the wind veered to the southwest—all our worst storms come from that direction—gradually increasing in force, until now it is almost a hurricane. And the rain! It comes, now in great, pattering drops; now in solid sheets; an almost resistless flood. My little house rocks and quivers like a ship at sea. I have fastened a rubber blanket over the top to keep the rain from splashing through. With all the wind and rain, it is still warm, and my little house is dry and comfortable. But how about the pickets, without shelter, fire or exercise; anything to protect them from the pelting storm or deepening mud? It is now four months since the Ninth Corps took this position—four winter months—and the men, during all that time, have been on picket as often as every third day, besides doing their other duties; and yet, a more stalwart, healthy-looking lot of men I never saw.

Inside of Petersburg, April 3d, 1865

Petersburg is ours, at last. The fighting yesterday was terrific, lasting from 3 o'clock in the forenoon until dark. The Seventeenth was not engaged; was detailed as Provost Guard. The First Division entered the city early this morning. I can write no more now. Everybody shouting. My heart overflows with happiness, too deep for words.

April 8th

We have remained all day in camp, expecting, each moment, the order to move. Last night was a night of rest, the first in seven long, weary days. Today we are ready to march, to fight, or do any work remaining to be done, to finish up the job we have in hand. I do not, however, anticipate any more fighting, unless with small bands of guerillas. Our men are scouring the woods in every direction, but with small success.

Good news comes pouring in. Last night an "official" from General Grant was read, telling us of the capture of six Major Generals, fourteen pieces of artillery and thirteen thousand prisoners. This evening it is reported that Lee, hard pressed in front and rear, has asked Grant for terms of surrender. Thus the good work goes bravely on. I read of great rejoicing in the North over our success. What, then, must be our emotions? Words cannot express them. I can only say, in all sincerity, I am glad I contributed my mite to bring about this glorious result.

April 10, 1865

It has just now been officially announced that Lee has surrendered the last remnant of his broken army. Everyone is wild with joy. As for myself, I cannot write! I cannot talk; only my glad heart cries "Hosanna! Hosanna in the Highest; in the Highest!"

[*Then the assassin's hand turned joy of victory into sorrow, and the army was plunged into the deepest mourning.*]

April 19th, 1865

Yesterday afternoon we received the sad news from our Nation's Capitol; news that caused each soldier's cheek to blanch, as if in presence of some dire calamity. Our President is murdered; ruthlessly struck down by an assassin's hand! The demon of Secession, in his dying agony, poured out the vials of its wrath on our Executive. Imagination cannot paint the whirlwind of revengeful wrath that swept over the army; the strong desire, openly expressed, to avenge his death by annihilating the people whose treason brings forth and nourishes such monsters. Woe to the armed Rebel, now and henceforth, who makes the least resistance.

To illustrate the feeling of the men, I will write down an incident that occurred in our regiment. We have one reptile left, and only one, to my knowledge. When the news reached us, he was heard to say, with an oath; "I'm glad of it. If I had been there, I would have helped to do it."

Before his words had time to cool, he was seized by the men near him; a tent rope was thrown around his neck, and he was hustled toward a tree, with intent to hang him. The officers interfered, and sent him under guard to the "bull pen."

Tomorrow is to be observed as a day of mourning throughout the army. Never was man more sincerely mourned than will be Abraham Lincoln, and in history his name will be enrolled beside our Washington.

[*Hostilities at an end, the 17th went back to Washington. There were still odds and ends to clean up—final reviews to be held, and equipment to be turned in before the final discharge. Those last days when the troops lived in that twilight between being soldiers and civilians were as trying to the patience as the waits and delays in the field. Finally, however, all was done that had to be done, and then . . . home!*]

Tenleytown, D.C., May 4th, 1865

The work of preparation progresses, but oh, so slowly. But the work is gigantic. The dismantling of this mighty engine of war; of returning this "citizen army" to its legitimate and proper field of action, transforming it to an army of citizens, is an herculean task. Officers are busy arranging their affairs for the final settlement.

Everything that has passed into or through their hands must be accounted for. There is but one "loop hole" for the dishonest officer. "Lost in battle," like charity, can be made to cover a "multitude of sins."

May 8th, 1865

There are rumors of grand reviews, triumphal processions, and all the rest of it; and our flag, too, must have all the various battles in which we were engaged inscribed upon it. And officers are in no hurry to lay aside their trappings. Why should they be? It clothes them with authority which, laid aside, they never more can wear.

May 19th, 1865

The grand review * has been officially announced to come off on Tuesday and Wednesday of next week, in Washington. The First Division, Ninth Corps, is being reviewed this afternoon by Generals Grant, Sheridan and others. Our brigade commander tells us this is to be our last demonstration; no more drills; no more reviews.

Probably the First Division will be required to do guard duty in Washington until after the review. That will all be over next week. Captain Sudborough tells me he has learned for a fact we will not be kept here longer than next week.

May 24th, 1865

The grand review is over. No doubt it was imposing, beyond the power of words to describe. Now we can begin our work in earnest.

June 8, 1865

We were discharged at Delaney House, D.C., on the third day of June, and next day took cars for Detroit, where we arrived on the seventh, and were disbanded. We are no longer an organized body. Each individual is at liberty to consult his own interests or inclinations. After exchanging photos and kindly regards with my late comrades, I took the midnight train for Jackson.

IX

The Road

To Gettysburg

IT WAS A BRIGHT, cloudless day and stifling heat pressed down upon the countryside. Shuffling feet of the column of marching men raised a smother of dust which settled on either side of the Emmitsburg road, dulling the green fields of wheat and corn.

The men marched easily. They carried only light equipment, their heavy gear having been left behind. They had rested well the night before on the grounds of a Catholic convent on the edge of Emmitsburg, Maryland. The word was that they would have only a half dozen miles to walk this day to a new bivouac on the banks of Marsh Creek. For men who had marched one hundred and sixty miles in the past seventeen days, it would be a mere pleasure jaunt. Canteens were filled with fresh, sweet water, and bellies were comfortable with a breakfast of pork, hardtack, and coffee—not the choicest of rations, to be sure, but filling and eaten at leisure.

There was something else which made the blue column feel good as it trudged along. It was in friendly country, north of the Mason-Dixon line. Someone near the head of the line had just shouted back that they had crossed from Maryland and now were in Pennsylvania. It was like being home again. The fields were fat with crops which hadn't been trampled flat by contending armies. The rail fences snaked across the pastures and hadn't been converted into camp fires. The round Pennsylvania Dutch faces of the farmers bore a cordial expression, unlike the hostile stares the men had known in Virginia. The only inconvenience was when they had to step off the road when an occasional column of cavalry jingled past and to suffer the taunts of the troopers, sitting easy in their saddles: "Jine the cavalry!" The standard reply of the foot-slogging infantry was invariably profane.

Colonel Henry A. Morrow rode up and down the length of his regiment—the 24th Michigan Infantry—keeping a watchful eye on his men, urging them to keep the column closed up, prodding the stragglers. Really, he didn't have much to worry about; the 24th sniffed some kind of work for them up ahead. The entire Army of the Potomac instinctively felt it.

Colonel Morrow was proud of the 24th. The regiment was proud of itself. There was reason for this feeling of self-admiration. The 24th wore the odd looking black felt western-style hats which told the world they belonged to the Iron Brigade.* No other outfit in the Army of the Potomac had headgear like that. The hats were as much a mark of distinction as the bright red, full-moon patches which proclaimed them as members of the 1st Division, 1st Corps. There was an esprit de corps in the 1st that ran from the top right down to the closing file of each regiment.

There was even pride in being part of the grand Army of the Potomac, now some hundred thousand strong and all on the move. There had been mostly bad times and precious few victories for the past year and a half, but the men felt things were going to be different now. The defeats had been the fault of bad generalship; the soldiers were supremely confident of their own ability. At long last, they assured one another, Lee and his butternuts had made a fatal error. They had jumped their reservation in Virginia, where they belonged, and had tramped into Pennsylvania. They were somewhere up ahead—none of the Federals knew exactly where. But they'd be caught pretty soon and taught their manners. Maybe they would be trapped. Then the war would be over and everybody could go home.

There was to be a lot of dying and a good deal of disillusionment before that misconception would be corrected three days thence.

It was the prospect of a showdown which was in the mind of Colonel Morrow as he guided his horse in the thick grass along the edge of the road. His own confidence grew when, occasionally topping a rise, he could see in the far distance, behind and to the southeast, heavy clouds of dust hanging in the air, telling that the other six corps of the Army of the Potomac also were on the move.

Jogging along, Morrow caught up with the head of one of his companies, led by a pink-cheeked drummer boy * who looked as if he properly belonged in some Michigan schoolhouse, scratching arithmetic problems on his slate. Morrow may have been moved to wonder what such a child, barely in his teens, was doing here in the ranks of war.

"Why aren't you beating your drum, boy?" he asked the youngster.

Startled, the lad looked up. "May I speak to the colonel, please, sir?"

Colonel Morrow reined in his horse and bent low in his saddle. With a con-spiratorial glance at the officer, half sly, half frightened, the boy lifted up the edge of his drumhead. Inside was stuffed the carcass of a fat goose, liberated from some farmyard.

The colonel straightened up. With a poker face, and with a voice that carried down the line, he said:

"All right, son. If you are feeling sick, you needn't pound that drum."

The boy grinned and Morrow grinned back at him. The colonel knew when, where, and how to wink at a breach of regulations. His men loved him for it.

The 24th Michigan * was the only all-Detroit and Wayne County regiment recruited during the war. In 1862 President Lincoln issued his call for 300,000 additional volunteers. Michigan's quota was six regiments, which were raised in the usual way by incorporating militia companies from various towns, or by sending officers into communities to recruit. This arrangement was successful, although recruiting was so slow in some cases as to give state authorities considerable concern. A large element of Detroit's population was opposed to the war, or at best lukewarm. In order to allay any out-state suspicion that Detroit was not doing its share, and to provide a bonus over and above the allotted quota, permission was sought and granted to raise a seventh regiment exclusively in Detroit and Wayne County. The 24th Michigan Volunteer Infantry was the result.

Recruiting started with a mass meeting in Detroit's Campus Martius on the evening of July 15. The purpose was to spark interest in the other regiments and to launch the drive for the 24th. The meeting was attended by an impressive number of dignitaries and civic leaders. There was no doubt that officially the city was solidly behind the effort to raise a local regiment.

By July 19 officers were fanning out into the townships and villages of Wayne County, conducting local recruiting rallies and signing up men. The response was surprising. Recruits, their patriotism and enthusiasm fired, flocked to the colors. The result was that by August 11 the regiment's full complement of 1,335 officers and men was filled. Of that number, 428 were from Detroit; the remaining 907 were from other communities of Wayne County. The vast majority were American-born, but in the ranks were 324 foreign born, including Germans, Irish, Canadians, Scots, Swiss and a few other nationalities.

All ages and many vocations were represented on the regimental rolls. Mechanics left the factories; boys came in from the farms. There were sailors from the Detroit waterfront. Schoolmasters and students left their classrooms. Ten printers took off their aprons at the *Detroit Free Press* and joined up with the foreman of the composing room, Lieutenant (later Captain) Malachi O'Donnell, of Company E.

There were blue bloods on the roster, too; men like young Frederick A. Buhl,* of a well-known Detroit family, whose father presented the regiment with its colors. In Company C was Private Edgar O. Durfee * who served fifty years as probate judge after the war. Lieutenant John Witherspoon * had been a member of the 1st Michigan (three months) Infantry. Wounded at Bull Run, he recovered in time to join the 24th as a sergeant in Company B. His second lieutenant's straps were still shiny new. Before long he too became a captain.

Having finished recruiting in record time, less than a month, the 24th was mustered at Detroit on August 15. Other new regiments were occupying all the available space at Fort Wayne, so the 24th assembled at the old state fair grounds, also known as the Detroit Riding Park. That was a tract of land bounded by present-day Alexandrine and Canfield, Woodward and Cass. It was named Camp Barns.

The regimental officers were, for the most part, men of local prominence. Henry A. Morrow,* judge of the Recorder's Court, was made colonel; the lieutenant colonel was the gigantic Mark Flanigan, a butcher by trade, who had been elected sheriff, but joined the regiment before his term of office expired. Digby V. Bell, collector of customs, was the quartermaster; Dr. Alexander Collar, from Nankin Township was assistant surgeon, and the Reverend William C. Way, a Congregational minister from Plymouth, was appointed chaplain.

Among the line officers were 2nd Lieutenant Henry R. Whiting, son of a former Michigan congressman. Captain William J. Speed's father was one of the founders of Western Union and built the first telegraph line into Detroit. Jacob M. Howard, Jr., was the son of Michigan's wartime United States senator.

The average age of the regiment was twenty-five years and three months. This represented an age span between thirteen-year-old Drummer Willie Smith at the bottom of the scale and seventy-year-old James Nowlin, a Romulus farmer, at the top. Willie thrived on a soldier's life which proved too rigorous for Nowlin. He succumbed to disease at Brooks Station, Virginia, December 9, 1862, without having been under enemy fire.

The regiment left Detroit on August 29. It had less than three weeks' training, hardly enough to smooth the rough edges, let alone transform the men into competent soldiers capable of standing up to Lee's veterans. But the men, unaware of their deficiencies, were noisily confident and, trained or untrained, would soon prove themselves the equals of any soldiers they would meet, blue or gray.

The regiment traveled by boat to Cleveland, thence by rail via Pittsburgh, and arrived at Washington on September 2. At Pittsburgh officers and men were feted at a civic banquet. Expressing their thanks, Colonel Morrow promised that whenever Pennsylvania troops should come to Michigan to join in the invasion of Canada, they would be received with equal hospitality.

The colonel may have been a good soldier. Obviously he was no diplomat.

Arriving at the capital, the 24th went into camp at Fort Lyons, Virginia, one of the receiving and training centers which made up Washington's defense ring. There it remained less than a month. Still as raw as recruits can be, the men were loaded aboard a train on October 1 and shipped to Frederick, Maryland. Four days later the regiment was tramping around in the mountains between Sharpsburg and Harper's Ferry, on the fringe of the Antietam campaign but never really in it.

Although it still lacked its baptism of fire, the 24th was fortunate enough to be attached at this time to the famed Iron Brigade.* The Iron Brigade was General John Gibbon's 4th Brigade, of Franklin's 1st Division of the 1st Corps, commanded by Major General John F. Reynolds. Gibbon's brigade, composed of the 2nd, 6th, and 7th Wisconsin, and the 19th Indiana, had performed so valiantly at Antietam that General McClellan had dubbed it the Iron Brigade, as proud a title as was borne, then or later, by any unit of the Federal army. Gibbon needed an additional regiment to restore his manpower depleted by the Maryland campaign. He asked McClellan for more Wisconsin men. Having none available, the commanding general offered what he considered the next best thing.

"I will send you a Michigan regiment," he told Gibbon. "They are as good as there are in the service." The order was dated October 9, 1862.

The rest of the Iron Brigade didn't share McClellan's enthusiasm for the green, untried Michiganders, and they made their disdain apparent. The 24th was treated like a delegation of poor relations and left strictly to itself. The other regiments visited back and forth and were on the most comradely terms, but they refused to fraternize with the Wolverines. There was obvious distaste for sharing laurels with an outfit which had yet to fire its rifles at the enemy.

If the 24th was aware of the snub, it managed to hold up its head and refused to admit any feeling of inferiority. It marched as well as its more seasoned brother regiments; it developed a fine proficiency in robbing farmers' hen coops, and it griped as loudly as the most professional veterans.

Then came the opportunity to show its worth.

General Ambrose Burnside succeeded McClellan in command of the Army of the Potomac. Prodded by Lincoln, who desperately wanted a victory, Burnside planned a campaign against Richmond. It was to open with a massive assault on Lee's army, which was strongly placed on the heights behind Fredericksburg.* Burnside moved his forces to the north bank of the Rappahannock River, built pontoon bridges, and on December 12, 1862, sent his army streaming across to death and defeat at the hands of the well-entrenched Confederates.

The Ist Corps, the Iron Brigade attached, was assigned to the Federal left, where it faced Stonewall Jackson's divisions and Jeb Stuart's dismounted brigades. Since Burnside's main attack was against Lee's center, the Ist Corps was not as heavily engaged as other corps. Nevertheless, the 24th got its first taste of battle and the opportunity to show its mettle.

The Iron Brigade was given its position, and the 24th found itself in line on a slight rise, which offered an attractive target for Jackson's artillerymen. The men were exposed, and soon the Confederate guns found the range. Here and there a man went down. Standing idle and taking what the enemy spooned out was a soul-testing experience for untried troops. To dive for cover was the natural instinct. Tension could have been relieved had the men even been able to fire their rifles in the enemy's direction. But orders were to stand firm; alignment of the brigade, division, and corps required each unit to stand fast.

It was asking a great deal of recruits to retain their composure under such conditions. Men of the 24th watched uneasily as a comrade slumped to the ground; they retched when a shellburst turned a friend into a shapeless, unrecognizable mass of bloody pulp, or a tentmate suddenly screamed in mortal agony. There was a wavering in the ranks which needed to be stiffened before it turned into a stampede.

Watching his men closely, Colonel Morrow caught the danger signal. Stepping in front of the regimental line and bellowing in a bull voice which could be heard above the din of battle, he proceeded to put the 24th through the manual of arms.*

There on the battlefield, while friend and foe alike looked on with wide-eyed amazement, the regiment went through its exercises—shoulder arms, port arms, present arms, order arms—with parade-ground precision. It was all that was needed to take the men's minds off their troubles. The regiment steadied and a few minutes later, when ordered to advance into some woods and clean out a nest of rebels, it did so with cool efficiency. Fredericksburg cost the 24th some good men. It lost seven killed, eighteen wounded and eleven captured or missing.

But from that moment, Wisconsin and Indiana accepted Michigan as comrades-in-arms. The 24th became a full-fledged member in good standing of the Iron Brigade.

After the Fredericksburg debacle, while the Army of the Potomac licked its wounds and Lincoln sought a new general to replace Burnside, the 24th camped north of the Rappahannock in relative peace and quiet.* There were visits from civilian dignitaries from home. These visitors usually climaxed their stay with oratorical exhortations to the regiment to do its duty, to stand by the Old Flag, and the like, expressed at length and in elegant well-rounded periods. On the verge of boredom, the men of the 24th may have found even these forensic passages mildly diverting. Interest was stirred more when some of the officers' wives came to visit.

"Fighting Joe" Hooker took over the command from Burnside, and, if he didn't exactly live up to his title, he did display a vastly needed administrative talent. He reshuffled the army, and in the process the Iron Brigade found itself designated 1st Brigade, 1st Division, 1st Corps. It had a new brigadier general, Solomon Meredith, and a new division commander, General James S. Wadsworth. Reynolds kept the 1st Corps. Both he and Hooker had a very high regard for the Iron Brigade.

Along toward the end of April 1863, Hooker unveiled a grand design which, on paper, looked like a sure thing. He proposed to cross the Rappahannock and slip around the left of Lee, who was still solidly established on the Fredericksburg heights. Hooker's march would take him to a place called Chancellorsville, where Lee would be forced to meet him. If Hooker could successfuly maneuver his superior force, he could work around in Lee's rear. The door to Richmond would then be open.

The battle of Chancellorsville began on April 29. Again the 1st Corps, much to the chagrin of all hands, was given little to do. It was used to create a diversion of sorts at Fredericksburg, and as a result it failed to get a share of the main fighting, which lasted until May 3. At first it appeared that Hooker might be successful. He outflanked Lee, but as the battle progressed he found his own right flank being turned by Stonewall Jackson. It was at Chancellorsville that Jackson was killed accidentally by one of his own men. Hooker lost his nerve and went on the defensive when his plans failed to work out. He finally retreated to his former position on the north bank of the Rappahannock. Before the withdrawal, however, the 1st Corps was marched to a new position covering Hooker's right flank. In that enterprise, the 24th Michigan gained a fleeting moment of glory when it became the last regiment of the entire Union army to recross the Rappahannock. For several hours it stood alone on the south bank of the river confronting the whole Confederate force.

During the lull which followed the battle of Chancellorsville, Hooker asked Reynolds to send a detachment down the Northern Neck of Virginia and clean out a pocket of rebels who were causing some annoyance. The Northern Neck, the peninsula between the Potomac and Rappahannock Rivers embracing King George and Westmoreland Counties, was also a rendezvous for deserters; there was a regular ferry service which transported them to the Maryland shore. Hooker suggested picked troops for the assignment and Reynolds promised to send the best he had. It was therefore a high compliment when he called upon Colonel Morrow to lead the expeditionary force composed of the best the Iron Brigade had to offer—the 24th Michigan and the 6th Wisconsin.

Highly pleased with themselves, and welcoming any break in the dull routine of camp life, this detachment of about a thousand men set out on May 21, 1863. It went as far as Westmoreland Court House and returned on May 26, after marching one hundred and thirty miles. It not only took care of the obstreperous rebels, it also brought back three captured Confederate officers and fifty men, and paroled three hundred more. It rounded up five hundred horses and mules, freed a thousand slaves and gathered in large quantities of corn and bacon earmarked for Lee's hungry army.

The 24th returned from this raid, barely out of breath, to find the Federal camp buzzing with rumor. Big events seemed to be shaping up. The Michiganders realized something was afoot when their camp was cleared of civilian visitors and strict orders were received to send unnecessary baggage to the rear.

Lee was getting ready to move. After his victory at Chancellorsville, he felt the time was ripe for him to go on the offensive. President Davis and other Confederate leaders believed the war would end if it could be carried into the North. At first dubious, Lee was won over to this idea and began to make his plans. Like the iron-nerved gambler that he was, he decided to toss his Army of Northern Virginia, as one would throw the dice, on an all-or-nothing invasion of the North.

He worked out his campaign carefully. It called for withdrawing his army quietly from in front of Hooker, slipping off to the west, and, with the Blue Ridge and Bull Run Mountains for a screen, crossing the Potomac and marching north into Pennsylvania. Stuart's cavalry was given the task of covering the mountain gaps and preventing the Federals from finding out where Lee was and where he was going. Thus, his movements clouded with secrecy, Lee headed for the general neighborhood of Chambersburg, Pennsylvania. Once there, it was his intention to improvise. Depending upon how fast the Army of the Potomac moved, he would have the choice of striking at Harrisburg, Baltimore, Philadelphia, or even New York.

Lee's maneuver was perfectly executed.* His entire army melted away from the Rappahannock. As far as the befuddled Federals could tell, he vanished from Virginia. His advance corps, led by General Ewell, crossed the Potomac on June 15 and moved into Pennsylvania while Hooker was still trying to decide whether he had a full-scale invasion to deal with or whether this was just a raid to capture food and horses. Finally Hooker worked up enough gumption to find out. He slowly started northward himself, following a route which would enable his army to shield Washington. All Hooker knew at the moment was that, whatever Lee was up to, he had a good head start. As for Lee's location and his intentions, the Army of the Potomac could only guess.

The 24th Michigan got its marching orders on June 12, almost a week after Lee had started north. With the Ist Corps, it set out leading the pursuit. The Army of the Potomac as a whole moved so ponderously that the exasperated Lincoln again was moved to look for a new general, more vigorous and less timid than Hooker. Reynolds looked like the best choice and the command was offered to him. The entire Ist Corps was unanimous in its opinion that no better selection could be made. But Reynolds rejected the offer because he was not promised complete freedom of action without interference from Washington.*

Not until June 25 did Hooker finally conclude that Lee was actually moving his entire force into Pennsylvania. On that day the 24th Michigan, which had been advancing by easy stages, ceased its dawdling and crossed the Potomac at Edwards Ferry, a few miles below Leesburg. It was ten days behind Lee and, by that time, an entire Confederate corps under Ewell was closing in on Harrisburg. Longstreet's and A. P. Hill's corps were well on their way to Chambersburg. If it was to be a foot-race, the Federal army was being badly outdistanced.

Having crossed the Potomac, the Ist Corps continued to move sluggishly north, never being permitted by Hooker really to extend itself. It marched around in the Maryland mountains between Middletown and Frederick and camped at Frederick the night of June 28. That was the day that Hooker was relieved of command and Major General George Gordon Meade was appointed in his place. On the following day, the Ist Corps made a long march and camped the night of June 29 at Emmitsburg, close to the Pennsylvania line.

The situation was complicated by the fact that at this time neither Meade nor Lee knew the exact whereabouts of the other. Each was groping blindly and cautiously. The Confederate army was spread out in a wide arc, its right at Chambersburg, its left in the vicinity of Harrisburg, Carlisle, and York. The

Federals were slowly advancing northward, still intent upon keeping Lee, wherever he was, between themselves and Washington. Meade's corps were strung out for miles along the roads.

On June 30, however, the situation began to jell. A civilian spy, coming up through Washington, told Lee of the Federal advance. On the same day, two brigades of Union cavalry under General Buford, scouting along the Chambersburg road near Cashtown, ran into Confederate outposts. Buford correctly guessed that he had located Lee's main force and so notified Meade that night.

Lee flung his couriers in lathered haste across the country with orders to his corps commanders to pull the army together. In response, the long gray columns began their concentration, marching down the roads from Hagerstown, Chambersburg, Carlisle, and York. Plodding toward them from the opposite direction came the Federals, strung out along the Emmitsburg, Taneytown, and Baltimore pikes. All these highways converged on the same point in the rolling farmlands of southern Pennsylvania. Where the roads came together, the two armies must inevitably collide head on.

Reynolds' Ist Corps was in the Federal van, moving up the Emmitsburg road. And as Colonel Morrow led his regiment toward its camp ground of June 30 at Marsh Creek, he must have reviewed in his mind those events of the past eleven months since the 24th Michigan had left Detroit. He and his men must have had an awareness of things impending; they must have speculated on when and where the showdown would take place.

They marched easily and they marched well, because they were veterans now. The rub of gear, the rattle of equipment, produced that cacophony which is the unmistakable sound of infantry on the march.

The regiment was north of Emmitsburg, and Marsh Creek lay just ahead. A country road ran off to the left, but the column kept on, straight ahead. By the roadside stood a signpost, pointing to the next town. The men glanced at it without much interest. Its faded letters spelled out a place of which few, if any had ever heard.

The sign read: "To Gettysburg."

X

Rendezvous

at Armageddon

THE WAN LIGHT of the moon touched the fields bordering the Emmitsburg road, where the 24th Michigan Infantry lay sleeping. To the east, low against the horizon, false dawn faintly tinted the sky. It was four o'clock, still half an hour until sunrise. The date was July 1, 1863.

Near neighbors to the 24th were the other regiments of the Iron Brigade. Strung out for a considerable distance along the road where it crosses Marsh Creek, the entire 1st Corps was bivouacked. The night was warm; the men slept under trees and bushes without blankets. Their campfires had burned out. Sentries walked their posts, the soft grass muffling their footsteps. All the usual night sounds of camp were muted: the stamping of hoofs in the picket lines; the creaking of a wagon; the distant baying of a hound in some farmyard across the ridges. The soldiers slept on, undisturbed.

Near Marsh Creek, Moritz Tavern stood back from the road, its harsh lines softened by night's shadows. The tavern was dark except for the front room where, by the light of lanterns, the 1st Corps staff worked its way through piles of paperwork.

Suddenly there was a drum of hoof-beats in the road and a rider, galloping up from the south, reined in sharply. He dismounted and entered the tavern. He was Major William Riddle, aide to Major General John F. Reynolds, 1st Corps commander and leader of the advanced elements of the Army of the Potomac.

Riddle strode across the room where the staff worked and rapped sharply on a door which opened into the rear chamber, where General Reynolds was sleeping soundly. Sleep was something Reynolds had had little of during the past few days; he had been in the saddle almost continuously, with only enough time to enjoy the luxury of a warm dinner with relatives in Frederick two days before. What rest he was able to get had mostly been catnaps, snatched when and where possible.

He had gone to bed around midnight in the tavern which he had appropriated for his headquarters. That was just after he had sent the new army commander, General George Gordon Meade, the first definite information of the whereabouts of Lee and his Confederates. A cavalry leader, Brigadier General John Buford, had reported during the evening that he had spotted the rebels between Chambersburg and Gettysburg, their forces apparently intent upon concentrating at the latter place. Reynolds in turn had sent Riddle with the news to Meade at army headquarters at Taneytown. Reynolds had then turned in to catch what rest he could until Riddle returned with orders.

Riddle did not stand on ceremony. After a pause in which his knock evoked no response, he pushed open the chamber door and walked in. Reynolds was coming awake slowly out of deep slumber; he was having trouble collecting his wits. His aide hated to waken his chief, but he carried urgent dispatches which he proceeded to read. Still groggy with drowsiness, Reynolds made him repeat the message from Meade three times so there would be no misunderstanding. The orders instructed Reynolds to start his Ist Corps immediately toward Gettysburg, six miles away, and to instruct Howard's XIth Corps to follow within supporting distance.

Headquarters in Moritz Tavern suddenly came to life. Couriers ran out of the building and dashed for their horses. In the regimental camps men got to their feet, officers shouting orders. Up and down the road, bugles began to bark their urgent messages.

The 24th Michigan rubbed the sleep out of its eyes. With the Iron Brigade, of which it was a part, it had marched up from below Emmitsburg the day before—an easy walk of about seven miles. It had gone into camp early, and during the afternoon the men had been paid. The evening had been given over to innumerable chuck-a-luck games.

The regiment fell in by companies and answered roll call. The morning report showed 496 officers and men available for duty. The adjutant dismissed them, fires were built up with the rails from some unlucky farmer's fence, and breakfast was cooked. It consisted of pork, hardtack, and coffee. The men boasted of their varied fare—for supper the night before they had eaten hardtack, coffee, and pork. Their next meal, if they lived to get one, would be coffee, pork, and hardtack. The menu may have been monotonous, but those Michigan boys knew it was better than Johnny Reb was likely to be getting.

Breakfast was finished quickly and the 24th lined up facing the road. Chaplain Way stepped to the front and center; the men stood uncovered while he asked divine blessing. That was a regular ritual in the 24th.

Other units were already moving. Cutler's 2nd Brigade of Wadsworth's 1st Division marched off up the road toward Gettysburg. General Meredith * rode past and his black-hatted Iron Brigade swung in behind him—the 6th Wisconsin in the lead, followed by the 2nd Wisconsin, 7th Wisconsin, 19th Indiana, and 24th Michigan.

In high spirits, the 24th had a good-natured word or two for the other divisions of the 1st Corps, lined up and waiting for the road to clear.

"Better stay there till we send for you," they shouted; "climate up there may be unhealthy."

It was about 6 or 6:30 a.m. The sun was up and already hot, promising a stifling day. The 24th congratulated itself on being posted near the head of the column. Let the others behind eat the dust.

Aware of the need for haste, Reynolds pushed the long blue column ahead at a fast clip. But despite the pace the men of the 24th had an opportunity to look at the countryside and to observe the terrain. The Emmitsburg road on which they were marching bisected a shallow valley formed by two almost parallel low ridges. That to the east, on the column's right, was Cemetery Ridge, deriving its name from the Gettysburg burying ground at its upper end on the southern outskirts of the town. A short distance to the right of the cemetery was another piece of rising ground covered with trees and underbrush. That was Culp's Hill. The lower end of the ridge, past which the 24th was now marching, ended in two hills, Little Round Top and Round Top.

The western wall of the valley was known as Seminary Ridge. It extended west and for a short distance north of Gettysburg. It was named for a Lutheran theological school which stood near its northern end on the edge of Gettysburg.

Gettysburg was the converging point of several roads which radiate from the town square. Main pikes to Chambersburg and Hagerstown extend out to the west, crossing Seminary Ridge near the Seminary itself. On the north side are the Mummasburg, Carlisle, and Harrisburg highways. On the east side of town are the York and Hanover roads. Running out from the south of Gettysburg are the Emmitsburg and Taneytown roads and the Baltimore pike.

At its upper end, Seminary Ridge slopes off to the west in a series of undulations. One of these is called McPherson's Ridge. Along its western base ambles a small stream, Willoughby Run.* In the angle formed by the converging Chambersburg and Hagerstown roads, where they cross Seminary Ridge, was a clump of trees known as McPherson's Woods.

103

It was in this area, in McPherson's Woods, that the battle of Gettysburg began and that much of the first day's fighting * took place.

The men of Reynolds' corps, hiking north along the Emmitsburg road, were not the only ones moving that Wednesday morning, July 1. Lee's Confederates were also headed toward Gettysburg. A. P. Hill's corps was strung out on the Chambersburg pike. Behind Hill, and moving at a leisurely gait, was Longstreet. Down the Carlisle and Harrisburg roads, coming in from the north, Ewell's corps was eating up the miles. It was composed of the fast-marching brigades which once had been led by Stonewall Jackson.

Pettigrew's brigade of Heth's division of Hill's corps was out ahead on the Chambersburg pike. Pettigrew had learned there was a supply of shoes in Gettysburg. His men needed them and he set out to get them on the afternoon of June 30. On the way he ran into Buford's yellow-legs on the outskirts of town, and he retired some eight miles to the village of Cashtown. That night he reported to General Hill, who confidently declared that the main Federal force was camped far away at Middletown, Maryland, and that the horsemen were only scouts. Heth, Pettigrew's superior, overheard the conversation.

"If there is no objection," Heth said to Hill, "I will take my division tomorrow and go to Gettysburg and get those shoes."

"None in the world," Hill replied. So early the following morning Heth moved out, expecting to do battle with a foe no more dangerous than a few shoe store clerks. For all that he, Hill, or Lee knew, Meade's army still was miles away.

But a surprise was awaiting the rebels. Buford, correctly surmising the direction of the Confederate advance, had assembled his two cavalry brigades and formed a thin line of dismounted men along the upper end of Seminary Ridge, across the Chambersburg pike. Actually it was little more than a skirmish line, supported by a couple of light field pieces. When the head of Pettigrew's column came in sight, Buford's men greeted it with a shower of lead, momentarily halting the Confederates. General Archer's brigade, following close behind Pettigrew, hurried to his assistance and a lively exchange of fire began.

Buford's fight started around 9 a.m. The head of Reynolds' column had just passed a wheat field and a peach orchard and was at the Codori farmhouse on the Emmitsburg road, a mile and a half south of the lower end of Gettysburg. As the leading brigade of the 1st Corps reached Codori's, the sound of spirited firing was heard off to the northwest. Good soldier that he was, Reynolds followed the rule book and instinctively turned toward the sound of the guns. With the Iron Brigade behind him, he left the Emmitsburg road and angled off across the fields in the direction of the sounds which told him the fight had started. He sent his pioneers and mechanics ahead with axes to . break down the fences in order that his infantry's advance would not be slowed.

Wadsworth's 1st Division was the first infantry on the field of Gettyburg and, except for Buford's skirmishing cavalrymen, opened that fateful battle. Reynolds galloped ahead with his staff, and at the seminary he met General Buford, whose outnumbered and outgunned troopers, though having a bad time, were still grimly holding on.

"There's the devil to pay," Buford told the Ist Corps commander, and Reynolds nodded in agreement. He looked over the field with a professional eye and took in the situation at a glance. An extended line of graybacks was moving across the fields, their left on the Chambersburg road. Most of them were on rising ground above Willoughby Run and were moving in what appeared to be brigade strength toward McPherson's Woods. Reynolds recognized the importance of the grove and the necessity for his people to occupy it before the Confederates got there. The woods would provide excellent cover for whatever troops were in them. Whoever held the grove would surely dominate the field. Reynolds sent his aides galloping off to urge his regiments to move up faster.

Cutler's brigade of Wadsworth's division came onto the field near the seminary and formed a battle line on the right of the woods and the Chambersburg road. They were closely followed by the Iron Brigade except for the 6th Wisconsin, which was detached to act as a reserve. The 2nd Wisconsin was first in line on the right, touching the left of Cutler's brigade at the Chambersburg road. Behind the 2nd came the 7th Wisconsin, then the 19th Indiana, and finally the 24th Michigan, which found itself on the extreme Federal left flank.

Colonel Morrow led his Michiganders forward at a run, but although the 24th moved with alacrity, it wasn't fast enough to suit Reynolds. He was desperately trying to head off Pettigrew's and Archer's Confederate brigades at McPherson's Woods. The Federal commander was all over the field, directing the placing of regiments, urging, coaxing, threatening. No matter how quickly his men moved into position, they were like sluggards to him.

The 24th Michigan hit the top of the hill alongside McPherson's Woods at approximately 10 a.m., out of breath from the hard run across the fields, but itching for a fight. Below them was Willoughby Run, with Archer's brigade massed just beyond. The rebels were beginning to get among the trees.

A spatter of rebel gunfire greeted the 24th; still Reynolds prodded them on.

"Drive them out of there," he shouted, pointing to Archer's men. "For God's sake, forward."

Morrow pointed out that his men had not had time to load their rifles. While Reynolds fumed, he halted the regiment momentarily while the ranks coolly and deliberately made ready. Then with a cheer, the 24th swept forward, charging across Willoughby Run, smashing the flank of Archer's brigade. The Confederates had expected to meet nothing more dangerous than militia. As the Michiganders dashed at them, they realized their mistake.

"There's them damned black hats again," yelled an observant and surprised Confederate. "Hell, that's no milishy!"

He was right. Stunned by the rush which brought the 24th to their flank and rear, and pounded in front by the 19th Indiana and 7th Wisconsin, Archer was in a trap from which he could find no way out. Most of his brigade threw down its arms and surrendered. Archer himself was taken. It was most humiliating. Archer was the first Confederate general officer to be captured since Lee had taken command of the Army of Northern Virginia.*

Over on the right, opposite Cutler, Davis' Confederate brigade was also in trouble. It had been pushed into a railroad cut and was being chopped to bits by the Second Brigade. That work was expedited when the 6th Wisconsin * was thrown in to help. Up to that moment it was a banner day for the Iron Brigade.

Unfortunately, some were no longer present to share in the brief triumph. Abel Peck, the 24th's color bearer, a man greatly admired for his almost saintly character, went down. He was the first man of the regiment to die. Big Mark Flanigan took a musket ball in the leg. He was through, and was carried back to a field hospital, where he underwent an amputation. The regimental adjutant, Captain William H. Rexford was wounded about the same time.

These were grave losses, but there was a still more serious one. As General Reynolds stood behind the 24th, pushing it into its initial charge, a Confederate sharpshooter in a tree caught him in his sights. The tall, impressive-looking Reynolds, straight and soldierly on his superb mount, was a sure target. He toppled forward to the ground, a bullet hole behind his ear. He was dead by the time his aides got him off the field.

General Abner Doubleday,* senior division commander of the 1st Corps, took charge. One of his first orders was to change the alignment of the Iron Brigade. In scooping up Archer's brigade, the 24th Michigan had swung around so as to half encircle the Confederates. That caused the left flank of the Union line to be exposed. The 24th was pulled back across Willoughby Run and assigned new ground between the 7th Wisconsin and the 19th Indiana. The latter, instead of the 24th, was now posted on the extreme left.

The change of position left the 24th with neither a breathing spell nor protection. The left of its line was on a downward slope. Opposite, on higher ground, there was a big build-up of Confederate strength, with regiment after regiment, brigade after brigade of Heth's division moving into place. The Michigan men were being exposed to a cruel fire. Three times Colonel Morrow sent a runner back to General Meredith, asking permission to take up a less exposed position. Each time the request was denied; the orders had come down from Doubleday that an unbroken front was to be maintained.

"The position must be held at all costs," Doubleday declared.

Pointing to the Iron Brigade, standing firm in the face of mounting punishment, a subordinate, probably Meredith, replied:

"If we can't hold it, where will you find men who can?" *

Where indeed? Rarely in any battle did troops unflinchingly face such a devastating fire.

It was obvious to everyone that the Federal situation was becoming desperate. The Ist Corps with about nine thousand men was the only Federal unit on the field at the time with the exception of Buford's troopers, who had moved out to cover the flanking roads and were no longer under fire. The closest assistance was Howard's XIth Corps, but it was several miles south and east of Gettysburg. Although coming up as fast as possible to take position on the right of the Ist Corps and cover the Carlisle and Harrisburg roads north of the town, Howard, at this early phase of the battle, was still nearly two hours away.

Meanwhile, the Confederates were piling up an almost irresistible force. Ewell's corps, consisting of the veteran divisions formerly led by Stonewall Jackson, were living up to their designation of "foot cavalry" by the way they were chewing up the miles. They were coming in from the north on the extreme right of the Federal Ist, which was thoroughly occupied at the moment and had neither the time nor the manpower to stop them. From the west, down the Chambersburg road, Hill's corps was rolling up in front of the Ist in such numbers that individual regiments of the Iron Brigade were standing off entire Confederate divisions. There was a brief lull in the battle about noon, but it was little more than a breathing space. It lasted only long enough for the Confederates to assemble and throw Heth's and Pender's divisions of Hill's corps against the 19th Indiana and the 24th Michigan.

About 1 p.m. Howard arrived with his XIth Corps. He got there just in time to collide head on with the barreling divisions of Ewell. In the hurry of placing his men, Howard left a gap between his left and the right of the Ist Corps. That gap was to prove disastrous before the day's fighting ended.

Around McPherson's Woods, still the key position of the battle, the fighting was renewed with ferocious intensity on the part of the reinforced rebels. The fire which they poured into the Iron Brigade was almost more than human nerve and sinew could stand. Men were cut down in windrows. General Meredith was hit and led from the field. Colonel Robinson of the 7th Wisconsin took command of the Iron Brigade, but there was little he could do. Each regiment was fighting its own desperate battle of survival.

Pettigrew's and Brockenbrough's brigades of Heth's Confederate division threw all they had at the 24th Michigan and the 19th Indiana. It was said of the 24th that they fought that day "with no other protection than the flannel blouses that covered their stout hearts." But flannel wasn't enough and neither were stout hearts. The flank of the 19th Indiana was turned and was slowly pressed back, leaving the Michiganders open to a withering cross fire. Through the battle smoke, the Federals caught a glimpse of a gray-uniformed colonel, ambling up and down his line on an ancient mule. He could be heard shouting above the din: "Give 'em hell, boys!" Some Billy Yank let go a pot shot at the colonel. The bullet knocked his hat off, but the officer deftly caught it before it hit the ground. That was typical of the sort of rebel coolness that made the 24th's work so difficult.

The 24th Michigan had stood about all it could. Colonel Morrow drew his regiment back fifty yards or so and staked out a new line, the third which the regiment had occupied up to that time. The men retreated, a step at a time, firing all the way. But the enemy kept the pressure on. Captain Speed was killed when he attempted to swing back two left companies to cover the exposed flank. Lieutenant Gilbert A. Dickey went down. Lieutenant Buhl was hit. The second color bearer fell and the colors fell to the ground with him. They were quickly caught up again, but it was an ominous sign of what was to come.

Morrow's men were barely able to plant their feet in their new position when the Confederates were on them again. They retired to a fourth position, fighting stubbornly and refusing to break under the crushing weight of the foe. But it was clear that the limit of endurance was near. A third color bearer was killed. One by one the officers were disappearing. Major Edwin B. Wight caught a shot in the eye and his fighting was done. Lieutenants Safford, Shattuck, and Wallace were killed. Altogether, twelve officers were casualties by this time. The ranks too were thinning fast; only about one-fourth of the regiment was still on its feet. Over on the right, the enemy had found the opening between the Ist and the XIth Corps, and Ewell's men were pouring into the gap. Howard's divisions were going to pieces under hammer blows. Some of the men were already streaming back toward Gettysburg.

Still the remnant of the Iron Brigade held on, refusing to admit defeat. There was no general direction; each regimental commander was improvising as the situation suggested. Nevertheless, the brigade was falling slowly back; the 24th was pushed farther from the woods into the open field. Another color bearer was shot in the chest and carried away. Colonel Morrow himself picked up the flag and planted it as a rallying point for his few survivors. With his men steadied and firing fiercely into the on-coming rebels, Morrow handed the standard to a private beside him. As the boy clutched the staff, down he went, and Morrow caught it again. Lieutenant Humphreyville fell, and more spaces were opened in the thin blue line.

Once more Morrow gave ground and took up a fifth position. That was the last stand for Captain Malachi O'Donnell. A bullet wrote "30" for the *Detroit Free Press* composing room foreman. Lieutenant Grace fell before the same volley. The hot fire was too much. Completely out of touch with the other regiments of the brigade, the survivors, pitifully few, crouched behind a rail fence in front of the seminary—their sixth and final position on the field.

Ordinarily Federal troops favored fighting from behind rail fences, especially if they had the opportunity to throw up earth or stones against them for protection. The 24th had no time to dig in and the fence behind which they made their last stand gave the men no protection. A bullet slammed into Colonel Morrow's head. Blood gushed from the wound and it was feared he had taken a mortal hurt. He was carried back to a field hospital in Gettysburg, where it was found the wound, though painful, was not fatal. But he was unable to return to the field and his loss depressed the men. By that time only four officers were left. Captain Albert E. Edwards, who possessed a charmed life and who went unhurt through the entire war, took command. Of the twenty-nine officers who had gone into battle that morning, eight were dead, fourteen were wounded, and three were prisoners. A total of nine color bearers had been killed or wounded, and now Captain Edwards was holding the flag. There really was little need of many officers because few of the men were alive or unhurt. Only a corporal's guard remained in action.

The collapse of the XIth Corps just about wrapped things up for the day. Howard's men simply turned and ran, a formless mob which milled around Gettysburg and was easily captured by the pursuing Confederates. Thousands were made prisoner while clogging the streets or attempting to hide in the houses.

The Ist Corps did not break but, deserted by the XIth, its condition was hopeless. Both flanks were exposed, and the rebels, pursuing Howard's people, were working into the rear. Reynolds had led 9,403 men into battle with him that morning. Now there were fewer than 3,500 left to oppose the full force of two-thirds of Lee's army—almost 50,000 effectives. The Iron Brigade had lost 1,153 officers and men; there were but 730 left to bear the brunt of attack by Hill's corps. It was just too big, too hopeless a job. Doubleday passed the word to disengage and withdraw.

Captain Edwards rallied the remnants of the 24th Michigan, and holding the colors aloft led the survivors back across the lower edge of Gettysburg to Culp's Hill. General Steinwehr, who commanded Howard's reserve, had noticed the importance of the hill and with admirable foresight had spent the afternoon ringing its summit with earthworks. It was to the safety of Steinwehr's lunettes that the 24th retreated. It rested on Culp's Hill in relative security.

Captain Edwards now had a chance to count noses. Besides himself there were three lieutenants and twenty-three men. Those twenty-six were all that followed him from the field. Later, some stragglers and wounded drifted in, and by nightfall there were ninety-nine men of the 24th on Culp's Hill. They were all who were left of the 496 who had begun the battle that morning.

On July 1, 1863, the 24th Michigan Infantry lost 316 men killed or wounded. Another eighty-one were missing. Some of the latter had been wounded and were captured as they lay in the hospitals and dressing stations which had been set up in the churches, schools, and other buildings in Gettysburg.*

The 24th Michigan suffered eighty per cent casualties in that single day. Of the four hundred Union regiments participating in the three days at Gettysburg—July 1 to 3—none surpassed the casualty rate of the 24th Michigan of the Iron Brigade. Both regiment and brigade losses were so heavy that neither was again particularly effective as a fighting unit. In time replacements filled out the depleted ranks, but the spirit which enabled the Iron Brigade to defy a major part of Lee's army could not be replaced. The scars were too deep ever to heal completely.

As for the 24th, it remained on Culp's Hill until the end of the fighting on July 3.* Except for protecting an artillery emplacement, it played no important role in the remainder of the battle of Gettysburg.

But if the 24th Michigan and the Iron Brigade suffered, the foe they opposed did not escape either. The surrender of Archer's brigade was a catastrophe to the Confederates, who were hard-pressed for manpower. Throughout the remainder of the day's fighting the 24th was confronted most of the time by Pettigrew's brigade, which included the 26th North Carolina. The latter brought eight hundred men on the field. It finished the day with ninety-two —-suffering a casualty rate of 88.5 per cent. That was the largest regimental loss suffered by any unit on either side during the entire war. At Gettysburg the losses dealt Pettigrew by the Iron Brigade were exceeded only by those of Armistead's brigade during Pickett's charge.

But the heroic Iron Brigade and the Ist Corps did more than exact an eye for an eye. They actually began the battle of Gettysburg. By their fierce obstinacy in holding their ground, they determined where the greatest battle of the war was to be fought. For a period of several hours, the Ist Corps held off the full weight of a major portion of the Army of Northern Virginia. By doing so, it gave Meade time to bring up the rest of his force and occupy the positions which Lee, on the second and third days, assailed without success. During the night of July 1, the other corps of the Army of the Potomac arrived on the ground which the Ist Corps had preserved for them. The sacrifices of Reynolds and his men enabled the rest of the Union army to prevent Lee from occupying Cemetery Ridge. Had he been successful, the main battle would have been fought elsewhere, with what results no one will ever know.

The fight at McPherson's Woods was an important factor in the outcome of the battle of Gettysburg. What would have been the fate of Meade's army and of the Union had the men of the 24th and their brigade comrades not stood fast, is one of the big ifs of history.

General Wadsworth knew what the 24th had accomplished. On July 4, the day after the battle ended and while Lee was turning back to Virginia, leaving at Gettysburg his shattered hope of Northern conquest, Wadsworth scratched off a note to Colonel Morrow.*

"Colonel Morrow:" the note stated, "the only fault I find with you is that you fought too long, but God only knows what would have become of the Army of the Potomac if you had not held the ground as long as you did."

That message was a worthy postscript to Michigan's moment of imperishable glory.

XI

Sabers at

Rummel's Farm

SIGNAL FLAGS wigwagged furiously at the observation post atop Cemetery Ridge. Out to the east, about three miles from Gettysburg on the Hanover Road, General David M. Gregg of the Second Cavalry Division, read the message and acted on it.

The flags informed him that a strong column of Confederate cavalry was under observation, moving out of Gettysburg along the York Pike, which runs parallel to the Hanover Road, about a mile and a half north of it.

The gray column was Stuart, in full force, bent on an errand intended to do Meade's Army of the Potomac no good. It was Friday, July 3, 1863, the final day of the test of strength between North and South on the field of Gettysburg. Behind the trees on Seminary Ridge, Lee was massing Pickett's division, which he proposed to throw in one massive, magnificent charge against the Federal center. The assault was expected by Lee to shatter the Union line.

Stuart's assignment was to work his horsemen into the rear of the Federals and to strike from behind at the same time Pickett hit their front. Stuart was to turn off the York Pike and move down to the Baltimore Road, where Meade's wagon trains and reserve artillery were assembled. When, as it was hoped and expected, Meade's line crumpled under the force of Pickett's charge, the rear echelons were to be disrupted by Stuart and the Union escape route cut off. The resulting confusion would seal the doom of the Army of the Potomac.

It didn't turn out as planned, thanks in large part to the inspired performance of the Michigan Cavalry Brigade, which was destined to play a leading part in the last act of the drama of Gettysburg.

The cavalry fight at Rummel's farm * helped build a new reputation and establish a new idol for the North to worship. Out of that engagement with Stuart's legions emerged into the center of public attention the flamboyant figure of George Armstrong Custer.

The Michigan Cavalry Brigade, formally listed on the army's table of organization as the 2nd Brigade, 3rd Division, Cavalry Corps, was composed of four regiments: the 1st, 5th, 6th, and 7th Michigan. Together they formed the largest exclusive Michigan group to serve as a unit during the entire war.

Before Gettysburg, only the 1st Michigan Cavalry could claim veteran status. The other three regiments were green and untried; they had seen no action more serious than picket duty brushes or skirmish line forays. The 1st was organized early in the war, in August 1861. By the following February it had been given its first taste of blood in the Shenandoah Valley. From that time on it was kept very busy indeed. It lost its colonel, Thornton F. Brodhead, of Grosse Ile, at Second Manassas. By the time Lee marched into Pennsylvania in June 1863, the 1st Michigan had taken more than its share of bumps.

The other three regiments came along much later. The 5th was mustered in August 1862, and the 6th the following October; the 7th did not complete its recruiting and leave the state until February 1863. Those regiments, along with the 1st, had men from virtually every Michigan city, village, and farm community. They came from Detroit, Grand Rapids, Ionia, Davisburg, Greenbush, Lansing, Pentwater, Saginaw, Port Huron, and nearly every crossroad in between.

The 5th, 6th and 7th spent most of the winter in Washington undergoing a rigorous training. The early stages of the war found the Union cavalry woefully inadequate, no match at all for the hard-riding, well-led squadrons which Jeb Stuart had welded into an admirably effective military instrument.

Union cavalry, at the outset, was composed of various local troops of Black Horse, Lancers, Hussars, and Dragoons, which looked lovely in resplendent dress uniforms, leading Fourth of July parades in their home towns, or escorting visiting dignitaries. They weren't much good for anything else, including fighting. McClellan thought so little of cavalry that he rarely employed it for anything other than guarding wagon trains or carrying messages. Infantrymen who knew what it meant to be mauled by the enemy, looked with jaundiced eye at their mounted comrades and with reason asked: "Whoever saw a dead cavalryman?" The story was told throughout the Army of the Potomac of an infantry division commander who posted a standing offer of five dollars for the body of every cavalryman spotted by his troops.

When General Hooker took over command of the Army of the Potomac from Burnside, he changed all that.

"Fighting Joe" Hooker may have left much to be desired as a field commander, but he brought to his new post qualities of administrative leadership and organizing ability of which the Union army was badly in need. One of his more important undertakings was to consolidate the cavalry into a single corps. Before that time it had been distributed through the army by regiments. To command this cavalry corps, he appointed Major General Alfred Pleasonton. After that, the business of horse soldiering began to look up, and the cavalry started to function as it should. One trooper later observed that "from the day of its reorganization under Hooker, the cavalry of the Army of the Potomac commenced a new life."

The Michigan Cavalry Brigade, with the exception of the 1st regiment, which was already in the field, arrived on the scene just in time to go through Hooker's process of reorganization. Considerable training was involved, so, instead of being rushed off to the front, the 5th and 6th Michigan were held in Washington. There, during the winter of 1862–63, they underwent rigorous and interminable drilling.

The 5th arrived at Washington on December 4, 1862, and was assigned a camp ground on Capitol Hill. The 6th came in about a week later and found a place at the other end of town on Meridian Hill, well out Fourteenth Street. When the 7th made its appearance, it camped in the same area as the 6th.

A few days after the 6th had settled itself in its Washington quarters, Congressman Kellogg of Grand Rapids rounded up the officers of the regiment, many of whom were his constituents, and marched them in a body to the White House for an audience with President Lincoln.

"Full dress was the proper 'caper,' " reported J. H. Kidd * of Ionia, who was one of the group, "and accordingly they were arrayed in their finest. The uniforms were new and there is no doubt that they were a gorgeous looking party as they marched up Pennsylvania Avenue, wearing shiny brasses, bright red sashes, buff gauntlets, and sabers glittering in their scabbards."

Reception of visiting officers was old hat to Mr. Lincoln. Repetition made it, for him, one of the horrors of war. It was a time-consuming nuisance he would gladly have avoided, but the political amenities could not be ignored even in the face of the burden of war and executive duties. He shook hands all around, uttered a perfunctory "How do you do?", and then sought escape to his study as quickly as possible.

Congressman Kellogg, however, was not to be robbed of his brief moment of reflected glory; he felt constrained to make the most of his opportunity to impress the boys from home. A speech came upon him.

"Mr. President," he called out, and Mr. Lincoln paused in the doorway. "These are the officers of a regiment of cavalry who have just come from my state of Michigan. They are 'Wolverines' and are on the track of Jeb Stuart, whom they propose to pursue and capture if there is any virtue in a name."

115

Old Abe listened to that bombast with an expression of intense weariness. When Kellogg, flushed with self-satisfaction, had finished, Mr. Lincoln replied.

"Gentlemen," he said gravely, "I can assure you that it would give me much greater pleasure to see Jeb Stuart in captivity than it has given me to see you." With that he vanished into another room.

The officers of the 6th may have been a little deflated, but their esteem for Lincoln was not lessened.

"We saw him," Kidd recalled, "as in a halo, and looked beyond the plain lineaments and habiliments of the man to the ideal figure of the statesman and president, struggling for the freedom of his country and the unity of his race, whom we all saw in the 'Railsplitter' from Illinois; and he seemed, in his absent-minded way, to be looking beyond those present to the infinite realm of responsibility and care in which he dwelt."

Kidd's ability to turn a phrase obviously qualified him for the time when, as colonel of the 6th Michigan, it would be his satisfying duty to produce reports couched in purple-tinted prose.

General Pleasonton's program of training consisted of teaching his recruits to fight dismounted with the superior Spencer repeating rifle * which they were issued. The Spencer, a seven-shot repeater, was considered the best rifle used in the Civil War, and it was highly regarded by the Federal troops who used it. A little later, the Spencer carbine was substituted for the rifle as the cavalry weapon. It was better suited to the horseman than the longer and hence more cumbersome rifle.

Pleasonton went further. Over-age horses and officers were retired and put out to pasture as fast as remounts and replacements could be obtained, so that, by the time a new cavalry regiment completed its training and was sent into the field, its horses were strong and frisky, and its officers, particularly above the field grade, were usually young, energetic, and daring. To get good officer material, Pleasonton took whatever attracted him; he was not above appropriating likely prospects from the young professionals and West Pointers attached to other branches of the service. A promising lieutenant with no duties more weighty than dancing attendance as aide-de-camp on a corps or division commander, might find himself requisitioned into the cavalry, hoisted into the saddle and given a regiment or even a brigade.

Thus it was with the man who, in time, came to command the Michigan Cavalry Brigade—George Armstrong Custer. He was not long out of West Point when the war started. In June 1863 he was still wearing a first lieutenant's straps and rattling around army headquarters doing staff work. Then he suddenly found himself advanced five grades in rank in a single jump, with a brigadier's stars on his collar. It was almost enough to take the breath out of a man and turn a head less giddy than Custer's.

Toward the end of February 1863 the three new regiments of the Cavalry Brigade were considered ready and crossed the Long Bridge over the Potomac into Virginia. Still needing seasoning (they had not yet seen an enemy soldier), they were employed on limited reconnaissance expeditions. It was Pleasonton's policy to send green troops out, whenever possible, in small detachments to drive off Confederate pickets. Pleasonton and Hooker believed the best way to give recruits experience and confidence was to let them tangle with the enemy under controlled conditions which would assure them of the pleasant taste of victory.

That is the way matters stood in June 1863, when Lee gambled and sent his Army of Virginia marching into Pennsylvania.

It is a familiar story by now that Hooker hesitated and permitted Lee a good head start before the Army of the Potomac aroused itself and started out in slow, cumbersome pursuit.

When Lee marched north, screened behind the Blue Ridge and Bull Run Mountains, Stuart took the Confederate cavalry off on an expedition of the kind in which he delighted. Superb horse soldier that he was, Stuart nevertheless relished the spectacular and sensational. On two previous occasions he had led his command completely around the Union army, raising hell in its rear and creating consternation all the way to the White House.

Lee's orders to Stuart at the beginning of the Gettysburg campaign were vague. The cavalryman was told to cover the mountain passes so that Lee's three infantry corps might march undetected and unmolested. Then Stuart was to ride north and make junction with Ewell somewhere near Harrisburg, covering the right flank of the Confederate army. He was also supposed to keep a watchful eye on enemy movements and inform Lee where the Federals were going and what they were doing.

Stuart failed to accomplish any of these assignments with the perfection expected of him. Attempting to cover the northward movement of the infantry, he discovered he had to deal with a new Union cavalry which could fight him on equal terms. Moreover, a routine, plodding march alongside the slow-moving foot soldiers was not to his taste. He devised the bold plan of doing what he had done before, making a circuit around the Union army. If successful, this would be a raid on the grand scale. It would place the rebel cavalry between the Federal army and Washington, cutting supply lines and creating general havoc and confusion. Then Stuart would finally rejoin Lee somewhere in Pennsylvania.

Embarking on his adventure, Stuart cut behind the Federals, crossed the Potomac, and headed north through Maryland. He passed almost within sight of Washington, throwing the city into near panic. Then he proceeded on a line of march far to the east of Lee's columns. He thus put himself completely out of touch with Lee, furnished the latter with no information whatever, and did not make contact with the main Confederate army until the second day of the battle of Gettysburg, July 2. By that time his men and horses were utterly exhausted and their chances for effectiveness substantially diminished. Some critics of the battle maintain that Stuart's failure to serve Lee properly cost the Confederates the Gettysburg campaign.

While Lee and Stuart were leaving Virginia, the Michigan Cavalry Brigade was at Fairfax Court House. The 3rd Division, to which it belonged, was then under the command of General Stahel, and the brigade commander was Colonel Joseph T. Copeland of Pontiac, who had taken the 5th Michigan out. The regimental post Copeland left vacant was filled by the promotion and transfer of Lieutenant Colonel Russell A. Alger, from the 6th Michigan.

The brigade got its marching orders at 2 a.m., June 25. Before the day was ended it had crossed the Potomac at Edward's Ferry, where the traffic was heavy with blue-coated corps setting out in pursuit of Lee. Generally, the brigade's route for the next few days was the same at that of Hooker's infantry, through Poolesville and Frederick, and on toward Emmitsburg and the Pennsylvania line.

This was an excursion which the Michiganders found to be very much to their taste. The countryside was peaceful and prosperous; for the moment the war seemed to have faded into the distance behind them. One trooper of the 6th Michigan became almost lyrical in his description of the Maryland and Pennsylvania scene.

"The rain of early morning," he wrote, "had left in the atmosphere a mellow haze of vapor which reflected the sun's rays in tints that softly blended with the summer colorings of the landscape. An exclamation of surprise ran along the column as each succeeding trooper came in sight of this picture of Nature's own painting."

He might have expressed his own and his comrades' feelings just as explicitly had he stated that all hands felt it was wonderful to be alive and to be jogging along with no one shooting at them.

Before long Stahel's division moved ahead of the main Union force, scouting the roads, seeking the whereabouts of the enemy. Thus it happened that on June 28, the 5th and 6th Michigan, riding up the Emmitsburg Road, became the first Union troops to enter Gettysburg.

The men of the two regiments felt ten feet tall when they rode into town. The amiable burghers of Gettysburg made their arrival a holiday and the streets were lined with cheering, waving men and women. It had been only a few days before that General Ewell had marched his ragged Confederate corps through the town; the men from Michigan now seemed like knights in shining armor, bringing deliverance and safety.

Church bells pealed out a welcome that carried the message of the brigade's arrival across the hills and fields. Flowers were tossed to the passing troopers; soon each soldier and each horse was hung over with garlands from the hands of smiling girls. Lines of men stood at the curbs, slicing into generous slabs giant loaves of warm, snowy fresh-baked bread. Tubs of home-made apple butter were brought out and the bread was smeared with it. Horses were given their heads while the men ate with both hands. War had never been that good before.

At the center square in Gettysburg the column turned to the right on the York Pike and went into camp in cool shady groves and rich meadows a short distance outside of town.

"The horses," said Major Kidd, "were up to their knees in clover, and it made the poor, famished animals fairly laugh."

But it wasn't a live cavalryman's good fortune to dwell long in Elysian fields. The next morning, having discovered no enemy, the brigade retraced its steps to Emmitsburg. Buford's 1st Cavalry Division moved into Gettysburg in place of the Michiganders and the next day, June 30, made contact with the rebels on the road west of the town. Had the Michigan cavalry stayed a day or two longer in Gettysburg, it would have been their destiny instead of Buford's to open the big show.

Back in Emmitsburg there was news awaiting the brigade. Hooker had been relieved of command of the Army of the Potomac and had been replaced by Major General George Gordon Meade. Of more immediate interest, however, was that both the 3rd Cavalry Division and the Michigan Brigade had been given new leaders. Pleasonton's reshuffling wasn't suspended even in the face of impending battle. Judson Kilpatrick, a West Pointer, had been promoted from the colonelcy of the 2nd New York Cavalry and, with the rank of brigadier general, had been given the division. The brigade went to Custer, who also received his star. Colonel Copeland faded out of the picture. The 1st Michigan at this time was added to the brigade.

As it was now constituted, the brigade had four regiments. The 1st Michigan was commanded by Colonel Charles H. Town of Detroit; the 5th by Colonel Russell A. Alger * of Grand Rapids; the 6th by Colonel George Gray of Grand

Rapids; and the 7th by Colonel William D. Mann of Detroit. Attached to the brigade was a six-gun battery of horse artillery, Battery M, 2nd United States Artillery, Lieutenant A. C. M. Pennington commanding.

The brigade did not stay long in Emmitsburg. The day—June 29—was still young when the brigade was sent out to the east, part of a force composed of Kilpatrick's and Gregg's divisions. It was reported that Stuart with his entire corps, accompanied by a long wagon train which he had captured, was in the vicinity, moving north along back roads in a hurried and desperate effort to make a junction with Lee's army, which Stuart expected to find somewhere north and east of Gettysburg.

The Union cavalry made contact, and wrangled and growled along Stuart's flank, fighting small engagements and succeeding in forcing the Confederate to make a considerable detour through Hanover, fourteen miles east of Gettysburg. Stuart's bypass carried him all the way to Carlisle looking for Ewell, who was by that time moving with the rest of Lee's army toward a concentration near Gettysburg. The result was that Stuart did not report to Lee until July 2.

Kilpatrick's division was scattered pretty well over the countryside; the Michigan brigade found itself working along the Hanover Road in closer proximity to Gregg's division than to Kilpatrick's other brigade.

While it was snapping at Stuart's heels on June 30, its new brigadier, Custer, caught up with it and provided the men with their first look at their new boss soldier.

The brigade could scarcely believe what it saw. The men blinked with amazement. Custer was a monument of splendor, a sight to behold. The dusty, road-worn troopers thought perhaps there had been a mistake: it was no soldier who had been sent to them, but a character out of an opéra bouffe. He was dressed in a uniform of his own contriving, the like of which had never been seen by the Union army. His trousers and short jacket were black velvet, with loops and ropes of gold braid or "lace," which almost covered the sleeves and splashed in a cascade down his trouser seams. He wore a blue navy shirt turned down over the collar of his jacket, with a flowing Windsor tie or neckpiece of brilliant crimson, tied in a large, careless knot, the ends loose over his chest. All this finery failed to hide the double row of brass buttons arranged in groups of twos, the mark of a brigadier general.

Custer's boots were knee length, of soft and highly polished black leather with golden spurs. His hat was soft, adorned with a gold cord. The wide brim was turned up on one side and fastened with a rosette encircling a silver star; the other side was turned down, giving him a rakish, piratical air. He wore his golden hair shoulder length, and a blond, full mustache drooped on either side of his mouth. A shining sword and an elaborate belt completed this portrait of cavalier grandeur.

His men may have thought Custer was trying to outdo in gaudiness the pride of the Confederate cavalry—Jeb Stuart, who was noted for his flamboyant and colorful costumes, brilliant sashes and ostrich-plumed hats. But there was method in the madness of both men. Like Stuart, Custer was a slapdash fighter who rode at the head of his men and charged in where the fighting was heaviest. The eye-catching uniforms were battlefield gonfalons, identifiable emblems which their men could easily follow and around which they could rally.

When Custer first came into view of the men of his brigade, they may have been inclined to snicker. But, for all his flair for showmanship, Custer had sound qualities of leadership. The troopers quickly learned to respect him; then respect grew almost into reverence.

James Kidd saw Custer for the first time on June 30, 1863, while the 6th Michigan was using its Spencer rifles to accelerate Stuart's march along the roads north of Hanover. Kidd declared that Custer was the most picturesque figure in the Union army, but he also maintained that his brigade commander was no vainglorious showoff.

"A keen eye," said Kidd, "would have been slow to detect in that rider with the flowing locks and gaudy tie, in his dress of velvet and of gold, the master spirit that he proved to be. That garb, fantastic as at first sight it appeared to be, was to be the distinguishing mark which, during all the remaining years of that war, like the white plume of Henry of Navarre, was to show us where, in the thickest of the fight, we were to seek our leader."

Although he was a native of Ohio, Custer's home was Monroe, Michigan, and that fact may have helped to prejudice the troopers of his brigade in his favor. He was only twenty-four years old when he won his stars, only two years out of West Point, where he won no distinction as a scholar. But he was brave and energetic, even if he did on occasion appear to act with hot-headed immaturity.

Kidd, who served under him until the end of the war and had a good opportunity to observe him, insisted the popular idea of Custer was all wrong.

"He was not a reckless commander. He was not regardless of human life. No man could have been more careful of the comfort and lives of his men. His heart was tender as that of a woman. He was kind to his subordinates, tolerant of their weaknesses, always ready to help and encourage them. He was brave as a lion, fought as few men fought, but it was from no love of it. Fighting was his business; he knew that by that means alone could peace be conquered. He was brave, alert, untiring, a hero in battle. . . .

"He was cautious and wary, accustomed to reconnoiter carefully and measure the strength of an enemy as accurately as possible before attacking. More than once the Michigan brigade was saved from disaster by Custer's caution."

Now, with the background filled in and the cast of characters assembled, the story becomes that of the Michigan Cavalry Brigade as well as that of George Armstrong Custer. It is the story of the cavalry at Gettysburg on July 3, 1863. War offers few real moments of glory; when one comes it may be brief and not recognized until long after the event. The Michigan Cavalry Brigade's grand climax—its reason for being, if destiny assigns reasons—came on the afternoon of the third day of the contest at Gettysburg. The place was called Rummel's Farm. It was near the juncture of the Hanover and Low Dutch Roads, two miles south of the York Pike, and three miles east of Gettysburg.

Stuart caught up with Lee on July 2 and Lee rebuked him for his failure to function as his "eyes and ears." Stung by the reprimand and resolved to redeem himself by tearing apart the rear of the Federal position at the moment of Pickett's grand charge, Stuart accepted a major role in the closing scenes of the drama. He had no doubts about his ability to play his part as he led the brigades of Hampton, Fitz Lee, Chambliss, and Jenkins out the York Pike about noon of the 3rd.

When he had gone about three miles Stuart turned off the York Pike to his right and placed his brigades in line on some rising ground known as Cress Ridge. In front of him were the farmhouse and barns of John Rummel, and beyond them were flat, open fields which extended for nearly three-quarters of a mile to the Hanover Road. Stuart placed his men behind a fringe of trees, then rode out to survey the scene.

Everything looked very peaceful; off in the distance a few blue-coated scouts could be seen, but they were nothing to worry about. From his position on the ridge, Stuart had a clear view of all the main roads behind the Federal lines at Gettysburg. There was no enemy activity in front of him; except for the grumble of guns off to the west, marking the artillery duel which preceded Pickett's charge, there might have been no war going on. Stuart ordered a field piece to the front and fired four random shots toward each cardinal point of the compass, a signal to Lee that he was in position and ready to make his move.

But there was a surprise in store for Stuart. His gun served as a signal to the Federals too, and out of the woods just beyond the Hanover Road came a swarm of Union skirmishers, who advanced dismounted almost up to Rummel's place. These were Alger's men of the 5th Michigan.

Both Gregg's and Kilpatrick's divisions had been in the vicinity during the morning. Kilpatrick had received orders to move his two brigades, including the Michigan, far around to the Union left near Round Top. He had started away, taking one brigade with him, and Custer was getting ready to follow. Then Gregg got the message from Cemetery Ridge that Stuart was on the move. Acting on his own initiative, he canceled Kilpatrick's orders and directed Custer to remain where he was on the Hanover Road facing Cress Ridge. Smelling a fight, Custer was only too happy to oblige.

Stuart sent a couple of squadrons of Jenkins' brigade to chase Alger's men away. Up to that point, Stuart did not know that the 6,000 men he had posted on the ridge were confronted by a substantial Union force of about 5,000.

The 5th Michigan took a position behind one of several fences which cut up the fields around Rummel's. The Confederates advanced to the fence and a sprightly exchange of fire took place. Outnumbered, the 5th worked their Spencer repeaters until the barrels were hot and their ammunition began to give out. Then Alger's men began to withdraw to their horses. At that moment Gregg sent the 7th Michigan forward to ease the pressure on the 5th. The 7th advanced mounted and ran into a fence where they were met by more of Jenkins' people and some from Chambliss' brigade. Unfortunately for the 7th, it had charged ahead without due caution. The fence stopped the front riders and those behind piled up on them. There was a milling mass of blue cavalry which provided the rebels with good targets. The 7th was forced back in considerable confusion, but the 5th, now mounted, returned to the fight, covering their comrades of the other regiment.

Other elements on both sides were feinting at each other, and small, limited brawls were boiling all over the field. Pennington's artillery was keeping things warm for the Confederates on the ridge and around Rummel's house. Stuart's guns, although barking furiously, were doing less damage, partly because of superior Federal marksmanship, partly because Confederate ammunition was defective and the shells were bursting short of their marks.

The fight was a big skirmish action up to this time, but the increasing number of blue coats who kept coming out from behind the cover along the Hanover and Low Dutch Roads made Stuart realize he was not going to turn Meade's flank without a scrap. Fretting at the delay and wearying of the inconclusive sparring on the field, the Confederate leader decided it was time to bring the issue to a head and clean the troublesome Federals out.

It was after 2 p.m. when Stuart called on Hampton and Fitz Lee to step in and settle things. Neither of these two brigades had up to that moment been engaged. Hampton took charge. His and Fitz Lee's troopers were the flower of the Confederate cavalry. It was taken for granted they were capable of anything, and no assignment had yet been beyond their ability.

Hampton formed his men in a column of squadrons, facing south toward the Hanover Road. Before him, for nearly three quarters of a mile, the field was flat and without obstruction. The Confederate bugles sounded, men settled themselves in their saddles, the guidons and battleflags fluttered, and the heavy mass of gray cavalry advanced at a walk.

From his observation point at the juncture of the Hanover and Low Dutch Roads, Gregg saw Hampton and Lee come out into the open and begin to move forward. His own regiments were scattered as a result of the small fights; the only complete unit immediately available was the 1st Michigan, standing easy behind a screen of trees and bushes on the Hanover Road. He ordered them out to meet the Confederates.

With parts of the 5th, 6th, and 7th regiments, the 1st Michigan stepped forward, also at a walk. Having heard Gregg's order, Custer rode over and placed himself at the head of the 1st Michigan and its supporting units of his brigade. Slowly the opposing forces approached each other. At the same moment, as if at a given signal, both bodies of horsemen increased their gaits to a trot.

Here, shaping up, was the grand spectacle of war, a cavalry charge in the classic manner. All over the battlefield, men in blue and gray who were not part of those advancing columns paused in the business of flaying each other and turned to watch.

The distance was rapidly narrowing. Then Custer, magnificent in his velvet pants and gold braid, riding four lengths ahead of the front files, rose in his stirrups and brandished his sword.

"Come on you Wolverines!" he shouted. His bugles bleated, calling for the charge. Hampton's replied. Each side swept toward the other, now at full gallop. Men bent low in their saddles; bright, gleaming sabers advanced. The earth shook under the drumming of thousands of hoofs; a mighty wave of sound rolled up, deafening, drowning out the rumble of guns at Gettysburg, where Pickett was sending his brigades up to the high-water mark on Cemetery Ridge.

Blue and gray slammed into each other with a crash. It was like a mighty explosion that rocked the field. Mounts were up-ended, their riders trampled into the ground. Sabers rang as they crossed. Horses screamed, men shouted. A cloud of dust arose. Columns broke up into a hundred dog fights, sabers slashing and biting.

Back and forth the battle swayed the full length of the field. First the Confederates chopped their way forward; Union blue rolled them back, only to have the process repeated time after time. Small groups on each side became ringed and isolated. Men would surrender, but within a few minutes the tide of battle would turn and captors became the captured. Shrill yells of rage and exultation mingled with cries for mercy.

Except for an occasional blast of canister from the opposing guns, not many shots were fired at first. Until the action had nearly ended it was almost exclusively a sword fight.

"Keep to your sabers, men; keep to your sabers," Confederate officers could be heard shouting. The rebels were not as handy with the saber as the Federals. In fact they had a particular distaste for it; they considered knife-sticking beneath the dignity of cavaliers. In earlier engagements Stuart's men, preferring pistols at short range, had been known to call out to Federal cavalrymen: "Put up your sabers! Draw your pistols and fight like gentlemen."

But there were no gentlemen on the field at Rummel's farm—only grim and determined warriors, hacking at each other's heads, intent upon destroying their enemies.

Along the fringes of the grinding battle small contingents of Gregg's men, particularly from McIntosh's brigade, began working in on the flanks. Here and there an officer gathered together a handful of men, sometimes not more than a dozen, and charged into the Confederate mass, riding back and forth, stabbing and slashing. Hampton got in the way of one group and took a saber cut across the head, which ended his fighting for the day.

A Pennsylvanian, Colonel William Brooke-Rawle, saw the Confederate brigades begin to fray around the edges. Custer kept up the pressure until, worn by weariness which bestowed no partisan favors, and acting as if by tacit agreement, each side began to break off and withdraw to its original position.

"The successful result of this magnificent cavalry charge," said Brooke-Rawle, "was attributed by the victors [Union] to the steadiness and efficiency with which they used the saber en masse against greatly superior numbers of the enemy, many of whom had exchanged that weapon for the revolver."

Stuart knew he was through. When the dust settled, he turned his glasses on the Federal position and saw in a field below the Hanover Road one of Gregg's brigades. It had been too far away to get into the battle, but now it was coming up fast and would be available if another fight started. The Confederates, men and horses, were tired from their previous hard days of riding and fighting, and there was no enthusiasm in the ranks for another try. The resistance of the Federal cavalry seemed to demoralize them.

Later both sides would claim victory—the Federals because they had checked Stuart, the Confederates because at the end of the battle they held the same ground they occupied at the beginning.

But there was more to it than that. The laurel wreath rightfully belonged to Custer and his valiant Wolverines. After all, Stuart was prevented from turning Meade's flank or synchronizing an attack on the Federal rear with Lee's last great effort to smash through the Federal front. From the crest of the ridge above Rummel's farm Stuart heard the noise at Gettysburg die down and he must have known that Lee had failed.

At twilight Stuart led his battered brigades back to the York Pike, where he camped for the night. Gathering together his people, Custer rode away to join Kilpatrick in accordance with his earlier instructions.

"Thus," wrote one historian, "ended the third and last day of Gettysburg."

Brooke-Rawle said Gregg's fight was the finest cavalry action of the war. Custer, more grandiloquent, said: "I challenge the annals of warfare to produce a more brilliant or successful charge of cavalry."

For many years after the war there was a tendency to overlook or at least to minimize the importance of the battle at Rummel's farm. Bigger events at Gettysburg overshadowed the work of the cavalry. But recent historians have been inclined to give it more attention.*

Whatever the verdict of history, the troopers of the Michigan Cavalry Brigade, riding away to rejoin their division on that fateful evening of July 3, 1863, had every reason to sit very tall in their saddles.

XII

Lady of

the Regiment

THE MORNING REPORT of the 2nd Michigan Volunteer Infantry for April 19, 1863, listed Private Franklin Thompson, Company F, absent without leave.

That notation created no particular stir among the regimental rank and file. There had been desertions from the 2nd before; there would be others.

The 2nd had been organized in April 1861 when the reverberations of the rebel guns firing on Fort Sumter echoed in indignant Northern ears. Since then the regiment had traveled far and had intimately known battle. It had been on the field at First Bull Run; it had experienced the tribulations and frustrations of the Peninsula campaign. The 2nd had counted its dead and wounded at Malvern Hill and Fredericksburg. With the IXth Corps, it had been sent west to help Grant and later to battle Longstreet in eastern Tennessee. In April 1863 it was at Lebanon, Kentucky, preparing to move south and join the siege forces around Vicksburg.

The news that another man had gone over the hill didn't cause the 2nd to miss a mess call.

Perhaps that observation should be amended—because Private Franklin Thompson wasn't a man. Franklin Thompson was the assumed name of a woman, Sarah Emma Edmonds.* And thereby hangs one of the strangest, most bizarre stories which the war was to produce. It is a story which was not fully known until around 1882, when the true identity of Franklin Thompson was revealed to the veterans of the 2nd Michigan.

The story began—and the reader is cautioned to have a few grains of salt at hand as it unfolds—at St. John, New Brunswick, in 1839, when Emma was born to a hardscrabble farmer named Edmonds and his wife. Some of the harshness of the Canadian maritime climate must have seeped into the soul of Farmer Edmonds. Even to his children he was a bleak, blue-nosed man—a dour Scotch-Irish immigrant, who firmly believed that offspring were sent into the world to provide inexpensive farm labor.

When she was little more than an infant, Emma was sent into the fields with her brothers and sisters to dig and sack potatoes, and no nonsense was permitted. Somehow, between chores, the youngsters got some schooling and absorbed a piety which sometimes became almost overpowering in later years.

Emma also possessed a vivid imagination with a decidedly romantic cast. She must have had a vigorously independent spirit. Before she was barely in her teens she got hold of a volume titled *Fanny Campbell, the Female Sailor.* It was the story of a British woman who, disguised as a man, became a sailor and enjoyed some high adventure. Fanny Campbell's tale made a deep impression on Emma Edmonds, and the girl decided that what Fanny could do, she also could do. She made up her mind that some day she would emulate Fanny.

The opportunity came a few years later, when her father insisted upon her marrying a neighbor, much older than she. Emma rebelled. With the conspiratorial aid of a male acquaintance, she obtained an outfit of man's clothing and lit out from home. Exactly when that happened isn't certain, but it was probably when Emma was about eighteen years old.

Displaying initiative and self-reliance, the girl—or now, by her own transformation, the youth—obtained a job as an itinerant Bible salesman for a Hartford, Connecticut, publisher. Her masquerade was effective and her secret was not discovered or suspected by her customers. She prospered sufficiently that she could buy a horse and buggy, and as she drove from one village to the next, stopping at each farmhouse she passed, she was accepted for what she professed to be, a personable and persuasive salesman.

Her Bible-selling Odyssey lacked a Homer; whether she worked in Canadian territory or went immediately to the United States is not known. Emma told how, becoming homesick, she returned to the family farm and was entertained by her mother and sister. Her identity was revealed only when the farm dog and horses recognized her. At least, that's the way Emma told it.

In the course of time, her travels took her to Michigan during the winter of 1860–61, and of her appearance there we can rely on the more factual account of Mrs. Lora Pratt Doty. Mrs. Doty, the daughter of an Oakland County farmer, Charles Pratt, recalled many years later the day on which Emma arrived at their Rose Township home.

"The girl disguised in men's clothing, came to my father's house selling Bibles and other religious books when I was a small child," Mrs. Doty said. "She asked to make her home with us while carrying on her sales work, and frequently assisted with the chores.

"She used the name of Franklin Thompson. Her features were almost too coarse to be those of a woman and too fine for a man. Once when she was helping my father he remarked that she handled a pitchfork like a woman. She dispelled his suspicions with the explanation that she had never done farm work.

"She was extremely devout. We had another boarder at our home, Elder Berry, who served as school teacher and Baptist minister. The two became great friends and corresponded throughout the war. It was through Elder Berry and his father that we learned the truth about our guest.

"Soon after the war broke out in the spring of 1861 our guest announced his intention of joining the Union forces and left us. After the war was over, Elder Berry wrote to her, still thinking she was a man, and told of his recent marriage. In a reply, she revealed her identity and explained that she and her father had quarreled at her home in Canada and that she had put on men's clothing to earn a living and avoid possibility of detection."

Mrs. Doty said Emma was eighteen at the time the war broke out. Actually, she was twenty-two when she enlisted in 1861.

Mrs. Doty apparently was in error when she said Emma was living at her parents' home at the time she joined the army. Some time before the spring of 1861 she had moved to Flint and boarded there with a Methodist minister, the Reverend T. J. Joslin. In Flint she—or Franklin Thompson—became acquainted with William R. Morse, who was captain of the Flint Union Greys, the local militia company. Probably through Morse's influence, Emma enrolled in the Greys, and on April 25, 1861, when the company was incorporated into the 2nd Michigan Volunteer Infantry for three months as Company F, Emma found herself in the army.

With the rest of the regiment, Company F rendezvoused in Detroit at the Agricultural Fair Grounds, then called Camp Blair, but soon moved to Fort Wayne, where it trained. At Fort Wayne the 2nd was re-recruited as Michigan's first three-year regiment, and on June 6, led by Colonel Israel B. Richardson of Pontiac, it departed for Washington. Arriving there June 10, it went into quarters at Camp Winfield Scott.

Only six weeks away was First Bull Run, where the 2nd would get its first taste of blood and glory.

When the regiment marched away, Franklin Thompson marched with it, none of his comrades sharing his secret. How a woman could enlist as a man, undetected, is something of a puzzle. Recruits were examined for physical fitness, but obviously the examination did not penetrate beneath the blouses of the applicants. The surgeons must have been most casual in their scrutiny.

If a recruit possessed a head, two arms, and two legs he was in. Non-soldierly appurtenances under the tunic must not have been exposed to the examining medic's gaze.

Perhaps Emma was not richly endowed with those appurtenances to begin with. But even so, it must have required some ingenuity on the part of the female soldier to conform to camp life and routine and keep her secrets under her blue uniform. A picture of Emma taken after the war shows her in mannish attire, and the likeness in the photograph would pass either for a fairly handsome man or a not quite so handsome woman. Franklin must have exhibited some feminine characteristics, because his comrades remarked about his small hands and feet and joshed him about being a "woman."

Perhaps Franklin Thompson's secret was not so well kept as Emma supposed. There is evidence that some comrades were aware of the masquerade. In 1863, immediately after her desertion, a soldier in the 20th Michigan Infantry, which was brigaded with the 2nd, put the following in his diary:

"We are having quite a time at the expense of our brigade postmaster. He turns out to be a girl and has deserted when her lover, Inspector Read, and General Poe resigned. She went by the name of Frank Crandall, and was a pretty girl. She came out with Company F of the second Michigan regiment, and has been with them ever since."

Where the diarist got the name Crandall has never been explained. Possibly it came to him through camp gossip. As for a love affair with Inspector Read, otherwise unidentified, that bit of information may have been derived from the same source. Once Franklin's true sex was learned, rumors of relations with men were almost inevitable.

Many years after the war Emma attended a reunion of the regiment at Flint. The results were not entirely happy as far as she was concerned. When the gathering was over and she had returned home, she wrote to one of her fellow veterans, stating she had been "properly punished for going to the reunion," and asking the cryptic question: "Who was the lady who volunteered the information?" Then, while expressing her pride and satisfaction at having been a member of the 2nd, she declared she had discovered "that the honor of membership has cost me more than I am willing to pay—that of slurs upon my character."

Of course she may have been referring to something done or said at the reunion, and it is entirely understandable, hindsight being a common and convenient thing, if some of the former soldiers with whom she had associated "remembered" incidents twenty years after the war which they neither knew nor realized while they were marching by Franklin Thompson's side.

There is substantial evidence that most members of the 2nd, officers and men, had no suspicion about Franklin's true sex. General Orlando Poe flatly stated in 1891 that "her sex was not suspected by me or anyone else in the regiment. . . ." Inasmuch as she served as Poe's orderly during the battle of Fredericksburg, he had an opportunity to observe her closely. Others in the regiment bore out what Poe said, and it is hardly likely that they were motivated by postwar gallantry. Quite the contrary. It would have been natural, had they entertained any suspicions during the war, to have pointed back to them in later years.

Suspected or not, Franklin Thompson performed his military duties in a manner which would have done credit to any member of the army. As Poe said of his orderly, she "carried messages through showers of shot and shell with a fearlessness that attracted the attention and secured the commendation of field and general officers. There was not even a shadow of humbug about the soldiership of Frank Thompson." In the early stages of the Peninsula campaign Emma was detailed to collect and distribute the regimental mail, and after Fredericksburg she was promoted to brigade postmaster, an assignment which lasted up to the time she deserted.

Emma's headquarters jobs allowed her more than the ordinary freedom of movement, and that was exactly what she preferred. It gave her the opportunity to roam around camp, visit hospitals, and help attend to the sick and wounded. That sort of service was to her liking, and, considering the deep religious convictions which she professed, it may have been the thing which impelled her to join the army in the first place.

After her desertion, Emma wrote a book under her own name. Titled *Nurse and Spy in the Union Army*, it had a large sale and the entire proceeds were donated to army relief. In her book she tells in considerable detail about helping the surgeons and chaplains, and it becomes quite obvious that Franklin Thompson was, in reality though unofficially, either a hospital orderly or a nurse.* She makes it clear that she derived her greatest satisfaction from that kind of duty. Speaking of her enlistment, Emma says:

"I was not merely to go to Washington and remain there until a battle had been fought and the wounded brought in, and then in some comfortable hospital sit quietly and fan the patients, after the Surgeon had dressed their wounds; but I was to go to the front and participate in all the excitement of the battle scenes, or in other words, be a 'Field Nurse.' "

While Emma roamed through camp and battlefield, distributing the mail, carrying messages, and looking after the wounded, her imagination far outranged her physical ambulations. Her book, presented as her wartime memoirs, is rather a collection of tall tales in which it is almost impossible to separate fact from fiction. She recounts adventures which, one concludes, are what she thought her readers would like, not what did or conceivably could have happened.

There is the story, for instance, of the regeneration of Nellie.

While on a private foraging expedition, said Emma, she came to a fine, old-style plantation house and was given a chilly reception by "a tall, stately lady . . . dressed in deep mourning which was very becoming to her pale, sad face. She seemed about thirty years of age, very prepossessing in appearance, and evidently belonged to one of the 'F.F.V.'s.' " That was Nellie!

Reluctantly, Nellie filled a basket with food, but, when Emma mounted her horse and started to ride away, Nellie pulled a gun and took a pot shot at what she must have supposed to have been a marauding Federal soldier.

Emma did not take kindly to being shot at, as she proceeded to demonstrate.

"I turned my horse in a twinkling, and grasped my revolver. She was in the act of firing a second time, but was so excited that the bullet went wide of its mark. I held my seven-shooter in my hand, considering where to aim. I did not wish to kill the wretch, but did intend to wound her. When she saw that two could play at this game, she dropped her pistol and threw up her hands imploringly. I took deliberate aim at one of her hands, and sent the ball through the palm of her left hand. She fell to the ground in an instant with a loud shriek. I dismounted, and took the pistol which lay beside her, and placing it in my belt, proceeded to take care of her ladyship after the following manner: I unfastened the end of my halter-strap and tied it painfully around her right wrist, and remounting my horse, I started, and brought the lady to consciousness by dragging her by the wrist two or three rods along the ground."

That treatment, according to Emma, was enough to take the secesh starch out of poor Nellie. Promising that if she was released she would turn Unionist and devote herself to aiding the Federal wounded, she was freed and was transformed into a veritable angel of mercy and "one of the most faithful and efficient nurses in the army of the Potomac."

After other equally melodramatic adventures, Emma undertook a new career, that of spy. General McClellan needed someone to work behind the rebel lines, gathering information. Who was best qualified for the undertaking? Why, Emma naturally!

She tells of being summoned to McClellan's headquarters, briefed on her duties, and given a phrenological examination to determine whether the bumps on her head established her aptitude for espionage.

Evidently her cranial knobs were of the right size and properly located. She exchanged her uniform for the costume of a Negro boy, blacked her face, and slipped behind the Confederate lines. So complete and perfect was her disguise that she was soon able to return to General McClellan with information about an impending rebel attack and the location of Confederate batteries.

The tale stretches credulity to the snapping point; can anyone believe that this Canadian girl, made up in blackface, using a minstrel-show dialect, could actually fool Confederate soldiers and Virginia Negroes?

There were other expeditions equally fantastic, and if one can believe Emma (which is practically impossible) she was a consummate actress and a genius at disguise and dialect. On one occasion she claims to have penetrated the Confederate defenses made up as an old Irish woman peddler, complete with a pack of pies and a rich brogue.

After the 2nd moved west to Kentucky, Emma really came into her own as a secret agent—at least that's the way she told it. She was employed in counter-intelligence, helping track down the leaders of a Confederate ring in Louisville who were sending information south and aiding Union deserters to escape.

Disguised this time as a Canadian youth and posing as a neutral, Emma obtained employment as a clerk for a suspected Louisville shopkeeper. While in his employ she was shanghaied into a rebel cavalry unit. As it started south it met a Federal cavalry patrol, and a fight followed. Luckily Emma was immediately recognized by the leader of the Union force and rescued, but not before she had managed to shoot down the Confederate officer who had abducted her.

The last part of her book is pure fabrication. It recounts her experiences in the Vicksburg campaign. Actually she was not at Vicksburg or any place close to it. She deserted before her regiment started south from Kentucky.

Why did she desert? The explanation she offers both in her book and elsewhere may well be the true one. She says she contracted malaria and found it increasingly difficult to perform her duties. She feared she would be sent to a hospital, where her real sex certainly would be disclosed. To forestall that, she applied for a medical discharge. When it was refused she went over the hill.

In her book, Emma does not mention that she deserted, but claims that she received a medical discharge.

"It was under these circumstances," she writes, referring to her illness, "that I made up my mind to leave the army; and when once my mind is made up on any subject I am very apt to act at once upon that decision. So it was in this case. I sent for the surgeon and told him I was not able to remain longer—that I would certainly die if I did not leave immediately.

"The good old surgeon * concurred in my opinion, and made out a certificate of disability, and I was forthwith released from further duty as 'Nurse and Spy' in the Federal army!"

In a letter dated September 6, 1897, Emma tells of having been thrown into a ditch by a mule she was riding while on her brigade postoffice duties. The accident resulted in injuries to her leg and side, probably fracturing some ribs. She refused medical attention at the time for obvious reasons. It may have been the effects of that accident, coupled with the malaria, which contributed to her bad health and led to her desertion. In after years she attributed a partial paralysis of her left leg to her mishap with the mule.

Leaving the army near Lebanon, Emma made her way to Oberlin, Ohio. There she laid aside her uniform and transformed herself back into a woman. She intended to enter Oberlin College, but that had to be deferred until after the war. While recuperating she wrote her book, which ultimately sold 175,000 copies. After regaining her health she went back to the army in Virginia, this time as a female nurse for the Sanitary Commission. Most of her service was in hospitals in and around Harper's Ferry.

The war finally over, she returned to Oberlin, but not for long. She made a trip to her old home in New Brunswick, and there she renewed acquaintance with Linus H. Seelye who as a boy was supposed to have loaned her his clothes when she first ran away. They fell in love; he followed her back to Ohio, and they were married in Cleveland, April 27, 1867.

Even as a married woman Emma found it difficult to settle down and remain long in one place. For years she and her husband were constantly on the move. For a while they lived in Charlevoix, Michigan, and Evanston, Illinois, then returned to Ohio. Before long they accepted employment with the Freedmen's Bureau and went to Lateche, Louisiana, where they operated a Negro orphanage. Their next move was to California, Missouri, then to Fort Scott, Kansas, where they remained twelve years. About 1893 they went to LaPorte, Texas, not far from Houston.

In the course of their migrations, Emma bore three children, all of whom died in infancy. They were replaced by two adopted sons, who survived to manhood.

About 1882, Emma applied for a service pension and in order to qualify she was obliged to submit affidavits from the officers and men of the 2nd Michigan who knew about her war service. She therefore began to correspond with several of her old comrades, and this was how they first became aware of the true identity of Franklin Thompson. Through those letters we learn a good deal about Emma's real war adventures. It was to further her pension claims that she went to Flint in 1884 to attend the regimental reunion.

A special congressional commission was appointed to examine her claims. Her pension was approved by the commission and by the military affairs committee of the House of Representatives. She was granted an honorable discharge, dated back to April 19, 1863. A pension of twelve dollars per month was allowed "for her sacrifices in the line of duty, her splendid record as a soldier, her unblemished character and disabilities incurred in the service."

Her trip to Flint to attend the reunion of the 2nd was underwritten by the former members of the regiment and, as a local newspaper reported, "the slender and wiry Frank Thompson of 1863 now appeared as a woman of above medium height, and had grown rather stout and fleshy." Her reception was described as a warm one, but the later letter in which she refers to her punishment for attending and the slurs on her character suggests the reunion was not an entirely happy occasion for her.

In 1897 Emma was in poor health and applied for an increase in her pension. That necessitated more letter writing to secure new affidavits. Her old friends of the 2nd responded nobly, but she returned one affidavit to Richard Halsted, asking him to amend it. He had stated that "she was my bunk mate considerable of the time." "Please," she asked, "just add:—But I *never knew* she was a woman."

At some time in the 1890's, Emma joined the George B. McClellan Post No. 9, Grand Army of the Republic. It has been said she was the only woman who was ever received into full membership by the G.A.R.

Thus, unqualifiedly recognized for her military service, and accepted on equal terms with the veterans of the Civil War, Emma lived her last years. She died September 5, 1898, at the age of fifty-nine. She was buried at LaPorte, Texas, with the full honors of a G.A.R. member. On Memorial Day in 1901 her body was moved to the G.A.R. plot in Washington Cemetery, Houston.

For all her romantic fabrications, Emma was a good soldier * and a worthy member of the proud 2nd Michigan.

1. Governor Austin Blair.
Michigan's wartime governor from 1861 to 1864, Austin Blair of Jackson, Michigan, directed the state's war effort, and staunchly supported the military and political policies of Abraham Lincoln. Courtesy Michigan Historical Commission.

2. Finney's Barn.
The livery barn of Seymour Finney's Temperance House, at the northeast corner of Griswold and State Streets, Detroit, was one of the important stations on the Underground Railroad. Courtesy Burton Historical Collection.

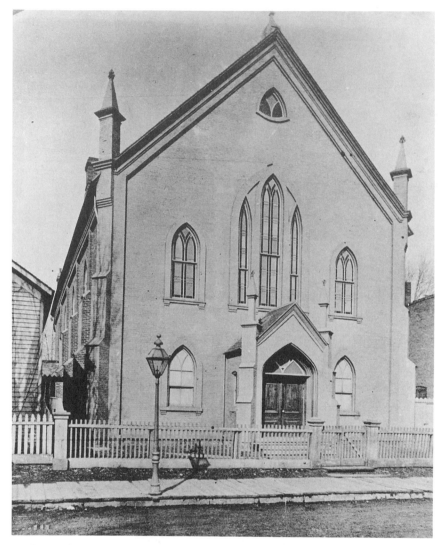

3. Second Baptist Church.
Located at the corner of Monroe and Beaubien Streets in Detroit, the Second
Baptist Church was founded in 1836 by thirteen ex-slaves. Its first pastor was
the Reverend William C. Monroe, who taught the first classes for black chil-
dren in Detroit in the church's basement. The first celebration of the
Emancipation Proclamation in the city was held here on January 6, 1863.
Courtesy Burton Historical Collection.

4. Citizens' Meeting.
On April 12, 1861, a Detroit telegraph operator received news that Fort Sumter had
been fired upon. Six days later, a citizens' mass meeting was held in front of the
newly built post office and customs house, at the northwest corner of Griswold and
Larned Streets, and a wave of patriotic fervor swept the city. Courtesy Burton
Historical Collection.

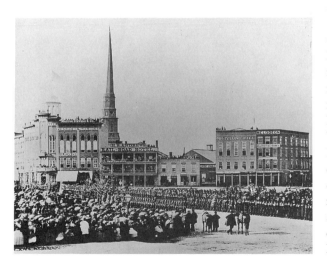

**5. First Michigan
Receives Its Colors.**
On May 11, 1861, the
First Michigan Infantry,
in an impressive cere-
mony, received its colors
in Detroit's Campus
Martius. Trained at Fort
Wayne on the Detroit
River, the First Michigan
departed for Washington
on May 13 and was the
first Western regiment to
arrive in the nation's
capital. Courtesy Burton
Historical Collection.

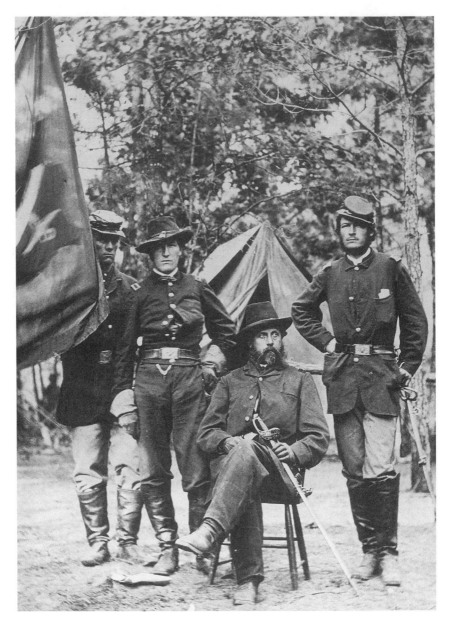

6. Colonel Orlando B. Willcox and Staff.
Shown here seated is Colonel Willcox of Detroit, commander of the First
Michigan Infantry. A West Pointer, Willcox was promoted in 1862 and com-
manded a brigade and division of the Ninth Corps, Army of the Potomac.
Courtesy National Archives.

7. Second Michigan at Fort Wayne.
Troops of the Second Michigan Infantry muster at Detroit's Fort Wayne in 1861. At Fort Wayne the Second was re-recruited as Michigan's first three-year regiment and departed for Washington on June 6, 1861. Courtesy Burton Historical Collection.

8. Captain William H. Withington.
As captain of Company B (Jackson Greys), First Michigan Infantry, Withington was captured at First Bull Run and spent several months in Southern prisons before he was exchanged. After the war he became one of Jackson's prominent citizens and leading industrialists. Courtesy Michigan Historical Commission.

9. Colonel Henry A. Morrow.
Judge of Detroit's recorder's court, Morrow was given command of the Twenty-fourth Michigan Infantry upon its organization in 1862. He led the regiment at Gettysburg, where he was wounded and captured in the first day's fighting. After the war Morrow remained in the regular army until his death in 1891. Courtesy Library of Congress.

Flag — 24th Mich. Vols
After Gettysburg.

10. Battle Flag of the Gallant Twenty-fourth.
The regiment recruited in Detroit and Wayne County belonged to the famous
Iron Brigade. It was one of the first Union regiments in action at Gettysburg
and on the first day, July 1, 1863, its loss was 316 killed and wounded, the
highest casualty rate of any Union regiment in the Battle of Gettysburg.
Courtesy Dearborn Historical Society.

11. General George Armstrong Custer.

A resident of Monroe, Michigan, Custer gained recognition as one of the great Union cavalry leaders of the Civil War. As brigadier general commanding the Michigan Cavalry Brigade, he won his first major victory on July 3, 1863, when he defeated Confederate General Jeb Stuart while protecting the flank and rear of the Union Army at Gettysburg. Courtesy Michigan Historical Commission.

12. Brigadier General Israel B. Richardson.
A West Point graduate and a Mexican War veteran, General
Richardson was living at Pontiac, Michigan, when the Civil War broke
out. He accepted command of the Second Michigan Infantry. His regiment helped cover the headlong Union retreat after First Bull Run.
General Richardson was mortally wounded at the Battle of Antietam in
1862. Courtesy Library of Congress.

13. Sarah Edmonds.

Under the name of Franklin Thompson, Canadian-born Sarah Edmonds enlisted in the Second Michigan Infantry at Flint in 1861 and served with the Army of the Potomac. She deserted in 1863, fearing that her true identity would be found out. After leaving the army, she wrote a highly colored account of her adventures: *Nurse and Spy in the Union Army*. Frontispiece from *Nurse and Spy*.

14. The S.S. *Philo Parsons*

Built in Algonac, Michigan, in 1861, she served the regular passenger and freight run between Detroit and Sandusky. Confederate conspirators planned to pirate her, capture the *U.S.S. Michigan,* and release Confederate prisoners from Johnson's Island in September 1864. Courtesy Dossin Great Lakes Museum; from a painting by Fr. Edward Dowling.

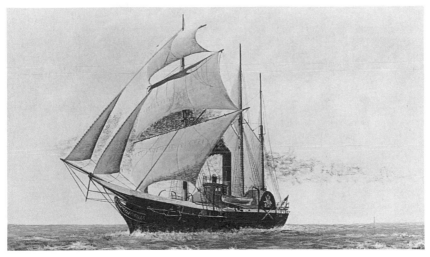

15. *U.S.S. Michigan.*

Launched at Erie, Pennsylvania, in 1844, the *U.S.S. Michigan* was for many years the only American ship of war on the Great Lakes. During the Civil War she served principally on patrol guarding the prison on Johnson's Island. Warned of the planned attack by Confederate agents aboard the *Philo Parsons,* the *Michigan* was prepared for a battle that never occurred. Courtesy St. Clair Shores Public Library; from a painting by James Clary.

16. Colonel R. H. G. Minty.
A one-time British cavalry officer, Minty became colonel of the Fourth Michigan Cavalry. Later promoted to brigadier general, he commanded the famous *Minty's Sabers*, which saw nearly four years of hard fighting with the Army of the Cumberland. Courtesy Burton Historical Collection.

17. Dr. Henry F. Lyster.
Dr. Lyster graduated from the medical school of the University of Michigan in 1860, and at the outbreak of the war he was appointed assistant surgeon of the Second Michigan Infantry. He later became surgeon of the Fifth Michigan Infantry. After the war he was a member of the Detroit Board of Education and one of the founders of Wayne State University (Detroit College of Medicine) medical school. Courtesy Burton Historical Collection.

18. Harper Hospital in the Civil War.
Detroit's Harper Hospital opened on October 12, 1864, as a general military hospital. Shown here is the hospital as it appeared in 1865. On December 12 of that year, the government turned the buildings over to a board of trustees and Harper was converted to civilian use. Courtesy Burton Historical Collection.

19. The Burning of the *Sultana*.
This Mississippi River steamer was destroyed by explosion and fire near Memphis, Tennessee, April 28, 1865. More than 1,200 Union soldiers, many of them from Michigan, returning north after having been released from Confederate prison camps, lost their lives in this disaster. From *Harper's Weekly*, May 20, 1865.

20. Ben Pritchard, the Man Who Captured Jeff Davis.
Captain Benjamin D. Pritchard of Allegan, Michigan, commanding a detachment of the Fourth Michigan Cavalry, led the pursuit which resulted in the capture of Jefferson Davis near Irwinville, Georgia, May 11, 1865. Courtesy Michigan Historical Commission.

21. Soldiers' and Sailors' Monument.

All across Michigan, in big cities and in small towns, citizens built impressive memorials to honor those who had served their country in the Civil War. Detroit was no exception. On April 9, 1872, the residents of the city dedicated this grand Soldiers' and Sailors' Monument. It stands to this day in Cadillac Square at Woodward Avenue. Courtesy Burton Historical Collection.

22. Grand Army of the Republic Parade.

In 1866 Civil War veterans formed the Grand Army of the Republic. The G.A.R. quickly attained a preeminent place among veterans organizations formed at the close of the war. By 1890 its membership had reached over 400,000. Here, stalwart veterans from the Detroit post are seen marching down Woodward Avenue past Grand Circus Park in the city's Memorial Day Parade, May 30, 1909. Courtesy Burton Historical Collection.

XIII

The Cruise

of the

Philo Parsons

$\mathbf{Q}$UIET MAY have reigned along the Potomac in September 1864, but all was not serene on the Detroit River.

Citizens of Detroit and other port towns on the Great Lakes were thrown into panic by a bizarre plot of Confederate agents. Their plan was to capture a Federal sloop-of-war on Lake Erie, free several thousand rebel prisoners in a camp near Sandusky, Ohio, and turn them loose to raid and pillage cities along the upper lakes.

That the attempt wasn't a success can be attributed to the smooth-working counter-espionage system operated from Detroit by Lieutenant Colonel Bennett H. Hill,* acting assistant Provost Marshal General, in charge of the Detroit district. Nevertheless, while falling short of its purpose, the elaborate and daring rebel scheme helped serve notice on the people of the Great Lakes area, farthest away from the actual fighting fronts, that they too were vulnerable to war.

Almost from the beginning of the Civil War, Michigan had an uncomfortable feeling that in one way or another it might be visited by hostile forces. At the outset the concern was not about the Confederates as much as it was about the British. The North recognized the possibility that Britain might enter the conflict on the side of the South. Were that to happen, Michiganders feared the British contribution would be a diversion directed at the Northern states. Such an enterprise might consist of an invasion based on Canada, and a logical place to strike at would be Detroit.

Michigan experienced its first case of war nerves when, on November 8, 1861, the Federal cruiser *San Jacinto* stopped the British mail steamer *Trent*

137

in West Indies waters and removed two Confederate commissioners, John Mason and John Slidell, who were on their way to England.

The British government reacted strongly to this breach of international rights; public opinion in England became violently anti-North. The British War Office dispatched troops to Canada, and the Admiralty sent emergency orders to the fleet.

The people of Michigan thought they could see an invasion coming. At the urging of Edmund Brush of Detroit and other leading citizens, the venerable Lewis Cass, Secretary of State under President Buchanan, transmitted a message enjoining the Federal government to release Mason and Slidell.* Other political leaders made similiar suggestions, President Lincoln followed their advice, and immediate danger was averted.

There were other alarms from time to time, but few of them had much substance before the summer of 1864. At that time, rumors circulated to the effect that Confederate conspirators aided by Northern sympathizers known as Copperheads,* planned a coup.

This time there was basis to the reports. Chicago was to be the target, and the occasion, the Democratic national convention, scheduled to be held in that city on August 29. About seventy former Confederate soldiers slipped into Chicago. At the appointed time they were to be joined by a large group of Copperheads and together they would raid Camp Douglas, near Chicago, and release five thousand rebel prisoners. This was to have been the signal for Southern sympathizers to rise in other parts of the North. Then the North would be overrun by friends of the Confederacy and others opposed to continuing the war. The North would be forced to make peace.

What spoiled the conspiracy was advance knowledge of the plot by Union agents and the failure of the Copperheads to rally their members.

The mastermind of this enterprise was the Confederate arch-agent, Jacob Thompson,* who directed an espionage and sabotage apparatus from Canada. An abler man might have been more effective than Thompson. Canadian sentiment toward the North was divided, but Canadian authorities did their best to maintain a scrupulous neutrality. They watched Thompson and his spies closely and kept Union officials advised of their activities. Thus, Federal intelligence was particularly efficient along the border and was able to thwart nearly every move Thompson made.

The Chicago-Camp Douglas plot having fizzled out, Thompson prepared to try again. He established headquarters at the Windsor Castle hotel, a famed hostelry in the town of Windsor, directly across the river from Detroit. There, surrounded by a collection of nondescript thugs, Canadian adventurers, and

Southern patriots, he dived deep into conspiracy of the best cloak-and-dagger variety.

Thompson's attention was fixed on Johnson's Island, which lay off Sandusky at the outer edge of Sandusky Bay not far from Cedar Point. After the outbreak of the war, part of this 275-acre sparsely settled island was made into a prison camp, primarily for Confederate officers. It was guarded by the 128th Ohio Volunteer Infantry, a regiment of men who were considered too old for field service. Members of the 128th sported long beards, and the regiment was known as the Grey Beard Brigade.

Usually based off shore from Johnson's Island in the shelter of Sandusky Bay was the 15-gun U.S.S. *Michigan,** the only regular American armed vessel on the lakes. In September 1864 there were about three thousand Confederates on Johnson's Island—a cadre which would have been most useful in restoring the depleted officer corps of the Confederate Army.

As he whispered the details to his co-conspirators, Thompson's new project sounded simple enough. He proposed to have a band of armed men seize a vessel, sail to Sandusky and capture the *Michigan* by surprise, and release the Johnson's Island prisoners. After that, the *Michigan* would sweep commerce from the upper Great Lakes and raid and pillage Ohio, Michigan, Wisconsin, and Illinois ports. The released prisoners either would escape into Canada and then make their way back to the South by way of the Bahamas or travel in a body across Ohio and Pennsylvania, leaving a trail of destruction behind.

To engineer this scheme, Thompson picked his men with what he considered great care. He planted agents in Sandusky who were to cooperate in capturing the *Michigan* either by bribing the crew or, failing that, by entertaining the officers at a party and drugging their food and wine. These agents also were to disrupt railroad operations into and out of Sandusky, so that the city would be paralyzed while the coup was being carried out.

From the beginning Thompson made errors which doomed his project before it got started. His first mistake was in failing to prevent leaks. Northern authorities had long been alert to the possibility of some such enterprise. Nearly a year earlier, in November 1863, the War Department was officially notified by Lord Lyons, the British minister at Washington, that he in turn had been warned by the Governor General of Canada that some such plot was afoot.*

It came, then, as no great surprise to Colonel Hill when one of the men whom Thompson regarded as a trusted aide, Godfrey J. Hyams * of Little Rock, Arkansas, slipped across the border and gave him almost complete details of the plot.

Thompson's second serious error was the selection of an agent to do the dirty work at Sandusky. He picked Charles H. Cole,* a former Confederate officer who was about as unreliable as they came. He was a drunkard, he talked too much, and he was generally incompetent to carry out any important assignment for which discretion was required. Thompson was well supplied with Confederate gold and Cole, recognizing a good thing, seemed principally interested in getting as much of it as he could.

Colonel Hill was a busy man. In addition to operating a counter-espionage system, he also had the duty of supervising the draft in Michigan, rounding up draft dodgers, bounty jumpers, and deserters, and maintaining a general security. But, busy as he was, he had time to listen to Hyams when he came to him surreptitiously on the evening of September 17.

The steamer which the plotters had determined to seize in order to launch their expedition, Hyams said, was the *Philo Parsons*,* a sturdy craft, which operated on regular schedule for passengers and freight between Detroit and Sandusky, with stops at the islands in the western end of Lake Erie.

The conspirators were to board the *Philo Parsons* as passengers at Detroit and Windsor on Monday, September 19. Once clear of the Detroit River and into Lake Erie, the ship would be taken over by the Confederates. They would then sail to Sandusky, arriving after dark. It was expected that by that time the officers of the *Michigan* would all be stupefied by drugged liquor, and Cole and his associates would be in control of the gunboat. A prearranged set of signals would tell the *Philo Parsons* that the *Michigan* was in rebel hands. All that would be necessary then would be for the crew of the *Philo Parsons* to board the *Michigan* and proceed with the work of liberating the prisoners on Johnson's Island.

Thompson delegated command of this enterprise to John Yates Beall, a young, daring, and colorful Virginia aristocrat. Beall was a graduate of the University of Virginia. He joined the Confederate Army at the outbreak of the war and was severely wounded in an early action. Afterwards unfit for regular service, he turned to secret service work, first operating on and around Chesapeake Bay, where he organized and led a sort of naval guerilla operation. Had Cole and some of the others associated with the scheme possessed even a small measure of Beall's ability, Thompson's plot might have come closer to success.

Forewarned, Colonel Hill lost no time in setting up counter-measures. On Saturday night, immediately after talking to Hyams, he sent a telegraph message alerting Captain Jack C. Carter, commanding officer of the *Michigan*.

"It is reported to me," Hill's message read, "that some of the officers and men of your steamer have been tampered with, and that a party of rebel refugees leave Windsor tomorrow with the expectation of getting possession of your steamer."

Captain Carter, although wide-eyed with disbelief at this report, did not dismiss it lightly. He thanked Hill for his wire and, while he discounted the possibility that his own men were involved, he declared himself ready for whatever might happen.

The following evening, Sunday, Hyams again came to Colonel Hill with further details. This time he named Cole as the chief agent at Sandusky and reported that he understood Captain S. M. Atwood, master of the *Philo Parsons*, had been "bought." This information proved incorrect.

A few hours earlier on Sunday, a man had gone aboard the *Philo Parsons* and introduced himself to Walter O. Ashley,* co-owner of the vessel and her purser and supercargo. The visitor said his name was Bennett G. Burley,* and he inquired about passage on the following day's trip. He said he was going to Sandusky with a party of friends who were then at Sandwich, a Canadian town a short distance below Windsor. Would the *Parsons* make a stop there and pick them up, Burley asked. What Burley neglected to tell Ashley was that he held a commission as master in the Confederate navy, issued by Secretary Mallory, Confederate Secretary of the Navy.

Ashley said his boat did not stop regularly at Sandwich. But he was anxious for business and assured Burley that if his friends were ready they would be picked up.

On Monday morning, September 19, the *Philo Parsons* lay at her regular berth, the Trowbridge & Wilcox dock, just east of the foot of Woodward Avenue. She had steam up and was loading a miscellaneous assortment of cargo under Ashley's supervision. She was scheduled to sail promptly at 8 o'clock. Two hours before that, Colonel Hill went aboard and, without giving Ashley any reasons for his being there, looked around and asked some questions about the passengers who had signed for the trip.

Hill was in something of a quandry. Should he arrest Burley and prevent the *Parsons* from sailing? Should he put his own men aboard and arrest the conspirators as soon as they showed their hands? Or should he do nothing, leaving the entire matter to Captain Carter to deal with?

He finally decided on the last course which, while it involved some risk, was undoubtedly the wisest. Had he stopped the *Parsons* from sailing he would have bagged only Burley, and there would have been no real evidence against him. The others, waiting in Canada, would have escaped. If he had put his own men aboard—and he explained he had too few available on such short notice—the conspirators might have learned about his counterplot and made no overt move. In that event it would have been virtually impossible to arrest everyone involved. The identities of most of those planning to go aboard in Canada were not known. Wholesale arrests in international waters might have included innocent Canadians and precipitated the kind of incident Colonel Hill and Union authorities were most anxious to avoid. So Hill made up his mind to permit the *Parsons* to sail, hoping that Carter would be able to pull the strings and close the bag.

Returning to his office, Hill again wired Carter, warning him that "the parties will embark today, at Malden [Amherstburg, a Canadian village at the mouth of the Detroit River and a regular stop for the *Parsons*] on board the *Philo Parsons* and will seize either that steamer or another running from Kelleys Island. Since my last dispatch, am assured that officers and men have been bought by a man named Cole. A few men to be introduced on board under guise of friends of officers. An officer named Eddy to be drugged." Hill stressed the point that he considered the situation to be of the utmost seriousness.

Captain Carter acted immediately. He promptly replied to Hill as follows: "Your dispatch of 19th received. I have Cole, and a fair prospect of bagging the party."

Without wasting time, Carter placed the *Michigan* under the tightest security. He anchored in a position to command both Johnson's Island and the entrance to Sandusky Bay, cleared his ship for action, and waited for what might happen.

Carter's statement to Hill that he had Cole indicates with what vigorous measures he acted, and belies later, melodramatic versions of the story to the effect that Cole actually got aboard the *Michigan* on the evening of the 19th and was entertaining the officers in their own wardroom when Carter entered, denounced him, and put him under arrest.

Meanwhile, back at Detroit, the *Parsons* cast off at 8 a.m. with Burley and forty or more other passengers aboard. Outwardly there was nothing to arouse anyone's suspicions. As Burley had been promised, a stop was made at Sandwich. Three passengers went aboard, dandified young men dressed in what Ashley described as the "Canadian style." What he meant was, that they were elegantly attired. One of the three was Beall, clothed in a black morning coat and silk rolled collar. These men proceeded to make themselves at home in the grand saloon, a well-appointed cabin equipped with a bar and a piano. About three-quarters of an hour later, the *Parsons* docked at Amherstburg.

There was a flurry of activity at the wharf. Cargo was unloaded, some more was carried aboard. Then a crowd of roughly dressed men, their number estimated at sixteen to twenty, trooped up the gangplank.* Ashley, who was collecting fares, had an opportunity to observe them.

"I took them," he said, "to be skedaddlers returning home, and did not think strange of it, as it is a very common occurrence."

"Skedaddlers" was the term applied to draft evaders or others who sought haven in Canada to avoid military duty. There was a lively traffic in this type of merchandise over the border.

The Malden passengers had no luggage except one "old pack trunk," tied together with a piece of rope. This they deposited in the main cabin. The paddles of the *Parsons* began to pound the water. She backed away from the Malden dock, swung around and, her walking-beam dancing, headed out into Lake Erie. Her next regular stop was the Bass Islands.

After leaving Amherstburg, the *Parsons* first touched at Middle Bass which, like most of the islands in that group, was a center of the grape-growing industry. Captain Atwood's home was on Middle Bass. He complained of not feeling well, and when the *Parsons* docked he went ashore, turning the command over to D. C. Nichols, the mate. Nichols and Mitchel Campbell, the wheelsman, carried on from there under the general supervision of Ashley.

Proceeding down Lake Erie, the boat touched briefly at Kelleys Island. It was about 4 p.m. when the *Parsons* pushed off on the last leg of her downbound run to Sandusky, about twelve miles below Kelleys.

Kelleys Island had barely been left behind when Burley and the passengers who had gone aboard at Sandwich and Amherstburg suddenly transformed themselves from peaceful travelers into Confederate soldiers and officers. They opened their pack trunk and distributed revolvers, hatchets, and knives. The other passengers were easily subdued by this display of arms, but beyond being herded into the cabin they were not otherwise molested. Then the crew was rounded up. Beall presented himself in the pilot house, pointed a gun at Nichols' head, and declared:

"I am a Confederate officer. There are thirty of us, well armed. I seize this boat and take you as prisoner. You must pilot the boat as I direct you and here are the tools to make you." Flourishing his gun, he directed Nichols to stay on course toward Sandusky.

Meanwhile, Burley had moved in on Ashley and ordered him into the ladies' cabin "or you are a dead man." Behaving more like a pirate than a belligerent, Burley demanded that Ashley hand over all the money in his possession. Ashley complied. He later stated that, while he realized he was under threat of bodily harm, he was not particularly frightened and did not anticipate any violence.

The rest of the crew, with the exception of the wheelsman, the engineer, and a couple of firemen, were put into the hold. There were later reports that one man was shot in the jaw, but there is no substantiating evidence. Some of the deck cargo, consisting of bars of pig iron and a carriage, was jettisoned, for some reason never explained—perhaps in order to lighten the ship and get more speed.

Now the *Parsons* was a Confederate ship, armed after a fashion and ready to do whatever mischief the opportunity provided.

It was much too early to approach Johnson's Island or the *Michigan*. According to expected arrangements, the *Michigan* would not be in rebel hands until nighttime, and a prearranged signal was to be flashed notifying Beall that Cole had been successful in taking the gunboat over. It was necessary, then, for the *Parsons* to slow down, or at least stand well off from Sandusky until the appointed time. This created a problem. The *Parsons* was a wood burner and her fuel was running low. It was impossible to cruise around for any length of time.

Beall had only one choice. He ordered the ship turned about and headed back to Middle Bass. It was late afternoon when the *Parsons* docked and began to take on wood. This return to Middle Bass gave Beall the opportunity to get rid of the civilian passengers, who were only taking up space and who would be in the way if a fight started. He ordered all ashore—there were about forty—after extracting their promises to raise no alarm for twenty-four hours. All but the most essential members of the crew were also set ashore, including Ashley.

About this time, the *Island Queen*,* a ship smaller than the *Parsons*, also engaged in the Sandusky-Islands trade, pulled into Middle Bass on her regular run from the Ohio shore. Her master, Captain Orr, laid alongside the *Parsons* at his customary berth, not realizing anything was wrong. He quickly discovered his mistake when the Confederates swarmed aboard and took over his ship.

The *Island Queen's* crew was set ashore along with its passengers. Among them were thirty or forty Federal soldiers who were on furlough or whose enlistments had run out. They were en route to Toledo. Taken completely by surprise, and being unarmed, they made no effort to interfere with Beall and his men.

As soon as all was ready, the *Parsons* pulled out with the *Island Queen* either in tow or lashed alongside. About three miles from Middle Bass, the *Island Queen* was cut loose and abandoned after her cocks had been opened. She drifted a short distance to Chickanola reef, where she settled in about nine feet of water, with most of her superstructure above the surface. She was in no immediate danger and was easily raised a couple of days later. Captain

Orr observed that it was the first time in his experience as a mariner that Chickanola reef ever served a useful purpose.

Unencumbered by passengers or deck cargo, and well supplied with fuel, the *Parsons* got up a full head of steam and proceeded toward Sandusky. She arrived off the harbor well after dark, and some time before midnight. Beall, Burley, and the other leaders stood in the pilot house anxiously scanning the entrance to the bay through their night glasses. It was bright moonlight. Johnson's Island was clearly distinguishable, and beyond, the dark, ominous shape of the *Michigan* could be seen.

Beall trained his glasses on the warship, which was obviously cleared for action. No crewmen were on deck. She showed no lights. Anxiously Beall studied her, waiting for the agreed-upon signal to be flashed from her masthead, telling him that Cole was in control and that the *Parsons* should move in. As time passed, with the *Parsons* rocking gently in the light swell, Beall realized something had gone wrong. Considering the clearness of the night, it was surprising that the *Parsons* was not discovered by Carter on the *Michigan*.

Finally the uncertainty and the tension of waiting wore down the nerves of Beall's men. The Confederates gathered in the main cabin and discussed their situation. A round-robin was circulated, written on the back of a bill of lading, in which the crew, while expressing admiration of Beall's skill and courage, pointed out the hopelessness of their position. They demanded that the venture be called off. All signed except Burley and one other man.

There was no choice left to Beall but to bow to his crew's insistence. He ordered full steam and sped back up the lake, running past the Bass Islands, as somebody later remarked, "like a scared pickerel." They entered the Detroit River about 4 a.m., with the pilot, Campbell, under instructions to hug the Canadian shore. At this point, Beall broke out a Confederate flag, which he ordered run up. The halyards fouled and the banner flew at half-mast—a neat bit of unintended symbolism. Beall may have displayed his colors simply out of bravado, but more likely he did it in order to establish his status as a belligerent.

Above Amherstburg, speed was momentarily checked while Nichols, Henry Haines, the engineer, and the firemen were put ashore on Fighting Island, from which they quickly escaped and made their way to the American shore. The *Parsons* continued to Sandwich, arriving there about 8 a.m., September 20. She was run alongside the shore, her main feed-pipe was opened, and water was let into her hull. As she slowly began to settle, the Confederates went over the side like a swarm of rats leaving a sinking ship. Before that, however, they wrecked the furniture and fixtures of the cabin with wanton maliciousness.

They were prevented from carrying away valuable articles by Canadian customs officers who hastened aboard as soon as the *Parsons* touched land. Ashley later reported the loss of the piano, which somehow was smuggled ashore.

Authorities at Detroit were quickly notified, a tug was dispatched to Sandwich and returned with the *Parsons* in tow low in the water. Once back at the Trowbridge & Wilcox wharf, she was pumped out and soon was as good as new.

Meanwhile, a hue and cry was being raised from Detroit to Sandusky. Ashley did not hold to his promise of twenty-four hours of silence. Immediately after the *Parsons* left Middle Bass with the *Island Queen,* he managed to get over to Put-in-Bay on South Bass by small boat. There he aroused the local militia officer who was none other than Captain John Brown, Jr.,* son of the hero of Harper's Ferry. Put-in-Bay citizens armed themselves and even hauled out an old cannon, relic of Perry's victory in 1812, which they mounted to command the harbor. Ashley and Brown sailed for Sandusky, where they reported what had happened to Captain Carter.

The commander of the *Michigan,* with Cole already in custody, alerted shore officials, who proceeded to make half a dozen arrests. Some of those taken into custody were described as prominent citizens, and included two men named Merrick and Rosenthal, and a woman. With Cole, they were taken to Johnson's Island for safekeeping. The news flashed out over the wires to Detroit, Cleveland, and Buffalo, and everywhere authorities were put on guard. Trains into and out of Sandusky were closely watched to prevent either an exodus of conspirators or an influx of Copperhead reinforcements. At Detroit Colonel Hill was prepared, if there was any further sign of trouble, to open the armory * and distribute arms to citizens. The *Michigan* cruised almost to Amherstburg looking for the *Parsons.* When he did not overtake the "pirate" ship, Carter returned to Sandusky, fearing to leave Johnson's Island unguarded for too long.

United States officials quickly started the legal machinery to grab the "pirates." The American consul in Windsor was notified, but "the birds have flown and, it is supposed, have taken passage for more congenial climes." Canadian customs officers had arrested two of the men and detained them for a short time but, with no formal charges immediately placed against them, they were freed within a matter of a couple of hours. Jacob Thompson checked out of the Windsor Castle Hotel, the others scattered. Many of them ultimately made their way to Halifax, Bermuda, and then back to the Confederate States. A few, Burley and Beall included, remained in Canada and attempted to carry out fresh plots against the Union.

Burley was traced to Toronto and extradition proceedings were begun by Alfred Russell, United States district attorney at Detroit. For some reason Burley instead of Beall was regarded as the ringleader, maybe because Burley, the proverbial bird in hand, was in custody and Beall was not. At any rate he was surrendered by Canada and taken to Port Clinton, Ohio, for trial on piracy charges. He was represented by able counsel, Sylvester Larned of Detroit and Judge Ranney of Cleveland. Their defense was that Burley was a Confederate officer, that the Confederacy was at war with the Union and that, therefore, Burley's activities constituted an act of war rather than piracy. The jury failed to agree and Burley was remanded to the county jail in Port Clinton to await a new trial. Before it could be held, a jail break was engineered by Southern sympathizers. Burley escaped and made his way to the British Isles. Eventually he became a noted journalist and correspondent.

Cole remained a prisoner, apparently without trial, until 1866, when he was released on a writ of habeas corpus. He then disappeared from history and his subsequent career is not known.

Beall was less fortunate. He and Thompson transferred their operations to the Niagara frontier. There, while attempting to wreck a train near Buffalo, Beall was caught. This was in December 1864. He was taken to Governor's Island, New York, where he was tried by a military court in January 1865, charged with being a spy and guerrilla. He was found guilty and sentenced to death, and on February 4, 1865, he was hanged, protesting that he was entitled to be dealt with, not as a spy, but as a regular prisoner of war.

Thus ended a reckless adventure, doomed before it got started. It failed largely because of the efficiency of Union counter-intelligence and the vigilance and prompt action of Colonel Hill. It accomplished nothing for the Confederacy except to throw the Great Lakes area into a temporary fright. In the long run it probably hurt the South more than it did the North by arousing the anger of many people in the Midwest whose zeal for continuing the war had begun to wane noticeably by 1864.

XIV

Escape by Night

LUCIEN B. SMITH was a typical Michigan farm boy. He grew up in the lush country close to the border of Lenawee and Washtenaw counties. His home was in Franklin Township in Lenawee. The village nearest his home was Tipton; not far away was Tecumseh. Adrian, twelve miles south, was the important city of the area and the seat of Adrian College, a small but highly regarded Methodist school.

When the war broke out Lucien was eighteen years old, and a freshman at Adrian College. Like most youngsters, he was aware of events because the war spirit ran high in that part of Michigan. He may have been less stirred by questions involving politics and abolition than by prospects of martial adventure. It is easy to imagine his feelings when the first soldiers from his neighborhood, some of them his college mates, marched away in response to President Lincoln's call for volunteers in 1861.

The countryside in which Lucien lived produced good soldiers. They were rangy, rugged boys whose fathers and grandfathers had been pioneer settlers in southern Michigan. That part of the country still bore some of the marks of the raw frontier. Lucien knew the strenuous life of the farm; he also hunted and fished and tramped the woods and fields. He was well conditioned to a hard outdoors life. Moreover, like most lads of his time, he knew horses.

In the summer of 1862 a new cavalry regiment was being recruited in Michigan. Recruiting officers came through Adrian—gallant fellows who had seen battle and could tell exciting tales of camp and field. One could almost hear the drums ruffle and thump and the muskets crack, and smell powder, as they painted glowing pictures of a soldier's life. With emotions stirred by patriotism and the blandishments of the recruiters, young Lucien decided college could wait. He rode over to Adrian on August 6, 1862, shortly before the beginning of his junior year, and enlisted in Company F, 4th Michigan Volunteer Cavalry.

Luckily for young Smith, the man chosen to command the 4th was himself a guarantee of plenty of action. He was Colonel Robert Horatio George Minty,* a sad-eyed professional soldier with a beautiful brown beard which, said his troopers, gave off electric sparks at the prospect of battle.

149

Colonel Minty was born in County Mayo, Ireland, in 1831, the son of a British cavalry officer. When he was eighteen he was given an ensign's commission in his father's regiment, and for the next four years he followed the flag of empire. After service in Africa, Honduras, and the West Indies, he resigned from Her Majesty's service in 1853 and went to Michigan, living first at Detroit and later at Jackson.

Soon after the outbreak of war Minty offered his services to his adopted state. Officer material was untried and soldiers who knew their business were at a premium. In October 1861 the 2nd Michigan Volunteer Cavalry was organized and Minty was made its major. He did not take the field with the 2nd however. He was soon promoted to colonel and assigned the task of raising an additional regiment—the 4th. His second in command was Major Horace Gray,* of Grosse Ile, a peacetime crony and hunting companion of George Armstrong Custer. Originally Gray was offered command of the 4th, but he declined in favor of a subordinate post, on the grounds that the colonelcy should go to a professional or experienced soldier.

Mustered at Detroit on August 29, 1862, the 4th, with Minty at its head and Lucien Smith in the ranks,* left the state for Louisville on September 26. It was soon attached to the 1st Cavalry Division of Rosecrans' Army of the Cumberland, and found itself in the thick of things around Nashville, Tennessee. It had embarked upon two and a half years of hard riding and almost incessant fighting. During that time it established a reputation as a tough outfit capable of almost any task. Few regiments from Michigan or any other state could match its record.

It was soon being said in the Army of the Cumberland that where there was trouble you were sure to find the 4th. The Confederates, particularly those under Nathan Bedford Forrest and "Fighting Joe" Wheeler, stated it a little differently. They said that wherever you found the 4th Michigan you found trouble.

Trounced by Rosecrans, the Confederate Army of the Tennessee moved slowly southward toward Chattanooga and northern Georgia, where General Braxton Bragg was watching for a chance to regain the initiative. Flushed with success and convinced that by maneuver as easily as by battle he could march straight to Atlanta, Rosecrans started in pursuit in early August 1863. His main force moved toward a point just west of Chattanooga where he intended to cross the Tennessee River and gain control of the roads which led to Ringgold, Dalton, and on south to Atlanta. To protect his left flank he sent a brigade of cavalry far to the east to watch enemy movements in the neighborhood of Sparta and Athens in the southeastern Tennessee mountains.

Minty was given command of the brigade which became known as the Sabre Brigade or Minty's Sabres. The Sabres boasted of never being repulsed in a saber charge. The three regiments which made up Minty's command were the 4th Michigan, the 4th United States Cavalry, and the 7th Pennsylvania. Command of the 4th Michigan passed to Major Gray after Minty's promotion. Lucien Smith, a hardened trooper by the late summer of 1863, rode under the guidon of Company F.

It was no easy task which the Sabres had been given. They had a vast territory to patrol. The terrain was a cavalryman's nightmare; the troopers rode up rocky slopes where there were no trails, along boulder-strewn ridges, and across tortuous ravines.

Near a Tennessee village with the intriguing name of Calf Killer Creek, the 4th Michigan flushed Forrest's old outfit, now commanded by a Colonel Dibrell. He had taken his regiment into what he thought was impenetrable country to rest and recruit. A lively running scrap of several days' duration followed. Dibrell and the 4th chased each other across hills where no self-respecting mule would go, but in the end Major Gray exerted so much pressure that the rebels were forced to run south to safety within Bragg's lines. The Sabres then circled back toward Chattanooga, and on September 13 crossed the Tennessee River and took up a position at a place called Lee and Gordon's Mills at the lower end of Chickamauga Valley.

During the next four days Rosecrans lumbered along with four army corps, passed through Chattanooga, and poured through the passes of Lookout Mountain and Missionary Ridge. His left was anchored at Rossville on the outskirts of Chattanooga, and his line, facing east, stretched southward, dangerously overdrawn, for a distance of about twenty miles along Chickamauga Creek.

Chickamauga Valley lay between Missionary Ridge, a long mountain spine on the west, and Pigeon Mountain and Pea Vine Ridge, which roughly paralleled Missionary Ridge. The valley itself was almost ten miles wide at the northern end but narrowed into a cul-de-sac in the south where Missionary and Pigeon came together.

If Rosecrans' overconfidence had been matched by knowledge of the enemy's movements, he would have been in good shape. Unfortunately, he badly miscalculated Bragg's movements and consequently found himself in serious trouble.

Far from being beaten, Bragg had assembled a formidable army of rugged veterans. His troops were massed behind Pigeon Mountain and Pea Vine Ridge, screened from Federal eyes. He was in process of being reinforced by Longstreet's corps, which had been detached from Lee's Army of Virginia and

151

rushed to northern Georgia. With Longstreet were such able fighting men as Hood's division. Longstreet made up Bragg's left; his right was commanded by the former bishop of Louisiana, the high-tempered, querulous Leonidas Polk.

Minty, probing for contact with the rebels, sent out the 4th Michigan, which returned with the first news of Longstreet's addition to the Army of the Tennessee. Rosecrans didn't believe the information, and simply ignored it.

Bragg had a plan of battle which should have worked. He intended to pour through the gaps in Pea Vine and Pigeon into Chickamauga Valley. Then he proposed to launch a series of sledge hammer blows at Rosecrans beginning on the left of the Federal line nearest Chattanooga, and, as the Union line curled back under a massive assault, to send successive attacks which would roll up the Army of the Cumberland, forcing it into the cul-de-sac, from which there would be no escape. Bragg came perilously close to succeeding in what turned out to be one of the bloodiest and hardest fought battles of the war.

On September 17 and 18, Minty led his brigade across Pea Vine and engaged the now advancing rebels in an attempt to slow them down. Belatedly recognizing his danger, Rosecrans made frantic efforts to pull his widely separated corps together in the vicinity of Lee and Gordon's Mills. That he was reasonably successful was in large measure due to the gallant work of the Sabres and particularly of the 4th Michigan.

The climax of the battle for the 4th Michigan came early—on September 18. Polk opened his attack on the Federal left as scheduled, but in order to get at his opponents he had to cross Chickamauga Creek, a deep, swift and—in most places—unfordable stream. He elected to make a crossing at Reed's Bridge near the north end of the valley. It was up to Minty's Sabres, reinforced by Wilder's brigade of mounted infantry, to stop him.

Minty accepted his responsibility. He fully appreciated the odds against him when he counted the flags of seventeen Confederate regiments bearing down on him. He retreated, fighting every foot of the way, down the road from Pea Vine Ridge. Slowly forced back, he made a determined stand at Reed's Bridge on the east side of Chickamauga Creek, where for several precious hours he managed to hold up the full force of Polk's advance, thus giving Rosecrans time to bring his corps together. Worn out at last, the Sabres crossed the bridge with Major Gray and the 4th Michigan fighting a rear guard delaying action. When he had to retire Gray pulled up the bridge, and the last of his men to cross the creek had to swim.

Finally, after three days of incessant fighting which had its culmination at the bridge, the completely exhausted Sabres were relieved. After a night's rest, they were attached to General Gordon Granger's reserve corps stationed around Rossville. There they covered the retreat of Rosecrans' army into Chattanooga.

As much as any Federal unit in the field, the 4th Michigan helped save the Army of the Cumberland from annihilation.*

Lucien Smith wasn't around to share the glory which Minty's Sabres won. Sometime during the hard fighting on September 18 he had been gobbled up by the rebels, and when the battle ended on the 20th he was in a prisoner of war compound, along with hundreds of equally unfortunate and unhappy Federals, contemplating a bleak future.

He did not have long to wait to learn what his fate was to be. On September 21 the prisoners were loaded aboard a train and started on a circuitous journey that took them through Atlanta and the Carolinas, to end in a stockade at Richmond. They arrived there September 29. Somehow they had bypassed Andersonville, which was already a specter of horror in the minds of Union soldiers. That they kept clear of that most notorious of all Confederate prisons was counted a stroke of rare good fortune. The feeling that any prison was better than Andersonville made life bearable.

Smith didn't remain long at Richmond however. Along with others who had been taken at Chickamauga, he was transferred on November 15, 1863, to a prison at Danville, Virginia. Located in the southwestern part of the state on the north bank of the Dan River, Danville is only a short distance from the North Carolina line.

Danville prison was no bed of roses, though it could have been worse. But in November a smallpox epidemic broke out.* Either Lucien was exposed to the disease or he took it lightly; in any event he was sent to the prison hospital, which was located about a mile outside of Danville on the south bank of the Dan River. Apparently the sick and convalescent were given decent care, although there was a shortage of doctors, nurses, and medicine. To meet one of those needs, convalescent prisoners were assigned duties as nurses and orderlies, and within a week Lucien was performing these duties.

Prisoner nurses and some of the other convalescents were quartered in a row of tents, six or eight men to a tent. Lucien drew Tent No. 1. A corporal, W. H. Newlin, of the 73rd Illinois Infantry, was put in charge. The other tent mates included a man from near Lucien's home, William Sutherland of the 16th United States Infantry, from Dundee, Michigan; Walton C. Trippe, 15th United States Infantry; John F. Wood, 26th Ohio Infantry; and Robert G. Taylor, 2nd Massachusetts Cavalry. If there were others in Tent No. 1, we do not know of them and they had no part in Lucien's subsequent adventures. All of the six named had been captured at Chickamauga except Taylor, who was made prisoner near Leesburg, Virginia, during the Gettysburg campaign.

Work in the hospital was not arduous nor was security very strict. Occasionally the prisoners were permitted to go into the woods under casual guard to gather persimmons. These excursions into the woods enabled the men to get a good idea of the characteristics of the countryside and to learn the lay of the land generally. It is understandable that as they rambled through the brush the thought of escape was much in their minds. Lucien's tent crew began to discuss the possibilities among themselves and to consider plans.

Nothing, however, was done immediately. Several weeks passed, the epidemic abated, and some of the hospital wards were closed. On February 19, 1864, Newlin and Sutherland were hauling wood, when Sutherland remarked: "It looks to me very much as if this hospital would be broken up soon." Newlin agreed. That evening Smith came off duty with the rumor that they were all to be moved to Andersonville. Then and there they agreed that the time had come to make their break for freedom if they were ever going to do it. It would be easier, they assured each other, to get away from the hospital than it would from the prison at Danville.

As fast as Wood, Taylor, and Trippe came off duty, they were told of the others' determination to leave that same night. Trippe, who was still weak from the effects of his sickness, and who had been caught after a previous unsuccessful escape attempt, had doubts about whether he should risk it but finally decided to go along.*

Each of the six men had an assigned task in getting ready. Two of them went to the laundry, to which they had access, and picked out the best clothes and stoutest shoes they could find. They also appropriated six haversacks. Others quietly approached the mess hall. The cook, also a prisoner, got together what provisions he could lay his hands on and the haversacks were filled. A few trusted friends were let in on the secret and they went through the wards collecting about two hundred dollars in Confederate scrip from the patients. Then each man changed into an outfit of clean clothes. The weather was cold, so each put on an extra shirt and blouse. All but Newlin and Trippe had overcoats; each one had a blanket. Lucien Smith somehow scrounged a bed quilt which he took along.

When they first discussed escape plans, they proposed to strike almost due west toward Knoxville, Tennessee, where General Burnside had established himself. Later they learned that Longstreet, after the fighting around Chattanooga, had moved to a place in the mountains called Bull Gap. That put the Confederates between Danville and Knoxville and made that escape route out of the question. So they decided to take a northwesterly direction toward the Blue Ridge Mountains and beyond into western Virginia to Charleston (now West Virginia), where there were Federal forces. They knew too that there was strong Union sentiment among the mountain people and counted on help from them.

About eleven o'clock on the night of February 19 they began to slip away from the hospital, two at a time in order not to arouse suspicion or attract attention. They fixed a rendezvous at a place in the woods with which they were all familiar from their persimmon hunting expeditions. Newlin and Sutherland went first, followed after a short interval by Smith and Taylor, and then by Wood and Trippe.

Without map or compass, barely provisioned and scantily clad against the winter cold of the mountains, the six fugitives set out through unfamiliar country, aiming by dead reckoning and luck for the Union lines at least four hundred miles away.

Once they had assembled at the rendezvous, they moved without delay in order to put as much distance between the hospital and themselves in the shortest possible time. They hoped to cross the Dan River the first night out, but, knowing the river was patrolled, they first turned southwest into North Carolina. It was their intention to make a wide circle around the area of Danville and then swing back, several miles upstream, to a crossing known as the Seven Mile Ferry.

As they approached that place, long after midnight, they nearly collided with disaster. But as they neared the river, some sixth sense gave them extra caution. Trippe suggested they hide in the woods while he reconnoitered ahead. As he rounded a bend in an old logging path they had been following, he all but stumbled into a picket of Confederate cavalry which was guarding the ferry. Trippe slipped back to his comrades with the warning of danger, and the six fugitives quietly faded into the woods and headed farther upstream.

"Had we arrived at the ferry ten minutes sooner, we should most certainly have been recaptured," Newlin later recalled.

It soon got on toward daybreak. The men found a safe hiding place in a dense thicket and bedded down, resolved to delay crossing the river until the following night. They held a brief council of war and concluded that their only hope of getting through safely to the Union lines was to remain hidden during the day and do their traveling, or as much of it as possible, at night.

It was on Saturday night, February 20, that they finally succeeded in crossing the partly frozen Dan. Following the highway, they struck boldly north. They stayed on the open road as much as they dared, detouring through woods and fields whenever they approached a house or settlement. Their chief concern was the dogs which invariably raised a hullabaloo whenever they neared a farm. On Sunday they finished the last of their provisions, but fortunately on the following day, February 22, they met a gang of Negro woodcutters who gave them a ham, a quantity of corn meal, some salt, and a few corndodgers, or small biscuits.

On the 24th they came close to the town of Rocky Mount and gave it a wide berth. This forced them to travel part of the day and proved hazardous, because they nearly walked into a Confederate supply train which had halted on the road.

The next day, February 25, they had another close call. While hidden in the woods, Trippe, the inveterate scout, did a little reconnoitering and unexpectedly bumped into a man wearing a cast-off Confederate uniform. Trippe frankly admitted he was trying to escape to the Federal lines and that he had several comrades with him. The Virginian expressed sympathy and the hope the fugitives would be successful. Trippe, however, was not impressed by the man's show of friendliness and sincerity. He warned his party and they started on their way at once, despite the fact that it was broad daylight. They had not gone far when they met some children, one of whom called out: "Uncle Jim has gone for the guards to catch you-uns." A little farther on they passed a farmhouse, and a woman warned them to make haste. She said her brother-in-law, the man Trippe had encountered, was a "mean man" and had gone to report to the home guards.

Fortunately they eluded this trap, but the exertion of walking for almost twenty-four hours took its toll. As they worked their way through woods and thickets in broken country between Roanoke and Lynchburg during the night of the 26th, they noticed that Taylor was lagging behind. They had to halt constantly to permit him to catch up. Finally, after one halt, Taylor collapsed. He was in a state of near exhaustion and it was obvious he would be unable to continue for some time. It was then they learned for the first time that, before his capture, Taylor had been wounded in the leg and had suffered a fracture. The break had not knit properly while he was in the hospital, and as a result of the forced marches of the preceding nights the bones had separated again.

It was decided they would camp where they were until Taylor was able to go on. Taylor, however, realizing his condition was hopeless and that he would only be a burden, gallantly declined his comrades' offer to wait until he could travel. He declared they should not endanger their escape because of him, and insisted that they go on without him.

Dividing their rations and money with him, they wrapped him in an overcoat and blanket and regretfully pushed on, leaving him sitting on the ground, propped against a fallen tree.

It was the last time they saw or heard of Taylor,* and ultimately they were forced to conclude he had perished in the wilderness. It was the first break in their ranks.

It was almost the end of February, and the party, reduced to five in number, trudged wearily on. They began to realize more clearly what they had undertaken. Their spirits flagged, and they discussed what they should do if cornered by a patrol. They even talked of breaking up into two groups in order to make themselves less conspicuous and improve their chances of getting through to their own lines. Finally they decided it would be better to stay together and continue as they had. They were constantly on the alert against bushwhackers who, they had been told, infested the hills. Provisions were hard to come by; they had to rely for food entirely on the generosity of Negroes. The Negroes themselves had little to spare, but no one else could be trusted. The farther they advanced into the Blue Ridge, the fewer blacks they encountered. To add to their misery, the weather turned foul. Cold rain drenched them and storms blotted out the stars, which were their only guide. On one occasion rain and extreme cold caused them to suspend their journey and remain for twenty-four hours in the woods under such shelter as they could contrive.

One night, at about this stage of their journey, their empty bellies grumbled and their thoughts were very much upon food.

"If we only had some meat and bread," Smith remarked, sadly, "now would be a good time to eat it."

One of the others agreed, pointing out that water was handy.

"I guess we wouldn't be particular about the place," Smith sighed wistfully, "if only we had something to eat."

On another occasion, driven by desperation, they grew bold enough to approach an isolated house and demand rations. They were in an ugly mood as they pounded on the door. Receiving no reply, Sutherland put his mouth to the string hole and shouted: "Is anybody at home?"

From inside a frightened voice could be faintly heard: "I guess somebody's about."

"Why don't you get up then?" Sutherland demanded roughly. "Nobody's going to hurt you."

They told their reluctant host they were Confederate soldiers on their way to Rocky Mount and wanted something to eat. But the owner of the voice, playing safe, refused to get out of bed. He bade them be on their way; they would be fed at the next house.

"If it was any other time, if it was daylight, I might do something for you," said the voice.

"I suppose," retorted Sutherland angrily, "we don't have to stand picket in the nighttime; we don't have to march, skirmish, and frequently fight in the nighttime."

"And skedaddle in the nighttime from such rusty Butternuts as you are," grumbled Smith, discarding the pose of being a rebel.

There were some lighter moments in their encounters. Once, turning a bend in the road, they suddenly came face to face with a lone countryman riding a bony nag. This citizen, observing the tatterdemalions, blankets over their heads and shoulders, their clothes worn and ragged, acted as though he had seen an apparition. He muttered something about going for a doctor and kicked his horse into a jog.

"He took sick mighty sudden," Trippe wryly commented.

Again, they knocked on the door of a Negro's cabin in the middle of the night, and when he answered from within, they whispered the magic password, "Yankees."

"Jist wait," replied the Negro, " 'til Ah gits my trouserloons on."

After that, "trouserloons" became a byword with them.

By March 3 they had crossed the Blue Ridge and were in a broad valley, with the rugged Allegheny Mountains looming ominously ahead. Up to this time they had made surprisingly good progress, often covering ten or twelve miles in a night. They held to a northwest direction, following roads when they could find them, clawing their way across wild and broken country when no roads could be found or when it appeared dangerous to travel on them. Still, they stood up remarkably well. Smith's boyhood training, tramping the fields and woods of his native Michigan, served him well. The others were similarly conditioned and considered themselves fortunate that they had no city-bred soldiers in their party.

The Allegheny Mountains presented a new obstacle, but they also promised one compensation. The men were now approaching country in which they could expect to find Union sympathizers to feed, shelter, and guide them. They had heard that the anti-secession mountaineers of western Virginia operated an underground system to aid the escape of prisoners. In what they now expected to be more friendly country, they decided to travel thereafter in daylight when it was at all feasible.

Almost immediately they had reason to regret their decision.

After having walked most of the previous night, they were awakened about 9 a.m. on March 4 by the sound of a wagon rumbling along a nearby road which they had not noticed when they made camp. Thinking there might be Confederate troops about, Smith crept through the woods to see what was ahead of them. He was gone a full half hour, and his waiting companions grew restless. Fearful that something had happened to him, they gathered up their blankets and coats. As they were about to move out, Smith returned, walking cautiously and making signs for quiet.

He explained in a whisper that he had suddenly found himself in a clearing near a cabin and that, before he could dodge out of sight, he was noticed by a woman tending a large iron cauldron over a fire. Determined to bluff it out, Smith walked boldly toward her and began a friendy conversation. As he was talking, he saw four or five men around the cabin, which was some distance away. Two of the men wore Federal uniforms, the others butternut.

"There is a company of soldiers near your house," Smith remarked to the woman, trying to sound as natural as possible.

She nodded her head. "A'nt you one of 'em?" she asked.

"Of course I am," replied Smith.

"Well," said the woman, "I thought it curious if you wasn't."

Realizing that he had to get away from there before he was seen by the men, Smith muttered something about having to go back to camp. He stepped into the brush and made a wide circle back to where he had left his friends.

Smith doubted that he had fooled the woman, and he and his party wasted no time getting away. They walked as fast as the nature of the country permitted, not being too particular about their direction.

As he suspected, Smith had not deceived the woman and during mid-afternoon they heard unmistakable sounds of pursuit. A bugle sounded not far away, leading them to conclude that a large party of troops was on their trail. It was at this moment, unfortunately, that they ran into a horseman who, observing them, wheeled his mount and rode off at a gallop with the obvious intent of raising an alarm.

The five Union soldiers, now thoroughly agitated, plowed through the woods toward a not-far-distant ridge, the top of which was strewn with large boulders which suggested a hiding place. Trippe, who had been captured after a previous escape attempt, was resolved not to be taken again, and he ran swiftly ahead, outdistancing the others.

As Trippe worked his way up the ridge, his companions saw movement in the bushes ahead of them. They dared not shout a warning to Trippe; they as-

159

sumed, in fact, from his frantic exertions that he was aware that pursuers were on his heels. Smith and the others slanted off in a new direction, and as they did so they saw several men in Confederate uniforms with bayoneted guns closing in on Trippe. At the same time, some of the soldiers spotted them and cried out: "Halt, halt, you damned Yankees, or we'll shoot." Knowing they were safely out of range, they did not check their flight. Looking back, they could see Trippe once more, dodging around the rocks. Then he disappeared from sight. That was the last they saw of him.*

There were just four left now—Smith, Newlin, Sutherland and Wood. Nearly exhausted by their dash, and dejected by the loss of Trippe, they finally found a secluded ravine, where they rested for half an hour. They were confident the chase had died out and they were safe for the moment. But distance had a strong attraction, and they soon pressed on again.

With all possible speed, spurred by the fear their pursuers might pick up their trail, they labored on. By nightfall they were in the foothills of the Alleghenys. Feeling somewhat safer, they approached a house whose occupants they concluded were three women. That emboldened them to knock at the door and ask for food. They were admitted and, when the women were convinced the four ragamuffin soldiers meant them no harm, were cordially welcomed and treated to a meal of cold meat and milk. They were encouraged to learn their benefactresses were Unionists and to be given directions to the house of James Huffman, four miles farther on. He could be relied upon to help them. As they were about to leave, a man crawled from under a bed, admitting he was a deserter from the rebel army, into which he had been conscripted. When the four men approached the house, he said, he feared they might be Confederates come to arrest him.

The fugitives left their friends with mixed emotions. They were keyed up by the excitement of the day and on the verge of physical collapse. Moreover, they were now entering country which, if possible, was wilder and more rugged than any through which they had yet passed. Their ultimate goal was at least a hundred miles ahead; the towns and even the houses in those mountains were farther apart. The area through which they still had to pass was nominally, at least, under control of the Confederacy. There was always the danger of being retaken. But to offset the gloomy aspects of their situation, they anticipated that at Huffman's they would be entering the underground system operated by friends of the Union.

These hopes were confirmed by their reception at Huffman's, where they arrived about 9 p.m. They were fed again and given a supply of rations to carry along. They were then directed to the home of William Paxton with careful instructions to avoid a rebel house on the way. Not far from Huffman's, they found a place in the woods and, too tired to continue—it was now almost midnight—they made camp and rested until the following evening.

Although Paxton lived only seven miles from Huffman, the travelers managed in that difficult terrain to lose their way in the darkness. By the time they discovered their error and retraced their steps, it was light again, so once more they holed up in the forest and slept through the day. They finally reached Paxton's around 9 o'clock of the evening of March 6.

Paxton was as hospitable as Huffman had been and set a table with what food he had in the house. To the famished Yankees, it was a feast. While they were eating a neighbor came in, explaining that he was returning home from a trip to the nearest village, Fincastle. Joining them at the table, he talked in a manner which left no doubt that he was an ardent secessionist. Still, he seemed to pay no attention to the Federal uniforms. It was not unusual for Confederate soldiers and veterans or members of the home guard to clothe themselves in discarded or captured Federal uniforms. Finally, however, Paxton's neighbor appeared to notice the garb of the four men and began to ask questions.

"Where do you belong?" he inquired suspiciously.

"They belong to the 22nd which you know is stationed at the bridge," Paxton replied quickly. "They have been home on furlough, their time is up, and now they are on their way to the bridge."

Whether or not this explanation satisfied the neighbor they had no way of knowing, but they silently resolved not to press their luck. As soon as they had finished their meal, they gathered up their scanty belongings and left. Paxton accompanied them outside, gave them a whispered warning to make haste, and directed them to their next station on the underground, the home of Robert Childs, eleven miles farther on.

Imagine their disappointment when, arriving at daybreak, they received a most chilly reception. Mrs. Childs refused to admit them; later in the day they tried again and she reluctantly permitted Newlin to enter. She explained that her husband was away but she expected him to return during the morning. Newlin told Mrs. Childs that they had been directed to her home by Paxton, at which she showed surprise and remarked that Paxton could be in a better business than helping prisoners to escape.

Despite his alarm at these words, Newlin told her where he and his friends were hiding and instructed her to send her husband to them as soon as he got home. He assured her no harm would be done to Childs.

At noon Childs came and was obviously not glad to see them. He said he could not understand how Paxton got the idea that he was a Union man. He insisted that he was and always had been a loyal Confederate. When bluntly asked if he would help the prisoners, he replied he would do nothing either to help or hinder them. With that, he returned to his house, which the now thoroughly dispirited Northerners kept under observation from their place in the woods.

After several hours Childs came back, but his manner and talk continued to be "secesh." The request for help was repeated and again refused.

"I suppose you haven't reported us, have you?" Smith asked.

"I haven't seen anybody to report to," Childs replied.

"Hasn't anyone been to the mill?"

"Oh, one or two," Childs said, "but they were in a hurry. I didn't say a word about you to anybody."

There was something about the man's protestations which wasn't very convincing. Finally, Sutherland blurted out:

"I'll be switched if I don't believe he is a Union man after all."

"Don't fool yourselves about that, boys," Childs replied.

But they kept on questioning him until finally Childs confessed his Union sentiments. He explained his first reluctance to reveal them. They were not the first escapees to come through, he pointed out. He even named some others, known to the present group, who had preceded them. Confederate officials, Childs went on, had got wind of the operation of the underground, and had dressed some of their own people in Federal uniforms and sent them wandering through the hills, posing as escaped prisoners. Childs referred to them as "bogus Yankees." As a result of their detective work several Unionists had been arrested and other people, taking warning, had become very cautious. He said he would immediately send word to Paxton to be more careful about whom he received and about mentioning names.

Having accepted the authenticity of Smith's party, Childs furnished them with enough food for a day's journey and told them how to find their way to the next stop at David Hepler's.

They reached Hepler's on March 8 and were well received. After spending the night with him, they were given new directions. Hepler walked with them to the top of an adjacent mountain and pointed to the home of William Lewis in the distance. Hepler assured them it was safe to travel by day, and he said Lewis would guide them all the rest of the way to the Federal lines.

At Lewis', however, they met an unexpected disappointment. Lewis was not at home; his place being occupied by Hepler's son. This young man had been conscripted by the Confederates, had deserted, and was hiding out in that remote hill cabin. He trusted no one, and was unmoved by assurances that his visitors were not "bogus Yankees."

Not knowing where to go from Lewis', they decided to retrace their steps to the home of the elder Hepler. There they remained three full days, resting and pegging new soles to their all but worn-out shoes.

They bade the friendy Hepler goodby for the second time on March 12. With a new set of instructions, they spent the next four days crossing the mountains into Greenbrier County, passing not far from White Sulphur Springs. On the 16th they found refuge with a Mrs. Mann, an elderly widow whose husband had been arrested as a Union sympathizer and had died in prison at Richmond. They slept that night in Mrs. Mann's hayloft. The following morning a young man summoned by the widow appeared and offered to guide them. He told them there were Federal outposts on the Gauley River, about four days' travel to the north. He agreed to escort them part of the way.

They were now in territory which was preponderantly Union in sympathy. Of course caution could not be relaxed. Confederate patrols and home guard units were constantly moving through the countryside, harassing loyal citizens and snatching up able-bodied men for conscription into the rebel ranks. There were informers lurking behind masks of loyalty and friendship. And there remained miles of rugged mountain travel before the sanctuary of the Federal outposts on the Gauley River could be reached. The men were close to the final stages of physical and nervous exhaustion. Their tempers were short even with each other as they thought of the possibility of recapture almost within sight of their goal.

Actually, while the physical and mental handicaps were great, their way was being smoothed by many helping hands. They were being well received, fed, and passed along with guides or good directions, and they were doing most of their walking safely during the day.

The night of March 17 they spent with James Alderman, who gave Smith a letter to deliver to his brother-in-law on the north bank of the Gauley. On the 19th they reached that stream, were ferried across by Alderman's kinsman, to whom Smith handed the letter. They were near Holcomb (now West Virginia), twelve miles east of Summerville and forty-eight miles from Gauley Bridge. They traveled the night of March 20, skirting wide of Summerville, where they were told there were rebel pickets. Their route was well marked out. All they had to do was follow the north bank of the Gauley River.

Early on the morning of the 21st they came upon the cabin of an old Irishman, who told them they were twenty-eight miles from their destination at

Gauley Bridge, and that the country between was patrolled by Union troops. He assured them that rebel sympathizers in that neighborhood would not bother them during the day, but warned that if they were seen at night they might be taken up and spirited back to Southern custody.

"Go on to the bridge, boys, and you'll be safe," the old man called after them as they started on; "don't stop outside the pickets."

They could almost smell freedom, and the fragrance buoyed their spirits and urged them on at a faster pace. The proximity of Gauley Bridge beckoned to them as an irresistible lure. As swiftly as they could, they put the miles behind them. They literally walked out of their shoes. Smith's feet began to give out, and he hobbled painfully behind. Once, when the others stopped, Smith caught up with them. They were bathing their feet in a cool mountain brook. Smith was in a black mood and snarled something to the effect that his companions "must be in a hurry to get someplace, keeping so far ahead all the time."

Wood added insult to Smith's injury with the jibe that, as infantrymen, they guessed they had forgotten that a yellow-legged cavalryman couldn't stand marching.

They had been on the road with almost no rest for twenty-four hours. The sun went down and darkness closed in, but they moved doggedly along. Suddenly the darkness was dispelled by the light of a fire blazing beside the road, and a voice ordered: "Halt!"

They had walked into a picket of the 5th Virginia (Union), which was on outpost duty at Gauley Bridge.

Their odyssey had ended!

The feelings of the four men can be imagined when they realized they were safe among their own people.

"We felt," said Newlin, "an indescribable but silent ecstasy of joy and thankfulness for our deliverance. . . . But in the height and fulness of our heartfelt rapture, we did not forget Taylor and Trippe, the early companions of our journey."

The pickets of the 5th Virginia passed them with an escort into Gauley Bridge, where they were fed and given a place to sleep. Almost as welcome as this haven was the news which they heard for the first time, that their comrades of the Army of the Cumberland had turned the defeat at Chickamauga into a smashing, decisive victory at Missionary Ridge.

The following day they were sent to Camp Reynolds, outside Charleston. There they were re-outfitted, and on March 25 they went aboard a steamer which carried them down the Kanahwa and Ohio Rivers to Cincinnati. They arrived there on the 29th. At Cincinnati they reported to the provost marshal and applied for furloughs, which were granted. Two days later they boarded trains for home.*

The four—Smith, Sutherland, Newlin and Wood—who successfully made their escape had accomplished a remarkable feat. They had crossed the state of Virginia and part of what is now West Virginia. Their route included some of the most difficult terrain in the eastern United States. They had been on the way a total of thirty-one days. They had made the journey in late winter, which is often bitter in the mountains. They lacked decent clothing; they were often hungry. Most of the time they were without guidance or direction except that provided by the stars. Their exploit was evidence of the stamina and resourcefulness of the northern country boy turned soldier.

Their route can be traced with approximation on modern maps. In a general way they paralleled what is today Route 220 from Martinsville to Roanoke. North of Roanoke, they passed the towns of Blue Ridge, Troutville, New Castle, White Sulphur Springs, Frankford, Holcomb, and Summerville. Much of their way was through populated country. That they avoided detection was due to their nimble wits and their willingness to travel by night.

As they parted, Lucien Smith remarked with evident relief that he wouldn't make that trip again for the whole state of Michigan. To which he appended, after a reflective pause: "Unless, of course, I had to."

XV

The Roundhead

and the

Cavalier

THIS IS the story of two men. One wore blue, the other gray. Neither knew the other. Their paths crossed only once and then for a matter of a few fleeting seconds—no longer than it took to lift a revolver and snap off a quick, almost unaimed shot.

In that brief encounter the man in gray received a mortal wound and the Confederacy was given a staggering blow.

The man who died was the gallant James Ewell Brown Stuart, one of the great cavalry leaders of all time. The man who flicked off the shot which took his life was Private John A. Huff, a member of Company E, 5th Michigan Volunteer Cavalry.

In a way, these two men, Stuart and Huff, epitomized the separate causes for which they fought, the social, political, and economic philosophies which fundamentally separated North and South and caused a sectional war.

Jeb Stuart was a professional soldier and an extremely good one. He was a product of the agrarian South, the last habitation of the cavalier, where the code of chivalry persisted—at least in the minds and hearts of its aristocracy.

By all standards of his day Stuart was an educated, cultured man steeped in the traditional code of honor to which he adhered. He was a knight although his armor consisted of gay, colorful uniforms, brilliant sashes, and fancy beaver hats with waving plumes. He rode with a retinue of lively fellows, his jesters, troubadours, and balladeers. He had an appreciative eye for a lovely lady, yet he followed a rigid moral and religious code.

Jeb Stuart was born in Patrick County in southwestern Virginia, February 6, 1833. If the ancestral home was not precisely typical of the Southern plantation, at least it was a large, self-sustaining farm, worked by slaves, so that its masters were left to the pursuit of genteel leisure and participation in public affairs. Stuart's kinsmen were numerous and influential. His ancestors—he was of the fifth generation of his family in Virginia—had been soldiers, lawyers, judges, legislators, clergymen. Genealogy, a fine art among the Virginia gentry, infused in Stuart a high sense of obligation to family, class, and state. It was natural that he should attend West Point and prepare for a military career as befitting a young squire of Old Dominion aristocracy.

Stuart was no dilettante in the profession of arms. At the outbreak of the war he had an established reputation in the Old Army. Nevertheless, when Virginia seceded, he resigned from the service of the United States. Before long he was commanding the Confederate Cavalry Corps. He was distinguished for personal courage, audacity, and an ability to maneuver and take quick advantage of every tactical and strategic opportunity. He was the idol of his subordinates and the darling of the people of the Confederacy, who saw in him their ideal of the beau sabreur. General Lee affectionately called him his "eyes and ears." At the time of his death, Stuart may have been Lee's most useful and trusted lieutenant; his loss was a disaster which undoubtedly hastened the collapse of the Confederacy.

Just as Stuart was the prototype of the cavalier, John A. Huff was typical of the roundhead. His antecedents, background, and position in society made him the complete antithesis of the gay, swashbuckling Confederate.

No member of the landed gentry was Huff. He was the commoner; he came from and never lost identity with the great mass of small farmers and artisans who constituted the backbone of the North and filled the ranks of the Union army. Huff had no more than an elementary education. He was stolid and plodding; his hands knew manual toil and he was not ashamed of it. He lived on the verge of poverty and accepted his position because he knew little or nothing of any other way of life. Undoubtedly he hated slavery, not because he gave studied consideration to its great moral and social aspects, but because he instinctively felt that it represented an inherent danger to what economic security he possessed. It can be assumed that he supported Lincoln and the Republican Party, and that he shared the common concern and indignation when the South seceded and threatened to destroy the Union. That is an assumption only; if Huff had any real political convictions, he left no record of them.

John A. Huff was born in Hamburg, New York, in 1820. His father was a carpenter and John learned that trade. How skillful a craftsman he was we have no way of knowing, but because he never achieved any great measure of success we may again assume that he was no more than just competent.

The family moved from Hamburg to Ohio, thence to Canada, and finally to Michigan, settling in or near the little village of Armada in Macomb County, a farming community thirty miles north of Detroit. The manner of his going to Michigan was also typical; he was part of that migration of New Englanders and New York Staters which swelled Michigan's population in the mid-1800's.

Huff was forty-one years old when the war broke out in 1861, married and doubtless restless. Beyond that little is known about him except that he had blue eyes, light complexion, and brown hair, and that he stood five feet eight and a half inches tall.

In one respect alone was he distinctive. John Huff was a superlative marksman, and it was his facility with firearms which took him into the army.

He enlisted in the late summer of 1861 for three years in Company B, 2nd Regiment, United States Sharpshooters. To say that he "joined" that unit would be stretching a point. One did not "join" the Sharpshooters; rather one qualified for membership and proved himself worthy of being a member.

Early in the war Colonel Hiram Berdan was authorized to raise a regiment of superior marksmen. The regiment consisted of ten companies of one hundred men each, and each company was supposed to be recruited in a different state. Actually, Michigan contributed three companies to the 1st United States Sharpshooters and might have furnished more except that a second regiment was soon authorized, with one company to be raised in Michigan.

Men flocked in from all sections of the state to apply for places in the ranks of the Sharpshooters. The most rigid standards were set up. Applicants were given severe tests of their shooting ability by a special commission appointed by the governor. Competition was keen among the woodsmen, trappers, lumberjacks, farmers, hunters, and gun enthusiasts who sought membership in this elite corps.

Company B was commanded by Captain Andrew B. Stuart of Lansing. John J. Whitman was the first lieutenant, and Darius C. Calkins was second lieutenant. Although the regiment was a Federal unit, each company was equipped by the state in which it was recruited. Each man was armed with a weapon of his own choice, the type of rifle with which he was most familiar and which he could use with the greatest efficiency. The result was a conglomeration of makes and sizes of hunting rifles most commonly employed in the West at that time.

Company B was mustered into Federal service October 4, 1861, as part of the 2nd Regiment, United States Sharpshooters.

There is no record of the kind of rifle with which Huff was armed, but whatever it was he was most expert in its use. The Sharpshooters were understandably considered to be the best shots in the Union army; by their manner of selection they had established the right to be so regarded. Among them all, John Huff must have been outstanding. He won a prize for shooting in competition with his comrades of the 2nd and was sometimes referred to as the finest shot in the army.

He may have merited that distinction, but at the same time it can be suspected that he was but an indifferent soldier. His record was not impressive. Less than sixty days after his regiment was mustered John Huff was in sufficiently serious trouble of some sort to be court-martialed and ordered to forfeit seven dollars of his pay.

The regiment was sent to Washington and from there into Virginia, where in 1862 it served in the Army of the Potomac under McClellan on the Peninsula. How much action Huff really saw can't be ascertained. The Sharpshooters did not fight as a regimental unit; instead they were assigned on a company basis to various brigades and divisions and scattered throughout the army. But it may be concluded that Huff spent little if any time on the firing line, because from August 1862 he was almost continuously in the hospital, first at Alexandria, Virginia, then at Chester, Pennsylvania. On January 17, 1863, both Huff and the army had seen enough of each other and he was discharged for disability, his record showing that he suffered "functional disease of the heart & dropsy of abdomen, contracted in the service."

He was sent home to Armada to recuperate or die.

Huff's recovery back in quiet and unwarlike Armada must have been remarkably quick and complete. Before the year was out he was back in uniform, this time as a member of Company E, 5th Michigan Volunteer Cavalry, one of the regiments of Custer's famed Michigan Cavalry Brigade.

Following the Gettysburg campaign of June-July 1863, Colonel Russell A. Alger's 5th Cavalry, together with the rest of the Army of the Potomac's Cavalry Corps, had been occupied in northern Virginia in the general vicinity of Culpepper Court House. It spent its time trying to outwit Jeb Stuart, but the results were not always gratifying from the Federal point of view. More often than not, Stuart did the outsmarting, much to the annoyance of all hands in blue, and destiny decreed the necessity of sending all the way back to a small Michigan village for the means of eliminating him. By some process of fate, the man selected was John A. Huff.

By late 1863 battle losses and normal attrition from hard campaigning made it necessary for the 5th to fill up its depleted ranks. Officers went back to Michigan to entice recruits, and in some manner Huff came under their spell. He signed the rolls late in the year, and on January 27, 1864, he was mustered in at the rendezvous station at Pontiac for a three-year hitch. On February 10, 1864, he reported to the regiment at Stevensburg, Virginia.

What caused Huff to re-enlist? His service with the 2nd Sharpshooters was so undistinguished as to suggest an extreme distaste for soldiering on his part. It seems unlikely then that an eagerness for more fighting impelled him to sign up again.

Was it patriotism? Not likely! Discharged soldiers were usually in no fever heat to rally 'round the flag again. They had done their part; they had papers to prove it. Let others be the heroes, was the natural attitude. Having been discharged as physically unfit, Huff was in no great danger of being drafted.

Possibly his re-enlistment can be explained by a notation on his service record that he received a sixty-dollar bounty. That sixty dollars was what the Federal government paid him. In addition, he was in a position to collect up to two or three hundred dollars more from the state and from his township. That much money would have looked good to a carpenter whose neighbors were not building many barns at the time. Actually it would have represented a substantial part of an ordinary year's cash income from his labor. If it was bounty that lured Huff back into the service, he was not alone. Hundreds of veterans and raw recruits alike found the money inducements attractive.

About the same time that Huff became attached to the Cavalry Corps, that branch of the Army of the Potomac received another recruit, one who was several notches in grade above the Michigan trooper. He was Major General Philip H. Sheridan, whose performance in the West had attracted the favorable attention of General Grant. Grant brought Sheridan to Virginia and placed him in command of all cavalry operations, replacing Pleasonton. That was in March 1864.

On May 3 Grant crossed the Rapidan and began the campaign of which the battles of the Wilderness and Spotsylvania were climactic. His forces consisted of the Army of the Potomac, which included the Cavalry Corps commanded by Meade, and independent units led by Burnside and others. For a week the fighting continued in the Wilderness, a desolate, tangled section of Virginia, west of Fredericksburg and south of the Rapidan and Rappahannock Rivers. During this phase of the campaign Meade employed the cavalry on various missions without much reference to Sheridan.

This was intolerable to the fiery little Irish cavalryman. At first Sheridan protested at being circumvented; finally he exploded in terrible wrath. He sought out Meade in the latter's headquarters and a violent quarrel followed.

Sheridan delivered what was, in substance, an ultimatum. Either Meade could run the cavalry or leave it strictly alone. If Meade ran the cavalry, Sheridan would find employment elsewhere, but he would emphatically not be interfered with or tolerate anyone's going over his head. The dispute was laid before Grant, who decided in Sheridan's favor. From that time on, the Cavalry Corps operated pretty much as an independent command, subject only to Grant. It became a strategic rather than a tactical branch of the army.

Meanwhile, of course, Trooper John Huff was concerned only with getting himself settled in his new life as a cavalryman. A taciturn, uncommunicative man, Huff had little to say to his comrades; he formed no close friendships. To the veterans of the 5th, he was just another replacement.

What did affect Huff though was Sheridan's next move. Having won his point, the cavalry leader left Meade's headquarters resolved to put into immediate practice the principle for which he hotly argued. He prepared at once to take his massed corps on an independent expedition which would lead to the doorstep of Richmond and, if luck was on the Federal side, into the city itself.*

Before dawn on May 9 the sleepy troopers were aroused and ordered to saddle up, and before the sun was over the tree tops a magnificent cavalcade was pounding down the Telegraph Road, which was a main turnpike connecting Fredericksburg and Richmond. Sheridan's force consisted of three divisions under Merritt, Wilson, and Gregg. He had, altogether, seven brigades and six batteries of horse artillery. His wagon train carried supplies for fifteen days. His column, stretching thirteen miles along the pike, counted between twelve and fifteen thousand riders.

It wasn't long before Stuart was aware of Sheridan's movements and took out after him. The Confederate leader could muster only a fraction of Sheridan's strength—about four thousand men. He borrowed two artillery pieces from the infantry with the solemn promise that he would give them loving care and return them intact. Dividing his force, leaving part to harry the Union rear, Stuart raced ahead on a route parallel to Sheridan's, seeking either to gain a strong position in front of the Federals or on their flank where he would be able to strike.

Custer's Michigan Brigade of Merritt's division was placed at the head of the Union column and the 6th Michigan provided the point. The 6th was followed by the 1st, the 5th—in whose ranks Huff rode—and the 7th, in that order. Behind them came the rest of the Cavalry Corps, splendid in its strength. The pace, after the line of march had been formed, was at a walk, leisurely enough so the endurance of men and horses was not taxed.

It was strange country to the Federals and they moved with caution and alertness. Even so there were difficulties. A local guide accompanied the advance party of the 6th Michigan, a detail consisting of eight men led by a Sergeant Avery. During the afternoon they reached Beaver Dam Road, which angled to the west from Telegraph Road. Orders were to leave Telegraph Road at this junction and proceed to Beaver Dam Station. The guide bore left instead of right as he should have. Several miles farther on Sergeant Avery became suspicious and accused the civilian guide of deliberately attempting to lead the army astray. He put a halter around the man's neck and prepared to swing him from the branch of a tree. Terrified, the guide admitted his error but denied that it was intentional. Fortunately the rest of the corps had gone in the right direction and was not delayed. Sergeant Avery's squad, retracing its steps, caught up with the main column and turned the guide over to the provost guard.

Toward evening the corps made camp on the south bank of the North Anna River—all except Custer's brigade, which dashed into the village of Beaver Dam Station. That was a railroad junction and an important supply depot full of commissary and medical stores. It was guarded by a small Confederate force, which was utterly surprised when the Michiganders swept down on them hooting, as Custer reported, like a band of Indians. The Michiganders made a rich haul. They recaptured four hundred Federal prisoners waiting to be loaded on railroad cars and shipped away to Confederate prisoner-of-war pens.

"We captured," said Custer, "three trains and two first class locomotives. The trains were heavily laden with supplies for the army. In addition, we captured an immense amount of army supplies, consisting of bacon, flour, meal, sugar, molasses, liquors, and medical stores; also several hundred stand of arms and a large number of hospital tents, the whole amounting to several million of dollars."

The loss of this materiel, which added up to one and a half million rations, hit Lee where it hurt acutely. The medical stores represented about all the Confederacy had left. They were the most important item on Custer's list of booty.

The men of the Michigan Brigade were instructed to fill their saddlebags with whatever choice items they could use. What was left was turned into a magnificent bonfire—trains, food, arms, all went up in smoke. It was said that for days the aroma of broiled bacon hung over the countryside for miles around.

The next day Custer rejoined the main column, and Sheridan continued southward at a deliberate pace. Stuart's couriers were flying to alert Richmond. The authorities there reacted to the danger by scraping up a makeshift force of men, boys, and government clerks, and sending them to man the fortifications covering the north approaches to the rebel capital. By this time Sheridan's objective was clear to Stuart. It was described this way: "In a word, a slow and steady march, straight toward the Confederate capital, all the time in position to accept battle should Stuart offer it. If he should not, to hold to the unyielding tenor of his [Sheridan's] purpose, and with exasperating persistence continue to invite it."

On May 10 the Federal column ambled along, the divisions closed up. That night, having crossed the South Anna, they made camp again. To Huff and his fellow troopers of the 5th it was all pretty routine. The horses were rubbed down and baited; hay was spread along the picket lines, rations were cooked, and the men rolled up in their blankets for an undisturbed night's sleep.

But while Huff was slumbering peacefully in bivouac with the 5th, Stuart was getting no rest. At Beaver Dam he had abandoned close and direct pursuit. Riding most of the night, he cut behind the Federal line of march and swung eastward to Hanover Junction, where he was back on Telegraph Road. Early on the morning of May 11 he moved down Telegraph Road to a place called Yellow Tavern. There Telegraph Road and Mountain Road, along which Sheridan was moving in a southeasterly direction, came together to form the Brook Road, which led into Richmond six or seven miles away. Yellow Tavern presented Stuart with two choices; he could throw his force, like a barricade, across Brook Road and challenge Sheridan's approach head-on, or he could take a flanking position. The size of his force made a head-on clash inadvisable, and the nature of the terrain made the flanking position, which suited Stuart's plans, more attractive. He hoped to set up a sort of ambush and strike Sheridan hard, thereby delaying the Federal advance until the Richmond defenses could be readied. Then, if things worked out as expected, he would have the Federals in a trap, under assault from front and rear. It is indicative of Stuart's supreme confidence in himself and his men that he actually believed he could wipe out Sheridan's command.

But the Confederates were working under a handicap. Continuous hard riding to reach Yellow Tavern before the Federals arrived left the Confederate men and horses bone weary, far from the best condition in which to fight.

Stuart laid the pattern of battle and Sheridan accepted it. About noon the blue column poured down the Mountain Road "like the rush of a mighty torrent," the red and white pennons snapping in the wind, the sun glinting off the saber scabbards of a mighty host. Devin's 6th New Yorkers and 17th

Pennsylvanians, in the van, hardly paused to look at the dismounted Confederates lined up along Mountain Road, their left extending across Telegraph Road. They pounded on past Yellow Tavern in a dash which took them right up to the Richmond earthworks. There they paused and were greeted by an enterprising urchin who came out to sell them the latest editions of the Richmond newspapers.* They could hear the bells clanging and locomotive whistles screaming the alarm within the city.

Hard behind Devin came Custer and his Michiganders. Custer wheeled into line opposite Stuart's left, with his saber regiments, the 1st and 7th on the extreme left and right, the rifle regiments, the 5th and 6th, in the center. A quick rush, and the battery which Stuart had promised so faithfully to cherish was Michigan property.

The fight narrowed down for the time being to some skirmishing while Custer adjusted his line. Looking out from the relative security of their prepared positions—a ridge screened by a fringe of trees—the Confederates decided "the enemy's cavalrymen were an insignificant looking set of men, but their horses and equipment were excellent." Stuart remarked more judiciously that the Federal cavalry fought better dismounted than did the Federal infantry.

A smart charge by Custer's regiments drove Stuart's left back four hundred yards to a more secure position. The Michiganders, the initiative firmly in their hands, maintained the pressure, and Stuart rode over to see for himself exactly what was happening. He stopped behind a low fence, the most advanced point in the rebel line. It was a hot spot too. Bullets were whipping around, and Stuart's bugler urged his chief to find a safer place.

"General," he said, "I believe you love bullets."

"No," Stuart assured him, "I don't love 'em any more than you do. I go where they are because it's my duty. I don't expect to survive this war."

It was a prophetic statement as the moment of climax approached, when the contest would momentarily be narrowed to one between two men—the Cavalier and the Roundhead.

The 5th and 6th Michigan pushed forward in an attempt to pierce the rebel line, but they met a galling fire which shattered their ranks. Caught in the blast, John Huff and a few of his fellow troopers dismounted and sought safety by running to their right on a line only fifteen feet in front of the fence behind which Stuart sat. When Stuart saw these men filing past he drew his revolver and began to fire, at the same time shouting to his own people: "Stand steady; give it to them!"

Stumbling over the rough ground, Huff ran hunched over, presenting as small a mark as he could make of himself. Somewhere his carbine had been dropped; his Colt's revolver was in his hand. There was a thin haze of smoke drifting over the field and partially obscuring targets, but it didn't offer much protection. The main thought in Huff's mind was to get away from the buzzing around his head which sang of sure death.

As he ran he suddenly looked up. There just above him, almost within hand reach, sat the Cavalier, his plume dancing, the joy of battle lighting up his face.

For a couple of seconds the eyes of the Cavalier and the Roundhead locked. They had never seen each other before; they would never see each other again. But in that brief glance the carpenter from Armada, the superb marksman, found the opportunity to fulfill his destiny. Without breaking stride, acting with a perfect reflex, he flicked his hand and his finger squeezed the trigger. A pencil of orange flame squirted from his revolver's muzzle; a handful of gray-white powder smoke fluffed into a ball.

Head down, not pausing to look back, Huff kept on running. He ran right out of the pages of history.*

On the other side of the fence, a hurt, stunned look came over the face of Jeb Stuart. The gaily plumed hat, the emblem of a score of victories, fell to the ground. The big bearded man sagged in his saddle. Hands reached out to support him and lead his horse away. The time of the Cavalier was close to its end. Stuart had taken a mortal wound in the belly. They put him in an ambulance and carried him into Richmond, where he died the next day.

Sheridan counted the fight a victory and led the Cavalry Corps away from Yellow Tavern. He did not try to force entry into Richmond. He said later that he could have taken the city, but admitted he could not have held it. He turned eastward towards the James River, where supplies were to be had. Twenty days later the corps was helping open a path for Grant, who was through in the Wilderness and was working his way to the James.

And what of John Huff, the Roundhead?

On May 31, at a place known as Hawes Shop, he was struck in the head by a rifle ball. He was taken to Campbell Hospital in Washington, and it was thought he would recover. They sent him to Armada, but his wound became worse and he developed pneumonia. He died at home on June 23, 1864.

He rests now in the little Armada cemetery, as obscure in death as he was in life.

He had played his role.

Fate had no further need of his services!

XVI

Out of

"Rat Hell"

COLONEL BILL McCREERY, 21st
Michigan Infantry, came back to consciousness on the battlefield of Chickamauga, completely disillusioned about the so-called "glory of war." *

He lay where he had fallen. The tide of battle had swept over him; now all
was quiet except for the moans of men who, like himself, had been wounded
and left behind. The Federal army had vanished, pushed back into the passes
of Missionary Ridge in a retreat which was almost a rout. As his senses returned McCreery probably wondered what had become of his regiment, his
brigade, and the whole army. But mostly his thoughts were about himself.

It was September 20, 1863, and it had been a bad day for Rosecrans' Army
of the Cumberland. The 21st Michigan, of Lytle's Brigade, had been given
its knocks. As the Confederate pressure mounted and it appeared that the
Army of the Cumberland might be destroyed, Major General Philip H. Sheridan, division commander, had passed down orders to his first brigade, led
by Brigadier General William H. Lytle. Those orders, in essence, were to stand
and die.

Lytle obeyed them literally and died. McCreery saw him fall and went to
his assistance despite the fact that he had himself been painfully wounded by
a bullet in his leg and another in his arm. With the help of three other men,
McCreery picked up General Lytle's body and started with it to the rear.
They had not gone far when a Confederate shell exploded near by. One man
was killed instantly; the leg of another was torn off. A fragment of the shell
slammed into McCreery's shoulder and he blacked out.

It was about five o'clock in the afternoon when he came to. He made an
effort to lift himself up, but he couldn't make it. The sun, still high, beat down
unmercifully and he had a consuming thirst. He wondered if this was the
end of things for him.

McCreery was a bull of a man who stood six feet and weighed more than one hundred and eighty pounds. He was broad-shouldered and thick-chested. He had a shock of black hair and a bushy black beard. Up to that day of disaster he had enjoyed the adventure and excitement of war, and he had proved himself a natural-born soldier.

He was twenty-seven years old. He had enlisted in Flint, Michigan, his home town, soon after the war started, and had risen from sergeant to colonel in three quick jumps. He had been wounded at Williamsburg during the Peninsula campaign, and as a result he carried a permanently crippled hand. That was the first of half a dozen wounds which he suffered before he was through.

As he lay on the field he noticed a man walking around among the dead and wounded. McCreery was unable to decide from his clothing to which side he belonged. He could have been either Union or Confederate. More likely he was a countryman, scavenging the field and looting bodies. McCreery called to him and the man came to his side. He was a Confederate soldier, prowling for plunder.

McCreery begged for water. At first the man just looked at him silently and thoughtfully. Then he asked if McCreery had a jacknife. The wounded officer told his visitor he could find one in his trousers pocket. In return the Confederate gave McCreery a pull at his canteen. McCreery then asked the fellow to find a surgeon for him. The man went away and soon returned with a Confederate chaplain and a stretcher. They carried the Yankee colonel half a mile, placed him on a horse, and took him to a field hospital which had been set up in an orchard. His wounds were dressed and a pallet was made for him on the ground in the open air. McCreery was grateful for the sympathetic attention he received. His spirits improved and he began to think about something to eat. A fellow prisoner, Private James Mead of the 21st, produced a couple of ears of corn and some coffee, and McCreery decided he had never tasted anything as good.

Mead looked after him during the several days he remained at the field hospital, and proved to be a good provider.

"I don't think he would steal, even from a rebel," McCreery said, commenting on Mead's talents as a forager. "But he had what the old soldiers used to call a 'terrible long reach' which proved to be of great benefit to me personally."

In time McCreery recovered sufficiently to be moved. He was sent to Dalton, Georgia, and put aboard a train with about four hundred other prisoners of war. After several days of bumping and jolting across the Carolinas he arrived at Richmond and was delivered to "that prison-house of torture and slow death, familiarly known as Libby Prison."

That was the real beginning of Bill McCreery's great wartime adventure.

Actually, he was not sent to Libby immediately. When he and his fellow prisoners arrived at Richmond they were taken to the Pemberton building for processing. The Pemberton building was a converted warehouse, in which incoming prisoners were classified, examined, and, as McCreery observed, "relieved of their valuables." Having gone through this routine, officers were assigned to Libby and enlisted men to Belle Isle, a large island in the James River near the western limits of Richmond.

Because of his wounds McCreery was given a thorough medical examination and assigned to a cot in that part of the Pemberton Building which was used as a hospital.

"It was paradise to what we had experienced, and personally I felt very comfortable," he said.

According to his own account of his stay in the Pemberton prison hospital, the prisoners were humanely treated and the Confederates did for them all that their resources permitted. The medical care must have been of good professional quality. At least McCreery mended quickly and satisfactorily.

Still it was prison. None of the inmates were there by choice and none of them were enthusiastic about it. Each man was permitted to write a six-line letter home twice a week. Incoming mail was permitted but it was carefully censored.

Understandably, as the patients gained strength their thoughts turned to escape. One attempt involved McCreery obliquely and resulted in his transfer to Libby.

During his convalescence he struck up a friendship with a Major Halstead, a member of a New Jersey regiment. Prior to service, Halstead had been a men's tailor in New York and, to hear him tell it, one of the best. One day he whispered to McCreery that he had perfected an escape plan and would be on his way home the following night.

Halstead confided that he had cultivated the chief surgeon, who had treated him well.

"Doctor," Halstead told the surgeon, "I have been trying to think of something I could do for you, to express even in a slight degree, the gratitude I feel for all the kindness you have shown me. With my present surroundings there is only one thing I can do. I am a first-class tailor, and can cut, fit, and make as good a suit of clothes as any man living. If you will bring me a good piece of Confederate gray cloth for a full suit—coat, vest, and pants—with whatever trimmings you may select, I will gladly take your measure and cut, fit, and make the suit with my own hands."

The doctor eagerly accepted this offer. The cloth, trimmings, shoulder straps, and buttons were procured.

"I took his measure," Halstead told McCreery, "and have made the finest Confederate major's uniform you ever saw—to fit my own dear self."

The following night, according to McCreery, Halstead arrayed himself in the new uniform and walked past the guards without a challenge. Several days later McCreery received a letter with a New York postmark. It was unsigned, and contained only the words:

"The tailor is himself again."

Naturally there was an investigation and, because he had been friendly with Halstead, McCreery was suspected of being an accomplice and was called on the carpet. The upshot was his transfer from the relative comfort of the Pemberton hospital to the more grim confines of the notorious Libby Prison.

Libby was a massive brick building which had been converted by the Confederates from a tobacco and sugar warehouse into a detention pen for Union officers. It was situated at the lower end of Twenty-first Street, fronting on Cary Street. Behind it on the south side, parallel to Cary Street, was Canal Street—a kind of towpath and dock running along the north bank of the James River. The building extended about one hundred and forty feet, or almost a full block, along Cary Street, and its depth between Cary and Canal was approximately one hundred feet. The front was three stories high with a basement underneath. Because the ground sloped down from Cary Street to Canal, the basement was at ground level on Canal Street, so that it was a four-story structure on the south.

The unadorned exterior was forbidding, and the interior was no more inviting, bare as it was of all comforts. Libby had been constructed as three units joined together. The inner walls divided each floor into three large rooms connected by doors. The basement too was divided into three sections.

The west main-floor division was used as a prison office; the center room was the common kitchen, where the prisoners prepared their own meals; and the east section was the hospital. Not having entirely recovered, McCreery was given a bed in the hospital where, as he said, "we were tolerably well provided for . . . and . . . it is at least charitable to say that they gave us all the attention that it was possible for the Confederacy to furnish."

By comparison with the rest of the prison quarters, the hospital was paradise. The building housed more than a thousand men and was frightfully overcrowded. The prisoners slept on the floor and those who had blankets were the fortunate ones. So closely were they packed together that there could be no privacy, and there were no facilities for exercise or physical recreation.

Glass was missing from several of the windows, and there was little heat. There was, however, an abundance of vermin.

The diet was no more attractive than the surroundings. It consisted of bread made from unsifted cornmeal and—to use McCreery's words—"beef so venerable that it ought to have exacted reverence from all beholders." Occasionally there were vegetables, rice, and soup, and sometimes "we had a small piece of bacon issued to us, but it was generally so full of animated life and industry that we could not use it except at a time of great need."

The men passed the time playing cards, checkers, and chess. They organized a theatrical company and a minstrel troupe. Those qualified to do so delivered lectures, conducted classes and gave instruction in the Bible, music, dancing, foreign and classical languages, and mathematics. Lawyer prisoners held moot courts; journalists published a manuscript newspaper. Still, despite all efforts to occupy themselves, the officers spent their days in utter, devastating boredom. It was the dreary day after day of doing nothing which frayed the men's minds and, more than actual mistreatment, caused them to damn Libby as a hell-hole. It is no wonder that the chief and endless topic of conversation was the possibility of escape or exchange.

McCreery had no sooner been established in the hospital than he again became involved in an escape plot. Occupying adjoining beds were a Captain Skelton and a Lieutenant Williams. These officers confided in McCreery that they could bribe a guard for sixty dollars and all three of them get away. Their plan did not sound practical to McCreery and he declined to join them, although he furnished the money from a hoard of three hundred dollars which he had hidden in the waistband of his underdrawers. The two men took the money, paid off the guard, and got away.

In order to help them, McCreery and another man managed to cover for them when the daily bed check was taken. As the sergeant in charge of quarters passed down the row of cots, McCreery and his companion would wait until they had been checked off and then would step across the aisle and stand by the cots of Skelton and Williams. This dodge worked successfully for four days; on the fifth they were caught at it, and McCreery was accused of complicity. He was hailed before Captain Turner, the commandant.

"I have never been vain enough to suppose that I knew a great deal," McCreery said of that interview, "but on that occasion I positively knew less than at any other time in my whole life."

Turner let go a stream of verbal abuse and threat of punishment which made McCreery lose his temper and make an angry retort.

"I said to him: 'Captain Turner, I am a Union soldier, but by the fortunes of war your prisoner. I have commited no crime, I have violated no law, and I have no apologies or explanations to make either to you or to your pretended government, and I ask no favors other than those granted my comrades. You ask me to tell you how Skelton and Williams made their escape and where they are now. I have only this to say. The roll call seems to disclose the fact that they are not here, and while I do not claim to be able to point out to you the exact spot where you will find them, I believe they are now safe under the protecting folds of the Star Spangled Banner, and if I ever have an opportunity to join them I shall most certainly do so without calling at your office and notifying you of my intention.' "

Almost choking with rage, Turner called a guard and pointed to McCreery. "This man," he said, "needs cooling off! Give him exercises! Set him to walking a crack, and if he don't walk right lively, give him the bayonet."

So McCreery walked, learning as he did so the value of a discreet tongue. After several hours of this punishment, Turner came by and informed him that he would be sent into the prison proper instead of being returned to the hospital.

"But I would like to get my things," McCreery protested in what he hoped would be a stall for time.

"What things have you got?" demanded Turner.

With all his possessions on his back, McCreery could think of nothing he could claim as baggage, but he thought he had to say something so he stammered out: "My night shirt."

"Night shirt be damned," Turner snorted, and stamped away.

Sans nightshirt, McCreery was escorted to the center section on the third floor, which was known as the Chickamauga room. There he began that dreary half-life which was the only kind of existence in Libby. He soon found old friends, made new ones, and engaged in the interminable discussions about how to escape.

Soon after McCreery's assignment to the Chickamauga room, a Connecticut officer said he knew a guard who patrolled outside the building and who could be bribed with three watches. Again McCreery declined to have anything to do with the plot, but he was on hand to observe the proceedings. The Connecticut man, aided by accomplices, made a rope out of a blanket, loosened the window bars, and slid to the street from the second floor. The rope was then drawn back up, and the sentry demanded the watches. The officer handed them over.

"Now, you damned scoundrel," the guard growled, "I will give you just two minutes to get back in the prison."

There was nothing for it but to lower the rope and haul the chagrined officer back in. The next day McCreery joshingly asked him how he found his friends in the Nutmeg State.

"He good naturedly replied that, so far as he knew, they were all well," McCreery said, "but he wanted one thing distinctly understood—the very next rebel he confided in would be a dead one."

Within a few days McCreery met a Colonel Thomas E. Rose, 77th Pennsylvania, of whom he later said "no truer, braver man ever lived." Rose had worked out an escape plan and was looking for reliable men to join him. McCreery seemed to have the qualifications and Rose invited him to become one of his band.

Rose had gone about arranging his escape in a businesslike manner, prowling around the prison at night, examining every possibility. He had once overpowered a guard and managed to get out on Canal Street but, realizing he would not get far, he abandoned that attempt and re-entered the prison.

On one of his night excursions Rose entered the kitchen, pried up a floor board, and descended into the middle cellar, which was not used and was seldom visited by the guards. Its isolation gave Rose the idea that a tunnel could be dug by men working free from interference in the basement.

He outlined his plan to about twenty officers, of whom McCreery was one. They were sworn to secrecy and assigned various tasks. They carefully studied the premises and concluded the tunnel should be started in the southeast corner of the east cellar. Outside the prison, along its east side, a narrow lane connected Cary and Canal Streets. Across the lane was a cluster of shacks and buildings used by the James River Towing Company. These were screened on the side facing Libby by a high board fence. Rose's idea was to run the tunnel under the lane with the exit behind the fence, which would cover the movements of the escapers from observation of the guards around the building and from the eyes of anyone looking out of the Libby windows on that side.

The first problem was to get into the east basement, which was directly under the hospital. It was not connected with the center section, but had to be entered from the street level.

A little experimenting and exploring showed Rose the way. He dug some bricks out of a fireplace in the kitchen, entered the chimney in the wall which separated the two sections, and opened a hole into the east basement. This he did with the aid of a broken chisel, a table knife, an auger, and a length of rope which he had picked up during his nighttime reconnaissances. It took several nights' work to open the passage, which had to be closed each day by replacing the loose bricks and smearing them with soot to hide all traces of the work. But at last the passage was ready, although navigating it required some back-bending contortions.

The east end of the basement was known as "Rat Hell." The floor was covered with straw, which provided cover for a horde of rodents. A spot in the southeast corner of the room was selected for the tunnel entrance and the digging began. After the shaft had been extended several feet it had to be abandoned. It had intercepted a sewer and there was danger that the tunnel would fill with drainage water and drown those working in it.

A new location was chosen and a new start was made in the center of the east wall. The conspirators were organized into work parties of five men each. One man dug; a second stood by to haul out the excavated dirt in a spittoon which had been added to their equipment; the third man used a hat or blanket to fan air into the shaft; the fourth stood by as relief man; and the fifth served as lookout.

The tunnel was started about December 20, 1863. At first digging was done only at night—although later some work was carried on by day. The crew would descend into the basement around 10 p.m. and remain there until 4 a.m. They hauled dirt out of the shaft, spread it on the floor, and covered it with straw. The tunnel was about eighteen inches square, barely large enough for a man to squeeze into, and only one man could dig at a time. It was back-breaking, miserable work. The air was foul and the digger was in danger of suffocating. There was an ever-present risk of a cave-in. Nevertheless, the work crews kept doggedly at it, increasing the length of the shaft about one foot each night.

Colonel Rose began to give some thought to what they would do when the tunnel was completed. Once out of the prison, what were the chances of passing safely through the guarded streets of the city and through the Confederate defenses on the outskirts without being apprehended?

McCreery suggested he make an outside reconnaissance. With Rose's approval, he wrote a letter to James Seddon, Confederate Secretary of War, stating that he had influential friends in Washington who would arrange his exchange on terms which would be favorable to the South. He requested permission to visit under guard the Confederate commissioner of exchange, General Robert Ault. His letter was forwarded through channels, and in a few days he received a favorable reply, granting his request for an interview with Ault. Captain Turner was quite impressed and treated McCreery with a certain amount of deference after receiving orders to provide an escort of two men for the Michigander.

McCreery and his guards set out at a leisurely pace. He still had some money and he stood treat for drinks and cigars. Ault received him courteously and suggested he write to Senator Zachariah Chandler of Michigan, asking his intercession with Secretary of War Stanton to arrange an exchange. Ault promised that his letter would be sent through the lines and that there would be another interview when an answer had been received.

Returning to the prison, McCreery suggested to his escort that they take a long, circuitous route. He had proved himself a good fellow; his guards, anticipating more drinks and cigars, were quite willing to oblige him. They stopped at the Spotswood Hotel and McCreery paid for the lunch. When everybody was in a comfortable and expansive mood, McCreery adroitly pumped his companions about the location of Confederate camps around Richmond, and carefully noted the layout of the streets with an eye to selecting the best escape route. One of the guards thoughtfully volunteered the information that the Union lines extended beyond Williamsburg and were only fifty miles from the rebel capital.

McCreery filed the results of his scouting expedition in his mind for future reference. Meanwhile, the work in the tunnel went on—dirty, sweaty, uncomfortable work. It had to be done with the most carefully guarded secrecy. Colonel Rose was afraid to let the general prison population know about the project. The conspiracy had to be protected against blundering friends as much as informers and guards.

Then something happened which nearly spoiled the whole enterprise. Somehow, in the course of the digging, the tunnel slanted toward the surface. Suddenly, one night, there was a small cave-in, right in the center of the lane. The man in the shaft could see a spot of light—worse, he could see two sentinels standing nearby, looking in his direction. It was obvious they had heard a noise and were trying to find out what caused it. Finally one of them remarked that they must have heard a rat and they resumed walking their posts. The digger backed out of the tunnel and reported what had happened to Rose. The Colonel immediately crawled in to investigate and plugged the hole with dirt and rubbish.

The error was corrected and the digging was resumed on the proper line. Rough measurements indicated the tunnel was about sixty feet long, which, according to calculations, should bring its end behind the board fence and under the yard opposite the prison. Rose decided it was time to break through. He entered the shaft on the evening of February 8. As he grubbed out some dirt he struck what he recognized as the butt of a fence post. That was all he needed to know. He realized that the tunnel had been pushed as far as necessary to bring its exit behind the fence. In a final agony of effort he opened the hole and emerged into the yard. It was about 1:30 a.m. on February 9. Climbing out and keeping in the shadows, he walked through the yard into Canal Street. Carefully observing the lay of the land, spotting the position of the sentries, he filled his lungs with free air and then re-entered the tunnel and crawled back to "Rat Hell."

His news that the job was completed was received with feverish excitement. Some of those in on the plan were all for making a break for freedom then and there. Rose vetoed that idea, pointing out that it was too near dawn. They would need more hours of darkness in which to get safely through the streets and out of the city. They would have to be patient and bide their time until that evening. Meanwhile there were preparations to be made.

Each man, it was decided, would have the privilege of inviting a friend to join the break-out party. Arrangements were also made, after the first group had cleared the prison, to inform all the other officers of the tunnel's existence. The digging party and those who had been taken into their confidence were divided into two squads. Rose's squad would be the first to leave. One hour after they had cleared the tunnel, the second party under Colonel H. C. Hobart of the 21st Wisconsin, would begin their escape. Hobart was to stand guard at the fireplace while Rose's men passed out of the prison.

Shortly after 6 p.m. on February 9, Rose's party assembled in the kitchen. Most of them were wearing civilian clothes, and their pockets were filled with as much food as they had been able to scrape together. Final instructions were given; the men were to pair off, each couple following the one ahead after an interval of three minutes. McCreery, in the first party, was teamed with Major Terence Clark of the 79th Illinois.

Now Rose led his band into the east basement on their last tortuous trip through the fireplace. When all were present they shook hands all around and Rose entered the tunnel, followed by his teammate. McCreery was one of the first to go, following Major A. J. Hamilton, 12th Kentucky Cavalry, and Captain I. N. Johnson, 6th Kentucky. McCreery pushed his big frame into the hole and laboriously squeezed through, clawing with his fingers, hunching his shoulders, and pushing with his toes. After what must have seemed like an eternity, he was through the sixty-foot passage, lying with Clark on the ground, gasping for breath.

The crisp winter air quickly revived them. Linking arms, they marched boldly into Canal Street, endeavoring to look like a pair of workmen leaving the yard after a long day's labor.

"As we passed out," said McCreery, "one of the sentinels guarding the prison not sixty feet away, cried out, 'Post No. Eight, seven o'clock and all is well.' We agreed substantially with the sentinel that up to that time all was well."

The exact route which McCreery and Clark followed through Richmond is not certain. They proceeded eastward and probably turned north off Canal Street at Twenty-second Street where they passed a hospital. At first they walked in the center of the street, then on the sidewalk, which was more shadowed. As they went by the hospital, they were challenged by a sentry. "Take the middle of the street," he ordered. "You know no one can walk on this yer' sidewalk in front of this yer' hospital after dark." They obeyed with alacrity.

As soon as they could they turned into a vacant lot and followed a ravine. In a short time they were in the southern suburb of Rocketts and found themselves in the midst of a military camp. Perhaps it was customary for civilians to come and go on business between the camp and nearby Richmond. At any rate, they passed through the camp without attracting the least attention.

"Our object," according to McCreery, "was to cross the Chicahominy as high up as possible, then cross the Yorkville [York River] Railroad, and follow down near the Williamsburg Pike. Of one thing we were certain; if we continued our course between the James and York Rivers, and were not molested, we would ultimately reach Fortress Monroe."

They walked rapidly and soon found themselves near Fair Oaks among old entrenchments where Union soldiers were buried. Being on this haunted ground gave McCreery a strange feeling of security, "as if we were among friends." They crossed the Chicahominy before daybreak and hid all day in a thicket, waiting until dark before resuming their journey.

On the second night they met Colonel Hobart and his teammate, Lieutenant Colonel T. S. West, 24th Wisconsin. From these men McCreery and Clark learned in part what had happened back in Libby.

The news about the tunnel's existence, despite efforts to keep it secret, spread like wildfire through the prison, creating a frenzy of excitement. The cellar was invaded by a throng of milling men, pushing and fighting like maniacs for a chance to get to the tunnel opening. Naturally the uproar aroused the guards, but not until one hundred and nine officers had gained freedom. Unfortunately, not all of them enjoyed it for long. Forty-eight were retaken. Ironically, Colonel Rose was recaptured near Williamsburg and was returned to Libby. He spent several more months in prison before he was exchanged.

McCreery and his three companions realized they were in a fairly desperate situation. Confederate cavalry was scouring the countryside and they could hear rebel search parties all around them. They had to move with the greatest stealth and to be on the alert every moment.

On Saturday, the fifth day since their escape, they almost blundered into a rebel cavalry picket, but managed to back away undetected. They decided that they needed a guide if they were to avoid walking into a trap.

Retracing their steps, they found a Negro who agreed to help them after they had convinced him they were Union soldiers. He took them into his cabin, gave them milk and cornbread, and then escorted them through the picket lines and directed them to Diascum Creek bridge. Upon reaching it, they found to their dismay that it had been burned and that there was no safe ford nearby. They managed, however, to wade to a small island where they felt comparatively safe.

Some time later Hobart, who was keeping watch, saw a man in rebel uniform rowing a boat downstream. Hailing him, Hobart told him he and his companions were farmers from near Williamsburg who had been to Richmond to sell produce. Their teams had been confiscated, he explained. Hobart asked the man to row them across the creek.

It took some persuading before he agreed; he was obviously suspicious of them. What probably influenced him was their truculent attitude and the fact that it was four against one. Reluctantly he ferried them to the shore, then lost no time in raising the alarm. Within minutes Confederate cavalry patrols were all over the area, but the four Union officers remained safely hidden.

They waited until midnight before starting out again. They knew they were close to the Union lines, and, as McCreery said, "we were now in danger of being shot as rebels by scouting parties of our own army." To minimize that danger they walked openly in the road, making no effort to conceal themselves.

"I led the advance," McCreery recalled, "and about 3 o'clock in the morning, coming near the shadow of a dark forest that overhung the road, we were startled and brought to stand by the sharp command 'Halt!' Looking in the direction whence the command proceeded, I discovered the dark forms of a dozen cavalrymen, drawn up in line across the road. A voice came out of the darkness, saying, 'Who comes there?' "

This was a critical moment. Were those who stopped them, those shadowy figures in the road, Union or Confederate? Were they safe at last, or on the way back to Libby? With a feigned confidence which belied his real feelings, McCreery said they were four travelers.

"If you are travelers, come up here, and that very quick," a gruff voice

xvi *Out of "Rat Hell"*

ordered. McCreery and his friends moved forward a few paces and found themselves surrounded. It was too dark to see the color of the uniforms, but McCreery decided they were gray. At that point he almost abandoned hope.

"It was a supreme moment to the soul!" McCreery remembered. "I at length gathered sufficient courage to inquire, 'To what regiment do you belong?'

"In broad United States accent, the answer came back: 'To the 11th Pennsylvania Cavalry!'"

McCreery, Hobart, Clark, and West were sent on to Fortress Monroe. Within a few days they were joined by about fifty others who had successfully escaped. At the first opportunity McCreery sent a telegram to his father in Flint, saying: "I have made my escape from Libby Prison, and am in God's country once more, ready for business."

After a short stay at Fortress Monroe all the escaped officers were taken to Washington and received by President Lincoln. They were lionized as heroes by the public, and their stories of the miseries of Libby brought about action by the War Department to speed up exchanges.

From Washington the officers were sent to their homes. The authorities decided it would be good for civilian morale to let the homefolks see these national celebrities and make a to-do over them.

McCreery arrived in Flint on February 26, 1864, and was given a civic welcome and testimonial banquet. Then he rejoined his regiment in the field.*

McCreery may not have realized when he poked his head and shoulders into the opening of the tunnel in "Rat Hell" that at the other end, besides freedom, lay public acclaim and enduring fame.

XVII

Death in the

Crater

THE SERGEANTS MOVED quietly among the men of the 3rd Division, prodding them awake, hissing admonitions of silence. The men rolled to their feet, grumbling and growling. They had slept in the open under a fringe of trees, without tents or blankets, their arms and knapsacks at their sides. But the grass was soft, the night warm and still. The Third had slept in worse places.

Had their eyes been able to pierce the darkness for any distance on either side, they would have seen other brigades and divisions also stirring. Ambrose Burnside's IXth Corps was coming to life.

A few stars shone faintly. A soft wind from the east gently rustled the trees and carried the brackish smell of the backwaters and salt marshes along the inlets of the James River five or six miles distant. It was an alien smell which fell strangely upon the nostrils of men accustomed to the pungent tanginess of the pines and tamaracks of the Michigan forests. Now and then, somewhere in the distance, the whump of a mortar would be heard or the single sharp crack of a sharpshooter's rifle.

As eyes became accustomed to the dark, they began to discern familiar outlines. Directly ahead, on slightly rising ground, stood the solid bulk of Fort Morton, one of the several strong points in the Federal lines composed of an intricate net of connecting trenches, rifle pits and bomb shelters. Beyond, but hidden by the gradual slope, was another arrangement of similar works—the first line, which at places almost touched the Confederate defenses. In some places less than one hundred yards separated the opposing lines. Four hundred yards away and slightly to the right, well within the rebel lines, could be seen dimly etched against the blue-black backdrop of night, the crest of a low hill. This eminence was crowned by a cemetery where for years before the war the people of Petersburg buried their dead. Still farther in the distance slept the beleaguered city.

The siege lines had been drawn around Petersburg only a few weeks before—a complex arrangement of strong points, traverses and laterals. The Union forces had dug two parallel lines fifty yards apart, connected by deep, wide lateral trenches called "covered ways." Wherever the Federals had inched their lines forward, they had met and been stopped by the iron defenses of the Confederates, which, having been planted first, followed every advantageous contour of the land. Day and night, sharp eyes looked across the narrow, intervening no-man's land. Fingers rested on triggers, and it was sudden and certain death to lift a head above the protective earthworks.

In front of where the IXth Corps lay, the rebel line bulged out slightly, forming what was called Elliott's Salient. It was manned by a brigade of North Carolinians, supported by the well-served artillery of the scholarly-looking, tight-lipped Pegram, the best of Lee's gunners.

As the 3rd Division got to its feet, the eyes of the men instinctively strained toward Cemetery Hill in the rear of Elliott's Salient. They knew that was their day's objective. None of them would reach it; the best of them would die in the attempt.

From the rear the cooks came up, carrying huge kettles of steaming coffee. Here and there a man dug into his knapsack for a piece of hardtack. But most of the troops had no interest in food. There were hard knots of nervousness in their stomachs. Some men pulled out their watches. It was 4 o'clock. The day was July 30, 1864.

The IXth Corps stood ready to embark on one of the biggest gambles of the war—a gamble which would end in dismal failure and spread an ineradicable stain of Michigan blood on the red soil of Virginia.

Petersburg was the key to Richmond. It was the junction of a complex of highways and railroad lines which connected with the capital of the Confederacy from south, west, and east. If those lines could be sealed off, Lee's army would starve and Richmond could not be held. At the head of the largest Federal force yet assembled, Grant smashed at the Petersburg defenses in a massive three-day attack on June 16, 17, and 18, but he failed to crack the rebel lines. So he dug in, shaping his siege lines into a horseshoe around three sides of Petersburg. Only that side of the city on the Appomattox River was left open. Grant would be there ten months, fighting it out on that line.

Neither side could reshape the opposing lines, although both tried and thousands of good men in blue and gray died in the attempts. Federal leaders looked at Elliott's Salient and Cemetery Hill beyond it. If they could wipe out the former and occupy the latter, they would be inside the Confederate works and the door to Petersburg would be open to them.

But how to do it?

Lieutenant Colonel Henry Pleasants, of the 48th Pennsylvania, one of Burnside's IXth Corps regiments, thought he had the answer. If you couldn't run over the Confederate defenses, how about going under them? His regiment was composed of anthracite miners from Scranton; they knew how to dig. He proposed to run a tunnel under the Confederate lines, fill it with explosives and blast the rebels right out of Elliott's Salient.

General Meade and others of the high command were dubious, but Burnside was persuaded the plan would work.* So on June 25 Pleasants' miners laid aside their rifles, took up picks and shovels, and started to dig. They ran a shaft into the hillside slightly in the rear of Fort Morton and then began to tunnel straight ahead. The shaft was about four feet high and four feet wide, shored up with whatever timbers could be begged, borrowed, or stolen. Meade thought so little of the plan that he refused to issue any material or equipment for the undertaking.

The tunnel started on a line thirty feet below the level of the Confederate works; about half way to its destination it angled upward until it was eighteen feet below the surface when it reached a point directly under Elliott's Salient.

Day by day, night by night, the Pennsylvanians grubbed forward until they had a tunnel extending five hundred and ten feet from its opening behind the Union lines. Then they dug two laterals, the whole work forming a gigantic underground T. The left lateral was thirty-seven feet long; the right, thirty-eight feet. Into the walls of the main shaft and the laterals they carved out eight magazines.

The Confederates suspected mining operations were going on under them and they sank countershafts and burrowed in several directions, but to no avail. They could hear the picks and shovels of the Pennsylvanians, but they could not intercept them. All they could do was wait and see what would happen.

Finally, on July 23, the mine was completed and the shafts and magazines were packed with eight thousand pounds of explosive. The Confederates within Elliott's Salient were literally sitting on a powder keg.

The detonation and assault were to be made on July 30. Grant had planned a heavy attack earlier in the month, but had delayed it to coincide with the explosion of the mine. He sent Hancock's Corps and two cavalry divisions across the James to create a diversion between Petersburg and Richmond, forcing Lee to withdraw some of the Petersburg defenders to meet the threat.

The blowing of the mine was to be the signal for a concentrated attack which was intended to carry to Cemetery Hill. It was to be a IXth Corps show, and careful preliminary arrangements were made. Ledlie's 1st Division moved into the front line on July 29 and took its position opposite the undermined rebel works. Potter's 2nd Division, composed mostly of New Englanders, was on Ledlie's right. Its job was to protect that flank. Willcox's 3rd Division was on the other side of Ledlie, to cover his left flank and occupy the Confederate lines left of the main point of attack. The 4th Division, Ferrero's, consisted of Negro troops,* the first to be used in combat against Lee's army. Their assignment was to follow through in Ledlie's wake and occupy Cemetery Hill. Two other Corps, the Vth and XVIIIth, were placed in reserve and were to be thrown forward on a broad front once the IXth had successfully cracked the line.

Willcox' division had two brigades—Hartranft's * and Humphrey's *— with a total of six Michigan regiments.* The 1st Brigade, which was Hartranft's, was composed exclusively of Michiganders. They were the 17th, 8th and 27th. Humphrey's 2nd Brigade had the 1st Michigan Sharpshooters and the 2nd and the 20th Infantry. In addition, it had the 50th Pennsylvania, the 46th New York, the 24th New York Cavalry (dismounted), and the 60th Ohio. The last two outfits were used on July 30 as reserve and provost guard units. All of the Michigan men in the two brigades were seasoned veterans of many campaigns and battles.

At 3 a.m. the assault troops began to move into position. Hartranft, in column, entered one of the covered ways between the Federal first and second lines. Humphrey's brigade stood behind Hartranft with the Sharpshooters at the head of his column and the 2nd and 20th Michigan next in line in that order. Lieutenant Colonel Byron M. Cutcheon * commanded the 20th. Colonel William Humphrey, the regular commander of the 20th, had been moved up to lead the brigade.

With all assigned positions occupied, the men crouched silently, waiting for the mine to be exploded. The detonation was scheduled for 4 o'clock. That hour came and passed and nothing happened. Men and officers turned to each other and in whispers asked what had gone wrong. Colonel Pleasants sent two of his men into the tunnel. They returned shortly with the report that the fuse had burned out at one of the splice points. They had fixed it and all was now ready again.

Once more the fuse was lighted—it was now 4:45 o'clock—and in another moment all hell broke loose. Directly in front of the IXth Corps creation itself seemingly erupted in a tremendous geyser of flame and fountain of earth. A brilliant, blinding flash lit the sky and the concussion shook the countryside, rocking the Union troops off their feet, deafening them momentarily with the frightful thunder clap.

"It was a magnificent spectacle," said one observer; "and as the mass of earth went up into the air, carrying with it men, guns, carriages and timbers, and spread out like an immense cloud as it reached its altitude, so close were the Union lines that the mass appeared as if it would descend immediately upon the troops waiting to make their charge. This caused them to break and scatter to the rear, and about ten minutes were consumed in re-forming for the attack."

It was about 5 a.m., then, when Ledlie's division moved out. Its rush across no-man's land to where the Confederate line had been, brought it to the lip of a huge, elliptical-shaped crater, a hundred and seventy feet long, sixty feet wide, and thirty feet deep. The red clay sides were almost sheer.

This was a great wonder! Instead of continuing their forward rush, which at the moment was unopposed, Ledlie's men slowed down and became sight-seers. They crowded around the hole, wide-eyed with amazement. Their curiosity proved fatal. About 287 Confederates and a few artillery pieces had been blasted to smithereens. But on either side of the hole, and to the rear, where they were protected by their trenches, the rebels recovered their senses and began to pour a heavy rifle fire into the broken up, confused, and leader-less mass of Ledlie's men milling around the edge of the Crater. General Ledlie, who should have been with them and directing them, was sitting comfortably and safely in a bomb shelter in the midst of Willcox's division.

The deadly fire of the Confederate sharpshooters was punching big holes in the surging mob which had been the 1st Division. To add to the danger and confusion, Confederate batteries came to life and began to pour their iron hail into the tangled blue mass. The division jumped for the nearest cover, which was inside the rim of the Crater.

This was the moment for Potter's division to go in. The New Englanders advanced gallantly, but the concentrated fire of the enemy artillery broke them up and they too were pressed into the pit on top of the 1st Division.

The Confederate fire was heaviest on the left of the Federal troops and, to protect that flank, Willcox now sent his brigades forward. Hartranft went first, leading the 17th, 8th, and 27th Michigan in that order. Moving fast and paying little attention to the murderous fire pouring in on them, the 1st Brigade hit the Confederate line to the left of the Crater and penetrated beyond. They smashed into a rebel battery and managed to turn one of the guns around to sweep across the enemy line to their left.

Humphrey's brigade left the covered way as soon as it was clear of Hartranft's men, and it took the ground which had originally been occupied by
Ledlie's division. Because it was made up of more regiments, the 2nd Brigade
was formed into two columns, the left one composed of the three Michigan
regiments—the Sharpshooters, the 2nd, and the 20th. The other column consisted of the 50th Pennsylvania, the 46th New York, and some miscellaneous
troops. The Michiganders were sent off on the left oblique behind Hartranft
for the purpose of supporting him. Their orders were to clear out the rebel
trenches, particularly the laterals, which gave the enemy well-protected positions from which they were delivering a devastating flank fire.

With a cheer, the men advanced in good order, climbing over the Federal
breastworks and breaking through three lines of abatis. Once clear and into
no-man's land, they went forward at a run which carried them two hundred
yards inside the Confederate lines. Their charge netted them about thirty
prisoners and another piece or two of artillery. Theirs was the deepest pene-
tration made that day.

Unfortunately it was not enough. They were exposed to enfilading artillery
fire, and angry blasts of canister tore deep gashes in their ranks. The 20th
Michigan left its own lines with one hundred and fifteen men; by the time
it reached the rebel positions it had lost nearly a quarter of that number. To
make matters worse, the Confederates were rallying a large number of troops
in a depression or swale between the Crater and Cemetery Hill. They were
protected by the contour of the land from Federal artillery. And to add injury
to insult, their riflemen in the lateral trenches had clean shots at the backs of
the Michigan soldiers who had pressed beyond them. Willcox's entire division
now was under galling fire from the front, rear, and left.

Still the Michiganders held on, trading death for death in heaping measure,
until the 46th New York, having had enough of the slaughter, panicked and
broke. They ran for the Crater, the most convenient cover. In their terrified
rush, they swept over the Pennsylvanians and other units of the 2nd Brigade,
forcing them also into the hole. This left the six Michigan regiments in the
two brigades unsupported and exposed to the full fury of the Confederate
counterattack. In order to ease the pressure the remaining division of the
Corps—Ferrero's Negro troops—was thrown in at the right of the Crater
where Potter should have been.

But it was too late. The Michiganders on the left, the colored men on the
right, fought desperately. Foot by foot they were pressed inward and soon
they too were sliding into the Crater. In the melee the casualties were frightful.
Colonel Wright of the 27th, was cut down with wounds which disabled him

permanently. Rather than surrender their colors the 20th cut up their standards and buried the pieces in the dirt at the bottom of the pit.*

The trouble was obvious. The sector chosen for the Union attack was too narrow for such a large body of troops. With an entire Corps crowded into a limited space, there was not enough room to maneuver and confusion reigned.

The Crater was solidly packed with a mob—no longer a Corps—of men who were as much concerned with avoiding being trampled by their own comrades as they were with what the enemy was doing. Several thousand of the IXth Corps were wedged into the bottom of the pit. All semblance of order and organization disappeared. Divisions, brigades, and regiments were hopelessly tangled.

Some of the Federals had avoided being pushed into the hole and they managed to get back to the safety of their own lines, but the number was pitifully small. Union artillery was turned loose and blue-clad sharpshooters in the advanced Federal rifle pits tried to clear the rim of the Crater of advancing Confederates. They were only partially successful. The rebels were members of General Billy Mahone's Virginia division, men who had followed Stonewall Jackson. They were superb fighters and masters of the art of counterattack. They worked their way to the edge of the Crater and fired down on the seething mass. It was like shooting fish in a barrel.

A few of the Union soldiers attempted to climb to the edge of the hole and organize some kind of defense. The odds were heavily against them. The walls were so steep that it was impossible to climb them unless the men turned their backs, dug in with their heels, and inched their way up backwards. Some managed to do this. A Confederate charge carried over the rim and into the Crater itself. The quarters were too close for rifle fire; the bayonet did its bloody work. The invaders, however, were overcome, and a Union defense line was established around the edge which succeeded in holding the rebels back at a respectful distance. Confederate mortars found the range though, and soon their shells were dropping on the besieged men.

General Burnside saw the complete collapse of his Corps' effort and about noon ordered a general withdrawal. But there was no easy way out. A few officers in the pit took counsel among themselves and decided the risk was too great. They resolved to hold on until dark, when the opportunity for safe escape would be better. Colonel Cutcheon of the 20th Michigan wriggled his way across no-man's land to the Federal lines. He asked for picks and shovels to be sent into the Crater in order to give the trapped men a chance to dig their way out through a protected trench. But no tools or sandbags were immediately available and his plan was abandoned. Cutcheon bravely returned to his men, empty handed.

The afternoon sun beat mercilessly down on the men in the Crater. They had not eaten since the previous evening. Their canteens were empty and there was no way to refill them. Neither was there any help for the wounded. It was more than most of the men could stand. The long wait until dark was a prospect which few relished. Let those wait who so desired! The others, singly and in small groups, risking death rather than remain longer in that hell hole, climbed the sides and dashed for the Union lines. After a while there weren't many left except the dead and wounded. One of the last groups to pull out of the Crater was the remnant of Hartranft's three Michigan regiments. Late in the afternoon the Confederates again charged the rim, and the Michiganders who had been defending it managed to scramble out and withdraw.

The Battle of the Crater was ended.

Approximately eight thousand men of the IXth Corps took part in the assault. Of that number, 473 were killed, 1,646 were wounded, and 1,356 were listed as missing. Many of the missing were eventually marked off as dead. The total loss in the Corps was 3,475, and other casualties brought the day's toll to 3,798.

From the Union standpoint, the Battle of the Crater was a boldly conceived but badly mismanaged undertaking. It failed for two reasons: First, because the sector chosen for the attack was too narrow to accommodate such a large number of troops; they were crowded in upon each other so that it was virtually impossible to maintain any sort of order; second, because of the failure at corps and division levels to provide leadership and hold units together. Much bitterness and much recrimination followed. There was the inevitable board of inquiry, which decided that General Burnside was lax. He was sharply censured. General Ledlie's peculiar conduct and his failure to accompany his division won him the scorn of the officers and men. He was transferred to another field of activity and served no more with the Army of the Potomac.

There was no censure for the Michigan regiments. It was universally agreed they had conducted themselves with brave distinction. General Willcox, who, unlike Ledlie, went into battle with his men, spoke well of the enterprise of the Michiganders. Colonel Cutcheon, who had a ringside seat, declared "there was no more gallant soldier than General Hartranft and no braver men than those he commanded. . . . Whatever may be said of other commands, it can be truly said of the Michigan regiments that they behaved with their customary gallantry, and none of them performed its duty more worthily than the 20th regiment."

General Willcox attributed a good share of his division's trouble to "the cowardice of the 46th New York Volunteers." All told, the 3rd Division with its six Michigan regiments lost forty officers and 666 men, of whom 258 were reported missing. That score represented a total loss of nearly fifty per cent of the men of the 3rd who went into battle that day.

It was a bleak day indeed for Michigan, and a bloody one for the Army of the Potomac. As a monument to death, the Crater stands with the Angle at Gettysburg and the slaughterhouse of Cold Harbor.

From the Lake Superior copper ranges, where the 27th was recruited, to the farms and villages of Jackson, Ingham, Muskegon, and Genesee, the evil genie of the Crater left the mark of his hand in blood on the lintels of hundreds of Michigan homes.

XVIII

"To Bind Up

the Nation's

Wounds"

MICHIGAN GOT ITS first taste of blood at Blackburn's Ford, July 18, 1861. Hardly more than a reconnoitering skirmish, that engagement took place on the same field upon which, three days later, the Battle of Bull Run was fought. The Blackburn's Ford tussle was brought on by an attempt of Tyler's division (Union) to force its way across the stream which gave its name to the first major battle of the Civil War.

One of Tyler's brigades was commanded by Colonel Israel Richardson of Pontiac, Michigan, and it included the 2nd Michigan Infantry.

There was considerable banging away on both sides as the 2nd probed for a foothold on the south bank of Bull Run. The Confederates held a strong position along the high banks, and the Union lines were dangerously exposed. Someone was bound to get hurt and somebody did.*

The lesser fates which decide the destinies of enlisted men in battle shuffled their cards and drew out one bearing the name of Private Mathias Wollenweber* of Company A, 2nd Michigan. He was selected for a dubious distinction—that of becoming Michigan's first Civil War battle casualty. As his name suggests, Wollenweber was of German extraction. He spoke English with a thick accent. To his comrades he was "Dutch" or "the Dutchman."

As the 2nd Michigan skirmishers moved across the fields toward Bull Run they were greeted by a spatter of gunfire from the opposite side. Wollenweber the unlucky was in the path of one of those musket balls; it took him smack in the side and laid him, gasping, flat on the ground. The wound was not deep, nor was it in a vital spot. But it hurt and it bled, and the terrified Wollenweber was sure he was done for.

But succor was at hand. While the injured man lay on the ground, reviewing his sins and assessing his chances for passage within the Pearly Gates, Dr. Henry F. Lyster,* assistant surgeon of the 2nd, rode across the field looking for business. If Wollenweber was to be enshrined in war's hall of fame as Michigan's first casualty, Dr. Lyster gained a pedestal beside him as the man who treated the first Michigan wound.

Henry Lyster, a Detroiter like Wollenweber, was a gay-hearted Irishman who had signed up with the 2nd partly for humanitarian reasons, partly from a desire for adventure, and partly because his brother William, adjutant of the regiment, persuaded him to. Up to the time of the fracas at Blackburn's Ford Dr. Lyster found war to be a pretty unstimulating affair. It consisted of listening each morning at sick call to the woeful self-diagnoses of a parade of goldbricks explaining why they should be excused from duty, and of prescribing for ailments, real and imaginary, which included everything from diarrhea to homesickness. Lyster considered himself a surgeon and felt imposed upon when all he was given to do was dispense pills. Since he looked forward to treating real wounds, he was as glad to see the stricken Wollenweber as the "Dutchman" was to see him.

In later years Lyster described, probably with joyous embellishment, what happened next. Dismounting—regimental surgeons had horses—he slipped his arm through his steed's bridle and bent to examine Wollenweber. The bullet had pinged the man just below the ribs and had bored into the side. There was a neat little round hole, and Lyster's first object was to determine how far the bullet had penetrated. It didn't impress him as a job requiring him to break out his instruments. His little finger would do nicely for a probe.

As he sought for the ball with his finger, said Lyster, the "Dutchman" let out yelps of anguish which startled the horse. The horse would toss its head and jerk Lyster's arm, which was slipped through the reins, giving Wollenweber further cause to sound off. This sort of surgical chain reaction continued for several minutes until Lyster had completed his examination and located the ball. Meanwhile, the soldiers on each side of the line paused in their lethal work to listen to the awesome sounds emanating from the "Dutchman" and all but drowning out the noise of battle.

Wollenweber recovered and may be considered fortunate. Three days later, during the Battle of Bull Run, Lyster performed the first amputation of the war on another Michigan soldier.

Lyster's treatment of Wollenweber, even allowing for some exaggeration in the doctor's telling about it, was not exactly typical. The surgeons who went to the front with Michigan regiments were generally as skilled as most practitioners of the time and as dedicated as any members of their profession. Though they were sometimes handicapped by inexperience, and almost constantly by a shortage of supplies and facilities, Union suffering and losses would have been much greater without them.

The army medical service at the outbreak of the war was as hastily organized as other branches. "Each regiment," announced the *Detroit Free Press* on May 9, 1861, "is allowed a Surgeon and a Surgeon's Mate, one Hospital Steward, two nurses, two matrons and one laundress."

Actually it didn't work out quite that way in practice. It is true that every regiment had a surgeon and assistant surgeon, each of whom bore commissioned rank, and one or more hospital stewards. Nurses were usually assigned from the ranks as needed, or from the bandsmen or company musicians. Matrons frequently were sent to general hospitals, but it was rare for one to accompany a Michigan regiment to the front. Cooks and laundresses were part of the hospital staffs and often were recruited from among the Negro women "contrabands" who attached themselves to the Union Army.

It is difficult to ascertain exactly how many Michigan doctors served with the regiments from the state. The number was fairly large. The *Medical History of Michigan,* in its chapter on the Civil War, refers to "an amazingly large number" and mentions by name one hundred and fifty-four. And there were many more.

Other doctors gave their services when emergencies arose, such as big battles with large casualty lists, for which special help was required. After the Battle of Chickamauga in 1863, when the rear-echelon hospitals filled up, practically the entire faculty and senior class of the University of Michigan medical school left for temporary service. Again, during Grant's campaign of 1864 along the Rapidan, the call went out for aid, and thirty-three Michigan doctors and several University medical students responded. These men served without compensation and stayed on the job until the regular army surgeons had caught up with their backlog of cases.

Naturally the ability and experience of the regimental surgeons from Michigan, as from the other states, varied—all the way from the highest of skills to practically none at all. In 1861, it has been stated, "surgery was on an equality with other branches of medicine." Nevertheless there simply weren't enough top-notch surgeons to meet the demands of war. The army took what it could get. Not uncommonly, young men serving as hospital stewards or nurses, having no formal medical training, took over the duties of assistant surgeons and progressed eventually to surgeonships. Some of these men came out of the war with "Dr." before their names and hung out their shingles when they got home. One of them was Orestus Watkins of Grand Rapids. He enlisted as a hospital steward with the 2nd Michigan Cavalry in 1861 and was mustered out as an assistant surgeon in 1865. The only medical training he received was in the army, and after the war he practiced successfully for many years.

More often though, nurses and hospital stewards discovered medicine as their true vocation while in the army and entered medical schools after the war.

When big battles caused the casualties to mount, field hospitals were set up for each division at some safe and accessible place behind the lines. Regimental surgeons were sent back to staff these hospitals, leaving the care of the front-line wounded to the chaplains, drummer boys, or whoever was available. In Virginia, where the battle lines in 1864–65 were fairly static, the field hospitals more or less assumed the status of base hospitals. They cared for all sick and wounded until they could be evacuated to large general hospitals in the North or be discharged as cured and fit for duty.

The field hospitals did a good job under difficult conditions. Usually they were understaffed and, when casualties were heavy, short on supplies. Patients and even medical staffs found much about which to gripe. Private David Lane, 17th Michigan Infantry, who was assigned as steward to a IXth Corps hospital near Knoxville during Burnside's East Tennessee campaign of 1863, made this complaint:

> This is called a United States General Hospital. It partakes of the nature of such an institution only so far as patients and shoulder-strapped doctors go toward making it one. And patients are becoming scarce, thank God. It is not a desirable place for convalescents, and, as soon as they are able, they gladly leave for their regiments. . . . They would run any risk to escape this den of filth, privation and starvation.
>
> Think of a hospital where the patients have no bedding but the blankets they brought with them; no clothing but the dirty rags they wore from the field; no dishes but their tin cups and butcher knives; where there is no "bed pan," and only two night vessels for one hundred forty sick men; where washing is put off, week after week, for want of soap, there not being so much as one piece to wash hands with. I went to every store, grocery and sutler's shop in the city this morning, seeking soap and finding none. Where wounded soldiers are fed on coarse bread and beef or vegetable soup twice a day, and not half enough of this to satisfy.
>
> It is no valid excuse that hospital stores cannot be procured here. They might have been sent from Kentucky before this time. Our troops—the Ninth Corps—in the field are in no better condition. They are encamped eighteen miles from here, unfit for duty for want of clothing; all are ragged; many have not a shoe to their feet or rags enough to cover them. Washington's army at Valley Forge is the only parallel in the history of this Nation.

. . . I have only one shirt, and that is nearly worn out. Army shirts—no better than those issued to us—cost six dollars at the sutler's. My shoes are nearly off my feet, and army shoes cost four dollars. I am destitute of socks, and socks cost one dollar. I do not wish to find fault, but the thought will arise, if sutlers can get their goods over the mountains, why cannot the Government?

Partly to relieve the conditions and shortages of which Lane complained, partly to provide the men in the hospitals and at the front with small luxuries to make life more bearable, there were a number of civilian organizations, some of them national and some purely local.

The most important of them was the Sanitary Commission, a semi-official organization created by government authority. Its purpose was to supplement by civilian effort the work of the regular army medical agencies, and particularly to attempt to improve the hygiene and sanitation of the Union army, both in camps and in hospitals. It drew upon some of the country's best medical talent as consultants and advisers.

One of the Sanitary Commission's major contributions was the recruiting and training of competent nurses, and many women went, if not to the front, very near to it, and ministered to the sick and wounded. These Sanitary Commission aides marked the first participation of women in the military effort on any considerable scale.

The Sanitary Commission has been compared to the Red Cross of later wars, and it was undoubtedly the most effective organization of its kind during the Civil War period. Its work was largely responsible for the claim that "the American sanitary measures were undoubtedly the most extensive and liberal ever undertaken by a people in any war, and accomplished much in ameliorating the suffering incident to a great and prolonged war."

Next in effectiveness to the Sanitary Commission was the Christian Commission, another national organization. The Christian Commission, as its name implies, was primarily religious, and it was really an outgrowth of the Young Men's Christian Association. It was described as "a powerful auxiliary in sanitary operations."

It solicited funds to carry on its work, and dispensed the money itself. One of its chief functions was to provide spiritual comfort to the men at the front or in the hospitals. For this purpose it sent Protestant ministers and laymen out to the troops. They established libraries and reading rooms stocked with church and hometown newspapers and periodicals, and provided writing paper and other needs. They helped nurse the sick and injured, and saw to it, whenever possible, that the dead were buried with Christian rites.

The Y.M.C.A. was not established in Michigan until 1863, and consequently the Christian Commission was somewhat slower getting started in that state than in some of the others. Nevertheless, it did send sixty Michigan agents, about half of them ordained ministers, to the front. The services of these men were about equally divided between the Army of the Potomac and the Army of the Cumberland.

In Detroit the Christian Commission fitted up a railroad freight house as a dining hall, and between June 4, 1865, and June 10, 1866, furnished meals and entertainment to more than twenty-three thousand discharged soldiers passing through the city on their way home.

The work of the Christian Commission can be described most clearly by its own statement of purpose, which declared:

> The plan of the commission is to minister both to the mental and spiritual, as well as the bodily wants of the army. It sends the living preacher, the Bible, the religious newspapers of all denominations, and all the time it is ministering to the temporal wants of the soldier, and working for the sick, wounded and dying. It searches for the wounded amid the thickets of the battlefield, and never leaves him till he is discharged from hospital, or a prayer consigns him to a soldier's grave.

Soon after the first Michigan troops arrived at Washington in 1861, citizens of Michigan residing at the capital, including the state's congressional delegation, set up a relief agency in that city. Called the Michigan Soldiers' Relief Association of Washington, D.C., it was the first such organization, and it continued to operate until the end of the war. Funds raised by private subscription, both in Washington and Michigan were used in many ways for the comfort of the men.

During the later stages of the Virginia campaign, for example, the Association established a depot at City Point, just outside the Petersburg siege lines, where it supplied Michigan men with fresh vegetables, pickles, tobacco, and soft bread, as well as necessary items of clothing. A soldier who was broke could apply to the Association's agent for a small sum of money, which sometimes financed a trip home when he had a furlough. The Association also maintained at City Point the Michigan Soup House, which provided hot meals behind the lines to hungry soldiers, whether they belonged to Michigan units or not.

One of the Association's most appreciated undertakings was its establishment in Washington of a hostel where men passing through town could obtain a night's lodging and food. A matron and cook were employed, and the records show that as many as seven hundred and twenty-five meals were served in a single day. It was estimated that more than eight thousand men were accommodated during the war in the Association's "house."

Another local organization was the Michigan Soldiers' Aid Society, formed in November 1861. Its major activity was to send boxes of food and clothing to the front. This Society was, in effect, an auxiliary of the Sanitary Commission, and its work was carried on by some of the most eminent citizens of Detroit. Between November 1, 1861, and June 1863, it sent 3,593 packages to the front.

Similar in purpose and operation was the Michigan Soldiers' Relief Association. It worked closely with the Ladies' Soldiers' Aid Society in raising money not only to benefit the men in the army but also to assist their needy families. Like the Washington group, this Association doled out cash to destitute soldiers and their dependents, and it also collected and shipped to the front large quantities of clothing, particularly shirts, socks, and handkerchiefs. Other items which it furnished were canned fruits, pickles, jellies, newspapers, books, sewing kits, and surgical dressings. In Detroit it maintained the Soldiers' Home in the old Arsenal Building on Jefferson at Wayne Street. During the war and for a few months after, this Home provided shelter for sick, incapacitated, and destitute veterans.

Other Michigan cities besides Detroit had their citizen groups working to make more bearable the lot of the soldier. One which was particularly successful was the Ladies' Soldiers' Aid Society of Kalamazoo which, in 1864, staged a huge Sanitary Fair. Much like the familiar church bazaar, Sanitary Fairs were quite common devices for raising funds, but that staged by the women of Kalamazoo outdid most others. It drew an attendance from all over the state and netted more than $12,000, all of which was distributed to various soldiers' relief organizations.

But private and semiprivate agencies were not the only source of relief. Soon after the outbreak of the war, Michigan and its local communities passed laws providing public assistance for soldiers and their dependents.

The responsibility for looking after dependent families was primarily a county function, and the laws stated that relief was not to exceed $15 per month. To be eligible for even that amount, the soldier had to be in actual service and his family was required to have been resident in the state for a year. The benefits of the law were extended to drafted men except those who furnished substitutes. To augment this aid, local communities, cities, and townships authorized supplementary funds for emergencies or special circumstances. For example, immediately after the Battle of Gettysburg the Detroit Common Council appropriated $2,500 for the relief of Michigan wounded.

After the war the chief object of public solicitude was the veteran, but while the battle raged most relief activities were for the benefit of the wounded and the sick, in that order. In the Union army there were 400,933 men treated for wounds, but more than six million cases of disease. Perhaps there is something heroic about a battle wound, while a case of jaundice lacks glamor. At any rate, the wounded got the best care; the sick, while not neglected, usually came out second best. Lane, the nurse and hospital steward, noticed that and protested what he considered outright discrimination.

"I am giving my attention mostly to the sick," he wrote from the 1st Division (IXth Corps) Hospital at City Point, Virginia, during the Petersburg siege. "It would seem strange to an outsider, but there is a distinction made between wounded and sick men that is not only unjust, but cruel. A sick man gets little sympathy, and less care, during an active campaign. The wounded must be cared for first, no matter how slight the wound, in one case, or how dangerous the illness in the other."

Possibly that attitude merely reflected a suspicion that the man who reported sick might be a malingerer.

We may thank Surgeon Wells B. Fox * of the 8th Michigan Infantry, for keeping and preserving a detailed account of cases of all types which he handled in some of the later campaigns of the war. The hundreds of sick and wounded whom he attended provide a fair representation of the hazards and ailments which assailed not only Michigan soldiers but Union troops generally.

Dr. Fox was born in Buffalo, New York, in 1823. His parents died while he was a small child, and he was either adopted by or apprenticed to an eminent physician of that city when he was eight years old. Later he studied medicine at Buffalo, attended Union College, and for two years was on the staff of the Erie County Hospital.

In 1849 Fox moved to Livingston County, Michigan, and began to practice in the village of Hartland. In August, 1862, he was appointed assistant surgeon for the 22nd Michigan Infantry, and on March 6, 1863, he became surgeon of the 8th Michigan. During the Petersburg campaign of 1864–65 he was surgeon-in-chief for the IXth Corps' 1st Division Hospital at City Point, where he did a brisk business. It was said that during his military service Dr. Fox performed nine thousand amputations and fourteen thousand other operations. Those figures certainly seem high; maybe they more accurately apply to operations performed under his supervision as chief of a large hospital.

At any rate Dr. Fox was a busy man, as the records of his cases prove. Cold Harbor, fought June 3, 1864, was one of the war's bloodiest engagements. During and immediately after the battle, 171 casualties, all Michigan men, passed through Fox's hands. His statistics, revealing what happened to men in battle, show that 152 wounds resulted from musket balls, one from grapeshot, fifteen from shells, one from buckshot, and two from solid shot.

That is probably typical of the wound pattern caused by the various types of weapons employed in the average Civil War engagement. It is interesting to note there were no bayonet wounds included in Fox's Cold Harbor list. Despite the popular picture of gallant Civil War charges, with hand-to-hand conflict and liberal doses of "cold steel," the truth is that the bayonet's chief use was for roasting meat over a campfire. There were only 922 reported bayonet wounds suffered by Union soldiers during the entire war. Fox mentions treating only one, and that, he notes, was the result of an accident by which Franklin Peck, 2nd Michigan Sharpshooters, somehow was pinked in the right forearm.

Peck's mishap falls into the category of the unusual, as do those of Private George L. Fisk, 17th Michigan, who was cut by a hatchet, and Private G. S. Smith, 27th Michigan, who was injured by a ramrod.

The hot sun was almost as great a hazard as the enemy's weapons. "Sunstroke is an every-day occurence, so common as to not excite remark," David Lane observed. In most instances, sunstroke was not considered important enough to enter on the medical records.

On August 19, 1864, Fox had another full day when the Battle of Weldon Railroad was fought as part of the Petersburg campaign. Following that fight, he took care of fifty-three Michigan wounded, eight of whom required amputations.

"The majority of those who died," said Fox, "met their death from the reaction and shock which always occurs to badly wounded men."

During the siege of Petersburg, which lasted nearly eleven months, and assumed the status of stalemated trench warfare, the ratio of disease to battle wounds increased materially. In fact Fox's hospital at City Point was filled with the sick but had comparatively few wounded patients.

"The winter of 1864–65, and up to the time of our mustering out," said Fox, "was characterized by a great amount of suffering and sickness endured by our men who had been through the war and had suffered all that falls to the lot of soldiers. Deprived of rations and halfclad fully one-half of the year, they had become physically impoverished to such an extent that their faces, from the rotund, had become gaunt and emaciated, the men of 25 years of age looked as though they were 40."

Under hardship and exposure, such men could easily fall prey to disease. Fox's records for the winter of 1864–65 list 316 sick patients from six Michigan regiments—the 1st Michigan Sharpshooters, and the 2nd, 8th, 17th, 20th, and 27th Infantry. These men were victims of thirty-seven different varieties of ailments.

The most common was diarrhea, for which forty-two were treated. Fevers, remittent and intermittent (including, perhaps, everything from the common cold to influenza), ran a close second, with thirty-four cases. Wet trenches and damp dugouts produced thirty-one cases of rheumatism and twenty-nine of pneumonia.

Nineteen times the diagnosis was "debility"; this may have covered a number of symptoms which during World War II would have called for psychiatric treatment. The other sicknesses treated by Fox were of a wide variety, with from one to half a dozen cases of each. Among them were bronchitis and anascara, six cases each; typhoid, hernia, and erysipelas, five; tuberculosis, epilepsy, jaundice, and pleurisy, four. The rest were about evenly divided among such common complaints as lumbago, hemorrhoids, dysentery, mumps, measles, heart condition, and boils. One case was diagnosed as old age, another as idiocy.

Fox makes no mention of any venereal cases—a strange omission, because the incidence was fairly high in both the Union and Confederate armies. The explanation may be that in the trenches before Petersburg, there was neither night life nor feminine company. It is possible, too, that Fox edited his records before their publication to avoid embarrassment and spare postwar feelings.

Of the 316 Michiganders who were received in Fox's division hospital, only nine died. Despite Lane's complaint of neglect and callousness, the smallness of the number bears testimony to the professional skill and dedicated attention of the Civil War medical services.

Terrible as the Civil War was in its waste of human and material resources, it did produce some tangible and lasting benefits to humanity.

Detroit was one of the beneficiaries. It was because of the war that the city acquired Harper Hospital, which was originally a military institution for the care of sick and wounded soldiers. At the end of the war it became a general hospital devoted to the service of the community at large.

At the outbreak of the Civil War there was no such thing as a general military hospital. Sick soldiers in the peacetime army were cared for in post or garrison infirmaries. As soon as casualties increased, however, it became necessary to establish hospitals well behind the lines, to which the wounded could be evacuated. These became the general hospitals, large institutions as a rule, and—unlike field hospitals, which cared only for men of a certain division or corps—they received all cases regardless of unit. By the end of

1862 there were a hundred and fifty-one such general hospitals, and the number increased steadily during the remaining years of the conflict.

At the beginning these hospitals were located within easy reach of the front—transportation being as important a consideration as other facilities. In the East they were to be found in the seaboard cities—Washington, Annapolis, Chester (Pennsylvania), and Philadelphia. Those serving the Western theater were located at such points as New Orleans, Memphis, Knoxville, and Columbus, Ohio.

About 1863 the people of Michigan began agitation for a hospital in their home state. Two considerations prompted this movement: one was local pride and the desire to have what other communities had; the other was a more valid one. Parents and friends of hospitalized Michigan soldiers had to travel long distances to see their boys. Wartime travel, under the most favorable conditions, was a hardship, and the expense a burden. How much better it would be, ran the argument, if Michigan's wounded could be cared for at home!

Citizens of the state presented their case in 1863 to Surgeon Charles S. Tripler,* medical director of the Department of Ohio, in which Michigan was included. He proved to be a willing ally and he laid the proposal before the Surgeon General, requesting immediate action. Tripler was supported by Dr. D. O. Farrand * of Detroit, assistant surgeon, U.S. Army, Dr. Joseph Tunnicliffe, military agent for Michigan at Washington, D.C., and Colonel George W. Lee, quartermaster at Detroit.

There were several delays, caused largely by disagreement about where the hospital should be located. There was spirited competition between Detroit and other leading cities. The Board of Regents of the University of Michigan made a strong case for Ann Arbor, with its medical school facilities. The Marine Hospital at Detroit, and the Federal arsenal property at Dearborn were considered, but rejected as inadequate.

A good site was available. In 1859 Walter Harper, a native of Ireland who had made a fortune in Philadelphia and had then moved to Detroit, donated one thousand acres of land and some other property to establish a Protestant hospital in the city. Shortly after Harper deeded his land another donation was made by Mrs. Nancy Martin, Harper's housekeeper, who had made considerable money operating a market stall in Detroit. From the proceeds of the trust which they established, a piece of ground was acquired in a beautifully wooded section on the east side of Woodward Road, well out in the city's northern precincts.

Now there was a suitable location but still no hospital. To remedy that deficiency, the Harper trustees offered the use of the land to the government, and in the spring of 1864 the Surgeon General agreed to build the necessary structures and assigned Colonel Lee to supervise the job.

The work was completed October 12, 1864, and Harper Hospital was opened as a general military hospital, primarily intended for the care of Michigan men. Lee put up eleven buildings: a large center structure, four barracks-like ward buildings on each side of it, and two smaller service buildings in the rear. The hospital occupied the site of the modern institution, fronting toward Woodward Avenue at what is now Martin Place.

When it opened Harper had about two hundred beds, but later the number was increased to five hundred and seventy-eight. The first patients were transferred from field hospitals in the South and from other Northern general hospitals. For the most part they came in small groups, although on July 2, 1865, the Harper staff was notified by the Army Medical Director of Transportation that one hundred and thirty-seven patients were being transferred from Philadelphia.

The end of the war naturally reduced the need for military hospital beds. Accordingly, the Federal government on December 12, 1865, turned over to the Harper Hospital board of trustees the buildings which had been constructed for military purposes. On January 1, 1866, Harper became a general public hospital and began to accept its first civilian patients.

The transition was gradual, however. The government, in transferring the buildings, stipulated that military patients would continue to be taken care of. The trustees also contracted with the Michigan State Military Board to care for veterans and to use the hospital as a soldiers' home. Immediately, twenty veterans who were being housed in the old Arsenal Building were transferred to Harper. The Michigan branch of the Sanitary Commission turned over to Harper its remaining assets—about $2,000—to be used for the care of Michigan veterans. The hospital continued to be a haven for old soldiers for the next twenty years. In 1883 it was still caring for a dozen men at the expense of the state.

Harper Hospital still preserves a day-by-day record of the men it looked after under its contract with the Military Board. The "Soldiers Record Book" lists 784 patients between March 1, 1867, and January 20, 1881. There was a variety of cases, ranging from delirium tremens to troubles of old age, with many complications resulting directly from battle wounds. One of the last patients listed in the book was Rees Williams, Company E, 7th Michigan Cavalry, who was treated for a period of sixty days for "old sabre wounds." Two admissions about which the researcher may speculate were Nat-tah-me-noting Jacko, and Joseph Shaw-em-as-ang, both of Company K, 1st Michigan Sharpshooters. Presumably they were Chippewa Indians who fought the white man's war. Jacko, admitted October 1, 1870, died in the hospital November 29. Joseph, who received "surgical treatment," left of his own accord six months after he was admitted, August 4, 1871. It is hoped Jacko found his way to the Happy Hunting Ground, and that Joseph returned to the woods and waters of northern Michigan, to live long in peace and contentment.

Many of the "soldiers' home" cases consisted of the destitute or mentally sick, and those whose illness was chronic were transferred from Harper to soldiers' homes maintained by the Federal government in Milwaukee, Columbus, and other places.

In 1884 a new building was erected on the original site, replacing the military structures. It was opened on June 19, and still (1960) forms part of the Harper Hospital complex.*

Thus a great modern institution of healing has arisen on the foundations of a Civil War hospital, a finer memorial undoubtedly then the statues and monuments of cast iron and sculptured stone which stand in scores of municipal parks and courthouse plazas across Michigan.

*The Harper Hospital Building was torn down on August 3, 1977.

XIX

Boat Ride

on the Styx

THEY HAD BEEN assembled on the levee at Vicksburg, about eighteen hundred of them. They were the backwash of the war, the casuals—the all-but-forgotten men, sick, lame, and blind —who had swarmed out of the Confederate prison camps. Now, after long months of imprisonment, they were on their way home.

The bank of the Mississippi was black with them as they stood waiting to board the steamer. They were a tatterdemalion lot. Their cast-off clothes, collected from the quartermaster depots, hung on their spare frames like scarecrow rags. Their faces were gaunt and lined with the marks of privation and sickness. Matted beards and long, lank hair gave a touch of wildness to their appearance. Scurvy had rotted their teeth; exposure had crippled limbs and made their joints swell.

To a man, their eyes were fixed on the river steamer *Sultana,* moored to the levee, waiting to take them aboard. The ship's white paint gleamed in the bright April sunshine; her decorative scrollwork made her look like a huge frosted cake. Three capacious decks, topped by her texas, suggested solid bulk and unbelievable luxury. Twin stacks, black and slender as pencils, reached toward the blue sky, crowned by a faint tracery of smoke. To the men on shore, the *Sultana* was a celestial chariot, heaven-sent, to bear them north to home and freedom.

It was April 24, 1865, and the war was over, or at least it was over except for a few mopping-up operations here and there. Lee had surrendered at Appomattox on the 9th. Johnston, with Sherman prepared to deliver a knockout blow in North Carolina, was negotiating for terms which would be agreed on within two days. Everybody's mind was set on getting home as quickly as possible.

Marching through Georgia and the Carolinas, Sherman had broken the spine of the Confederacy, and his sweep had overrun several of the places, like Andersonville, where the Confederates had established their prisoner-of-war camps. The approach of the Union troops toward the prisons had caused some fast reshuffling; threatened compounds had been evacuated and the hapless prisoners had been shifted to other camps beyond the reach of the Federal columns.

In the final stages of the war the rebel supply system had broken down completely; it was hard enough for the South to feed its soldiers, let alone the thousands of Federal prisoners who were penned up. With its superior manpower, the North had long since suspended exchanges. Toward the end a new arrangement had been worked out. Unable to feed and care for its prisoners, the Confederacy had agreed to move them to camps within territory controlled by the North. Those camps were administered by Confederates, but supplies of food and medicine were furnished by the United States. One such camp, Camp Fisk, was set up on the Big Black River, about six miles from Vicksburg.

Following the almost complete collapse of the rebel armies in the east and in Tennessee and Georgia, the men held at Camp Fisk were considered liberated and ready to be sent north. Transportation was arranged. They were to go up river to Cairo, Illinois and from there to Camp Chase, at Columbus, Ohio, where they would either be discharged or hospitalized, according to their condition.

These were the men waiting on the levee. They had been brought in from Camp Fisk by rail early on the 24th to be loaded aboard the *Sultana*. Of course, there were the usual delays; it would hardly have been a normal military operation if everything had gone off smoothly without the interminable waits. So the men stood as patiently as possible. Names were checked, lines formed and re-formed while long queues shuffled up the gangplanks at a pace which suggested the loading process would last throughout eternity.

The contingent from Camp Fisk was composed of men from Michigan, Ohio, Indiana, Tennessee, and West Virginia. About four hundred and twenty were Michiganders, representing twenty-two regiments.* Nearly a quarter of the Wolverines—one hundred and sixteen to be exact—were members of the 18th Michigan Infantry, a regiment which had been raised in 1862 in that part of the first congressional district which comprised Hillsdale, Lenawee, and Monroe counties.

Among the crowd of milling, expectant soldiers, only casually supervised by a small detachment of troops of the transportation section of the Quartermaster Corps, was Private Chester D. Berry of Marshall, Michigan. He had enlisted in Company I, 20th Michigan Infantry, August 18, 1862. He was eighteen years old when he volunteered; now at twenty-one he had seen hard campaigning and experienced the bitterness of imprisonment—and prison was far worse than battle. Watching his comrades die like flies at Andersonville, he had not expected to survive, but he made a solemn pact with himself that if he lived he would enter the ministry and in that way endeavor to repay God for preserving his life.

Berry's luck as a combat soldier ran out at Cold Harbor, June 2, 1864. Gobbled up by the Confederates, he was carried off to Richmond, and then transferred to Andersonville, where he arrived June 16. There he suffered as so many thousands of Union prisoners did: short rations, inadequate medical care, and brutal administration. By the beginning of September, the daily food allotment for each man was two tablespoonsful of coarse corn meal, an equal amount of stock peas, and two ounces of fresh beef.

"The beef first, then the peas were eaten raw," Berry said, "and the meal made into a gruel and drank."

Another in the crowd on the levee was Joseph Stevens who had served with the 1st Michigan Sharpshooters and then with the 4th Michigan Infantry. A Hillsdale, Michigan, boy of about twenty-one, he had been captured at Petersburg and, like Berry, became an alumnus of Andersonville. His story of imprisonment had a grisly tone. Recounting his trip to Andersonville, Stevens said:

> We were then taken to the stockade in which were imprisoned at that time thirty thousand Union men. Here I met a number of my old comrades who were in my company captured the preceding year. My friends warned me of a gang of raiders, men who had become desperate. When new prisoners came these men would rob the poor fellows and sometimes cut their throats. We formed a company to capture the leaders of this notorious gang. We captured six of them and turned them over to the rebels for safekeeping until we could send word to Gen. Sherman to ask what we could do with them. His answer was, "court martial them and do what you think best." They were then court martialed and sentenced to be hung, and the balance of the raiders to run the gauntlet. . . .
>
> The food they gave us was corn cobs, all ground up, and made into mush and there wasn't near enough of that to keep the boys alive any length of time. Those that lived had to speculate by trading their brass buttons, boots, etc., with the guards. There were from one hundred to one hundred and fifty boys dying every day. A large wagon drawn by four mules was used in drawing out the dead. They were laid in as we pile cord wood and taken to the burying ground, generally putting fifty in a grave, and returning would bring mush in the same wagon, where worms that came from the dead could be seen crawling all over it; but we were starving, therefore we fought for it like hungry dogs.

Another member of the waiting crowd, a Hoosier, recalled that food could be purchased at Andersonville, but it came high—"one Irish potato would bring from 75 cents to $1.25—a tablespoon of coarse salt 20 to 40 cents and a handful of wood 25 cents, and all in good United States money, too."

The other prisons, particularly Castle Morgan at Cahaba, Alabama, were no better than Andersonville. At times they were even worse.

Samuel Stubblefield, Company F, 18th Michigan Infantry, along with a score of his comrades, was captured near Athens, Alabama, by Forrest's cavalry. They were held at Cahaba from October 1864 until March 1865. It was a bitter winter, and much of the time the compound was under water to a depth of four feet.

"I slept two nights on a sixteen inch wall which was fifteen feet above the water, and some of the boys did their cooking among the braces of the roof," Stubblefield said.

Ogilvie E. Hamblin, Company E, 2nd Michigan Cavalry, was wounded at Raccoon Ford on the Tennessee River and captured by Hood's army. He was given medical attention at the Confederate hospital at Florence, Alabama, but he had a low opinion of the surgeons who amputated his arm. The doctors, he insisted, were novices and cut off his arm for practice. Eventually Hamblin wound up at Cahaba, where he found conditions similar to those reported by W. N. Goodrich from Monroe County, who served in Company E, 18th Michigan. Goodrich said he and his fellow prisoners subsisted on an unvarying diet of cornmeal for a period of six months. Commodore Smith, a Hillsdale boy, also of the 18th, was reduced to a skeleton during his half year in Cahaba.

"My weight when captured," he declared, "was 175 pounds, and when I reached our lines at Vicksburg, Miss., March 16, 1865, my weight was 94 pounds, although I had not been sick a day while in prison."

J. Walter Elliott, 10th Indiana Infantry, had an equally dismal story to tell about Cahaba. He was able to buy a bushel of corn for thirty-two dollars and divided it with his fellow prisoners. Another time, he said, a wagon load of corn on the ear was driven into the prison corral "and thrown out to us as though we were a lot of fattening hogs." It was the first food in four days, so the prisoners were not fussy about grubbing on the ground for it, but several men died as the result of eating it raw. Elliott was one of a group of prisoners transferred from one compound to another by rail, a twenty-four-hour ride "in a close, crowded box car, in which fresh horse dung was half a foot deep."

George F. Robinson of Charlotte, Michigan, was a private in the 6th Michigan Infantry. He was imprisoned at Meridian, Mississippi, a replica of Andersonville and Cahaba. Newly arrived batches of prisoners were hailed as "fresh fish" and promptly robbed of everything they possessed. Robinson thought he could save his hat and haversack by burying them and sleeping on the earth, which covered them. But during the night someone dug them up without disturbing him.

"I tell you," he said, "I was the most beat man you ever saw." Later he was transferred to Cahaba. He took with him his entire worldly possessions consisting of a shirt, a pair of drawers, and one shoe.

The relocation center at Camp Fisk began to receive prisoners during the last two weeks of March 1865. Orders for the Andersonville contingent to be shipped there came through March 20 and produced a spontaneous celebration which one prisoner described as resembling an old-fashioned camp meeting.

"How each of us laughed and cried, shook hands with and hugged his fellows, and . . . we all joined in singing 'Rally Round the Flag, Boys.' "

There was still another celebration, a moving experience, upon arrival at Camp Fisk, where "we hailed the glorious flag of our country as it floated on the breeze. . . . Tears flowed at sight of that proud emblem, while Big Black river, Jordan-like, divided the forlorn C.S.A. from our Canaan. We crossed; we gathered at the river; we sang and danced and rested under the shade of the trees . . . Out from the gates of hell—out from the jaws of death—going home."

As welcome as the sight of Old Glory to the Camp Fisk arrivals were barrels of sauerkraut and kegs of pickles—ambrosia to the scurvy-ridden. Alonzo Van Vlack, 18th Michigan, arrived with legs which "were one raw sore from my knees down to my feet, with scurvy." Walter Elliott observed that the best part of his welcome was being taken to the commissary, "where barrel after barrel of pickled cabbage was rolled out and the heads knocked in, and we, marching round and round, gobbled out and ravenously devoured the cabbage and licked the vinegar from our fingers, the sweetest dainty to my bleeding gums that ever I tasted."

Although there were at least three steamers waiting when the Camp Fisk prisoners reached Vicksburg, the entire column was marched aboard the *Sultana*.

Commanded by Captain Mason, the *Sultana* had arrived from New Orleans the day before. She was a commodious ship which had been built in Cincinnati in 1863 and was, therefore, relatively new. She was a side-wheeler of 1,719 tons displacement. A packet, designed to carry both cargo and passengers, she had cabin accommodations for about seventy-five persons. Her normal crew, which probably included some roustabouts, consisted of about eighty men. Before the troops were put aboard, several hundred hogsheads of sugar were stowed in the hold, and sixty horses and mules were stabled on the lower deck. The *Sultana* already had aboard about two hundred civilian passengers, including a number of women, members of the Christian Commission. In the miscellaneous cargo was a crate containing a nine-foot alligator.

The men filed aboard—as one declared, "driven on like so many hogs until every foot of standing room was occupied." The manifest called for a maximum of 1,400 soldiers, but apparently no one bothered to count noses. Nor did it appear strange to any of the men at the moment that so many were being embarked on the *Sultana* while other boats stood by empty. The minds of the liberated men were obviously fixed on getting home—how they got there and the inconvenience involved were of little concern. After all this was nothing compared to Andersonville.

Whether anyone realized it or not, the *Sultana* was dangerously overloaded. When the gangplanks were raised and the *Sultana* nosed out into the current of the Mississippi, she carried 1,866 troops, a number which later was said to be "unnecessary, unjustifiable," by Brigadier General W. Hoffman, commissary general of prisoners. In addition, there were the two hundred or so civilian passengers, two companies of infantry who acted as provost guards, and about thirty-five unattached officers. The exact number, passengers and crew, was never precisely determined, but from the best official estimates it was approximately 2,300, all crowded in cabin and deck space never intended to accommodate more than 800.

Around midnight all were aboard who were going aboard. At 1 a.m., April 25, the gangplanks were pulled in and with a cheery whistle blast the *Sultana* backed away from the levee, pointed her nose upstream, and began to plow a furrow in the Mississippi. To the men on her crowded decks, home seemed at the moment to be just around the next bend in the river.

It quickly became obvious that the trip to Cairo was not going to be a pleasure excursion. Every available foot of deck space was occupied; there was no room to walk around or exercise except at the hazard of treading upon some recumbent figure. Men bedded down wherever a place big enough could be found. Blankets were spread on the deck. To wander away from one's "home" spot for any reason was to find it occupied upon return.

William Fies, a Buckeye, recalled that he found a place on the cabin deck next to the rail. Later, when the ship's captain came up from below on his way to his stateroom, he was compelled to crawl around on the rail to avoid stepping on the tightly packed men. Ogilvie Hamblin and a comrade did like so many others; they bedded down on deck and removed all their clothes except their undershirts and drawers, making themselves as comfortable as possible. Robinson found a choice spot on the promenade deck between the smokestacks. Since it was cool on the river at night, those who found places close to the boilers thought themselves fortunate. The crowd was so large that the hurricane deck began to sag and officers of the ship hastily installed temporary stanchions to help support the unaccustomed weight. A kitchen of sorts was set up on the main deck aft, and whoever wanted to cook waited his turn. Most of the men were satisfied with cold rations. Hot water for coffee could be drawn from the boilers.

Despite the discomfort nobody complained, and the *Sultana* proceeded briskly up river, arriving at Helena, Arkansas, at 7 a.m., April 26. During a short stopover at Helena someone on shore took a picture of the ship which reveals her passengers, thick as ants on a picnic cake, seemingly piled up one on top of another.

After a run of exactly twelve hours from Helena the *Sultana* arrived at Memphis. Part of her cargo was unloaded there, some of the soldiers helping out as stevedores to earn a little money. Guards were posted to prevent unauthorized persons from going ashore, but many of the men still managed to slip over the side. They went uptown to visit restaurants and saloons. After laying over at Memphis about four hours, the *Sultana* crossed the Mississippi to the Arkansas side and loaded coal, then resumed her journey about 1 a.m., April 27.

The river was calm but the sky was overcast and the night was dark. The shores were hidden behind a curtain of blackness. There was a light sprinkle of rain, not enough to be more than a minor discomfort. There was almost no wind. The big paddles pounded the water with a rhythmic beat, and a crewman assured one passenger that they were making good time. Most of the men, wrapped in their blankets, slept.

About eight miles above Memphis the *Sultana* was opposite Tagelman Landing and was passing a group of small islands—really nothing more than sandbars covered with some vegetation and choked with driftwood. They were known as Paddy's Hen and Chickens Islands. The river being high, they were almost submerged. Low places along the Tennessee and Arkansas banks were also covered with water. In some places the overflow made the ground marshy for a considerable distance inland.

It was then about 2 a.m. Suddenly there was a tremendous explosion, a blast which shook the vessel from top to keel. The port boiler had burst, spewing steam, scalding water, and flaming embers the length and breadth of the ship. Dazed men, jarred out of their slumbers, found themselves engulfed in holocaust. Many, in the first moments, thought they had been fired upon from the shore by guerrillas.

The blast brought down the two smokestacks and their crash caused the top deck to collapse, crushing scores of men. Then a sheet of flame swept over the forward section and spread upward and aft until, in a short space of minutes, the *Sultana* was a blazing torch.

The first impulse was to leap overboard, and many did. George Robinson was badly scalded and injured by the falling deck. Nevertheless he managed to make his way to the rail.

"I looked around," he said, "and my God, what a sight! There were three or four hundred, all in a solid mass, in the water and all trying to get on top. I guess that nearly all were drowned, but that was not the worst sight. The most horrid of all was to see the men fast in the wreck and burning to death. Such screaming and yelling I never heard before or since."

Another survivor recalled that there were so many people in the water "you could almost walk over their heads."

Nathaniel Fogelsong of the 18th Michigan, like hundreds of others, couldn't swim, but he climbed over the stern and clung to the rudder. He had a difficult time holding on because others kept jumping from the deck on top of him. Finally a shower of sparks and hot ashes forced him to shift his hold to a piece of driftwood. Others hesitated to jump, remembering the alligator and visualizing the beast swimming around feasting on the thrashing men in the water. For the moment they preferred the flaming deck. Somehow, the horses and mules quartered on the lower deck were turned loose and got into the water. More than one man was saved by clinging to a mane or tail.

Those who did not lose their heads in the first moments of panic attempted to help the injured and extricate the trapped. Some tore shutters and doors loose and pitched them, along with crates, cracker barrels, and bales of hay, into the water for the non-swimmers to cling to. Eager hands grasped anything which would float.

Several men, seemingly oblivious to their own danger, went about the deck literally tossing into the water those who were unable to help themselves.

"We proceeded to perform carefully, but hurriedly, the most heart rending task that human beings could be called upon to perform—that of throwing overboard into the jaws of certain death by drowning those comrades who were unable on account of broken bones and limbs to help themselves," said a private of the 18th Michigan. "We were wanting to render every kindness,

222

to dress their wounds and soothe their sufferings. But, alas! this was impossible, the only alternative was to toss them overboard."

Walter Elliott came across a friend, his legs so badly crushed that he could not walk. He begged Elliott to save him.

"I can't help you," Elliott replied; "I can't swim."

"Throw me in the water is all I ask," the injured comrade implored. "I shall burn to death here."

With the aid of another soldier, Elliott carried the man aft and pitched him into the river. He disappeared immediately beneath the surface.

The women were a problem and some of them were treated less than gallantly. One survivor confessed that a woman passenger appealed to him for help, but he curtly told her "it was everyone for himself." He did, however, pause long enough to help her adjust a life preserver. Then she jumped, saying: "May the Lord bless you."

Another woman, a member of the Christian Commission, set a noble example for some of the panic-stricken men by passing quietly among them, trying to calm them. Even after the flames had forced her to the bow, she continued to direct those thrashing wildly around in the water to objects floating within their reach, endeavoring to quiet them so they could save their lives.

"The flames now began to lap around her with fiery tongues," a survivor recalled. "The men pleaded and urged her to jump in the water and thus save herself, but she refused, saying: 'I might lose my presence of mind and be the means of the death of some of you.' And so, rather than run the risk of becoming the cause of death of a single person, she folded her arms quietly over her bosom and burned, a voluntary martyr to the men she had so lately quieted."

Chester Berry frankly admitted he was no hero, and he bore a troubled conscience for a long time after the disaster. As he crossed the deck he saw a soldier weeping and wringing his hands, the victim of utter fear and despair. Supposing the miserable fellow was injured, Berry stopped and spoke to him.

"I took him by the shoulder and asked where he was hurt," Berry said. " 'I'm not hurt at all,' he replied, 'but I can't swim, I've got to drown.' "

Berry urged him to pull himself together and offered him a board he had picked up, telling him it would keep him afloat in the water.

"But I did get one," the man replied, "and some one snatched it away from me."

"Well, then," said Berry, "get another."

"What would be the use," wailed the man; "they would take it from me. I tell you there's no use; I've got to drown, I can't swim."

"By this time I was thoroughly disgusted," Berry declared, "and giving him a shove, I said 'Drown then, you fool.' "

"I want to say," Berry admitted, "I have been sorry all these years for that act."

Thirty minutes after the explosion the *Sultana* was burned to the water line and was drifting, a smoldering hulk. Those who had not been killed were floating around in the chill dark waters of the Mississippi, still far from being safe. Many were fighting for survival, not against the flood, but against their comrades. More than one was pushed off a plank or had a board or box snatched from him by a stronger man. Good swimmers, trying to aid drowning friends, were dragged to their deaths by those they sought to save. Lack of visibility was the undoing of others; with nothing to guide them, floundering men swam or pushed their way upstream thinking they were headed for shore. Many discarded all their clothes in order to be less burdened, and chill and exposure took a heavy toll. Private William Fies managed to swim despite a dislocated shoulder.

George Robinson clung to the carcass of a mule and managed to remain afloat. He drifted past another soldier attempting to climb on a beer keg. He would crawl up on it praying loudly all the while. Then the keg would roll and pitch him into the water. Up he would come again, sputtering and cursing, and repeat his efforts to climb on the keg. "Damn this thing," Robinson heard him say, "it will drown me yet."

One of the horses which the *Sultana* carried swam to a log to which several men were clinging, and put its neck over the floating timber for support. Unable to see clearly in the dark, the men thought they were being joined by their friend the alligator. They promptly surrendered the log to the sole possession of the horse and swam away to look for more congenial company.

Throughout the night the river was full of men, some drifting downstream, others making their way to shore. Many floated into half-submerged trees on sand bars and islands and crawled into the branches. There they sat, naked and shivering, until daylight. The morning brought out the river folk, some of them in Confederate uniforms, who pushed skiffs or canoes along the banks and plucked the stranded men out of the trees. More than one man drifted past Memphis; several were taken from the river six or seven miles below the city, having been carried by the current twelve or fifteen miles altogether.

The explosion was heard in Memphis and rescue boats put out immediately, but it was difficult to find survivors in the dark. The Federal ironclad *Essex* was alerted about 3:30 a.m. and sent out small boats. Someone in Memphis sent blankets to the ship, and one thoughtful citizen donated a keg of whisky. The commander of the *Essex* was a teetotaler, and ordered the whisky poured out into the scuppers, much to the horror of Quartermaster Thomas Love, who reported the incident. The crew managed to sop up some with rags and buckets, and "got quite jolly." Boat crews from the *Essex* worked all of April 27 and saved hundreds.

"All that day," Love said, "we found men almost dead, hanging to trees about two miles out into the river, and among those that I rescued was one man so badly scalded that when I took hold of his arms to help him into the boat the skin and flesh came off his arms like a cooked beet."

An officer of the gunboat *Grosbeak* said bodies were still being taken from the river eight or nine days later, and some of them were found as far south as Vicksburg.

William McFarland, 42nd Indiana Infantry, was picked up by the small steamer *Silver Spray*. While he was aboard the boat went to the aid of a lanky Tennessean perched astride a drifting log. He called out, asking how far it was to Memphis, and was told the city was only a mile downstream.

"Go to hell with your boat, then," he shouted. "If you couldn't come to help me before now you had better have stayed away." With that, he slid from his log and began resolutely swimming downstream in the direction of Memphis.

While river craft of all kinds were busy pulling men out of the water, parties were organized to search for those who had reached shore and worked their way inland. Because of high water there was much swampy ground inland and many perished there. Those who did not were almost eaten alive by swarms of mosquitoes, flies, and gnats.

Memphis was quickly mobilized for relief, and as the survivors landed from the rescue craft they were met by women of the Sanitary and Christian Commissions. Scores of men were set ashore without a stitch of clothing, naked as the moment they were born. The women unblushingly helped them off the boats and wrapped them in blankets. Every available vehicle in the city was sent to the waterfront, and as fast as one was loaded it was driven to an army or civilian hospital.

It took some time to tote up the score of the missing, but the final official count placed the toll at 1,238, of whom 1,101 were soldiers and the rest civilian passengers and crew. Actually, the number lost may have been considerably higher, since there were hundreds of men aboard whose names were not on the lists of the transportation officer at Vicksburg. Unofficial estimates which are generally accepted as more nearly correct place the number of dead in excess of 1,400, and even that figure may be too low.

The entire country, North and South, was shocked at news of the disaster. The war was considered to be over, and people believed they were done with reading casualty lists. The loss of life on the *Sultana* was greater than in most of the war's bloodiest battles.

Of course investigations were started immediately to learn the cause and find out who was responsible. The findings were not pleasant.

The first quick opinion was that Southern sympathizers had sabotaged the *Sultana* by planting a grenade in her coal bunker. Those rumors were soon discounted and attention was turned to the more reasonable possibility that the boilers were defective. Inquiry showed the boilers had been inspected at St. Louis on the down trip and had been found to be in satisfactory condition. That would have been about a week before the explosion. At Vicksburg, on the up-bound trip, a leak was found in one boiler but it was immediately repaired by a competent boilermaker. However, later examination of the wreck revealed the boiler was broken at the bottom, indicating that it had been exposed to fire without having sufficient water. If this was the cause of the blast, there certainly must have been negligence on the part of the second engineer who was on duty at the time and who was killed.

But although either malfunction or negligence might account for the explosion, responsibility for the terrible loss of life lay elsewhere.

The investigators found the answer at Vicksburg. Major General N. J. T. Dana, commanding the Department of Mississippi, testified that he had given orders to embark the men on whatever boats were available, and that at least two loads had gone north before the *Sultana* arrived. He learned later, he said, that two other ships were waiting and should have been loaded ahead of the *Sultana*, but agents of the contract line operating that vessel had bribed transportation officers to detain the other two. They were not contract carriers, and preference was given the *Sultana*. General Dana further declared that the transportation officers had not adequately inspected the vessel, and that they had reported to him that no more than 1,400 men would be put aboard.

Other, unofficial, statements elaborated upon the bribery story. Following the fall of Vicksburg in 1863, many Federal troops were sent north, and so eager were they to get transportation that they were willing to pay any fare that steamboat captains demanded. When General Grant learned that his men were being gouged, he established a flat rate to Cairo of $5 for enlisted men and $10 for officers. Loads were limited to one thousand passengers on each ship.

Under those regulations, which were still in force, the *Sultana* should have been paid $5 per man, although there seems to have been some official willingness to relax the rule about the number she could carry. Through connivance of the transportation officers and the ship's captain, it was agreed to take aboard about 2,000 men at a rate of $3 each. The captain was to receive $6,000—that is, $1,000 more than his legal fee if he carried only one thousand men at $5 per head. The quartermaster made out the voucher for two thousand men at $5 per man and cashed it, receiving $10,000. Out of that sum the captain was paid his $6,000 and the extra $4,000 went into the pockets of the transportation officers.

General Hoffman's report named the following as responsible for the overloading: Colonel R. B. Hatch, chief quartermaster; Captain George A. Williams, commissary of musters; and Captain W. F. Kernes, master of transportation. General Hoffman was aware of the bribery story, but he made no accusations on that score. The records do not disclose what action, if any, was taken by the War Department against the three men whom Hoffman named.

The shattered hulk of the *Sultana*, sitting in the mud on the bottom of the Mississippi, remained a tragic monument to infamy. The death list of those who had already suffered war's worst horrors made it the greatest marine disaster in history prior to the sinking of the *Titanic* in 1912.

XX

The Great

Manhunt

WHEN THE 4th Michigan Cavalry
went into camp at Macon, Georgia, April 21, 1865, the weary troopers felt that
they had been assigned squatters' rights in the Elysian Fields. For thirty days
without rest or pause the 4th had romped across Alabama and Georgia, trading punches with Nathan Bedford Forrest's Confederate cavalry. It had been
no Sunday school picnic, and the Wolverines had saddle sores to prove it.

The 4th Michigan belonged to the 2nd Brigade, 2nd Division, Wilson's
Cavalry Corps, Military Division of the Mississippi. Under Colonel Robert
H. G. Minty, the regiment had earned its spurs in eastern Tennessee in 1863–
64. Since those days it had covered a lot of miles and had been on intimate
terms with battle and sudden death. Minty had moved up to command, first
the brigade, then the division. His promotions left the regiment to the paternal
care of Lieutenant Colonel Benjamin Dudley Pritchard.*

Although he claimed Allegan, Michigan, as his home town, Pritchard had
graduated into the 4th from the law school at the University of Michigan.
Starting as a captain, he had risen rapidly. He won two citations and had a
scar from a wound received at Chickamauga. He was thirty years old in 1865.
He had a boyish expression which he tried to disguise with a General Grant-
type beard, but he wasn't entirely successful, because his eyes were soft and
gentle. That was deceptive. There was nothing boyish, soft, or gentle about
Ben Pritchard.

First under Minty, then under Pritchard, the 4th Michigan became a real
iron-pants horse-soldier outfit. There were those willing to make affidavit
that the army had none better.

Officers like Minty and Pritchard had to be hell-for-leather types if they
expected to keep up with their corps commander, Brevet Major General James
H. Wilson. Not long out of West Point, Wilson had served his apprenticeship
under Sheridan up in Virginia. When things there settled down to a war of

attrition between Grant and Lee, Wilson was sent West to raise all the assorted varieties of hell he could. It was an assignment very much to his taste.

Wilson assembled his cavalry corps at Gravelly Springs, in the northwest corner of Alabama. On March 22, 1865, he crossed the Tennessee River and started his columns south, ostensibly to relieve pressure on a Federal expedition against Mobile. Wilson's orders were flexible—he could go pretty much where he pleased as long as he caused the Rebs enough pain and anguish. He turned his enterprise into one of those rip-roaring cavalry raids of the kind at which the Federal horsemen became so proficient in the latter part of the war.

His force consisted of three divisions of two brigades each, and three batteries of artillery, numbering about 13,000 men. It was a hard-bitten veteran force with which he moved into central Alabama, and it made a public nuisance of itself by indulging in a spree of bridge burning, tearing up railroads, and destroying public stores.

Forrest endeavored to stop them but he was slow getting started. His own force was divided and it took him some time to assemble his brigades. As a result, he failed for once to "get thar fustest with the mostest," and he took a smart licking at the hands of the Yankees. Out-generaled and out-fought at every turn, the Confederates lost men by the thousands, most of them taken prisoner. Wilson, on the other hand, lost only ninety-nine killed, five hundred and ninety-eight wounded and twenty-eight missing during the entire month of his raid.

After whipping Forrest near Selma, Wilson took that city and then turned east, threatening Montgomery. When his advance rode into that first capital of the Confederacy, the mayor came forward hat in hand, and surrendered the place without argument. Wilson then pointed toward the state line and picked off Columbus, Georgia. From there it was an easy canter into Macon, which had been bypassed when Sherman marched from Atlanta to the sea.

Its mission accomplished, the 4th Michigan settled down in camp to enjoy the good things of life. Men and horses looked forward to a period of fattening up in that spring-kissed countryside. Pickets could loll in shady groves beside murmuring streams where the magnolias and jessamine blossomed. No bugles would disturb the rest of honest troopers, and only farriers and officers would have work to do. The sutler's tent, close by, was well stocked.

From all accounts, the war was breaking up pretty fast and the men of the 4th assured one another that the prospects of getting home looked better every day. Of course they would get back to Michigan too late for the spring plowing, but they allowed that wouldn't be too grievous a disappointment.

But cavalrymen, like other mortals, weren't able to read the future. Could they have done so, Pritchard's men would have known they had one more job to do—one which would just about close the book on the Civil War.

Six days after the 4th Michigan arrived at Macon, the word drifted down through the Federal chain of command that Jefferson Davis, the president of the Confederacy, was fleeing south, and orders were issued alerting the forces in Tennessee, the Carolinas, and Georgia.

"Capture Jefferson Davis; get him dead or alive!" the Union armies were told.*

As was his custom, Davis was seated in his pew in St. Paul's Church, Richmond, on Sunday morning, April 2. Midway through the service a messenger entered, walked down the aisle, and handed the President a message. Davis read it, then rose, his face strained and gray, and without a word walked out of the church.

The message, from Robert E. Lee, was to the effect that the Richmond defenses were fast crumbling and that the city would have to be evacuated that day. It was a message which spoke the final word of the Confederacy's doom.

The rest of that Sunday was spent in feverish preparation. All day long Lee's veteran corps marched through town on their way west, some said to Lynchburg, while others predicted a move toward Danville and an attempt to make a junction with General Joseph E. Johnston who, with about 30,000 men, was contending Sherman's passage through North Carolina. In government offices, records and archives were packed; the Confederate treasury, or what was left of it, was removed from bank vaults and loaded on ordinary freight cars. Army supplies were distributed to the public; ordnance stores were blown up, burned, or dumped into the James River.

That night about 8 o'clock, accompanied by his cabinet and other government officials, President Davis boarded the train for Danville. There he issued a confident proclamation which promised that Virginia would not be abandoned. Nobody really believed that unless it was Davis himself.

The move to Danville was part of a prearranged evacuation plan, and the word from Lee putting it into operation was not entirely unexpected. A week before, Lee had warned Davis that he might be driven out of his lines at Petersburg, the key to the defense of Richmond. Mrs. Davis and her four young children had quietly departed on March 29, going to Charlotte, North Carolina, to visit friends—the public was told.

After April 2, events moved toward a climax. Fighting what amounted to a rear guard action, Lee retreated toward Appomattox Court House. Inexorably Grant drew a noose of steel and iron around him, and at last, his army all but fallen apart, without supplies and threatened at every turn by vastly superior Federal forces, Lee gave up the good fight and asked for terms. That was on April 9.

With Lee's surrender Danville became untenable. Once more Davis packed up and moved south, going this time to Greensboro, North Carolina, where for the time being he was under Johnston's protection. However, it soon became apparent that he was not safe there either. Johnston was negotiating with Sherman for favorable terms, including amnesty for political leaders. Although Sherman personally was inclined to be lenient, Washington was not, particularly where Davis was concerned. Following Lincoln's assassination feeling ran high, and there was suspicion that Davis was implicated in the plot. Sherman was informed, and through him Johnston, that the capitulation would have to be on the same terms as those which Grant gave Lee. That left no room for Davis, who started for Charlotte on April 18. It was while he was at Lexington, North Carolina, that he received the news from Johnston.

Accompanying Davis was about all that remained of the Confederate government: John C. Breckinridge, Secretary of War; Judah P. Benjamin, Secretary of State; S. R. Mallory, Secretary of the Navy; John H. Reagan, Postmaster General; George Davis, Attorney General; Samuel Cooper, Adjutant General; and several lesser functionaries. This party was now traveling by wagon train, hauling over the mountain roads personal and official records and the treasury. The escort consisted of four cavalry brigades numbering between three and four thousand men.

Davis hoped to join Generals Richard Taylor and Forrest, who were still operating in Alabama, or, if that was not practical, to move across the Mississippi River into Texas, where there was a Confederate force. There was some vague talk of the possibility of escaping to Mexico and forming an alliance with Maximilian against the United States. Mrs. Davis and the children, who had left Charlotte and moved on to Chester, South Carolina, were supposed to go to Jacksonville or some other Florida port and escape to the West Indies and then to Europe.

Leaving Charlotte, Davis' train and escort pushed on to Abbeville, South Carolina. There Davis called what is said to have been the Confederacy's last council of war, summoning the commanding officers of the brigades which were accompanying him. He asked their opinion as to the course he should follow and what his destination should be. A bitter-ender, Davis clung to the delusion that the South still could be aroused to resistance, and he told his officers that the troops of his escort "are enough for a nucleus around which the whole people will rally when the panic which now affects them has passed away."

His officers were astounded. They did not share his hopes or his opinions, and they told him so. Davis was shocked by their frankness, and in despair admitted that all was indeed lost. Nevertheless he was still resolved to get to Texas instead of attempting to flee the country. The cavalry escort remained with him for the time being.

Meanwhile the Federal dragnet was closing in on Davis and his party. On April 27 General Halleck who was then in Richmond, was tipped off by Union intelligence that Davis had fled south from Danville, taking between six and thirteen million in specie. Halleck notified the War Department, which in turn alerted the departmental commanders.

The first Federal force to move in on Davis' trail was that of General George Stoneman, Jr., commanding the cavalry corps of the District of East Tennessee. He was another graduate of the Sheridan school of slam-bang tactics. His troops were strung out along the western slopes of the Great Smokies, but under his field commander, General William J. Palmer, three brigades moved into South Carolina and put out feelers for the fleeing Confederates.

Palmer picked up Davis' track on April 28, learning the make-up of his party and the direction in which it was moving, but his men were spread out over too much territory for him to be able to close in. Any force he could hurriedly assemble would be outnumbered by the Confederate cavalry escort, small groups of which could effectively hold bridges and ferries while the main body moved swiftly ahead. Those were exactly the tactics which the rebels employed. Palmer could do no more than march along on a course parallel to that of Davis, maintaining contact and waiting for an opportunity to move in and strike. He hoped to concentrate enough strength at Anderson, thirty miles northwest of Abbeville, strongly picket the Savannah River crossings, and prevent Davis from entering Georgia.

In this he was not successful. Davis was moving about forty-eight hours ahead of Palmer, who had to be satisfied with rear guard contacts. There was some light skirmishing at river crossings, but their chief effect was to delay Palmer while Davis pressed on. However, these small affairs gave Palmer one advantage. He was able to snare a few prisoners from whom he could obtain information. From the captives and from intensive questioning of civilians, Palmer knew all about Davis' strength, his routes, and the fact that he had about $10,000,000 in treasury funds.

From this intelligence, Palmer deduced that after leaving Abbeville Davis would attempt to cross the Savannah at Petersburg, Georgia, where there was a pontoon bridge, and head for Athens, about fifty miles to the southwest. Once there, he could fairly easily slip away to points west.

Accordingly, Palmer speeded up his own column. Striking south from Anderson, he crossed the Savannah River and entered Athens himself on May 4. From there he fanned out his patrols to the east in a wide arc. Thus, while he was groping for contact with Davis and his main escort, he had effectively cut off escape routes to the west and forced the fugitives to take the only road left open to them which was directly south, or southeast.

Meanwhile Davis and his friends had crossed the Savannah and instead of turning to their right toward Athens, they bore left and entered the town of Washington May 3. There they rested overnight and used the time to take care of some necessary business.

His group was breaking up. Soon after crossing into Georgia, Breckinridge and Judah Benjamin slipped away. Eventually they reached the seacoast and escaped from the country. It was obvious to Davis, now that Palmer had raised the alarm, that a change in his plans was necessary. His only way to avoid capture lay in moving south as swiftly as possible, hoping to find an opening through which he could cut across southern Georgia. The alternative was to get to the coast somewhere in Florida and improvise from that point. As a matter of fact, once Palmer had succeeded in straddling his path to the West, all of Davis' subsequent movements were improvisations.

During the pause at Washington, however, the picture was not yet entirely clear to Davis. Just how Palmer's blockade was set up wasn't apparent. He still believed himself to be ahead of Palmer—as indeed he was. That explains the one-night lay-over in Washington. The wagons carrying what was left of the treasure were brought up—some five million in bonds and Confederate currency and almost two hundred thousand in coin, had fallen into the hands of one of Palmer's patrols a day or two before. The cavalry escort was paid off, officers and men each receiving $32 on account without distinction of rank, and what remained, except for what was held out for Davis' personal traveling expenses, was deposited in a local bank.

Davis left Washington on May 4, the same day Palmer reached Athens. Mrs. Davis, with the children and a small escort, traveling in wagons and ambulances, had pushed straight south, leaving Washington the day before her husband arrived there. The President's party had been whittled down to a troop of twenty hand-picked men under Captain Given Campbell of Kentucky. Of his cabinet, only Postmaster General Reagan remained with him. There were a few aides and servants, bringing the total of the group to about thirty.

Some members of the escort which was disbanded at Washington were of the opinion that Davis was no longer really trying to escape. Brigadier General Basil W. Duke, who led one of the cavalry brigades, said he believed the President quitted the main body of troops in order that they might have an opportunity to surrender while it was still possible to get favorable terms.

"He and his party were admirably mounted, and could easily have out-ridden the pursuit of any party they were not strong enough to fight," said Duke. "Therefore, when he deliberately procrastinated as he did, when the fact of his presence in that vicinity was so public, and in the face of the effort that would certainly be made by the Federal forces to secure his person, I can only believe that he had resolved not to escape."

This judgment was colored by Duke's loyalty to his chief. Nevertheless, Davis did leave Washington and go toward Atlanta by train. At Union Point, he learned that Palmer's men were at Madison, the next station west. It was then that Davis finally abandoned the railroad and turned south, joining Mrs. Davis near Milledgeville. It was then too that Davis moved out of Stoneman's area and entered the sector for which Wilson was responsible.

Wilson had been thoroughly briefed by Stoneman and he also possessed information picked up by his own command. Somewhere between the Savannah River and Washington, a patrol of the 1st Ohio Cavalry, attached to Wilson's 4th Division, actually managed to mingle with Davis' escort and rode along with it for several miles looking for an opportunity to kidnap the Confederate leader. From other good and reliable intelligence Wilson concluded that Davis would move in a southeasterly direction—the only route, really, which remained open to him.

Knowing approximately where Davis was and where he was going was one thing. Tracking him down and capturing him was something else. Like Stoneman, Wilson was handicapped by having his divisions and brigades dispersed over a large area. He was responsible for maintaining a line which extended from northwest of Atlanta to the Gulf coast below Tallahassee, Florida, a distance of almost 350 miles. As a result, his men were spread thin, and a quick concentration of a force sufficiently large to permit him to fine-comb the mid-Georgia country was out of the question. So it became a game of hide-and-seek between Davis and such relatively small forces as Wilson could handily muster.

Wilson, however, possessed an advantage of which he made the most. Two rivers slanted across central Georgia, running almost parallel in a generally southeasterly direction. One was the Oconee, the other the Ocmulgee. If Davis was heading for the Florida coast, as Wilson surmised he would do, he would have to cross those streams. If the fords and ferries could be picketed in time, particularly along the Ocmulgee, which was below the Oconee, there was a good possibility that Davis would be picked up.

Accordingly, Wilson proceeded to lay his trap. He instructed the chief of his 1st Division, General John T. Croxton, to send a battalion off toward the city of Savannah. The most likely route for Davis after he left Union Point was almost due south to Dublin, which lay on the Oconee, fifty road miles east and a bit south of Macon. To head him off at that point if possible, Croxton sent one of his best officers, Lieutenant Colonel Henry Harnden, and a detachment of one hundred and fifty men of the 1st Wisconsin Cavalry to Dublin. In the event Davis was not there, Harnden was ordered to continue on down the river, all the way to Savannah if necessary, leaving pickets behind to cover the main crossings. Harnden's orders were elastic enough to permit him to use his own discretion whenever conditions, in his estimation, warranted a change of plan.

Harnden began his march on May 6, and reached Dublin at 5 o'clock the next afternoon. Having covered more than fifty miles, his men and horses were exhausted, so he made camp for the night. Scouts were sent out to pick up what information they could. They got very little. The white people refused to talk, a fact which made Harnden suspicious. The Negroes, apparently under orders from the whites to say nothing, were also reluctant to tell the cavalrymen what they knew. But they were obviously excited about something, which increased Harnden's belief that Davis' whereabouts were known to the inhabitants of the area.

During the night a Negro slipped into the Wisconsin camp and informed Harnden that during the day a train of eight wagons had crossed the river and passed through Dublin. There were quality folks in the party, said the informant, and he had heard a lady addressed as Mrs. Davis, and a man as Mr. Davis. Under Harnden's questioning, it developed there were really two parties, Mrs. Davis and the President traveling separately. The latter had bypassed the town and joined his wife a short distance below it.

Now Harnden realized he was very close to his quarry. But in a sense his difficulties only increased. The country was sparsely settled and covered by piney woods. Roads were little better than deer tracks through the forest, and the whole district was laced by small streams which, if they flowed at all, moved so sluggishly as to form an almost continuous chain of swamps. It was an ideal place in which to elude pursuit, and a hard one in which to find a fugitive.

At dawn's light on May 8, Harnden rolled his men out and rode seven miles southeast of Dublin where he again was told that Davis had passed that way. A little later, the information was wrung out of a reluctant citizen that a wagon train was parked eleven miles farther on. The citizen guided them to the place; sure enough, it had been a campsite, but it was now deserted.

Harnden had trouble keeping to the trail; no sooner would he pick it up than he would lose it. He kept falling farther and farther behind Davis. On the 8th, he covered forty miles without catching sight of the fugitives. Once more he was forced to make camp and give his weary riders an opportunity to catch a few hours' sleep.

The next morning, May 9, he was up early and soon again picked up the trail, learning that Davis was on his way to Abbeville on the Ocmulgee River. Harnden crossed into the "town," which consisted only of three shabby houses and a scattering of other buildings. By questioning the inhabitants he learned that Davis was on the road to Irwinville, another spot which can be found only by a careful scrutiny of the map. Harnden sent his men ahead; he himself turned back to make contact with some Union troops which he heard were coming up behind him.

In the meanwhile, having sent the 1st Wisconsin out to cover the Oconee River, Wilson issued some additional orders. Minty was assigned to patrol the Ocmulgee, with instructions to use his best men for the task. Naturally he picked his own old outfit, the 4th Michigan. Minty relayed to Colonel Pritchard the instructions he had received from Wilson: "Move down the Ocmulgee river and take possession of all its ferries below Hawkinsville, picket the river as far as the strength of the regiment will permit, and scout through the country on both sides of the river, for the purpose of capturing Jeff. Davis and party and any other government parties who might be fleeing in that direction." Like Harnden, Pritchard was told to use his own judgment if he thought it advisable to leave his sector.

Pritchard received his orders in the afternoon of May 7, the day after Harnden had moved out. The camp of the 4th Michigan suddenly changed from a scene of tranquillity to one of orderly activity. Equipment was checked, light rations were issued, and horses were saddled. At 8 p.m., with the dusk closing in, the bugles rang out "Boots and Saddles" and, grumbling at having to leave the comforts of Macon, the 4th rode out on the Hawkinsville road in a column of twos. Pritchard at the head, was followed by twenty officers and 419 men, all rested and well mounted. Pritchard had told no one where they were going or what their mission was. But there was plenty of speculation in the ranks, and the men guessed correctly what was in the wind.

Pritchard walked his regiment through the woods all night, halting at 8 a.m.

on May 8 after having covered thirty-six miles. He rested five hours, then marched another fifteen miles, halting again three miles below Hawkinsville. By that time he had been on the road well over twenty-four hours and had gone fifty-one miles. Supplies were supposed to have caught up with him at Hawkinsville, but they didn't appear. The 4th pulled its belt a couple of notches tighter and prepared to go hungry for the next forty-eight hours. It wasn't the first time the Michigan horsemen had missed a meal.

Early on May 9, with the mists rising wraith-like from the swamps, Pritchard saddled up again and moved down the river toward Abbeville. It was the 4th Michigan that Harnden had heard was behind him and that he had ridden back to meet.

Before Pritchard and Harnden met, however, the 4th entered Abbeville, advancing fairly close on the heels of the 1st Wisconsin, which had a full day's head start. At Abbeville, the Michiganders picked up the same information as Harnden had obtained the day before.

"I learned," said Pritchard, "that a train of twelve wagons and two ambulances had crossed the Ocmulgee river at Brown's ferry, $1\frac{1}{2}$ miles above Abbyville [sic], about 12 o'clock on the previous night; had stopped at Abbyville long enough to feed their animals, and moved on again before daylight in the direction of Irwinville."

Harnden rode into Abbeville in the late afternoon, and he and Pritchard compared notes. Apparently each officer was careful not to tell the other all that he knew or guessed. Both were on a hot trail; each was hoping to claim for himself the glory of catching the prize. The Wisconsin colonel did admit that his men were on their way to Irwinville, but he tried to make Pritchard believe they were farther ahead than was actually the case. Pritchard, on the other hand, allowed Harnden to think the 4th Michigan would spend the night in Abbeville, although this was not actually his intention. Harnden's command had been whittled down to seventy men as the result of picketing the river. Pritchard offered to loan him a company or two. Harnden declined with thanks. The two officers then parted; Harnden rode back toward Irwinville; Pritchard led his regiment along the river two or three miles below Abbeville.

There Pritchard came upon a Negro attempting to repair a wagon. From him he learned that during the previous night a body of mounted men had crossed the Ocmulgee, paying the ferryman with gold coin. The Negro pointed out to Pritchard a way to get to Irwinville by following the river ten or twelve miles and then cutting across country to the southwest. Pritchard verified these instructions with residents of the neighborhood and decided to follow them. He assumed that Harnden would reach Irwinville well ahead of him, and might drive Davis to the east, right into his arms.

So, about 4 p.m., the Michigan column started out, riding twelve miles downriver to a place known as Wilcox's Mills. There was an hour's rest; then the march was resumed. But Pritchard had left most of his command bivouacked at Wilcox's Mills and taken with him only one hundred twenty-eight men and seven officers. He felt it necessary now to advance as fast as possible. He dared not risk being impeded by the confusion which a large body of men and horses might create in unfamiliar territory in the dark.

It was eighteen miles from Wilcox's Mills to Irwinville, through a "desolate pine forest," as the 4th's adjutant, Lieutenant Julian G. Dickinson,* noted. The trail was faint, the country was uninhabited. Nevertheless, Pritchard pushed his column hard and, about 1 a.m. of May 10, the detachment entered Irwinville. There were no signs of Harnden, which puzzled Pritchard. After all, the Wisconsin troopers had a head start of many miles on the 4th.

Although it was a county seat Irwinville consisted of only a half-dozen slab-sided buildings. Dickinson called it "a sort of four corners in the wilderness." Pritchard routed the inhabitants out of bed and tried to get information from them. They were suspiciously reticent. Finally a Negro told Pritchard that a body of men had been in the settlement earlier that night buying food and forage. They were camped, he said, about a mile and a half north of town on the Abbeville road.

Pritchard sensed that the gray fox had been run to earth, and he moved in quickly for the capture or the kill. With the Negro informant for a guide, the column moved up the road. About half a mile from where he expected to find Davis' camp, Pritchard called a halt. Second Lieutenant Alfred B. Purinton, of Company I, was told to take twenty-five men, dismounted, swing through the woods to the left, and circle around to the north side of the camp. He was to block the road and prevent escape in that direction. He was cautioned to be as quiet as possible, but if he was discovered Pritchard would attack at once and come to his help. If after a reasonable time no alarm had sounded, it would be assumed that Purinton had gained his position. He was to remain posted there until he heard Pritchard move in on the camp; then he was to close in from the opposite direction.

"I had not decided at this time whether to move upon the camp at once or to wait until daylight," Pritchard said later, "but upon further consideration, decided to delay it, as it was now after 2 o'clock in the morning, the moon was getting low, and the deep shadows of the forest were falling heavily, rendering it easy for persons to escape undiscovered to the woods and swamps in the darkness."

Pritchard waited an hour longer. Between 3:30 and 4 a.m. the first dawn was faintly coloring the sky. Now if ever was the time. Quietly the men swung into their saddles; with the stealth of night animals creeping upon their prey, the 4th formed into column and advanced. Gradually it was possible to make out through the gloom the outlines of the camp three or four rods up the road—the cluster of tents, the park of wagons. Pritchard rose in his stirrups and swung his arm in the signal to advance. The troopers kicked their steeds into a gallop and the column charged down upon the sleeping, unsuspecting, and unguarded camp. So suddenly was it done, so complete was the surprise, that not a gun was raised in resistance; not a person escaped. A chain of mounted guards was thrown out, and dismounted sentries were posted by the tents and wagons.

Now it was Pritchard's turn to be surprised. Before he had had an opportunity to examine his prize, a spatter of firing broke out from the direction where Purinton was posted. Leaving Dickinson in charge of the camp guard, Pritchard gathered up the rest of his men and charged off to see what was causing all the commotion.

He found a brisk little battle going on, and it was getting hotter. What had happened was that in the dawn shadows Purinton had become tangled up with the 1st Wisconsin. Afraid of missing Davis in the dark, Harnden had bivouacked for the night about two miles north of the Confederate camp. About 3 a.m. he had renewed his pursuit and, unaware that the Michiganders had arrived first, he assumed he had caught up with Davis' escort. It was a case of mistaken identity and trigger-happy men of each Union regiment went into action on the premise that it was safer to shoot first and ask questions afterward.

Pritchard arrived on the scene, formed a line of dismounted skirmishers, and began to push forward. Suddenly he realized the error. The gunfire didn't have the familiar sound of Confederate musketry. It was too rapid, too well spaced. It could come only from Spencer repeating carbines such as the Union cavalry carried. Pritchard ordered a cease-fire and called out asking who was in front of him. "1st Wisconsin," came the reply. Unfortunately the mistake was not discovered until two Michigan troopers had been killed and one Michigander and three Badgers had been severely wounded.

While this fight was going on Dickinson took the opportunity to take inventory.

"On the right of the road," he described the camp, "in line facing the clearing or parade, stood three wall tents; beyond the clearing there was what appeared to me to be a swampy thicket. On our left in the woods, at some distance from the road, was a miscellaneous collection of tents and ambulances."

None of the Confederate party was in sight except one man, partially dressed. Everyone else was in his tent. Dickinson tried to question the man, but he appeared too bewildered to give a coherent reply. Some of the troopers of the 4th were nosing around the wagons, seeing what there was in the way of loot.

Suddenly Trooper Andrew (or Andreas) Bee, a Company L cook who had been posted as a sentry, called Dickinson's attention to three persons, their arms linked, walking rapidly across the clearing, away from the tents and toward the thicket.

"Adjutant," Bee shouted in his thick Norwegian accent, "there goes a man dressed in women's clothes!"

The disguise was quite apparent. A pair of cavalry boots, not customarily an item of female garb, was the give-away. Dickinson rode toward the group and ordered them to halt. When his command was ignored, he motioned Corporal George M. Munger of Company C, Corporal William H. Crittenden of E, and Troopers James F. Bullard of C and Daniel H. Edwards of L to intercept them. The four men barred their path and leveled their carbines. Dickinson called to them not to shoot. The adjutant then investigated and identified the three as Mrs. Davis, her colored maid, and the President.

Mrs. Davis put her arms around her husband and warned the soldiers to be careful or they would "make Mr. Davis very angry and he might harm someone."

That was identification enough for Dickinson. He knew the search was ended.

"Davis had on for disguise a black shawl drawn closely around his head and shoulders, through the folds of which I could see his gray hair," Dickinson reported. "He wore on his person a woman's long black dress, which completely concealed his figure, excepting his spurred boot heels. The dress was undoubtedly Mrs. Davis' traveling dress which she afterwards wore on her return march to Macon. At the time of the capture, she was attired in her morning gown, and a black shawl covered her head and stately form." *

The apprehension of Davis threw the camp into an uproar. The children were crying, and several officers came out of their tents but made no effort to resist or escape. Dickinson ordered everyone back in the tents and set a three-man guard over Davis.

About this time Pritchard returned. He asked Davis how he should call him. He could call him what or whoever he pleased, Davis replied curtly.

Pritchard said he would call him Davis, and after a moment's hesitation the President admitted that was his name. He then asked if Pritchard was in command, and the officer replied that he was.

"I suppose," said Davis bitterly, referring to the looting of the wagons, "that you consider it bravery to charge a train of defenseless women and children, but it is theft; it is vandalism."

Diplomatically, Pritchard ignored that outburst.

In another part of the camp, one of the troopers found Davis' horse and appropriated it.

"Mr. Davis," he remarked, "you won't need this horse any more. Hadn't you better give him to me?"

One of the Confederate officers spoke up angrily. "How dare you insult the President in this manner?" he demanded.

"President, hell," growled the trooper. "What's he president of?"

Mrs. Davis asked Dickinson what would be done with her husband, and whether the family would be permitted to accompany him. That, replied the adjutant, was up to his commanding officer and higher authorities. Mrs. Davis requested certain personal things in one of the wagons and Dickinson promised to have them brought. Others, however, had been there first. An officer rode up "with something from the wagon, in the shape of a canteen of most excellent fluid, of which he freely offered me a share," Dickinson recalled.

Pritchard proceeded to count heads and find out exactly what had been caught in his net. Besides President and Mrs. Davis and their four children, there were Mrs. Davis' brother and sister, Midshipman J. D. Howell of the Confederate navy, and Miss Maggie Howell. In addition to the family, the captives included Postmaster General Reagan; Colonel Burton Harrison, Davis' private secretary; Colonel William Preston Johnston and Colonel F. R. Lubbock, aides; Major V. R. Maurand, Richmond Light Artillery; Captain George V. Moody, Mollinson's Light Battery; Lieutenant Hathaway, 14th Kentucky; thirteen privates; two maids, one white, the other colored, and five other Negro servants and drivers. The party had about fifteen horses, twenty-five to thirty mules, three ambulances and several wagons containing personal baggage and commissary stores.

Some gold and silver coin disappeared. Pritchard said it was taken by one of his men, a Tennessean, but he was searched and nothing was found on him. Later he was reported to have been flush and to have distributed several gold pieces among his officers and comrades.

That about wrapped it up. Pritchard allowed the prisoners an hour's time to prepare breakfast. Then, placing Davis, the women, and the children in two ambulances, Pritchard mounted the other captives on their own horses. He reserved the other ambulance for his wounded and one of the wagons for his dead.

Closely guarding the Davis party, the 4th Michigan and the 1st Wisconsin turned back toward Abbeville, where camp was made the night of May 10.

In the morning Pritchard gathered up the rest of his regiment, which he had left at Wilcox's Mills and the column took the road back to Macon.*

With Jefferson Davis safe in the custody of Michigan, the war was indeed ended!

XXI

The Last Man

AT LAST the bloody work was done!

One by one, in Virginia, in Tennessee, in North Carolina and in Georgia, the Michigan regiments furled their banners and boarded the trains for home.

Most of the soldiers—they were veterans now—went through Detroit, where they were mustered out and paid off. This formality concluded, they drifted away by twos and by squads for a last drink together in one of the saloons on Woodbridge or Franklin Streets. They had their pictures taken and exchanged copies with their mates. They promised to write, to keep in touch. Then they went their separate ways. Most of them left by railroad, and when they reached the end of the line they went on by stage or by shank's mare, with maybe a lift from a farmer driving his wagon in the right direction.

Then they were home.

Some didn't stay home. The wandering fever was in the bones of many, and they went off to far places in the West, where one hundred and sixty acres of prairie land awaited the veteran who would homestead and break the sod. Some went farther west—to California or Oregon, or down into the Arizona or New Mexico Territories. Others who had known nothing but soldiering in their entire adult lives went back to the army, where they felt more at home than on the farms or in the cities.

But most of them tried to pick up where they had left off. The passing months found them in the fields, in the lumber camps and mines, in the law offices and banks and school rooms. In time they established their Grand Army of the Republic posts; they saw to it that they got pensions, and they became the backbone of the Republican Party, which ruled Michigan with only an occasional interruption for the next eight decades.

Year followed year, and the blue contingents in the Memorial Day parades became smaller. Those who insisted upon marching did so with steps that became slower and more faltering. Each Memorial Day there were more graves in the village cemeteries upon which to drop the flowers.

Then there were new wars, and remembrance of Shiloh and Antietam and

Gettysburg grew dim, and the talk was of strange-sounding places like Santiago, Chateau Thierry, Guadalcanal, and Bastogne.

Only a few old men were left who remembered, and their memories were confused and clouded. Of all who so bravely marched away under the banners of Michigan, only four were left at the end of 1945.

At the close of 1946, there was only one!

He was Orlando LeValley.*

LeValley was born September 19, 1848, on a pioneer farm in Lapeer County, Michigan. He wasn't quite thirteen years old when the war started but he was determined to be a soldier. He applied at the recruiting office but was turned away.

"Go home and grow up a little, Bub," they told him. "Then come back. The war will wait for you."

It did wait, and on October 3, 1864, when he was a few days past sixteen, Orlando LeValley was mustered in for one year as a substitute for a certain Perry Kroll, who had been drafted from Thetford in neighboring Genesee County. At last Orlando was a soldier, and he had a substitute's bounty to boot. He was assigned to Company E, 23rd Michigan Infantry, and joined the, regiment at Johnsonville, Tennessee, November 11, 1864. He was just in time to get a baptism of fire in the battles of Franklin and Nashville. In June 1865 he was transferred to Company F, 28th Michigan Infantry, and was discharged at Raleigh, North Carolina, October 14, 1865.

LeValley went home and with his bounty money he bought an eighty-acre farm near Caro in Tuscola County. In due time he married and sired six children.

The years slipped by. It was 1948, and April. A very old man felt the warm winds awaken the fields and bring the buds back to the apple trees. And he recalled another April when the land awoke from its winter's sleep to the rattle of drums and the tramp of a marching host. But that was so long ago, and now there was little reason to make the effort to remember. He was ninety-nine years old, and somewhere in the distance, faintly, he heard the roll being called.

As a good soldier, he answered to his name.

"He was tired and lonesome," they said of him.

In the Michigan state capitol the clerk responsible for such details reported to Governor Kim Sigler that on April 19, 1948, Orlando LeValley had died, and, in accordance with the statutes, the records of the Michigan Department of the Grand Army of the Republic were officially closed.

They paid him much honor.

All the business places in Caro, the county seat, closed for the funeral on April 20. The Governor and other high dignitaries came to pay their respects. A military escort accompanied LeValley to the Fairgrove Cemetery. Taps were blown, and a firing squad split the air with its farewell volleys.

But they stirred only faint echoes of the roar of Sumter's guns which had shattered the peace of the Michigan countryside on another April day, eighty-seven years before.

APPENDIX

Chapter I

"The Eastern Papers," said the *Detroit Free Press* of June 25, 1867, "announce the death in Brooklyn of COL. NORMAN J. HALL, late colonel of the gallant Seventh Regiment of Michigan Volunteers, whose record as a soldier is one of the proudest among those our state delights to honor."

Norman J. Hall was born in New York in 1836 and spent his early years in Monroe, Michigan. He was appointed to West Point in 1854, graduated with the class of 1859, and was assigned to the famous 4th U.S. Artillery as a brevet second lieutenant. In 1860 he was with the 1st U.S. Artillery as second lieutenant, and it was with that rank and as a member of that regiment that he was assigned to the Fort Sumter garrison.

After the surrender of Sumter, Hall was promoted to first lieutenant, 5th U.S. Artillery, with which he served in various areas in the early stages of the war. For a while he was on General McClellan's staff. Michigan sought competent officers for its new regiments, and on July 7, 1862, Hall was requisitioned and given command of the 7th Michigan Infantry with the rank of colonel of volunteers. He led the regiment with distinction at Antietam and Gettysburg, but gained his greatest renown for his conduct at Fredericksburg on December 13, 1862.

General Burnside's efforts to cross the Rappahannock at Fredericksburg were thwarted by Confederate sharpshooters posted in the town, who prevented Union engineers from laying pontoon bridges. It became necessary to cross a force over in boats to dislodge the snipers, an extremely hazardous undertaking. Hall, temporarily in command of a brigade consisting of the 7th Michigan and the 19th and 20th Massachusetts, volunteered to carry out the assignment, and succeeded in doing so under heavy fire. The incident was celebrated in the following ballad which became popular in Massachusetts:

> 'Where go they?' 'Across the river!'
> 'Who are they?—I'll know to a man!
> Our own Nineteenth and Twentieth,
> And the Seventh Michigan.'
>
> Twixt death in the air above them
> And death in the waves below,
> Through balls, and shells and shrapnel,
> They moved—my God how slow!
>
> Cheer after cheer we sent them,
> As only armies can—

> Cheers for old Massachusetts,
> Cheers for young Michigan.

At Antietam, the 7th counted losses of seventy per cent, and at one stage of the battle Hall rallied his men by carrying the regimental colors himself. At Gettysburg on the third day Hall displayed impressive initiative when, without waiting for orders, he moved his regiment to the assistance of the troops that were crumbling under the weight of Pickett's charge. His movement was credited with having helped check the enemy at the so-called "highwater mark."

Soon after Gettysburg, Hall was assigned to Boston as provost marshal general for New England. His valor earned him several promotions and he ended the war as lieutenant colonel in the regular army. He died May 26, 1867, at the age of thirty-one.

[Reference: Details of Hall's service may be found in *Record of Service of Michigan Volunteers* (Kalamazoo, 1915), VII, 48; also in Charles Lanman, *Red Book of Michigan* (Detroit, 1871), p. 149; and Roy Meredith, *Storm Over Sumter* (New York, 1957). There is an account of Hall's crossing the Rappahannock at Fredericksburg in *Battles and Leaders of the Civil War* (New York, 1887), III, 121.]

LAFAYETTE C. BAKER is the subject of brief sketches in Margaret Leech, *Reveille in Washington* (New York, 1941), p. 430; and John Robertson, *Michigan in the War* (Lansing, 1882), p. 155.

A shoemaker by trade, CHRISTIAN RATH was born in Württemberg, Germany, on October 22, 1831. A political refugee, he came to the United States in 1849, enlisted in the United States Navy for two years, and at the expiration of his service established himself in Jackson, Michigan. In 1853 he married Eveline Henry of that city. He joined the army June 17, 1862, as a second lieutenant, 17th Michigan Infantry. He was wounded at Antietam. He became first lieutenant in 1862 and captain in 1863. On May 12, 1864, he was taken prisoner at Spotsylvania but escaped the same day. On July 8, 1865, he was made brevet major and lieutenant colonel "for special and efficient service during the confinement, trial and execution of conspirators." He was discharged July 19, 1865, and returned to Jackson where he continued to live until his death, February 14, 1920. [Reference: *Detroit News*, Feb. 15, 1920.]

THE MICHIGAN CAVALRY BRIGADE'S Western service had all the trimmings of a Wild West thriller. Its units operated in Dakota, Wyoming and Montana Territories, and they were active along the Powder River, in the

Black Hills, and at Virginia City. In 1866 one detachment of the 6th Michigan rebuilt Fort Connor and renamed it Fort Reno. It became a major post in what is now Wyoming. Units of the brigade, particularly the 1st Cavalry, had several encounters with the Sioux and Arapahoes, and lost several officers and men. The fact that it was retained in service long after most of the Union Army had been disbanded caused considerable dissatisfaction among the men, and their treatment was the subject of a bitter controversy between the State of Michigan and the War Department. [For an account of this episode see Robertson, *op. cit.*, pp. 611–613.]

THE CONGRESSIONAL MEDAL OF HONOR was awarded to members of twenty-four different Michigan regiments, the largest number, eight, going to the 17th Infantry. Two Michigan men won the medal twice. They were Lieutenant Colonel Frank D. Baldwin, of Constantine, 19th Infantry, and Major Thomas W. Custer, of Monroe, 6th Cavalry. Major Custer was the brother of General George A. Custer, and was a member of the general's command which was wiped out at the Little Big Horn, June 25, 1876. [For Medal of Honor citations see *American Decorations* (U.S. Government publication), Washington, 1927.]

THE NUMBER OF MICHIGAN REGIMENTS fielded during the war may seem small in comparison to that of other states like New York, Pennsylvania, Ohio, and Illinois, whose regimental designations ran over one hundred. But those other states, when their regiments were depleted by casualties or expiration of enlistments, permitted them to lapse and raised new ones with new designations to replace them. Michigan, however, kept its regiments intact, filling their vacancies with replacements instead of assigning recruits and drafted men to brand-new units. This policy is said to have saved the state millions of dollars and increased the effectiveness of the soldiers by giving recruits the advantage of serving alongside veterans. [Reference: Vivian Thomas Messner, *The Public Life of Austin Blair* (typescript), Burton Historical Collection, Detroit Public Library, pp. 13–14.]

Not all Michigan men volunteered. Some were drafted. The exact number of men conscripted in Michigan through the various draft calls cannot be easily ascertained. The best figures available, those of the adjutant general of Michigan, indicate that after deducting those paying commutation, providing substitutes, or being rejected for physical reasons, and those who simply failed to report, there were 4,281 men actually inducted by conscription. That relatively small number is explained by the fact that voluntary enlistments were allowed as credits against the states' draft quotas, and Michigan's response to the numerous calls for volunteers was sufficiently great that the state's draft quotas were materially reduced. [Reference: Robertson, *op. cit.*, pp. 66–67.]

Oddly, only 145 Indians served in Michigan units even though during the war period the state had a relatively large Indian population. Early in the war a proposal to recruit Indians was, as a newspaper reported, "fortunately nipped in the bud" by the legislature. "Every man knows the system of warfare adopted by these demi-savages, and the civilized people of the northern states will hardly consent this year to become responsible for the performance of any such allies." [*Detroit Free Press*, May 14, 1861.] Wisconsin, on the other hand, enlisted many Indians, who were successfully used as sharpshooters and scouts.

Chapter II

Many of the SLAVES WHO REACHED CANADA were given small farms. These were provided by philanthropic and abolition societies in the United States and Canada. One such organization was the Elgin Association for the Improvement of the Coloured People, at the head of which was the Reverend William King. The Elgin Association helped to establish a colony in Raleigh Township, west of Chatham, Ontario. Other Negro colonies were set up in other parts of Ontario, including the area east of Windsor and Amherstburg. Descendants of those Negro settlers are still numerous in that part of Canada. [Reference: Fred Hamil, *The Valley of the Lower Thames* (Toronto, 1951).]

UNDERGROUND RAILWAY SIGNALS of which examples are quoted, were described by William Lambert in the *Detroit Post*, May 15, 1870.

THE "CENTRAL MICHIGAN" line was under the general supervision of Erastus Hussey. The Adrian Division was in charge of Mrs. Laura Smith Haviland. Hussey, a Quaker, was born in Cayuga County, New York, December 5, 1800. He settled at Plymouth, Michigan, in 1824 and moved to Battle Creek in 1833 where he became a successful merchant. It was about then that he began his work for the Underground Railway, and he estimated that he personally assisted 2,000 slaves to escape. At one time, he recalled, there were forty fugitive Negroes hiding on his premises. Hussey was a presidential elector for the Abolition ticket in 1844; he published a Free Soil paper, and helped organize the Free-Soil Party in 1848. In 1854, he was one of those who issued the call for the meeting "under the oaks" at Jackson where the

Republican Party was organized. He served as clerk of Calhoun County, was elected to the Michigan House of Representatives and then to the Senate. As a legislator, he introduced laws to help slaves and to nullify enforcement of the Federal Fugitive Slave Law. In 1860 Hussey was a delegate to the Republican national convention at Chicago at which Lincoln was nominated. He died at Battle Creek, January 21, 1889. [Reference: *Michigan Pioneer and Historical Collections*, Vol. XXXVIII.]

SEYMOUR FINNEY was born at New Windsor, New York, August 28, 1813. He learned the tailor's trade at Geneva, New York. In 1834 he moved to Wayne County, Michigan, and in 1850 purchased the Finney House and the barn at Griswold and State. It is said that slaves were sometimes hidden in the barn while their pursuing masters were guests of the hotel. Finney was an active abolitionist, free-soiler, and Republican. He served as alderman in Detroit for fourteen years. He died at Detroit, May 26, 1899. [Reference: George B. Catlin, *The Story of Detroit* (Detroit, 1926), p. 325. See also Biographical Index, Burton Historical Collection.]

THE PERSONAL LIBERTY LAW was introduced as a bill in the Michigan Senate in 1855 by Erastus Hussey, and was designed as Michigan's answer to the Federal Fugitive Slave Law of 1850. [For details of this law see *Laws of Michigan*, 1885, p. 412.]

THE ESTIMATE OF 40,000 TO 50,000 SLAVES being helped by the Underground Railway in Michigan was made by William Lambert. The figure is almost certainly too high. Estimates of the national figure rarely exceed 100,000. It is said that the first slave to ride the Michigan Underground came through about 1829, which marks the beginning of operations. The last was helped in April 1862, according to recollections of Detroit operators. [Reference: *Detroit Advertiser and Tribune*, Jan. 17, 1886.]

THE CROSSWHITE CASE is the subject of an article in *Michigan Pioneer and Historical Collections*, Vol. XXXVIII.

JUDGE ROSS WILKINS was one of Michigan's most distinguished jurists. Born at Pittsburgh, February 19, 1799, he was educated at Dickinson College and began to practice law in Pittsburgh. He was prosecuting attorney there when he was twenty-one years old. He was a personal friend of Andrew Jackson, who appointed him territorial judge for Michigan in 1832. He was active in the constitutional conventions of 1835 and 1836 which prepared the way for Michigan statehood. He was a member of the Board of Regents of the University of Michigan, and Recorder for the City of Detroit. In 1837, he was appointed United States District Judge for Michigan, a post which he held until his resignation in 1870. He died in Detroit May 17, 1872. [Reference: Biographical Index, Burton Historical Collection.]

CALVIN TOWNSHIP, Cass County, has had an almost all-Negro population since ante-bellum days. It was settled as a philanthropic enterprise with funds for farms for Negroes; the funds were originally provided in the will of a wealthy Southerner who opposed slavery. As recently as 1956, when its population was about 1,000, it was the only Michigan township which regularly elected Negroes to all offices. [Reference: Richard Dorson, *Negro Folktales in Michigan* (Cambridge, 1956).]

JOHN BROWN'S MEETING IN DETROIT with Douglass and other Negro abolition leaders is concisely described in *Negroes in Detroit* (typescript of compiled sources), Burton Historical Collection. See also Oswald Garrison Villard, *John Brown* (Boston, 1910).

Except for Brown, all those who attended the meeting at Webb's were Negroes active in the Underground Railway. All but Brown and Douglass were residents of Detroit, although at the time of the meeting Willis was residing at Chatham. What information is available on these leaders was furnished by Mr. Fred Hart Williams, of Detroit.

William Webb's two-story frame house stood on the north side of East Congress Street between St. Antoine and Hastings Streets. Webb was the proprietor of a second-hand store which adjoined his home. Little is known about Webb's origins. He was about forty-nine years old at the time of the meeting. Soon after that he moved to Pittsburgh, but returned to Detroit in 1867 and opened a grocery store.

Elijah Willis was born in Virginia in 1828, and was either taken or sold into Kentucky. When his owner announced his intention of selling Willis' wife and children, Willis arranged for their escape and later, after two unsuccessful attempts, managed his own. He established himself in Canada, where he published an abolition paper. After the Civil War he went to Detroit and became a real estate dealer. He died in 1899. (Robert Willis, son of Elijah,

APPENDIX TO *Chapter II*

practiced law in Detroit and for many years "Old Bob," as he was called, was a familiar and colorful figure in the courthouse. Robert Willis died July 9, 1937. He is said to have been the first Negro to graduate from the University of Michigan.)

Dr. Joseph Ferguson, a physician, was a free man in Richmond, Virginia, probably his birthplace, before he moved to Detroit.

The Reverend William C. Monroe was pastor of the Second Baptist Church, located on East Lafayette between Brush and Beaubien Streets, from 1836 to 1847. In that year Mr. Monroe was ordained a priest of the Episcopal Church and founded St. Matthew's, Detroit's first Negro Episcopal Church. He also taught in the city's only public school for Negroes from 1851 until about 1860. He left Detroit and went as a missionary to Haiti, where he died.

William Lambert was born free in Trenton, New Jersey, November 17, 1820. As a youth he was taken to Buffalo, where he found employment as cabin boy on Great Lakes vessels. He settled in Detroit in 1838 and opened a tailoring and cleaning shop at 10 East Woodbridge. He was one of the first Negroes to engage in work of the Underground Railway and was one of its most active workers. He died in Detroit, in April, 1890.

George de Baptiste had an interesting and dramatic life. He was born of free parents in Fredericksburg, Virginia, about 1815. At eighteen, he was employed as valet by a professional gambler with whom he traveled extensively. About 1838 he settled at Madison, Indiana, where he probably had his first experience working for the Underground Railway. He is said to have been engaged as servant or valet by William Henry Harrison, and accompanied him to Washington when he was elected President in 1840. De Baptiste attended Harrison in his final illness and, according to tradition, supported the President's head in his arms when Harrison died. De Baptiste went to Detroit about 1846. For a while he worked as a barber, and for a time is supposed to have owned and operated a small ship, the steamer *T. Whitney*, which ran between Detroit and Sandusky, Ohio. Later he established a baking and catering business which was quite successful. De Baptiste was the "firebrand" of the abolition movement, ready at all times to resort to force and direct action.

The member of Brown's band who came from CHATHAM was Osborn Perry Anderson. A free Negro, he had settled in Canada and worked as a printer. Although he was in the thick of the Harper's Ferry fighting, he was one of those who made his escape. He lived until 1872. [Reference: Allen Keller, *Thunder at Harper's Ferry* (Englewood Cliffs, N.J. 1958).]

PUBLIC REACTION TO BROWN'S EXECUTION, as far as the majority of people in Michigan was concerned, was well summed up in the following editorial in the *Detroit Advertiser and Tribune,* December 3, 1859:

> He [John Brown] was the common topic of conversation.
> We scarcely met a man during the day, no matter what his politics, who did not recur to his mournful fate. Some spoke harshly of the old man, but the majority expressed an undisguised sympathy for him in his extremity. The people of the South have to thank their own senseless extravagance for much of this feeling. Their folly has given bold relief to the heroism of John Brown. It is not sympathy with the old man's crime, but it is the natural homage that mankind have ever paid to devotion to liberty, to courage, to fortitude, sincerity, and an indomitable trust in the mercy and providence of God. . . . He was, for all this, misguided, and died for his own criminal folly, and he was willing to die for it; but in his own idea he gave his life for the freedom of the black slave. Thus he will stand in history.

Chapter III

THE *DETROIT ADVERTISER,* Michigan's most vociferous Republican newspaper, strongly supported the Lincoln administration and its war policy throughout the conflict. The *Detroit Free Press,* the Michigan organ of the Democratic Party, followed a policy of supporting the government, but being critical of the administration. At the beginning, the *Free Press* felt the war was unnecessary and a great evil. But by May 11, 1861, it had become reconciled to the fact that there was no alternative but to fight, and it stated that "two confederacies will never live in peace between the Great Lakes and the Mexican Gulf. The American people must recognize the fact now. There will be only one government south of the St. Lawrence."

HARDEE'S *TACTICS* was a two-volume work, properly titled *Rifle and Light Infantry Tactics,* by William J. Hardee. It was the standard training manual for both North and South. Hardee was commandant of cadets at West Point just before the war. He resigned his commission as lieutenant colonel after the attack on Sumter, and in June 1861 was appointed brigadier general in the Confederate army. In 1862, he was made lieutenant general. Although Jefferson Davis considered him the best corps commander in the Confederate service, he lost the confidence of General John B. Hood during the Atlanta campaign, and thereafter received only minor assignments. [Reference: Ellsworth Eliot, Jr., *West Point in the Confederacy* (New York, 1941), p. 348.] Hardee's *Tactics* was officially designated by Governor Blair as the drill manual for Michigan's infantry regiments. (See Blair's proclamation, April 16, 1861.)

Despite his great record as Michigan's war governor, AUSTIN BLAIR'S political fortunes went into a postwar decline. In 1866 he was elected to Congress, where he served three terms. His war-period service, he believed, entitled him to a greater reward from the Republican Party, and in 1871 he sought a Senate seat, but it was denied him. Embittered by what he regarded as a rebuff, he affiliated with the Independent Republican movement in 1872, supporting Horace Greeley for president. He ran for governor on the same ticket and was overwhelmingly defeated. In 1885 he was an unsuccessful candidate for justice of the Michigan Supreme Court. From 1882 to 1890, he sat on the Board of Regents of the University of Michigan. He died at Jackson, August 6, 1894.

Despite his rejection by the voters in his later life, Austin Blair is remembered today as one of Michigan's great political figures. His statue, erected after his death by a grateful state which ultimately recognized his worth, stands in front of the main entrance to the Capitol in Lansing. [Reference: *Dictionary of American Biography* (New York, 1929), Vol. II; Messmer, *The Public Life of Austin Blair*.]

THE ACCOUNT OF GOVERNOR BLAIR'S WAR MEETING in Detroit, April 16, 1861, and subsequent events can be found in the daily newspapers of the period. [Other details, particularly concerning the loan fund, are given in Robertson, *op. cit.* See also C. W. Davis, *The First Michigan Infantry* (Quincy, c. 1903); and *History of the Detroit Light Guard,* by Frederic S. Isham and Purcell & Hogan (Detroit, 1896).] Soon after the Detroit meeting, Governor Blair called a special session of the Legislature. On May 10 it passed the Military Bill, which authorized raising ten regiments; approved an emergency loan of $1,000,000; created a Military Contract Board to supervise purchases of army supplies, and drafted regulations for the discipline of Michigan troops. One provision of the latter prohibited flogging or branding, a fact which in itself suggests that these were accepted forms of military punishment. [Reference: *Detroit Advertiser,* May 13, 1861.]

CAPTAIN GEORGE GORDON MEADE, who on the eve of the Battle of Gettysburg was given command of the Army of the Potomac, was not the only member of the Union "high brass" to have lived at one time or another in Detroit. From 1849 to 1851 Lieutenant Ulysses S. Grant was a member of the 4th U.S. Infantry detachment stationed at the Detroit Barracks. During part of that period Grant lived on East Fort Street near Russell. The house which he rented was restored and moved to the Michigan State Fair Grounds, where it now stands, the property of the Detroit Historical Commission. Meade was stationed in Detroit from 1857 to 1861. [Reference: *Detroit Advertiser,* April 15, 1861.]

Chapter IV

CAPTAIN WILLIAM WITHINGTON'S story is continued in chapter V. He was later captured at Bull Run, and exchanged January 30, 1862. Upon returning to Michigan, he recruited the 17th Michigan Infantry and became its colonel August 11, 1862. The following October he was commanding the First Brigade, 1st Division, IX Corps; later he commanded the Second Brigade. He was critically wounded at South Mountain on September 14, 1862, when the 17th saw its first action. As a result of his injuries he was forced to resign March 21, 1863. In 1865 he was breveted brigadier general in recognition of his gallantry at South Mountain. After the war he was a prominent Jackson industrialist and civic leader, and served one term (1873–74) in the Michigan House of Representatives. He died at Jackson June 27, 1903. [Reference: *Record of Service of Michigan Volunteers* (Lansing, 1915), Vol. XVII; *Portrait and Biographical Album, Jackson County, Michigan* (Chicago, 1890).] Withington's notebook, referred to in Chapter IV, is now in the Fort Wayne branch of the Detroit Historical Museum.

THE LIGHT GUARD did not pass out of existence when it became Company A, 1st Michigan Infantry. A new Light Guard was organized in 1861 and served throughout the war as a home guard unit. After the war the Light Guard resumed its former social-military status. In later years it provided the nucleus for the 1st Infantry, Michigan State Troops, and the 31st Infantry, Michigan National Guard. It is regarded as the military ancestor of the 125th Infantry, Michigan National Guard, which served with distinction in both world wars as part of the 32nd Division, and which, after World War II, became the 225th Battle Group. Today's fine new National Guard infantry armory in Detroit is known officially as the Light Guard Armory. The account of the organization of the 1st Michigan is based largely upon contemporary newspaper articles in the *Detroit Free Press* and the *Detroit Advertiser*. [See also Isham and Purcell & Hogan, *History of the Detroit Light Guard;* and Robertson, *Michigan in the War.*]

THE 2ND MICHIGAN INFANTRY was organized April 25, 1861, and was made up of those militia companies which were not selected for the 1st Infantry. They were the Scott Guard (Detroit), Hudson Artillery, Battle Creek Artillery, Adrian Guard, Niles Color Company, Flint Union Greys, Constantine Union Guard, East Saginaw Guard, Kalamazoo Light Guard, and Kalamazoo Blair Guard.

Because of lack of room at Fort Wayne, the 2nd Infantry trained at the Agricultural Fair Grounds in Detroit until after the 1st departed for Washington, when it moved into the Fort. At the Fair Grounds, officially designated Cantonment Blair, the regiment was quartered in Floral Hall and the Hall of Domestic Manufactures. It was the sad fate of the 2nd to have been overshadowed by the 1st Infantry, and while the latter was in Detroit little attention was paid by the public or the press to the 2nd.

The 2nd Infantry was commanded by Colonel Israel B. Richardson of Pontiac, a West Point graduate and veteran of the Mexican War. One of Michigan's outstanding officers, Richardson rose to the rank of major general of volunteers. He died at Sharpsburg, Maryland, November 3, 1862, from wounds received at the Battle of Antietam, September 17, 1862.

The 3rd Infantry was organized at Grand Rapids about the same time as the 2nd, but was not mustered in until mid-May 1861. The 4th Infantry was authorized May 16 and was mustered at Adrian. Both the 3rd and 4th were in the field in time to take part in the Bull Run campaign of July 1861.

After the 2nd Infantry was organized, there still remained a few militia companies which were unassigned. Impatient for service, several of these, together with other independent companies organized after the call for volunteers, offered themselves to other states and served in regiments belonging to Missouri, Illinois, New York, Ohio and Indiana. [Reference: Robertson, *op. cit.*, pp. 472–473.]

DESCRIPTION OF THE ARMS of the 1st Michigan is based upon information in Charles Winthrop Sawyer, *Our Rifles* (Boston, 1944), p. 150.

THE COLDWATER LIGHT ARTILLERY became the envy of other troops quartered in Fort Wayne when some of its members found a young woman, described by the newspapers as beautiful (naturally), wandering naked in some woods near the Fort. Her clothing was discovered hanging on the branch of a tree. She was immediately taken in charge by the Light Artillery, whose members established her in a vacant house near the Fort and resisted attempts of civil officials to remove her to a hospital or the poor house. For several days the soldiers "nursed her with all the tenderness of women." She was finally identified as Georgiana Bishop of Cincinnati. It was said that she followed either her brother or sweetheart to Detroit. "She is apparently about 20 years of age," said the *Detroit Advertiser* (June 1, 1861), "and very handsome. . . . The artillerists take turns attending upon her."

THE EXCLAMATION ATTRIBUTED TO LINCOLN—"Thank God For Michigan!"—is admittedly apocryphal, and there is no available documentary evidence that Lincoln made such a remark. But the story of Lincoln's relief at the arrival of the Michigan troops can be substantiated, and his exclamation of satisfaction was repeated to two or three generations of Michigan children. Those now at middle age or beyond will recall hearing the story from their elders and from Civil War veterans. The quotation may therefore be regarded, in my opinion, as authentic Michigan folklore.

And it is by no means unlikely that Lincoln did utter those words, or something very similar to them. There is no doubt that he was delighted to see this first Western regiment in Washington. He received the officers of the 1st Michigan at the White House and visited the regiment in its quarters. He was serenaded by the regimental band, and requested that it alternate with the Marine Band in giving public concerts.

On the occasion of the serenade by the 1st Michigan band at the White House two days after the regiment's arrival at Washington, the President appeared at an upper window and greeted the regiment, remarking that it was "the first installment from Michigan and the great Northwest." (*Detroit Advertiser*, May 23, 1861.)

In Washington the 1st Michigan was quartered in the Woodward building on North D Street, close to Pennsylvania and Ninth. Later it went into camp in a field northeast of Willard's Hotel, not far from the White House. (*Detroit Advertiser*, May 23, 1861.)

Chapter V

This account of the 1st Michigan's CAPTURE OF ALEXANDRIA, and the events following, including the Battle of Bull Run, are based primarily upon contemporary newspaper dispatches in the *Detroit Free Press* and the *Detroit Advertiser* between May 25 and August 3, 1861. Other useful references are Robertson, *Michigan in the War*, pp. 169, 170–173; Isham and Purcell & Hogan, *History of the Detroit Light Guard*, pp. 43–55; *Battles and Leaders*, I, 167–261; Davis, *The First Michigan Infantry*.

THE BATTLE OF BULL RUN, or First Manassas, might also be properly called the BATTLE OF THE COLONELS. There were few general officers in command on either side, and most of the leadership was by colonels. The Confederate organization at Manassas had no real divisions; its largest tactical unit was the brigade, commanded by colonels in every case. Union divisions and brigades also were led by officers of the same rank. Some of those colonels, Union and Confederate, later counted among the most famous generals of the Civil War. The Confederate roster included Wade Hampton, Jeb Stuart, Edmund Kirby–Smith, R. S. Ewell, James Longstreet, Jubal Early and, of course, Thomas J. "Stonewall" Jackson. On the Union side, William Tecumseh Sherman, Henry J. Hunt, David Hunter, John Reynolds, Ambrose Burnside, W. B. Franklin, and Oliver O. Howard all rose to high rank and commanded armies or corps. Hunt became chief of artillery of the Army of the Potomac. [Reference: *Battles and Leaders*, I, 194–195.]

Although the 1ST MICHIGAN was the only Michigan regiment actively engaged at Bull Run on July 21, the other three regiments, the 2nd, 3rd, and 4th performed valuable service by covering the retreat of the army. They were among the last of McDowell's force to reach Arlington. They arrived there July 22 in good order. The 4th Michigan acted as a sort of military police unit, rounding up fugitives near Fairfax. It was observed that the flight of the Union soldiers was not so precipitate but that the fleeing men "eagerly stopped long enough when an audience could be found, to recount exciting tales of their bloody experiences, telling how their regiments had been 'cut to pieces' when actually few of them lost more than half a dozen men." [Reference: *Detroit Advertiser*, July 25, 1861.]

Both COLONEL WILLCOX and CAPTAIN WITHINGTON were awarded the CONGRESSIONAL MEDAL OF HONOR for heroism in the Battle of Bull Run. Although the Medal of Honor was created in 1861 for Navy enlisted men, and extended in 1862 to army enlisted men, it was not authorized for army officers until 1863. The fact that the citations of Willcox and Withington were post-dated to July 21, 1861, technically places these men among the very first to win that coveted decoration. [Reference: *American Decorations.*]

For what is known of WILLCOX'S experiences as a prisoner of war, we have to rely upon Withington's field memorandum book, now in the Fort Wayne branch of the Detroit Historical Museum. Withington's references to

Willcox end abruptly at the time of the former's exchange on January 30, 1862. Willcox remained a prisoner nearly seven months more. Soon after the two men separated, Willcox was shifted to prison at Salisbury, North Carolina and then to Libby Prison, Richmond.

On August 20, 1862, the day after Willcox was exchanged, he was promoted to brigadier general of volunteers, his commission being dated back to July 21, 1861. After a short visit to Detroit, he was sent back to the field, in command of a brigade of Burnside's IXth Corps, to which he was attached for the remainder of the war. He commanded the Corps' First Division at South Mountain and Antietam, where he was cited for gallant conduct. His seniority was high, so that frequently during Burnside's absence Willcox had temporary command of the Corps. It was under his direction that the IXth was shifted from Virginia to Kentucky in the spring of 1863. Thus Willcox saw service in both principal theaters of the war. After the IXth Corps returned to Virginia from the West, Willcox had a division in the Wilderness campaign, at Spotsylvania, Hatcher's Run, and the siege of Petersburg. His was the first division to enter that city after Lee evacuated it. Willcox was made brevet major general of volunteers August 1, 1864, and brevet brigadier general and major general, United States Army, March 2, 1867.

Mustered out January 15, 1866, Willcox returned to Detroit, resuming his law practice for about six months. The attraction of military life was strong, however, and after applying for reinstatement in the regular army he was commissioned colonel of the 29th U.S. Infantry, July 28, 1866, and was assigned to duty in Virginia.

In March 1869 he was transferred to command of the 12th Infantry at San Francisco, where he was stationed until 1878 except for a few months when he was on recruiting duty. In 1878 he was given charge of the army's Department of Arizona, where he remained until 1882, directing the campaigns against the Apaches. The next four years found him in command at Madison Barracks, New York. In 1886 he was promoted to brigadier general in the regular army, and was assigned to the Department of Missouri, with headquarters at Fort Leavenworth.

General Willcox retired April 16, 1887. After extensive travel abroad, he returned to the United States and was given the post of governor of the Soldiers' Home at Washington, D.C., a position he held until 1905, when he moved to Cobourg, Ontario, where he died May 10, 1907, at the age of eighty-four.

Despite General Willcox's outstanding Civil War service, and the distinction he earned, very little is known about his private life. In his native Detroit he is all but forgotten, and on the rare occasions when he is mentioned his name is invariably misspelled.

[For the best available biographical data, see *Dictionary of American Biography* (New York, 1936), Vol. XX; and *Summary of History and Services* of Orlando B. Willcox (unsigned and undated), Burton Historical Collection.]

Chapter VI

GENERAL GORDON GRANGER was born in Wayne County, New York, in 1822, and was a member of the West Point class of 1841. He earned recognition as a cavalry officer early in the war and his advancement was rapid. He commanded the 2nd Michigan from the time of its arrival at St. Louis, his appointment being dated back to September 2, 1861 when the regiment was authorized. He became a brigadier general of volunteers March 26, 1862 and major general September 17. He served with the Armies of the Mississippi and the Cumberland, and distinguished himself at Chickamauga, where he commanded a corps which covered Rosecrans' withdrawal from the field. Most of his service was in the Western theater of war. After 1865 he reverted to the regular army rank of colonel, commanding various infantry regiments until about the time of his death, January 10, 1876. [Reference: Robertson, *Michigan in the War*, p. 837.]

LIEUTENANT FRANK E. WALBRIDGE enlisted from Kalamazoo and was made regimental quartermaster. He was promoted to captain June 9, 1862. He died at Kalamazoo April 6, 1863, at the age of thirty-five. [Reference: Robertson, *op. cit.*, p. 955.]

SHERIDAN'S COMMISSION as colonel of the 2nd Michigan did not catch up with him, and he officially became a brigadier general before he became a colonel. The war was over and Sheridan was commanding occupation forces in New Orleans in 1866 when, as a gesture and to straighten out his record, the Michigan commission was presented to him. [Reference: Robertson, *op. cit.*, p. 626.]

Among SHERIDAN'S CLASSMATES AT WEST POINT were Major General James B. McPherson, killed while serving under Sherman before Atlanta; Major General John M. Schofield, who commanded the Army of the Ohio; and Lieutenant General John B. Hood, one of the Confederacy's brightest stars. [Reference: Philip H. Sheridan, *Personal Memoirs* (New York, 1888), I, 13.]

SHERIDAN'S CREDO is given in detail in his *Memoirs*, I, 153–154.

THE SIZE OF CONFEDERATE FORCES AT BOONEVILLE has been variously estimated. Sheridan says it was between 5,000 and 6,000. Robertson says there were 7,000. Burr and Hinton place the number at 4,000. O'Connor, who agrees with Sheridan, points out that in the early stages of the war Confederate divisions were much larger than those of the Union, being almost the equivalent of a Federal corps. The difference between the number of men mustered into the 2nd Michigan and the comparatively small number under his command on July 1, 1862, was attributed by Sheridan to sickness, which had materially reduced his effective force. [Reference: Sheridan, *Memoirs*, I, 156; Robertson, *op. cit.*, p. 615; Frank A. Burr and Richard J. Hinton, *The Life of General Philip H. Sheridan* (New York, 1890), p. 55; Richard O'Connor, *Sheridan the Inevitable* (Indianapolis, 1953), pp. 65, 365n.]

LEONIDAS S. SCRANTON, born in 1822, joined the 2nd at Grand Rapids, September 2, 1861. He was promoted to captain in 1862 and to major later the same year. He resigned and was honorably discharged November 9, 1864. He died prior to 1911. [Reference: Robertson, *op. cit.*, p. 925.]

CAPTAIN ARCHIBALD P. CAMPBELL was soon commanding a brigade, Alger the regiment; in time Alger too became a general. Scranton, who felt the first blow at Booneville, eventually commanded the 2nd Michigan with the rank of major.

Campbell, born in 1832, entered the service from Port Huron as captain in the 2nd on September 2, 1861, and was honorably discharged for disability September 29, 1864. Although a capable officer, Campbell won his fame obliquely by the gift of a horse to Sheridan. The steed, a three-year-old Morgan gelding, was jet black except for three white feet. It stood sixteen hands high. The horse was foaled on a St. Clair County (Michigan) farm and was presented to Campbell by the citizens of Port Huron. Campbell found the steed unmanageable and regarded it as vicious. Sheridan, however, fancied the animal and in August 1862, after some fighting around Rienzi, Mississippi, Campbell gave it to Sheridan, who named it Rienzi. It caused him no trouble. Sheridan described the horse as strongly built, with great powers of endurance, "and so active that he could cover with ease five miles an hour at his natural walking gait." Sheridan rode Rienzi throughout the war and during some of the Indian campaigns which followed. Horse as well as rider achieved fame in Sheridan's famous ride of October 19, 1864, from Winchester to Cedar Creek, celebrated in the poem by T. Buchanan Read:

> There with the glorious general's name,
> Be it said in letters both bold and bright—
> "Here is the steed that saved the day,
> By carrying Sheridan into the fight,
> From Winchester, twenty miles away."

Rienzi died at Chicago in October 1878 at the age of twenty-one. Its remains were sent to a taxidermist at Rochester, New York, for skillful mounting. It stood for a time in the Military Institute on Governor's Island, New York, and is now displayed in the Smithsonian Institution.

[Reference: Sheridan, *Memoirs*, I, 177; Burr and Hinton, *op. cit.*, 214; W. L. Jenks, *St. Clair County* (Chicago, 1912), p. 448.]

THE COLT REVOLVING RIFLE did not give all Union troops as good results as it did the 2nd Michigan at Booneville. This arm was developed in 1855, but was not issued from the factory until 1857. It was .56 caliber, the five-chamber revolving magazine operating on the same principle as the more efficient Colt hand gun. Quite a large number of the rifles were purchased by the states for militia use, and it is said that many militia companies so equipped entered the war without ever having fired the weapon. It was not popular with the troops on account of the flash and loud report so close to the face. Misfires were common, and there was a tendency for several chambers to go off at once, causing a terrific recoil. There is no indication that the Colt revolving rifle was used by the regular army, or even in substantial numbers by volunteers. [Reference: Sawyer, *Our Rifles*, pp. 153–154.]

AFTER BOONEVILLE, the 2nd Michigan's service, except for a short campaign in Kentucky, was in eastern Tennessee, northern Georgia, and Mississippi. Among the more important battles in which it participated were New Madrid, March 13, 1862; Island No. 10, March 14–April 27, 1862; Chickamauga, September 18–20, 1863; Nashville, August 30, 1864; Franklin, September 27, 1864. It carried a total of 2,425 officers and men on its rolls; it had two officers and forty-five men killed in action; twenty-three men died of wounds, and two officers and 266 men died of disease. The regiment was mustered out at Macon, Georgia, August 17, 1865. [Reference: Robertson, *op. cit.*, pp. 624–625.]

Chapter VII

THE RIOT OF 1863 has been the subject of many articles and is described in several histories of Detroit. Most accounts are in general agreement. The best source of information about what happened, and from which all other descriptions of the riot are drawn, is the newspapers of the day—the *Detroit Advertiser and Tribune* of March 6 to March 10, and the *Detroit Free Press*, March 5 to March 9, 1863. For some emotional trimmings, see *The Late Detroit Riot*, a pamphlet published in Detroit in 1863 by Negroes, in which the testimony of several victims of the riot is given in the first person. A facsimile copy of this pamphlet is in the Burton Historical Collection, Detroit Public Library.

LIEUTENANT VAN STAN may have been the John T. Van Stan who, prior to the war, was a house painter and lived at 106 Woodbridge Street. There also was a Constable Van Stan, probably the same man, during the early war years. [Reference: James D. Johnston, *Detroit City Directory 1855–56.*]

THE TRIAL OF FAULKNER and the fatal shooting of Langer are given a different locale by George B. Catlin in his *Story of Detroit*. Catlin says the trial was held in the old Federal Building at Larned and Griswold, and that the Langer shooting occurred at Griswold and Michigan while Faulkner was being escorted back to jail. This is at variance with the contemporary accounts, which place the trial in the old city hall, outside of which the mob first gathered. The provost guard, according to the newspapers, marched up Monroe to Gratiot to the jail. This would have been the logical route. It is difficult to understand why a criminal trial of that nature would have been held in the Federal Building. Catlin cites no authority for his statements which, under the circumstances, seem less credible than contemporary newspaper versions.

Chapter VIII

THE 17TH MICHIGAN was assigned the position of honor in the parade held for Colonel Orlando B. Willcox upon his return from captivity.

The *Detroit Advertiser* described it this way:

> Then came the 17th Regiment of Michigan Infantry, headed by the City Band. This is the first time the 17th have appeared in the streets of Detroit, and their fine, soldierly bearing called forth encomiums from the spectators. This fine body of men have now left this city for Washington and we feel

confident that they will do their part in sustaining the high reputation Michigan soldiers have so nobly earned in the battlefield.

The *Detroit Free Press* of the same date, August 27, 1862, was equally generous in praise of the appearance of the 17th, which, it noted, was the first regiment to leave Michigan in response to President Lincoln's 1862 call for 300,000 volunteers.

JOHN CONLEY, twenty-one years old when he joined Company G, 17th Infantry, was a resident of Battle Creek. He may have been an accomplished chicken thief, as Lane suggests, but he was also a good soldier. He was wounded at Antietam, on September 17, 1862, and returned to duty April 20, 1863. At Spotsylvania he was taken prisoner (May 12, 1864), but was with the regiment again at the end of the war. [Reference: *Record of Service of Michigan Volunteers*, Vol. XVII.]

GENERAL ORLANDO METCALFE POE deserves greater recognition than he has received, both for his wartime and peacetime services. Michigan particularly should remember most gratefully the contributions he made to his adopted state. Unfortunately, there has been a tendency to overlook Poe's great achievements.

Born at Navarre, Ohio, March 7, 1832, Orlando M. Poe entered the United States Military Academy in 1852 and graduated sixth in his class in 1856. His high standing earned him the coveted engineer's assignment, and his first duty was as a second lieutenant of the Topographical Engineers. With headquarters at Detroit, which thereafter was to be his home, he supervised lighthouse construction and river and harbor improvements on the upper Great Lakes until 1861. In that year he married Eleanor Carroll Brent, daughter of Captain Thomas Lee Brent, United States Army.

At the outbreak of the war Poe was detailed to organize Ohio volunteers, but his ability and experience as an engineer caused him to be added to General McClellan's staff. His major assignment was to lay out the defenses of Washington. On September 16, 1861, his connection to Michigan was renewed by his appointment as colonel of the 2nd Michigan Infantry. At the head of that regiment, he participated in the Peninsular campaign of 1862, winning a citation for bravery and promotion to brigadier general of volunteers.

For some months in 1862–63 he commanded a brigade in the IXth Corps, and it was then that the incident at Fredericksburg occurred which Lane mentions. Poe's volunteer commission expired March 4, 1863, and because of the Fredericksburg affair the Senate refused to grant confirmation when renewal was recommended. Poe therefore reverted to his regular army rank of captain.

His services as an engineer, however, were in demand, and he was soon acting as engineer officer of the XXIIIrd Corps, building fortifications at Knoxville, whose defense he directed during the siege of 1863. He then became chief engineer for General William T. Sherman, on whose staff he remained until the end of the war. He ultimately regained his rank of brevet brigadier general.

After the war Poe returned to Detroit, having general supervision in the Corps of Engineers over work on the upper Lakes. For a while he also represented the army in the construction of the transcontinental railroads. In 1883 he was made superintending engineer of improvement of rivers and harbors on Lakes Superior and Huron. In that capacity he not only directed channel work in the Detroit and St. Clair Rivers, but also designed and constructed the famous Poe Lock in the St. Mary's River ship canal.

[Reference: *Dictionary of American Biography* (New York, 1934), Vol. XV.]

THE IRREPRESSIBLE BILLY (WILLIAM H.) DUNHAM was a corporal in Company K. He was from Blackman, Jackson County, and a near neighbor to Lane. He enlisted August 9, 1862, at the age of nineteen. He was mustered out with the regiment at Delaney House, D.C., with the rest of the regiment, June 3, 1865. His subsequent history is not known. [Reference: *Record of Service of Michigan Volunteers*, Vol. XVII.]

THE GRAND REVIEW was the greatest military spectacle ever staged in the United States. For two days, May 23 and 24, 1865, tens of thousands of Union veterans marched up Pennsylvania Avenue in Washington, passing in review before President Johnson and high ranking military and civil officials. The first day's contingents consisted largely of Grant's Army of the Potomac; they were followed the second day by Sherman's Western troops, many of whom purposely straggled along in loose formation, leading foraged livestock, appearing much as they had on their march to the sea, when they earned the sobriquet of "Sherman's bummers." [For graphic illustrations of the Grand Review see *Frank Leslie's Illustrated Newspaper*, and *Harper's Weekly*, both for June 10, 1865.]

Chapter IX

The origin of the BLACK HAT, the distinguishing symbol of the IRON BRIGADE, is difficult to trace. Apparently, it was first worn by the Wisconsin regiments of the brigade and may have been favored by the Western troops. Contemporary pictures show members of other Western regiments wearing that style, but they seem to have discarded it for the kepi or forage cap which was worn by most Federal troops. The 24th Michigan was issued the kepi when the regiment was organized and received the black hats only when they became part of the Iron Brigade. Possibly the men also had kepis which they wore in camp or on fatigue duty; pictures show the men of the regiment wearing both kinds.

The patch designating division and corps was an innovation of General Hooker's. Use of such insignia was ordered in a general headquarters circular which he issued on March 21, 1863. When the Iron Brigade was designated 1st Brigade, 1st Division, 1st Corps, its members proudly pointed out that if the entire Union army was formed in line, the Iron Brigade would be on the extreme right. Its designation entitled it to carry the division colors, a triangular banner with the red corps badge imposed upon a white field.

[Reference: Walter H. Hebert, *Fighting Joe Hooker* (Indianapolis, 1944), p. 180; O. B. Curtis, *History of the Twenty-Fourth Michigan of the Iron Brigade* (Detroit, 1891), p. 142.]

The story of the DRUMMER BOY and his goose is told in Robertson, *Michigan in the War*, p. 449. The drummer may have been Willie Young, of Detroit, who enlisted in Company G when the 24th was organized. Willie was then thirteen years old, the youngest member of the 24th Michigan. He served throughout the war and was discharged June 30, 1865. The roster of the regiment listed Willie's occupation as student. He was no doubt looked down upon as a mere child by such of his elders as Herman Krumbach, a Company B musician, and Private William C. Young of Company H, both of whom had attained the ripe age of fifteen. Herman, listed as a plumber, apparently did not remain with the regiment; there is no record of his being mustered out, nor does his name occur among the casualties. Private Young, however, fought to the end. Like his drummer boy namesake, he was listed as a student. He was discharged as a corporal in 1865. Both Krumbach and William C. Young were from Detroit. The Detroit city directory, just before the war, lists a Herman Krombach, foreman, Michigan Boot and Shoe Store, who lived at 282 Croghan Street. It is more than probable that he was the father of young Krumbach. At the same time, sixteen Young families are listed, making it difficult to identify either of the two youthful soldiers of that name.

COMPOSITION OF THE 24TH, together with a detailed record of its service, from the time it was recruited until the end of the war, is to be found in O. B. Curtis, *op. cit.* This is one of the best regimental histories which the war produced and is often cited in accounts of the battle of Gettysburg. Orson B. Curtis, at the age of twenty-two, enlisted at Wayne, Michigan and was assigned to Company D. His occupation was given as student. He was seriously wounded at Fredericksburg, where he lost his left arm. He was discharged at Washington, March 2, 1863. After the war, he was a government employee. He died at Detroit January 11, 1901.

FREDERICK A. BUHL was the son of Fred Buhl, a prominent Detroit businessman and head of the firm of F. Buhl, Newland Company, furriers and manufacturers of hats, gloves, and other items. The family home was at 86 West Congress Street. Young Buhl joined the 24th as a second lieutenant at the time of its organization and became a first lieutenant December 13, 1862. After recovering from wounds received at Gettysburg, he transferred to the 1st Michigan Cavalry with the rank of captain. He was severely wounded August 25, 1864, at Shepardstown, Virginia, while serving with the Michigan Cavalry Brigade under General George A. Custer. He died September 15, 1864, and was buried at Annapolis, Maryland.

Captain Buhl's father presented the regimental colors to the 24th before it left for the front. The flag was carried through all campaigns up to and including Gettysburg. After that battle it was so tattered that it was retired and returned to the state.

[Reference: Robertson, *op. cit.*, pp. 438, 786.]

Just as the war produced heroes from the ranks, so did the postwar period produce great civic leaders from the corps of veterans. One of them was EDGAR O. DURFEE, of Company C, 24th Michigan Infantry. Durfee was born on a farm in Wayne County on the outskirts of Detroit, October 28, 1842. As a youth he worked on the family farm and had little time for formal schooling. He enlisted at the age of twenty and suffered several wounds at Gettysburg, one of which resulted in the amputation of his arm. After he had recovered, he was given employment in a government office in Washington. He remained there until 1870, when he returned to Detroit. He became a self-taught lawyer, but without having practiced he was elected judge of the Probate Court in 1876, and held that office continuously thereafter until his death, at the age of eighty-four, on April 28, 1927. During his tenure of almost fifty years on the bench, he won national renown for his knowledge of probate law and his opinions were accepted throughout the country as authoritative.

For many years Judge Durfee was the acknowledged head of the Republican

Party in Wayne County and as such he enjoyed the bitter enmity of his Democratic counterpart, Major George Penniman, also a Civil War veteran. With advancing age, Penniman's mind began to fail and it became necessary for his family to have him declared incompetent. The petition had to be approved by Judge Durfee, who was thus placed in an extremely embarrassing position, and apologized in court to Penniman for doing what the law required of him. Penniman quietly asked, when the order was signed, if he was thereby adjudged insane.

"That is correct," replied Durfee, sadly.

"And as an insane person, I can't be held responsible for anything I do?" Penniman asked.

"That's right," Durfee stated.

"Then, you old so-and-so," shouted Penniman, "I'm going to tell you exactly what I think of you." And he proceeded to do so, in purple language, while the unhappy Durfee squirmed on the bench, with no choice but to sit and listen.

[Reference: Biographical Index, Burton Historical Collection.]

CAPTAIN JOHN WITHERSPOON was one of those who left the *Detroit Free Press* composing room to become a soldier. He was twenty-two years old when he enlisted in 1861 in the 1st Michigan. At Gettysburg, he was one of the four officers of the 24th who came through the battle unhurt. He was made second lieutenant in Company C on December 13, 1862, first lieutenant on September 1, 1863, and captain the following November 22. He was wounded in the Wilderness, May 5, 1864. After the war he homesteaded at St. Edward's, Nebraska, and was killed there during a cyclone. His family returned to Detroit, where his grandson and namesake, John Homer Witherspoon, became a popular civic figure, occupying the various public offices of assistant corporation counsel, police commissioner, and city controller. [Reference: Curtis, *op. cit.*, p. 5.]

COLONEL HENRY A. MORROW was one of those men who seemed to have a natural bent for soldiering and made the transition from civil to military life as if he had been born to do so. He was born at Warrenton, Virginia, in 1829. Ironically, he saw much action in and around his native town, and on more than one occasion marched his regiment past the house in which he was born and the cemetery in which his parents were buried.

As a youth Morrow went to Washington, where he attended the Rittenhouse Academy and won appointment as a page in the United States Senate. There he attracted the favorable attention of Michigan's senior senator, Lewis Cass, whose protégé he became.

When Morrow was seventeen, the Mexican War broke out and he enlisted in the Maryland-District of Columbia volunteer regiment. He was engaged at Monterey and in the Tampico campaign.

He returned safely to Washington and on advice of Cass he went to Detroit, where he studied law and was admitted to the bar. With the political backing of Cass he became city recorder, and in 1857, when the Recorder's Court was created, he was elected its first judge. In private practice he was associated with A. W. Buel and had offices in the Rotunda Building on Griswold Street. His home was at 161 Woodward Avenue.

Morrow's war record was impressive. He was appointed to command the 24th Michigan by Governor Blair, a recognition of his civic and political prominence. He was three times wounded: at Gettysburg, at the Wilderness, May 5, 1864, and again at Petersburg, February 6, 1865.

On August 1, 1864, he was breveted brigadier general "for gallant and distinguished service during the present campaign before Richmond, Virginia." On March 13, 1865, he was breveted major general "for distinguished and conspicuous gallantry before Petersburg." During the latter campaign he was often in command of his brigade.

Mustered out of service July 19, 1865, he returned to Detroit and received appointment to the post of collector of the port. He resigned after a year to accept a commission as lieutenant colonel in the regular army. Assigned to the 36th U.S. Infantry, with the rank of brevet colonel, he spent several years in Louisiana and other parts of the South aiding in reconstruction. In 1872–73, he was stationed in Utah, at that time with the 13th U.S. Infantry. The year 1877 saw him in command of troops sent to Scranton, Pennsylvania, to preserve order during the railroad riots. Soon afterwards, in 1879, he was promoted to colonel and given command of the 21st U.S. Infantry, a post he held until his death at Hot Springs, Arkansas, January 31, 1891. He was buried at Niles, Michigan, February 6, 1891.

[Reference: Curtis, *op. cit.,* p. 477; *Detroit Free Press,* Feb. 6, Feb. 7, 1891.]

HOW THE IRON BRIGADE won its designation is told by Curtis (*op. cit.,* p. 452) in the following statement attributed to General George B. McClellan: "During the battle of South Mountain my headquarters were where I could see every move of the troops taking the gorge on the Pike [National Road]. With my glass I saw the men fighting against great odds, when General

Hooker came in great haste for some orders. I asked him what troops those were fighting on the Pike. His answer was: 'General Gibbons' brigade of Western men.' I said, 'They must be made of iron.' He replied: 'By the Eternal, they are iron. If you had seen them at Second Bull Run as I did, you would know them to be iron.' I replied: 'Why, General Hooker, they would fight equal to the best troops in the world.' This remark so elated Hooker that he mounted his horse and dashed away without his orders. After the battle, I saw Hooker at the Mountain House near where the Brigade fought. He sang out, 'Now General, what do you think of the Iron Brigade?' "

Some idea of the fighting qualities of the Iron Brigade can be gained from examining its casualty lists. "Out of over 2,000 regiments in the Union army," Curtis states, "the records of the regiments of the Iron Brigade make a most honorable showing. In percentages of killed and died of wounds, the 2nd Wisconsin stands first; the 7th Wisconsin stands sixth, and the 24th Michigan stands nineteenth."

William F. Fox in *Regimental Losses in the American Civil War* (Albany, 1889), says: "In proportion to its numbers this brigade sustained the heaviest loss of any in the war. Its aggregate losses are exceeded in only one instance."

The account of the assignment of the 24th Michigan to the Iron Brigade is from Curtis, *op. cit.,* p. 142.

For a more detailed account of the role of REYNOLDS' 1ST CORPS (including the Iron Brigade) at Fredericksburg and later at Chancellorsville, see Edward J. Nichols, *Toward Gettysburg* (University Park, Pa., 1958). This excellent biography of General John F. Reynolds provides much information about the campaigns and battles, up to Gettysburg, in which the 24th Michigan participated.

The episode of the MANUAL OF ARMS is from Curtis, *op. cit.,* pp. 86–104.

It was during A PERIOD OF TEMPORARY IDLENESS for the 24th Michigan, during the winter of 1862–1863, that Henry J. Raymond, the famed editor of the *New York Times,* received the fright of his life. His brother, James F. Raymond, a musician, had joined the 24th as bandmaster. In January, 1863, Henry Raymond, while visiting headquarters of the Army of the Potomac, received a telegram stating: "Your brother's corpse is at Belle Plain." The anguished editor hurried to the camp at Belle Plain to recover, as he thought, the body of his brother. However, he found James hale and hearty. A careless telegrapher had added an "e" where there should have been none. [Reference: Robertson, *op. cit.*, p. 449.]

An account of LEE'S MOVEMENTS, his invasion of Pennsylvania, and Hooker's belated pursuit, together with the movements of the 24th Michigan, will be found in Edward J. Stackpole, *They Met at Gettysburg* (Harrisburg, 1956), pp. 12–43; Nichols, *op. cit.*, pp. 182–185; Curtis, *op. cit.*, pp. 140–143.

The 24th Michigan, highly partisan where REYNOLDS was concerned, believed the top command should have been his on any terms. ". . . his soldiers knew that he held in reserve a latent force of clear- and cool-headedness that could always be relied upon. They trusted him implicitly. And when the news reached the Ist Corps that Hooker had been relieved, it was not strange that many of us jumped to the conclusion that our Reynolds would be selected. . . ." [Reference: Nichols, *op. cit.*, p. 192; Curtis, *op. cit.*, p. 422.]

Chapter X

Both WADSWORTH and BRIGADIER GENERAL SOLOMON MERE-DITH were political generals, and, while there has always been a tendency to downgrade Civil War officers who won high rank by preference, some of them proved most capable. Both Wadsworth and Meredith turned out to be competent commanders.

James Samuel Wadsworth was born at Geneseo, New York, October 30, 1807. He attended Harvard, but left school without graduating in order to manage his family's extensive estate.

At the outbreak of the war he was made major general of volunteers by the governor of New York, but the commission was not recognized by the Federal government. Nevertheless, Wadsworth went to the front and offered to serve in an unofficial capacity on the staff of General Irwin McDowell. He was accepted and he so distinguished himself in the first battle of Bull Run that he was commissioned brigadier general of volunteers on August 9, 1861. During the early part of McClellan's campaign on the peninsula, he was in charge of the defenses around Washington. In 1862 Wadsworth was candidate for governor of New York but he was defeated. After the battle of Fredericksburg he was assigned the command of the 1st Division, Ist Corps, and after

Gettysburg he was given the 4th Division, Vth Corps. At the Battle of the Wilderness, May 6, 1864, he was killed at the head of his division.

[Reference: *Dictionary of American Biography* (New York, 1936), Vol. XIX.]

Solomon Meredith was born in Guilford County, North Carolina, on May 29, 1810. In 1829 he moved to Indiana and settled on a farm near Richmond. An ardent Whig and an active abolitionist, he entered local politics. He was twice elected sheriff of Wayne County, Indiana, and served a term in the legislature. He was also United States marshal from 1849 to 1853.

At the outbreak of the war he was given command of the 19th Indiana Infantry, which became part of the Iron Brigade. He was made brigadier general in 1862 and put in command of the Iron Brigade. In 1864 he was breveted major general.

After the war Meredith engaged in the mercantile business at Cambridge, Indiana, and was given several political appointments, including that of surveyor of Montana Territory, 1867–69. He died at Cambridge in 1875.

[Reference: Andrew W. Young, *History of Wayne County, Indiana* (Cincinnati, 1872), p. 270; *Indiana Magazine of History*, June 1929, p. 191.]

WILLOUGHBY RUN wanders southward along the base of Seminary Ridge. About two miles below McPherson's Woods it is crossed by Pitzer road, which runs from the Peach Orchard west to the Hagerstown road. The fields along Pitzer road between Willoughby Run and Seminary Ridge, where on July 3, 1865, Pickett massed his troops for his celebrated charge, are now part of the farm of former President Dwight D. Eisenhower.

THE FIRST DAY'S FIGHTING at Gettysburg is described by Douglas Southall Freeman in *Lee's Lieutenants* (New York, 1944), III, 81, as a "reconnaissance." It was, in truth, just that, particularly from the Confederate standpoint. Yet, again from the Confederate point of view, it was costly. Federal losses the first day were about 9,700 men—nearly 6,000 being Ist Corps casualties, and the rest XIth Corps. Confederate losses were approximately 5,000—far more than Lee could afford.

One of the most vivid contemporary accounts of the Battle of Gettysburg is that written by Frank Aretas Haskell, of the 6th Wisconsin of the Iron Brigade. During the battle, Haskell served as aide to Brigadier General John Gibbon, who led a division of Hancock's IInd Corps. Haskell's first-hand description of the three-day fight is regarded as a primary source by students of the battle. Written in 1863, a few days after the battle, it has been several times reprinted under the title of *The Battle of Gettysburg*. Haskell says, "the first division, General Wadsworth, was the first of the infantry to become engaged."

ARCHER'S UNHAPPY EXPERIENCE is described by Freeman, *op. cit.*, III, 80. "As fate would have it," says Freeman, "Archer encountered the Iron Brigade, a command of Michigan, Wisconsin and Indiana soldiers who deserved their name."

THE 6TH WISCONSIN was commanded by Colonel (later General) Rufus Dawes, the father of Charles G. Dawes who was Vice President of the United States under Herbert Hoover, 1929–33.

GENERAL ABNER DOUBLEDAY, "a literate and analytical soldier," began the war for the Union. At least he fired the first shot from inside Fort Sumter in answer to the opening Confederate bombardment on April 12, 1861.

Doubleday was born at Ballston Spa, New York, June 26, 1819. He attended school at Auburn and Cooperstown, where he prepared for a career as a civil engineer. At Cooperstown he revised the rules of the game of "one old cat," and thereby gained immortality as the inventor of modern baseball.

He entered West Point in 1838 and graduated in 1842. As an artilleryman, Doubleday saw service in the Mexican and Seminole wars and thereafter was assigned to various Atlantic coastal defenses. A captain, he was stationed at Charleston, South Carolina, in 1860–61 as second in command to Major Robert Anderson. He was a member of the Fort Sumter garrison and lived through the bombardment, which ended when Anderson surrendered on April 14.

Doubleday was rapidly promoted during the early part of the war and soon had a division under Reynolds. Although he took over command of the Ist Corps upon Reynolds' death, his own division was not as heavily engaged as Wadsworth's, and on the second day of the battle Doubleday was actively involved on Cemetery Ridge. He was replaced in command of the Ist Corps by General Newton at the close of the first day's fighting, a bitter disappointment to him, as he felt he had earned permanent command. Newton, however, was his senior.

After Gettysburg Doubleday served out the rest of the war in Washington. In 1866 he reverted to regular army rank of lieutenant colonel, but was promoted to colonel the following year. He was stationed in the West, and while in San Francisco he obtained a charter for that city's first cable car.

Doubleday retired in 1873 and made his home at Mendham, New Jersey. He died there January 26, 1893.

Doubleday's troops nicknamed him "Old Forty-eight Hours," a tribute to his promptness and vigor as a commanding officer.

[Reference: Meredith, *Storm Over Sumter; Dictionary of American Biography* (New York, 1930), Vol. V.]

In the early stages of the battle, the IRON BRIGADE HAD THE ASSISTANCE OF HALL'S BATTERY of six three-inch guns which were planted across the Chambersburg road. This battery was formally known as the 2nd Maine Battery and was commanded by Captain James A. Hall. When this artillery unit came on the field, the placing of the guns was personally directed by General Reynolds, an old artilleryman himself. In his postwar reminiscences, Hall stated that he gained the distinct impression that Reynolds, who had been given broad discretion by Meade in deciding where and when to fight, determined to bring matters to an issue by selecting Gettysburg as the place for a showdown. [Reference: Nichols, *Toward Gettysburg*, p. 204.]

Hall held his position during most of the morning, then was forced to withdraw under concentrated Confederate fire which threatened to overwhelm him.

Curtis (*History of the Twenty-Fourth*) designates Hall's unit as Battery B, 4th U.S. Artillery. Apparently he is in error. But Hall was attached to the 1st Division, 1st Corps, at Fredericksburg and at Chancellorsville, and therefore was well known to the 24th Michigan. One of the "characters" of Hall's Battery, known throughout the entire army, was one of its horses, Old Bobtail. This animal, it was said, entered the service at Fort Leavenworth in 1857 under the name of Tartar. It acquired the name of Old Bobtail at Second Manassas where it was walloped on the rump by a solid shot, which knocked off its tail. It was said that thereafter, at the sound of guns, Old Bobtail always turned his injured parts away from the direction of the firing, and no amount or kind of persuasion could force him to change position.

COLONEL MORROW WAS CAPTURED along with hundreds of other FEDERAL WOUNDED when the Confederates overran Gettysburg at the end of the July 1 fighting. Morrow removed his insignia and, posing as a doctor, aided the Union wounded. He was recognized but was permitted to remain in the town. During the evening of July 1 he met General Ewell, and in the course of their conversation the Confederate corps commander remarked that he thought the 24th Michigan was foolish not to have surrendered in preference to being so badly cut up. To that Morrow replied: "General Ewell, the 24th Michigan came here to fight, not to surrender." [Reference: Curtis, *op. cit.*, p. 187.] Later that evening Morrow personally complained to Major General John B. Gordon, one of Ewell's division commanders, that some of the 24th's wounded had been left on the battlefield. Gordon immediately ordered out ambulances and permitted Morrow to accompany them. On July 3 Morrow was an interested spectator of Pickett's charge from the vantage point of the seminary cupola. His captivity ended when the Confederates evacuated Gettysburg, leaving many of the wounded behind. [Reference: Robertson, *Michigan in the War*, p. 449.]

AFTER THE CLIMACTIC FIGHTING of July 3 both armies rested. Lee maintained his positions all day Saturday, July 4, waiting for a counterattack which did not come. On the night of July 4 he began his withdrawal, heading back toward Virginia. Meade waited most of July 5 before starting his belated and ineffective pursuit. Meanwhile, the Army of the Potomac rested on Culp's Hill and Cemetery Ridge. The 24th Michigan improved the time during this interlude by reorganizing itself into four companies. According to Curtis (*op. cit.*, p. 192), the regiment was not actively engaged on the second and third days of the battle except to protect a battery on Culp's Hill.

After Gettysburg, the 24th Michigan, along with the rest of the Iron Brigade, served in a number of campaigns and battles, but never with the same distinction which it earned at Gettysburg. The 24th was at the Wilderness, Spotsylvania, and North Anna in May 1864; it was at Cold Harbor, June 1, 1864; and, from June 18, 1864, to February 1865, it took part in the siege of Petersburg. On February 11, 1865, the exhausted and depleted 24th was pulled out of the line and sent to Springfield, Illinois to rest and recruit. In the following weeks, the regiment was built up to its original strength, its new additions being mostly conscripts. It was quartered at Camp Butler (Springfield) beginning February 20.

The regiment saw no more action, but it performed one final duty. Early in May, the body of the martyred Abraham Lincoln was taken home. The funeral and burial were on May 4, and, when the body was carried to the cemetery, it was the 24th Michigan which provided the military escort. At that time, the regiment was commanded by Colonel Albert M. Edwards. On June 19, 1865, the 24th left Camp Butler for Detroit, where it was mustered out of service on June 30.

THE TEXT OF GENERAL WADSWORTH'S NOTE to Colonel Morrow is given in Curtis, *op. cit.*, p. 168.

Chapter XI

THIS ACCOUNT OF THE MICHIGAN CAVALRY BRIGADE at Rummel's Farm is drawn from the following sources: Burke Davis, *Jeb Stuart, the Last Cavalier* (New York, 1957) ; Luther S. Trowbridge, *Operations of the Cavalry in the Gettysburg Campaign* (Detroit, 1888) ; Robertson, *Michigan in the War;* Hebert, *Fighting Joe Hooker;* J. H. Kidd, *Personal Recollections of a Cavalryman* (Ionia, 1908) ; Sawyer, *Our Rifles;* Stackpole, *They Met at Gettysburg;* William Brooke-Rawle, "The Right Flank At Gettysburg," in *Annals of the War* (Philadelphia, 1879).

The story of the cavalry brigade is told as completely as anywhere in the personal recollections of BRIGADIER GENERAL (BREVET) JAMES H. KIDD which he published in 1908 under the title of *Personal Recollections of a Cavalryman.* Kidd joined the 6th Michigan Cavalry at Grand Rapids, August 28, 1862, at the age of twenty-two. He was then a student at the University of Michigan, before that he had attended the State Normal College at Ypsilanti.

Kidd was born at Ionia, February 14, 1840. Upon joining the 6th he was commissioned captain and assigned to Company E, which he helped to recruit. In May 1863 he was promoted to major. Kidd saw his first real action in the Gettysburg campaign and was wounded at Falling Waters, Maryland, July 14, 1863, during Lee's retreat. On May 19, 1864, he became colonel of the 6th. He was again wounded at Winchester and received his brevet rank for meritorious conduct in the Shenandoah campaign.

After Appomattox the 6th was sent west and employed for several months against the plains Indians. Kidd was mustered out of service with his regiment at Fort Leavenworth, November 7, 1865.

After the war he returned to Ionia and engaged in the lumbering and manufacturing businesses. In 1867 he was appointed register of the United States Land Office, and in 1890 he became postmaster of Ionia. He remained active in military affairs, serving as brigadier general and inspector general of the Michigan State Troops, the militia organization which preceded the National Guard. He was also interested in G.A.R. and Masonic affairs. In 1890 he became proprietor and publisher of the *Ionia Sentinel.* Kidd delivered the dedicatory address at the unveiling of the Michigan Cavalry Brigade monument at Gettysburg, June 12, 1889.

General Kidd married Miss Florence S. McConnell, granddaughter of Edward Mundy, who was Michigan's first lieutenant-governor and who was also the state attorney general and supreme court justice. Kidd died at Ionia in 1913.

THE SPENCER REPEATING RIFLE AND CARBINE are credited by several authorities for the poor showing of the Confederate cavalry during the Gettysburg campaign. The fire-power advantage which these weapons gave the Federals provided an edge which Stuart was unable to overcome. Kidd states the Spencer was a seven-shot repeater; Sawyer in *Our Rifles*, p. 155, says it was an eight-shot, while Carl P. Russell in *Dictionary of American History*, I, 145, says "the magazine capacity was 9 rounds." Experts account for the apparent discrepancy by pointing out that the magazine held seven rounds and the chamber another. To load with nine rounds would have required some adaptation. (Information furnished by the Fort Wayne Military Museum, Detroit, 1958.)

We last met RUSSELL A. ALGER in 1862, performing heroics as a captain with the 2nd Michigan Cavalry under Colonel Philip Sheridan in northern Mississippi.

Alger stands high on the roster of Michigan's distinguished citizens, with a record of public service which has been carried on by his descendants.

Russell Alexander Alger almost became President of the United States. He possessed the premier qualification—birth in a log cabin. He was born in Lafayette, Medina County, Ohio, February 27, 1836, the descendant of Revolutionary War forebears and the child of a frontier family which knew extreme poverty. Alger's father died in 1848 and Russell became the support of several brothers and sisters, so that he had time for only a scant education.

In 1857, however, he left home and went to Akron, where he found employment and time to read law. He was admitted to the bar in 1859 and began practice in Cleveland. His health impaired, he moved to Grand Rapids, Michigan, that same year and entered the lumbering business because it would enable him to work out of doors.

He prospered from the start, but when the war broke out he put his career aside and joined the 2nd Michigan as a captain. He won promotion to major in 1862 and later that year, when the 6th Michigan Cavalry was organized,

Alger was made its lieutenant colonel. As the result of the army reorganization of 1862–63, he was shifted to the 5th Michigan Cavalry as its colonel.

Alger's record was one of great activity. He had a flair for command and was as courageous and vigorous as any cavalry officer could be expected to be. In addition to his mishap at Booneville, Mississippi, in 1862, he was wounded at Boonsboro, Maryland, during the Gettysburg campaign, July 8, 1863. Later he served under Sheridan, mostly in the Shenandoah Valley.

Alger was mustered out September 20, 1864, under somewhat peculiar circumstances. It was charged that he loaned General Sheridan $10,000 and that in return Sheridan arranged for his separation from the service. Custer and other superiors accused him of being absent without leave; Alger insisted his absence and ultimate discharge were due to illness which kept him in the hospital and made him unqualified for further duty. As a result, there was always a cloud on Alger's record, and the accusation, while never formally presented, was used against him politically. However, it did not prevent him from being made brevet brigadier general, October 16, 1865, and brevet major general, June 11, 1866.

After the war, Alger established himself in Detroit and amassed a fortune in lumber, mining, and banking. He was always interested in politics, and in 1884 he was elected governor of Michigan. In 1888 he was a strong contender for the Republican presidential nomination, but the whispers about the war scandal helped ruin his chances. He remained a favorite of the veterans and was both national and Michigan department commander of the G.A.R.

Alger was philanthropically inclined and his favorite charities were those which helped underprivileged boys. He made it an annual practice to buy new suits for Detroit newsboys, and out of that custom grew the Old Newsboys-Goodfellows movement which, beginning in Detroit, was taken up nationally. In 1893 Alger took six hundred Detroit boys as his guests to the Chicago World Fair.

In 1897 President McKinley selected Alger to sit in his cabinet as Secretary of War. In that capacity he directed the military effort in the Spanish-American War. Because of scandals involving equipment and supplies for the troops, McKinley asked for Alger's resignation in 1898.

That did not end his political career. Still regarded as Michigan's favorite son, he was appointed to the United States Senate in 1902 and, while still in that office, died in Washington, January 24, 1907.

[Reference: Henry Hall, ed., *America's Successful Men of Affairs* (New York, 1896), II, 17; *Dictionary of American Biography* (New York, 1928), Vol. I.]

THE CAVALRY FIGHT on July 3, 1863 in which the Michigan Cavalry Brigade played such an important part, may or may not have been of great strategic significance or affected the outcome of the battle of Gettysburg. It is undoubtedly true that the battle ended when Pickett withdrew after the repulse of his charge against the Union center.

Regardless of how the later arm-chair strategists may argue, the outcome of the campaign and the events of the days subsequent to July 3 would have been very different if Stuart had been successful in demoralizing Meade's rear. The worried, harassed and hesitant Meade most certainly would have reacted differently if Stuart had been loose behind him. The range of speculation is limitless. It is arguable that under such circumstances Lee would not have broken off the battle, even if Pickett had not been successful.

There has been a tendency to give scant attention to the cavalry fight. The following paragraphs are quoted in order to place the action in slightly better perspective.

Edward J. Stackpole (*They Met at Gettysburg*, p. 278) : "So much has been written about Pickett's charge and its dramatic role in featuring the high watermark of the rebellion that the cavalry fight behind the Federal line, which occurred about the same time as Pickett's charge was being driven home, was not only dwarfed by comparison, but has been correspondingly neglected by historians. Yet that spirited clash between four Confederate brigades under command of Major General J. E. B. Stuart and three Union brigades commanded by Brig. Gen. David McM. Gregg could have played an extremely significant part in the third day's activities."

J. H. Kidd (*Personal Recollections of a Cavalryman*, p. 156) : "For more than twenty years after the close of the Civil War, the part played by Gregg, Custer and McIntosh and their brave followers in the battle of Gettysburg received but scant recognition. Even the maps prepared by the corps of engineers stopped short of Cress's Ridge and Rummel's fields. 'History' was practically silent upon the subject, and had not the survivors of those commands taken up the matter, there might have been no record of the invaluable services which the Second cavalry division and Custer's Michigan brigade rendered at the very moment when a slight thing would have turned the tide of victory the other way. In other words, the decisive charge of Colonel Town and his Michiganders coincided in point of time with the failure of Pickett's assault upon the center, and was a contributing cause in bringing about the latter result."

General Charles King, U.S.A. (in Kidd, *op. cit.*, p. 158) : "And so, just as Gettysburg was the turning point of the great war, so, to my way of thinking, was the grapple with and overthrow of Stuart on the fields of the Rummel farm the turning point of Gettysburg. Had he triumphed there; had he cut his way through or over that glorious brigade of Wolverines and come sweeping all before him down among the reserve batteries and ammunition trains, charging furiously at the rear of our worn and exhausted infantry even as Pickett's devoted Virginians assailed their front, no man can say what scenes of rout and disaster might not have occurred."

Chapter XII

It is unfortunate that SARAH EMMA EDMONDS did not see fit to write a factual account of her wartime experiences. Her story, as she told it in her book, *Nurse and Spy in the Union Army* (Hartford, 1865), is of little historical value aside perhaps from providing some insight into her personal character. Anything else in her book must be weighed carefully and compared to other information about her. What a great opportunity she wasted in failing to utilize her talent to provide a valuable document about camp life and battlefield as seen through a woman's eyes!

A far more accurate and comprehensive account of Emma's experiences is given by Dr. Betty Fladeland, in a scholarly article titled "Alias Franklin Thompson," in *Michigan History* (December 1958), pp. 435–462. Most available source material and references are provided by Dr. Fladeland in the footnotes accompanying her article.

Other references are the *Detroit Free Press*, October 6, 1935, containing Mrs. Lora L. Doty's recollections of Emma Edmonds. Robertson, *Michigan in the War*, p. 205, and *Record of Service of Michigan Volunteers* (Kalamazoo, 1911), Vol. II, are also useful. The latter gives Emma's age at the time of her enlistment in 1861 as twenty years. This is at variance with Dr. Fladeland's probably correct account (p. 435), based on pension records, which gives 1839 as Emma's birth year.

THE 2ND MICHIGAN was unusually blessed in its complement of "ANGELS OF MERCY." In addition to Emma Edmonds, the 2nd had the services of Anna Etherage as a nurse.

"Anna Etherage," says Robertson (*op. cit.*, p. 204), "a native of Detroit, was about 21 years of age when the war broke out. Her father once a man of wealth, her early days were spent in the lap of luxury, with every wish gratified. But misfortune came and swept away his property. Broken in fortune and depressed in spirit, he removed to Minnesota, where he died, leaving Anna at the age of twelve in comparative want. On the breaking out of the war she was visiting her friends in Detroit, and at once volunteered and went as a nurse with the 2nd Michigan Infantry to the field, serving with it for some time, but afterward became attached to the 5th Infantry, and continued her service until the war closed, returning with that regiment to the State on its muster out. She was furnished with a horse, side-saddle, and saddle-bags, and at the commencement of a battle she was accustomed to supply herself with lint, bandages, etc., mounts her horse, gallops to the front, passes under fire regardless of shot or shell, engages in the work of staunching blood and binding up wounds. On one occasion a soldier was torn to pieces by a shell while she was binding up his wounds, and on many fields has her dress been shot through and through by bullets and fragments of shell. Yet she never flinched, and never was wounded. She is of German descent, small of stature, fair complexion, but while in the service much bronzed by exposure; brown hair, a vigorous constitution, and decidedly good looking. Her demeanor was modest, quiet, and retiring, her habits and conduct correct and exemplary. No vulgar word escaped her lips, and she was held in the highest veneration and esteem by the soldiers. On the march she was with the ambulances, caring when needs be for the sick and wounded, and in the bivouac she wrapt herself in her blanket and slept on the ground with the hardihood of a true soldier.

"She has the honor to wear the 'Kearny Badge,' which was presented to her while in the service by that gallant General."

Certainly Emma Edmonds must have known Anna Etherage, raising the suspicion that some of the adventures told in *Nurse and Spy* as Emma's own were, in reality, those of Anna. In fact Emma describes a nurse whom she calls Miss Mary Safford and who sounds remarkably like Anna Etherage.

[Reference: Edmonds, *op. cit.*, p. 360.]

THE "GOOD OLD SURGEON" who gave Emma her mythical medical discharge may have been a fictionalization based upon the character of Dr. Alonzo B. Palmer of Ann Arbor, surgeon for the 2nd Michigan Infantry.

EMMA EDMONDS was by no means the only WOMAN SOLDIER in the Union army. She had her counterpart in Mary Owens Jenkins, of Company K, 9th Pennsylvania Volunteer Cavalry. Mary Jenkins served eighteen months under the name of John Evans.

Her home was near Youngstown, Ohio, and it is said she joined up to be near her lover, William Evans, also of the 9th. He was killed at Gettysburg and

"John Evans" was wounded. Her true sex was revealed in the hospital and she was immediately discharged.

After returning home she married Abie Jenkins and settled near North Lawrence, Ohio, where some of her descendants were still residing in 1959. Mary Owens Jenkins was buried at Massilon, Ohio, and her grave is marked by a monument erected in 1937 by the Sons of Union Veterans.

[Reference: Betty Ingraham, in the *Akron Beacon-Journal*, March 1, 1959.]

Chapter XIII

LIEUTENANT COLONEL BENNETT H. HILL, a graduate of the United States Military Academy and a native of the District of Columbia, was a member of the 5th U.S. Artillery. Early in the war he was assigned by the War Department as Acting Assistant Provost Marshal General of Michigan. He was described as an officer "of great executive ability, truly loyal and patriotic." [Reference: Robertson, *Michigan in the War*, p. 42.]

The message transmitted by Cass and urging the release of MASON AND SLIDELL was said to have been of "determining weight" in influencing the administration's decision. Meeting Brush after the war, Seward is reported to have exclaimed, "Brush, you saved the nation!" [Reference: Frank B. Woodford, *Lewis Cass—The Last Jeffersonian* (New Brunswick, 1950), pp. 336–339.]

Activities of the KNIGHTS OF THE GOLDEN CIRCLE, or the Sons of Liberty, or COPPERHEADS, as they were popularly called, are described and a more detailed account of the Chicago-Camp Douglas plot is given in Wood Gray, *The Hidden Civil War* (New York, 1942).

JACOB THOMPSON was born in North Carolina, May 15, 1810. He acquired extensive plantation properties in Mississippi and represented that state in Congress. President Buchanan called him into his cabinet as Secretary of the Interior. Thompson was a member of the cabinet cabal which worked assiduously to weaken the Union. He was described as a "ruthless, ambitious leader" who "was not excessively troubled by principle." After brief service in the Confederate army with the rank of colonel, Thompson was appointed by Jefferson Davis as a member of a three-man commission sent to Canada for the purpose of stirring up as much trouble for the Union as possible. Thompson concentrated on plots against the Midwestern states. After the war he spent some time in Europe, then returned to the United States, where he died March 24, 1885. [Reference: Allan Nevins, *The Emergence of Lincoln* (New York, 1950), I, 76–77; also Gray, *op. cit.*]

THE U.S.S. *MICHIGAN* was the Navy's first iron-hull vessel and for many years she was the only American ship of war on the Great Lakes. Designed by Samuel Hart, Navy constructor, she was built and launched at Erie, Pennsylvania, in 1844. Her hull plates were made in Pittsburgh mills and hauled by ox-sled to Erie. Her dimensions were: length, 168 feet; main deck beam, 27 feet; draft, 10 feet. She displaced 600 tons. Her wheels were 20 feet in diameter. Originally she was equipped with square sails to give added driving power, but later these were eliminated. She was primarily used for patrol purposes, and had a part in preventing participation by United States citizens in Canada's Patriots' War and the Fenian Revolt. In 1851 she was employed to help break up the Mormon kingdom which "King" Joseph Strang established on Beaver Island in Lake Michigan. In 1909 her name was changed to *Wolverine* and she was employed as a training ship by the Naval Reserve. In 1928 the *Michigan* or *Wolverine* was decommissioned and allowed to deteriorate in Misery Bay, Erie. Her wheel, bell, and a few other fittings were placed in the naval museum at Newport News, Virginia. In 1948 she was sold to private interests. Unsuccessful efforts were made to preserve her as a monument or museum, and in 1949 she was scrapped at Hamilton, Ontario. [Reference: Dana Bowen, *Lore of the Lakes* (Daytona Beach, Fla., 1940).]

THE EARLIER RAID ON JOHNSON'S ISLAND was planned in 1863. Captain John Wilkinson, the noted Confederate blockade runner, left Wilmington, North Carolina, and went to Halifax with a party of twenty-six picked men. They made their way to Montreal, where they proposed either to hire or seize a vessel, sail up the St. Lawrence and through the Welland Canal, and capture the *Michigan*. A Canadian vessel was chartered for the purpose and grappling hooks were put aboard. However, Federal spies learned of the plot and notified British officials, who threatened Wilkinson with severe penalties for violation of neutrality. The expedition was abandoned and Wilkinson went back to blockade running. This is the incident about which the governor-general of Canada alerted the United States through the British minister at Washington. [Reference: Robert Carse, *Blockade* (New York, 1958), pp. 167–174.]

GODFREY J. HYAMS was on the closest of terms with Thompson and had his implicit trust. Colonel Hill said that Hyams had twice been a candidate for

Congress, had been a prominent local politician in Kentucky and Arkansas, had served in the Confederate army, and was wounded three times. His feeling that he had been unjustly treated by Judah Benjamin, Confederate Secretary of War, probably accounts for his defection. Hill employed him in counter-espionage work, even to the extent of sending him to Washington to report directly to the War Department. Hill also notified his superiors that "I have it in contemplation to employ him to travel about at different points in Canada, reporting to me on all matters that will be interesting to the government." [Reference: Martha Mitchell Bigelow, *Piracy on Lake Erie*, in *Detroit Historical Society Bulletin*, Oct. 1957.]

CHARLES H. COLE apparently hoodwinked all the Confederates who employed him. Thompson, who first sent him around the Lakes to survey security measures taken by the port cities, believed his story that he had been a member of General John Morgan's command and had escaped from prison after Morgan's raid into Indiana and Ohio had been broken up. On another occasion, he claimed to have been a lieutenant in the Confederate navy, although Confederate Navy Secretary Mallory later denied that he had held a commission. Cole made his headquarters in Sandusky at the West House, where he posed as a representative of a Pennsylvania oil firm. He entertained lavishly, and did succeed in making friends with some of the officers of the *Michigan*. Papers found on him at the time of his arrest indicated he was a captain in the Confederate army, had taken the oath of allegiance to the United States, had been paroled at Memphis, Tennessee, and had subsequently been in correspondence with rebel refugees and agents in Windsor, Niagara Falls, Toronto, and other Canadian cities. [Reference: Bigelow, *op. cit.; Detroit Advertiser and Tribune*, Sept. 25, 1864.]

THE STEAMER *PHILO PARSONS* was built at Algonac, Michigan, in 1861 by Charles Heinman for Michael B. Kean of Detroit and Patrick Kean, of Algonac. On December 27, 1862, she became the property of Kean, Dustin & Ashley, predecessors of the Ashley & Dustin Line. Originally she was of 221 tons burden; 135 feet length; 20 feet beam; and 8 feet draft. She was later lengthened to 145 feet, which gave her a 21-foot, 8-inch beam and 6-foot draft. She then displaced 250 tons. She was a sidewheeler. From 1866 the *Parsons* was employed on Lake Michigan, and she was burned at her berth in the north branch of the Chicago River during the great Chicago fire of October 21, 1871. [Reference: Letter of Captain Frank E. Hamilton, Kelleys Island, Ohio, to the author, June 26, 1958.]

WALTER O. ASHLEY was one of the best-known steamship men on the Great Lakes. He was born at Claremont, New Hampshire, October 26, 1835, and went to Michigan at the age of twenty-one. He was engaged as a clerk on various ships in the Detroit-Sandusky trade and later went into partnership with his brother-in-law, Captain Selah Dustin, in owning and operating vessels. The Ashley & Dustin Line flag eventually flew from such well-known ships as the *Jay Cooke*, the *Wyandotte*, the *Frank E. Kirby*, and the *Put-in-Bay*. The firm continued to operate until about the time of World War II. Ashley died in Detroit, September 27, 1899. His home was at 114 Adelaide Street. [Reference: Biographical Index, Burton Historical Collection.]

BENNETT G. BURLEY'S commission as acting master was dated September 11, 1863, and was signed by S. R. Mallory, Secretary of the Navy, C.S.A. This commission was introduced, along with a supporting affidavit by Mallory, at Burley's extradition hearing for the purpose of establishing his status as a belligerent. [Reference: Robertson, *op. cit.*]

THE CONFEDERATE CAPTORS OF THE *PARSONS*, referred to in contemporary accounts as the "boarding party," had arrived at Amherstburg on Saturday, September 17. They inquired if there were any Kentuckians in town and, being told there were, they apparently sought out their compatriots and went into hiding. At least, they were not reported seen again on the streets of Amherstburg until the following Monday morning. [Reference: *Detroit Free Press*, Sept. 21, 1864.]

THE *ISLAND QUEEN* was built at Kelleys Island, Ohio, by Daniel Dibble, and launched December 2, 1854. Until 1875 she was engaged in the Sandusky-islands and Detroit River operations. Her specifications were: tonnage, 167; length overall, 121 feet; beam, 20 feet, six inches; draft, 7 feet. In 1875 she was converted into a barge and after 1876 was used on Lake Michigan. She was wrecked at Grand Haven, Michigan, some time after 1876. [Reference: Letter of Captain Frank E. Hamilton, Kelleys Island, Ohio, to the author, June 26, 1958.]

JOHN BROWN, JR., was associated with his famous father in the Kansas troubles, but was not with him on the Harper's Ferry raid in 1859. After serving briefly in the Federal army, Captain Brown, to escape notoriety, went to Put-in-Bay in 1862. He made his home there until his death, May 5, 1895.

He was buried at Sandusky. [Reference: Theresa Thorndale, *Sketches and Stories of the Lake Erie Islands* (Sandusky, 1898).]

COLONEL HILL'S OFFICE was located in the ARMORY Building on the east side of Griswold Street, between Michigan Avenue and Fort Street. This is the site of Detroit's old city hall. In 1864 the mayor's office also was in the Armory Building.

Chapter XIV

COLONEL R. H. G. MINTY was breveted brigadier general December 23, 1862, when he assumed command of the Sabre Brigade, First Cavalry Division, Army of the Cumberland. He became a major general, United States Volunteers, March 13, 1865. At the time he mustered out, August 15, 1865, he was offered the permanent rank of major in the regular army but declined. After the war he settled at Elizabethtown, Kentucky, where he was general manager of the Elizabethtown & Paducah Railroad. Later, as a railroad official, he went west, and died at Jerome, Arizona, in 1906. He was buried at Ogden, Utah. [Reference: *Record of Service of Michigan Volunteers in the Civil War*, Vol. XXXIV; J. G. Vale, *Minty and the Cavalry* (Harrisburg, 1886); *Dictionary of American Biography* (New York, 1934), Vol. XIII.]

MAJOR HORACE GRAY was born September 12, 1812, at Watertown, New York. He left home at the age of twelve to seek his fortune. In 1830 he went to Detroit, and by the time he was nineteen he was a partner in a flourishing mercantile enterprise. He acquired a large tract of land on Grosse Ile, where he built his home—Gray Gables—which was a showplace until it was destroyed by fire in the 1930's. Gray was sheriff of Wayne County, Michigan, in 1853–54. He married Miss Mary Frances Bury, daughter of the Reverend Richard Bury, second rector of St. Paul's Episcopal Church (now Cathedral) in Detroit and one of the prime movers in the organization of the Episcopal Diocese of Michigan. Gray was commissioned in the 4th Cavalry August 14, 1862, and resigned for reasons of health February 22, 1864. After that he served in Detroit in various capacities under the provost marshal and Detroit district commander. He died November 25, 1895, and was buried in Elmwood Cemetery, Detroit. [Reference: Robertson, *Michigan in the War*; Paul Leake, *History of Detroit* (Chicago, 1921), II, 619.]

AMONG SMITH'S COMRADES in the 4th Michigan was a young hospital steward of his own age—James Vernor of Detroit. Vernor was promoted to second lieutenant of Company M, September 20, 1864. He served with the 4th throughout the war. Returning to Detroit, he earned fame by concocting a popular soft drink which made the name "Vernor's" famous, and which became a household staple throughout much of the United States. James Vernor was active in civic affairs, serving as president of the Detroit Common Council and acting mayor. Detroit's Vernor Highway was named in his honor. He died in Detroit October 29, 1927. [Reference: Robertson, *op. cit.*]

THE 4TH MICHIGAN CAVALRY'S valiant conduct at Chickamauga was commemorated when the state of Michigan dedicated a monument in honor of the regiment on the battlefield on September 18–19, 1895. A bronze bas-relief on the granite marker depicts the action at Reed's Bridge, September 18, 1863. [Reference: Charles E. Belknap, *History of the Michigan Organizations at Chickamauga, Chattanooga and Missionary Ridge* (Lansing, 1899), p. 274 and illustration facing p. 275.]

Confederate records show 818 SMALLPOX CASES admitted to the Danville Prison Hospital between November 23, 1863, and March 27, 1865. Early in 1864 there were 800 prisoners at Danville, of whom 285 had smallpox. [Reference: H. H. Cunningham, *Doctors In Gray* (Baton Rouge, 1958), p. 196.]

A DETAILED ACCOUNT OF THE ESCAPE and subsequent adventures of the six prisoners was written by Newlin in 1866 and published in 1887. It has been possible to authenticate from official records most of Newlin's story. [Reference: W. H. Newlin, *An Account of the Escape of Six Federal Prisoners* (Cincinnati, 1887).]

AFTER THE WAR Newlin made an attempt to find out what had happened to TAYLOR, but was unsuccessful. "From all the information ever obtained," he wrote, ". . . the reasonable conclusion is that he perished at or near the place where we left him, his remains being found and decently buried near the Blue Ridge Mountain. . . . His reasons for preferring to be left alone were satisfactory to him, and were not all disclosed to us. The explanation of this last rather singular circumstance may be found in the fact that the comrade was an Englishman and had been in this country but a few weeks before enlisting." [Reference: Newlin, *op. cit.*, p. 4.]

Through correspondence with Huffman after the war it was learned that their benefactor had made inquiries about their MISADVENTURE OF MARCH 4. Huffman located and talked to the woman with whom Smith had conversed, and she said the Confederate patrol returned without having killed or captured anyone. Still later inquiry disclosed that Trippe had eluded the patrol but, after wandering around for several days, was finally caught. He was sent to Richmond to prison and held there until September 1864, when he was paroled, exchanged, and discharged. In 1885 he was living near Burlington, Kansas. [Reference: Newlin, *op. cit.* pp. 4, 7.]

Newlin attempted to trace his COMRADES OF THE ESCAPE AFTER THE WAR and there was some correspondence between them.

When his furlough was over, Lucien B. Smith rejoined the 4th Michigan Cavalry and served with it for the duration. With the rest of the regiment, he was mustered out at Nashville, Tennessee, July 1, 1865. He returned to Michigan and settled at Dundee, Monroe County, where he taught school for a while and then opened a shoe store. In 1867 he married Miss Amanda Densmore, who was also a Dundee school teacher. Smith was popular with his fellow townsmen; his services as a fiddler were for many years in demand for square dances. Smith was born February 23, 1843, and died at Dundee September 18, 1917. Two of his brothers were killed serving with the Union army. He was a charter member of William Bell Post, No. 10, G.A.R. [Reference: Records, Department of Michigan, Grand Army of the Republic, Lansing. Additional information was furnished by Mr. Sidney Moore, Detroit. Mr. Moore is the grandson of Lucien B. Smith.]

Sutherland rejoined his regiment, but there is no record of his later service. After the war he too lived near Dundee.

Wood, like the others, went back to his unit. Newlin was not successful in finding out anything about him for several years. Later, however, he learned that he had died of wounds June 20, 1864.

Newlin included little autobiographical information in his account of the escape. It is known only that he rejoined the 73rd Illinois and was promoted to second lieutenant June 9, 1864. He saw considerable service around Atlanta and was in the battle of Franklin. He was slightly wounded in July 1864 and later that year suffered sunstroke. He apparently served until the end of the war. After that he lived at Danville, Illinois. [Reference: Newlin, *op. cit.*, pp. 4, 126ff.]

Chapter XV

THE ACCOUNT OF SHERIDAN'S RICHMOND RAID and the shooting of General J. E. B. Stuart by John A. Huff is drawn from the following sources: Theodore F. Rodenbough, Brevet Brigadier General, U.S.A., "Sheridan's Richmond Raid," in *Battles and Leaders of the Civil War*, IV, 186–190; *War of the Rebellion Records*, Ser. I, Vols. XXXVI, XLII, LI; John W. Thomason, Jr., *Jeb Stuart* (New York, 1943), pp. 497–499; Davis, *Jeb Stuart, the Last Cavalier*, pp. 385–409, 437–438; Kidd, *Personal Recollections of a Cavalryman*, pp. 278–306; Robertson, *Michigan in the War*, pp. 595–597; Freeman, *Lee's Lieutenants*, III, 420–424.

Unfortunately, none of these references are as clear as could be desired concerning the action of Custer's Brigade, the terrain, and the plan of battle as it developed. This may be explained in part by the confusion which resulted from the extensive skirmishing which comprised most of the battle. James H. Kidd, who was on the spot as commander of the 6th Michigan Cavalry, confessed that during much of the fight he did not know exactly where he and his regiment were in relation to important features of the terrain. Custer too, in his report, confused the names of roads along which the fighting took place.

The raid, of which the Yellow Tavern fight was a minor episode except for the killing of Stuart, was a success from the Federal view, even though Richmond was not entered. The Confederate cavalry was not destroyed; it is a question whether it was seriously hurt. But Sheridan's mission was to divert Stuart from attacking Federal wagon trains and otherwise disrupting Grant's communications in the Wilderness, and from that standpoint, the raid was wholly successful. Moreover, the loss of Stuart to the Confederacy made it really a disaster to the South.

THE STORY OF THE NEWSBOY meeting Devin at the gates of Richmond can be found in Alfred Hoyt Bill, *The Beleaguered City* (New York, 1946), p. 217.

What is known about JOHN A. HUFF and his part in the shooting of Stuart comes from the service records of Huff as a member of the 2nd Regiment United States Sharpshooters and the 5th Michigan Volunteer Cavalry, furnished by the National Archives, 1958. Additional material is found in the *Record of Service of Michigan Volunteers* (5th Cavalry). For information about Company B, 2nd Sharpshooters, see Robertson, *op. cit.*, p. 744.

One question never satisfactorily answered concerns the weapon which Huff used when he shot Stuart. All the above references speak of a revolver. As a cavalryman, Huff undoubtedly carried one; his ability as a marksman would most surely have qualified him to use it effectively. But where was his rifle or carbine? In the melee, did he drop or lose it? As a sharpshooter, he would have held on to it if at all possible. Must it be assumed then, that he lost it when he was dismounted during the charge against the Confederate position? Otherwise, is it not possible that he was armed with a rifle or carbine when he ran across the field in front of Stuart? Had he been so armed at the moment, he would have used his shoulder gun almost instinctively.

As a matter of fact, Robertson, *op. cit.*, p. 597n, gives an otherwise unverified account of the shooting. He quotes Custer as stating: "I have reason to believe that the rebel General J. E. B. Stuart received his death wound from the hand of Private John A. Huff, of Company E, 5th Michigan Cavalry . . ." Robertson then offers this highly improbable story:

"The 5th Regiment had charged through and driven the enemy out of the first line of woods near 'Yellow Tavern', and had reached an open space, when the command was given to cease firing; just at that instant a rebel officer, who afterward proved to be General J. E. B. Stuart, rode up with his staff to within about 80 rods of our line, when a shot was fired by a man of the 5th. John A. Huff, of Company E, remarked to him: 'Tom, you shot too low and to the left;' then turning round to Colonel Alger, who was near him, he said: 'Colonel, I can fetch that man.' The Colonel replied, 'Try him.' He took deliberate aim across a fence and fired. The officer fell. Huff turned around to the Colonel and coolly said: 'There's a spread-cagle for you.' "

Chapter XVI

The search for a graphic ACCOUNT OF WILLIAM B. McCREERY'S ADVENTURES need not extend beyond the Colonel's own story. It can be found in a paper which he read at a meeting of the Loyal Legion at Detroit, February 6, 1889, and which was published by the Loyal Legion under the title *My Experiences as a Prisoner of War, and Escape from Libby Prison* (Detroit, 1893). Other references fill in some of the details. Among them is "Colonel Rose's Tunnel at Libby Prison," in Frank E. Moran, *Famous Adventures and Prison Escapes of the Civil War* (New York, 1904), pp. 184–242.

Eugene T. Petersen wrapped up the escapade in a lively package, "The Grand Escape," in the *Michigan Alumnus*, LXIV, No. 12, 258–267. Dr. Petersen is director of the museum at Mackinac Island, Michigan, and a distinguished authority on Michigan history.

Also useful are *Record of Service of Michigan Volunteers*, XXI, 70–71; the *Detroit Evening News*, October 22, 1879; and the *Detroit Free Press*, January 5, 1875. Material on Libby Prison, with a reproduction of a Richmond, Virginia, street map of 1861, may be found in Bill, *The Beleaguered City.*

COLONEL McCREERY'S CAREER was distinguished not only during his period of military service but after the war as well. He was born at Mt. Morris, New York, September 27, 1836. His parents moved to Flint, Michigan, when he was a year and a half old. His father engaged in farming, lumbering, and milling, and the family prospered.

Young William attended an academy at Lodi, Michigan, and then read law in Flint. He was admitted to the bar in 1860. He entered service May 25, 1861, with the Flint Union Greys, which became Company F, 2nd Michigan Infantry. Appointed sergeant at the time of his enlistment, McCreery was soon promoted to captain, and on November 20, 1862, he was transferred to the 21st Michigan Infantry with the rank of lieutenant colonel. He became colonel of the regiment February 3, 1863.

His injuries forced him to resign September 14, 1864, and he left the army with an unusual citation from Major General George Thomas, which stated:

"On account of wounds (six in number) received at various times in action while in discharge of duty, the honorable scars of which he now wears. In accepting the resignation of Col. William B. McCreery, the major general commanding takes occasion to express his high appreciation of the soldierly qualities and faithful discharge of duty which have ever characterized Col. McCreery's actions, at the same time regretting the existence of the disability which compels the withdrawal of so valuable an officer from the service." [Reference: Robertson, *Michigan in the War*, p. 883.]

McCreery became a leading citizen of Flint. He became associated with his father, but soon branched out, heading a lumber company, a mercantile enterprise, and establishing a bank in Flint. In 1865 he was elected mayor of Flint, and in 1875 he was elected by the Republican Party to the first of two consecutive terms as treasurer of the State of Michigan. Before that, in 1871, he held the office of United States district collector of internal revenue.

Colonel McCreery was an active member of the G.A.R. and, upon joining the post at Flint, he gave his occupation as farmer and banker. In 1865 he married the daughter of William M. Fenton, a former lieutenant governor of Michigan (1848–1852), in whose office McCreery read law. He died at his home in Flint on December 9, 1896.

[Biographical material furnished by the Michigan Section, Michigan State Library, Lansing, and the *Detroit Free Press,* Dec. 10, 1896.]

Chapter XVII

FOR A DESCRIPTION of the terrain, the defenses around the CRATER, and the mining operations, as well as of the battle itself, see Major William H. Powell, U.S.A., "The Battle of the Petersburg Crater," in *Battles and Leaders of the Civil War,* IV, 545–562. The Confederate view is found in Freeman, *Lee's Lieutenants,* III, 541–545.

USE OF COLORED TROOPS was bitterly resented by the Confederates, and not many Negro soldiers were taken prisoner. Many of General Ferrero's men, caught by Mahone's division at the Crater, were massacred. One rebel soldier wrote that all the colored soldiers would have been killed had not General Mahone personally intervened. The story was told of how Mahone ordered one particularly bloodthirsty Confederate to cease slaughtering any more of the colored prisoners. "Well, general," the man replied, "let me kill one more." Whereupon he deliberately drew his knife and slit the throat of another Negro. [Reference: Bell Irwin Wiley, *The Life of Johnny Reb* (Indianapolis, 1943), pp. 314–315.]

COLONEL JOHN FREDERIC HARTRANFT was the non-Michigan brigadier in Willcox's division. A native of Pennsylvania, he commanded the 4th Pennsylvania Infantry from 1861 to May 1864, when he was given a brigade. Like Colonel Cutcheon, Hartranft also was awarded the Congressional Medal of Honor for services at First Bull Run. He was breveted major general for conspicuous gallantry at Fort Stedman. Colonel Hartranft died October 17, 1899. [Reference: *Michigan Pioneer and Historical Collections,* XXX, 128.]

COLONEL WILLIAM HUMPHREY was one of the most able officers Michigan sent to the war. Born at Canandaigua, New York, June 12, 1828, he went to Adrian, Michigan in 1838 and was a resident of that city for the rest of his life. He entered service April 19, 1861, as captain in the 2nd (Three Months) Infantry and remained with it when it was reorganized into a three-year regiment. He was frequently promoted; made colonel in 1863, he was soon commanding a brigade. On November 16, 1863, while leading a brigade composed of the 2nd, 8th, 17th, and 20th Michigan and the 79th New York Highlanders, plus a battery of artillery, he acted as Burnside's rear guard during the retreat from Lenoir Station, Tennessee, and fought off an entire division belonging to Longstreet during the withdrawal. He was twice wounded at Spotsylvania on May 12, 1864, but a month later he was again at the head of his brigade. Then on the night of June 12 he was assigned to cover Grant's shift from Cold Harbor across the James, and for several hours Humphrey's brigade was the only Federal unit confronting Lee's entire army. He was breveted brigadier general August 1, 1864, and was mustered out September 30, 1864. Both before and after the war, he was a teacher. He died at Adrian on January 15, 1899. [Reference: John I. Knapp and R. I. Bonner, *Illustrated History and Biographical Record of Lenawee County, Michigan* (Adrian, 1903); *Record of Service of Michigan Volunteers*, Vol. II.]

SIX MICHIGAN REGIMENTS which were the backbone of Willcox's 3rd Division were made up of veteran troops who, by the time the Crater was exploded, had seen much hard campaigning. Except for the 1st Michigan Sharpshooters, these regiments had long worked together and their records are somewhat similar.

The story of the 2nd Michigan is told in Chapter IV.

Like the 2nd, the 8th Michigan was made up of militia companies from the central part of the state. Counties represented were Ingham, Kent, Gratiot, Barry, Genesee, Shiawassee, and Jackson. Known as the "Wandering Regiment," the 8th saw service in South Carolina, Georgia, Mississippi, Tennessee, Maryland, and Virginia. It was mustered at Fort Wayne September 23, 1861, and discharged at Detroit, August 3, 1865.

The record of the 17th has been described in Chapter VIII.

The 20th Michigan was raised in the third congressional district, comprising the counties of Washtenaw, Jackson, Calhoun, Eaton, and Ingham. It was mustered August 19, 1862, at Jackson camp ground. Its first action was at Fredericksburg, December 12, 1862, and, after service in the West and Tennessee in 1863, it returned to the Army of the Potomac and finished out the war in the lines before Petersburg.

The 27th Michigan included several companies from the Upper Peninsula, the rest being from Port Huron and Detroit. Trained at Port Huron and Ypsilanti, the 27th was mustered at Ypsilanti April 10, 1863. Its first service was in the West, including Vicksburg; thereafter its fortunes were the same as those of the 20th. It was discharged at Washington July 26, 1865.

The 1st Michigan Sharpshooters was recruited as a "show" regiment, composed of picked men from all areas of the state. Because of the high requirements, recruiting was slow, beginning in the fall of 1862 and not being completed until July, 1863. Its first rendezvous was at Kalamazoo; it later trained at Dearborn. The regiment was sent in pursuit of the raiding Confederates under General John Morgan, and its first engagement was with Morgan's rear guard at North Vernon, Indiana, July 14, 1863. Thereafter, its service was entirely in Virginia. The regiment disbanded at Jackson, August 7, 1865.

[Reference: Records of these regiments will be found in Robertson, *Michigan in the War*, index.]

COLONEL BYRON M. CUTCHEON had a distinguished career both in war and peace. He was born in Pembroke, New Hampshire, May 11, 1836. With his family he moved to Ypsilanti in 1855 and, after teaching school in that city and in Birmingham, he entered the University of Michigan, graduating in 1861. In July 1862 he raised B Company of the 20th Infantry and was mustered as a second lieutenant. He rose steadily, becoming colonel of the 20th in 1863, succeeding Colonel Humphrey when the latter was given a brigade command. Cutcheon also commanded a brigade from October to December 1864, and again in January and February 1865. In November 1864 he was given the 27th Michigan Infantry. As his actions at the Crater suggest, Cutcheon was a brave and gallant soldier, and he was awarded the Congressional Medal of Honor for courageous conduct at Horseshoe Bend, Kentucky, May 10, 1863. His citation was "for distinguished gallantry in leading his regiment in a charge on a house occupied by the enemy." He was breveted brigadier general of volunteers March 13, 1865, and was honorably discharged by a War Department special order. After the war, he studied law and practiced in Ypsilanti, Ionia, and Manistee, where he served as postmaster. He became president of the Michigan Soldiers' Home, was elected a member of the Board of Regents of the University of Michigan, and was a member of Congress from 1882 to 1891. In that year he moved to Grand Rapids, where he died in 1908. Among other achievements was a long-standard history of Michigan, of which Cutcheon was co-author. [Reference: Ernest B. Fisher, ed., *History of Grand Rapids and Kent County* (Logansport, Ind., 1900) ; *American Decorations*.]

THE INCIDENT OF THE COLORS is described by Robertson, *op. cit.*, p. 408.

Chapter XVIII

GENERAL REFERENCES from which material for this chapter was drawn include: Wells B. Fox, *What I Remember of the Great Rebellion* (Lansing,

1892); C. B. Burr, ed., *Medical History of Michigan* (Minneapolis, 1930); Silas Farmer, *History of Detroit and Michigan* (Detroit, 1884); *Minutes of the Meetings of the Board of Trustees of Harper Hospital, 1859–1874*; Jean Louise Datson, *The History of Union Hospitals During the Civil War*, Wayne State University thesis, 1947; Messner, *The Public Life of Austin Blair*; Robertson, *Michigan in the War*; Agnes G. Deans and Anne L. Austin, *The History of the Farrand School for Nurses* (Detroit, 1936); Lane, *A Soldier's Diary, 1862–65—The Story of a Volunteer*, privately printed (1905), copy in possession of Michigan State Historical Commission, Lansing; Carl R. Fish, "Social Relief in the Northwest During the Civil War," *American Historical Review* (January 1917), pp. 309–324; Henry F. Lyster, *Recollections of the Bull Run Campaign After Twenty-Seven Years* (Detroit, 1882).

MATHIAS WOLLENWEBER, either because of the wound he received at Blackburn's Ford, or the way Dr. Lyster treated it, was discharged November 2, 1861, on a surgeon's certificate of disability. He had enlisted in Company A, 2nd Michigan Infantry, April 18, 1861, for three years. He was then nineteen years old. Beyond that not much is known about him. Just before the war, the Detroit city directory listed an Anthony Wollenwaber, a mason, living on Maple Street in Hamtramck Township. It is possible he was the father of Mathias.

DR. HENRY FRANCIS Le HUNTE LYSTER was a member of one of Detroit's most prominent families and he became a recognized leader in the medical profession.

He was born in County Wexford, Ireland, November 8, 1837, the son of the Reverend William N. Lyster, who went to Detroit in 1846 and became the first rector of Christ Episcopal Church.

Henry Lyster entered the University of Michigan and graduated with a medical degree in 1860. He entered the army as an assistant surgeon attached to the 2nd Infantry at the time of its organization, April 25, 1861. He was commissioned surgeon, 5th Michigan, July 15, 1862. The following year he became brigade surgeon. He participated in many important engagements in Virginia and was wounded in the Battle of the Wilderness.

After the war Dr. Lyster was a member of the University of Michigan medical school faculty. He was one of the founders of the Wayne State University (Detroit College of Medicine) medical school. He was a member of the Detroit Board of Education and the Michigan State Board of Health.

Dr. Lyster married Winifred Lee, the author of the song "Michigan, My

Michigan." He died at Niles, Michigan, October 3, 1894. [Reference: *Record of Service of Michigan Volunteers,* Vol. V; Burke A. Hinsdale, *History of the University of Michigan* (Ann Arbor, 1906), p. 280.]

DR. WELLS B. FOX was also carried on the muster rolls, for some unexplained reason, under the name of Benjamin F. Fox. He joined the 22nd Michigan as assistant surgeon at the time it was organized, August 21, 1862. He transferred to the 8th Michigan as surgeon March 6, 1863, and was mustered out at Delaney House, D.C., July 30, 1865. After the war he lived at Bancroft, Michigan. He died subsequent to 1892. [Reference: *Record of Service of Michigan Volunteers,* Vol. VIII.]

DR. CHARLES STUART TRIPLER was born in New York City in 1806 and graduated in 1838 from the College of Physicians and Surgeons in that city. He immediately entered the regular army as assistant surgeon and was promoted to surgeon within a year. He was assigned for a while to the Military Academy at West Point, then was stationed at Detroit. In the Mexican War he was medical director of General Twiggs' division. Later he saw duty at several posts in the West.

When the Civil War broke out Dr. Tripler was appointed medical director for General Patterson's army in the Shenandoah, and, when General McClellan took command of the Army of the Potomac, Tripler was made its general medical director and organized its medical services.

In 1862 Tripler was appointed to duty in Michigan with the rank of brevet colonel. He had general medical supervision over Fort Wayne and the Detroit Barracks. Later he became chief medical officer for the Department of Ohio. Although his headquarters were at Columbus, he maintained his residence at Detroit, where he was well known and highly regarded. Just before the war, he lived at 52 W. Fort Street. He died in Cincinnati in 1866.

[Reference: *Leartus Connor Medical Biographies,* Manuscripts, Burton Historical Collection.]

DR. DAVID OSBORNE FARRAND was born at Ann Arbor, Michigan, in 1837. He earned a liberal arts degree from the University of Michigan and later studied in Munich. With his brother, Jacob S. Farrand, he entered the wholesale drug business, but decided to become a doctor and entered the New York College of Physicians and Surgeons, from which he graduated in 1862. He was commissioned assistant surgeon in the regular army, but most of his service was under the medical department with jurisdiction over Michigan. It was largely through his efforts that Harper Hospital was built by the government, and when it opened he served as its medical director. In 1865 he transferred to Fort Wayne as medical officer. He resigned from the service July 1, 1866, with the rank of brevet captain.

After the war Dr. Farrand became a civic leader in Detroit. He entered partnership with the venerable Dr. Zena Pitcher, the dean of the medical profession in Michigan. Dr. Farrand continued to be closely affiliated with Harper Hospital and was responsible for the establishment of its nursing school, which was named for him. He was one of several doctors who organized a preparatory medical school which was the forerunner of the Detroit College of Medicine, which, in turn, became the medical college of Wayne State University.

Dr. Farrand was surgeon-in-chief for the Michigan Central Railroad, and was author of the bill that created the modern Detroit Board of Health. He died March 19, 1883.

[Reference: Burr, *op. cit.*, II, 806.]

Chapter XIX

Because of the lack of exact information about the number of passengers aboard the *Sultana* and the number of lives lost, it is impossible to determine accurately how many MICHIGAN MEN were killed.

The 18th Michigan Infantry had the largest Michigan contingent aboard the ill-fated vessel; therefore it is reasonable to assume that its losses were the heaviest, although this cannot be definitely established. *Record of Service of Michigan Volunteers*, Vol. XVIII, states that "there were 68 members of the Eighteenth killed or drowned, and only a small number survived." Unofficial lists indicate that 116 men of the 18th embarked on the *Sultana* at Vicksburg.

The *Sultana* accounted for the largest category of the 18th's losses in the entire war, except for those who died of disease. The *Record of Service* says the 18th's total enrollment was 1,308 officers and men. Eight were killed in action; three died of wounds; twelve died in Confederate prisons; two hundred and eight died of disease; and sixty-eight were lost in the *Sultana* disaster.

Twenty years after the loss of the *Sultana*, efforts were made to locate as many survivors as possible. Those who could be contacted and were able to go met at Fostoria, Ohio, December 30, 1885, and formed an organization. Its purpose was to provide a suitable memorial and present Congress with pension claims. Inasmuch as there is no record of any memorial having been erected, it must be assumed that the pensions were the group's chief interest.

To support the claims, survivors were asked to submit written statements of their recollections of the disaster. The leading light in that enterprise probably was the REVEREND CHESTER D. BERRY, of Tekonsha, Michigan. He compiled the statements and in 1892 published them in book form. The title of the volume, published at Lansing, Michigan, was *Loss of the Sultana and Reminiscences of Survivors.*

It is largely from this volume, now a rare item, that this account of the disaster is drawn. It was supplemented by information in an article, "The *Sultana* Disaster" by Joseph Taylor Elliott, 10th Indiana Infantry, prepared for the *Indiana Historical Society Publications,* and published in 1913 in Vol. V, No. 3, pp. 163–199. Taylor's story is also told in Berry's book.

Accompanying the Elliott account in the Indiana Historical Society Publications is an account of the rescue operations by the "Late Acting Master's Mate, U.S. *Grosbeak,* U.S.N." Both Berry's book and the Indiana Historical Society Publications articles contain the reports of the investigating officers to the War Department.

Chapter XX

THIS STORY OF DAVIS' FLIGHT AND CAPTURE is derived from several sources. One of the best is an article by Francis F. McKinney, entitled "The Capture of Jefferson Davis" in the *Michigan Alumnus Quarterly Review,* Vol. LX, No. 21 (August 7, 1954). Another is Robertson, *Michigan in the War,* which on pp. 679–683 contains the text of Colonel Benjamin D. Pritchard's official report of the Davis incident to the Secretary of War, dated Washington, D.C., May 25, 1865. Other useful references are Ishbel Ross, *First Lady of the South—The Life of Mrs. Jefferson Davis* (New York, 1958); Julian G. Dickinson, *The Capture of Jeff Davis* (Detroit, 1888); *Battles and Leaders of the Civil War,* IV, 762–767; *Annals of the War,* pp. 147ff, 554ff.

LIEUTENANT COLONEL BENJAMIN DUDLEY PRITCHARD earned a deserved reputation as a reliable and competent officer, and his capture of Davis was the climax of his military career.

Pritchard was born at Nelson, Portage County, Ohio, January 29, 1835. His father, Lambert Pritchard, was a well-to-do farmer. Ben attended Western Reserve College and then entered the University of Michigan law school, from which he graduated in 1860. He was admitted to the bar and established him-self in Allegan, Michigan, where he began to practice in association with William L. Williams, one of the city's leading citizens.

When the 4th Michigan Cavalry was being organized Pritchard recruited Company L and was rewarded with a commission as its captain when the regi-ment was mustered on August 13, 1862. He served with distinction in all of the major Tennessee and Georgia campaigns. He was wounded at Chickamauga on September 18, 1863 and, partly because of his gallantry in that battle, he was promoted to lieutenant colonel November 26, 1864. His part in Davis' capture won him the rank of brevet brigadier general, his appointment bearing the date May 10, 1865. He was mustered out of service July 1, 1865.

After the war Pritchard returned to Allegan, where he engaged in several enterprises, including his law practice until 1868. After that he devoted most of his attention to farming, real estate, and banking. He organized the First National Bank of Allegan in 1872 and served as its president more than thirty years. During a war leave, he married Mary B. Kent of Ohio. They had two children.

Like many veterans, Pritchard took an active interest in postwar politics. His military reputation served him well in that regard. In 1866 he was ap-pointed a commissioner of the state land office, and in 1878 he was elected treasurer of the State of Michigan on the Republican ticket. He was re-elected in 1880 for a second term, which expired at the end of 1882.

Pritchard died at Allegan, November 26, 1907.

[Reference: *History of Allegan and Barry Counties, Michigan* (Philadel-phia, 1880), p. 123; *American Biographical History of Eminent and Self-Made Men, Michigan Volume,* Part 2 (Cincinnati, 1878), pp. 99–100; *Allegan County Cemeteries* (typescript in Michigan State Library, Lansing), IV, 29; Robertson, *op. cit.,* p. 910.]

JULIAN G. DICKINSON was born in Hamburg, New York in 1843. For several years before the war he lived in Jonesville and Jackson, Michigan, and it was at Jackson that he enlisted in Company I, 4th Michigan Cavalry, July 10, 1862, and was mustered in for three years August 29, 1862. The following October he was made adjutant's clerk; he was promoted to sergeant, Septem-ber 1, 1863, to sergeant major, March 1, 1864, and to adjutant (with the rank of first lieutenant), July 15, 1864. For his part in the capture of Davis, he was breveted captain to date from May 10, 1865. He was discharged at Edge-field, Tennessee, August 15, 1865. After the war, Dickinson attended the Uni-versity of Michigan law school, and was admitted to the bar in 1866. He practiced in Detroit, with offices in the Newberry Building, and attained a prominent place in the social and business life of the city. He died in 1916. [Reference: *Record of Service of Michigan Volunteers*, Vol. XXXIV; *Burton Scrapbook No. 10*, Burton Historical Collection.]

THE SO-CALLED DISGUISE WORN BY DAVIS has long been a controversial subject. The fact that he did wear a woman's garment has been established, and was the subject of a good deal of adverse publicity in the North. Mrs. Davis testified that when Davis started to leave their tent, he picked up a waterproof cloak which he thought was his own. In the dark, however, he took that of Mrs. Davis, which was very similar to his. Mrs. Davis threw her shawl over her husband's head. It was not unusual in those days for men to wear shawls around their shoulders. Lincoln frequently wore one. But it does seem strange that Davis would cover his head with a shawl. The War Department confiscated the raincoat and, after it was delivered to Federal authorities at Washington, there was never any further claim that it was a woman's dress. Besides the raincoat and shawl, Davis was wearing a Confederate uniform and cavalry boots when captured. [Reference: Ross, *op. cit.*, p. 393; McKinney, *op. cit.*, p. 352.]

THE 4TH MICHIGAN CAVALRY AND ITS DISTINGUISHED PRISONER reached Macon at 3 p.m., May 13. Two days earlier, near Hawkinsville, Colonel Pritchard received information that the United States government had offered a reward of $100,000 for Davis' capture.

Just before reaching Macon Pritchard was informed that he would take the prisoner to Washington and was told to select a detail of three officers and twenty men for an escort. They left Macon by train the night of the 13th, going first to Atlanta and then to Augusta, then proceeded to Savannah by ship. Several other important prisoners were placed in Pritchard's custody, including Alexander H. Stephens, Vice President of the Confederacy, Major General "Fighting Joe" Wheeler, and Clement C. Clay and his wife.

At Savannah the party transferred to another ship, which took them to Fortress Monroe, where they arrived May 19. There Pritchard received instructions to turn Davis over to General Nelson A. Miles, commandant of the fortress. Pritchard continued on to Washington, where he gave a full report to the President and the War Department. He remained in Washington until July 1, when he was discharged.

Payment of the reward was held up until 1868, when an appropriation was made by Congress. The $100,000 was divided as follows: General Wilson,

Colonel Pritchard, Colonel Harnden, and Captain Yoeman (1st Ohio) received $3,000 each. The balance was distributed in equal shares to members of the various units which participated in the chase and capture.

[Reference: See Pritchard's report in Robertson, *op. cit.*, pp. 681, 684.]

Chapter XXI

ORLANDO LeVALLEY was the last known Michigan survivor of the Civil War. It cannot be said positively that no others were living at the time of his death. Somewhere, perhaps in another state, perhaps even in Michigan, there may have been a Michigan veteran who outlived LeValley. Unless a veteran was a member of the G.A.R., or qualified for a pension, his death might easily have passed unnoticed.

At 9:40 a.m., July 13, 1951, Joseph Clovese, age 107, died in the Veterans Administration Hospital in Dearborn, Michigan.

Clovese was born a slave on a plantation in St. Bernard Parish, Louisiana. He ran away when he was about eighteen, and attached himself to the Union army operating in the vicinity of Vicksburg, Mississippi. On November 1, 1863, he enlisted in a Negro regiment, the 63rd Infantry, and served until January 9, 1866.

Clovese continued to live in the South for many years after the war, working as a laborer along the Mississippi and as a deck hand on steamers running between New Orleans and Biloxi. In 1948 he came North to make his home with his niece, Mrs. Valerie Daniel, in Pontiac, Michigan.

A civic observance was held in Pontiac in honor of his 107th birthday on January 28, 1951. Tributes were paid him by his fellow townsmen, and he received a warm letter from President Harry S. Truman, who wished "that your pathway ahead will be bright with days of serene contentment."

Serenity was one of Joe Clovese's notable attributes.

"Ever since I can remember," he told an interviewer, "ever' time I sits down to eat I say 'Thank God and bless the cook.'"

During the remaining days of his life, Clovese was troubled by reports of the fighting then going on in Korea.

"There wouldn't be no trouble in Korea," he said sadly, "if folks would do more prayin' and lovin'"—which is a suitable observation with which to close a book about war.

[Reference: The death of Orlando LeValley was, of course, thoroughly reported by Michigan newspapers of April 20, 1948. LeValley's service record is given in *Record of Service of Michigan Volunteers in the Civil War*, Vol.

XXIII. Information concerning Joseph Clovese was obtained from the *Detroit News*, Jan. 29, 1951, and July 13, 1951, the *Detroit Free Press*, Jan. 29, 1951, the *New York Times*, July 14, 1951, and records of the Veterans Administration Hospital, Dearborn, Michigan.]

Index

Titles in the Great Lakes Books Series

Orvie, The Dictator of Dearborn, by David L. Good, 1989

Seasons of Grace: A History of the Catholic Archdiocese of Detroit, by Leslie Woodcock Tentler, 1990

The Pottery of John Foster: Form and Meaning, by Gordon and Elizabeth Orear, 1990

The Diary of Bishop Frederic Baraga: First Bishop of Marquette, Michigan, edited by Regis M. Walling and Rev. N. Daniel Rupp, 1990

Walnut Pickles and Watermelon Cake: A Century of Michigan Cooking, by Larry B. Massie and Priscilla Massie, 1990

The Making of Michigan, 1820–1860: A Pioneer Anthology, edited by Justin L. Kestenbaum, 1990

America's Favorite Homes: A Guide to Popular Early Twentieth-Century Homes, by Robert Schweitzer and Michael W. R. Davis, 1990

Beyond the Model T: The Other Ventures of Henry Ford, by Ford R. Bryan, 1990

Life after the Line, by Josie Kearns, 1990

Michigan Lumbertowns: Lumbermen and Laborers in Saginaw, Bay City, and Muskegon, 1870–1905, by Jeremy W. Kilar, 1990

Detroit Kids Catalog: The Hometown Tourist by Ellyce Field, 1990

Waiting for the News, by Leo Litwak, 1990 (reprint)

Detroit Perspectives, edited by Wilma Wood Henrickson, 1991

Life on the Great Lakes: A Wheelsman's Story, by Fred W. Dutton, edited by William Donohue Ellis, 1991

Copper Country Journal: The Diary of Schoolmaster Henry Hobart, 1863–1864, by Henry Hobart, edited by Philip P. Mason, 1991

John Jacob Astor: Business and Finance in the Early Republic, by John Denis Haeger, 1991

Survival and Regeneration: Detroit's American Indian Community, by Edmund J. Danziger, Jr., 1991

Steamboats and Sailors of the Great Lakes, by Mark L. Thompson, 1991

Cobb Would Have Caught It: The Golden Age of Baseball in Detroit, by Richard Bak, 1991

Michigan in Literature, by Clarence Andrews, 1992

Under the Influence of Water: Poems, Essays, and Stories, by Michael Delp, 1992

The Country Kitchen, by Della T. Lutes, 1992 (reprint)

The Making of a Mining District: Keweenaw Native Copper 1500–1870, by David J. Krause, 1992

Kids Catalog of Michigan Adventures, by Ellyce Field, 1993

Henry's Lieutenants, by Ford R. Bryan, 1993

Historic Highway Bridges of Michigan, by Charles K. Hyde, 1993

Lake Erie and Lake St. Clair Handbook, by Stanley J. Bolsenga and Charles E. Herndendorf, 1993

Queen of the Lakes, by Mark Thompson, 1994

Iron Fleet: The Great Lakes in World War II, by George J. Joachim, 1994

Turkey Stearnes and the Detroit Stars: The Negro Leagues in Detroit, 1919–1933, by Richard Bak, 1994

Pontiac and the Indian Uprising, by Howard H. Peckham, 1994 (reprint)

Charting the Inland Seas: A History of the U.S. Lake Survey, by Arthur M. Woodford, 1994 (reprint)

Ojibwa Narratives of Charles and Charlotte Kawbawgam and Jacques LePique, 1893–1895. Recorded with Notes by Homer H. Kidder, edited by Arthur P. Bourgeois, 1994, co-published with the Marquette County Historical Society

Strangers and Sojourners: A History of Michigan's Keweenaw Peninsula, by Arthur W. Thurner, 1994

Win Some, Lose Some: G. Mennen Williams and the New Democrats, by Helen Washburn Berthelot, 1995

Sarkis, by Gordon and Elizabeth Orear, 1995

The Northern Lights: Lighthouses of the Upper Great Lakes, by Charles K. Hyde, 1995 (reprint)

Kids Catalog of Michigan Adventures, second edition, by Ellyce Field, 1995

Rumrunning and the Roaring Twenties: Prohibition on the Michigan-Ontario Waterway, by Philip P. Mason, 1995

In the Wilderness with the Red Indians, by E. R. Baierlein, translated by Anita Z. Boldt, edited by Harold W. Moll, 1996

Elmwood Endures: History of a Detroit Cemetery, by Michael Franck, 1996

Master of Precision: Henry M. Leland, by Mrs. Wilfred C. Leland with Minnie Dubbs Millbrook, 1996 (reprint)

Haul-Out: New and Selected Poems, by Stephen Tudor, 1996

Kids Catalog of Michigan Adventures, third edition, by Ellyce Field, 1997

Beyond the Model T: The Other Ventures of Henry Ford, revised edition, by Ford R. Bryan, 1997

Young Henry Ford: A Picture History of the First Forty Years, by Sidney Olson, 1997 (reprint)

The Coast of Nowhere: Meditations on Rivers, Lakes and Streams, by Michael Delp, 1997

From Saginaw Valley to Tin Pan Alley: Saginaw's Contribution to American Popular Music, 1890–1955, by R. Grant Smith, 1998

The Long Winter Ends, by Newton G. Thomas, 1998 (reprint)